Palgrave Studies in Educational Media

Series Editors
Eckhardt Fuchs
Georg Eckert Institute for International Textbook Research
Braunschweig, Germany

Felicitas Macgilchrist
Georg Eckert Institute for International Textbook Research
Braunschweig, Germany

Managing Editor
Wendy Anne Kopisch
Georg Eckert Institute for International Textbook Research
Braunschweig, Germany

Editorial Board Member
Michael Apple
University of Wisconsin–Madison
Madison, WI, USA

Tânia Maria F. Braga Garcia
Federal University of Paraná
Curitiba, Brazil

Eric Bruillard
ENS de Cachan
Cachan, France

Nigel Harwood
School of English
University of Sheffield
Sheffield, UK

Heather Mendick
Independent Scholar
London, UK

Eugenia Roldán Vera
Departamento de Investigaciones Educativas
CINVESTAV
Mexico City, Mexico

Neil Selwyn
Faculty of Education
Monash University
Clayton, VIC, Australia

Yasemin Soysal
University of Essex
Colchester, UK

There is no education without some form of media. Much contemporary writing on media and education examines best practices or individual learning processes, is fired by techno-optimism or techno-pessimism about young people's use of technology, or focuses exclusively on digital media. Relatively few studies attend – empirically or conceptually – to the embeddedness of educational media in contemporary cultural, social and political processes. The **Palgrave Studies in Educational Media** series aims to explore textbooks and other educational media as sites of cultural contestation and socio-political forces. Drawing on local and global perspectives, and attending to the digital, non-digital and post-digital, the series explores how these media are entangled with broader continuities and changes in today's society, with how media and media practices play a role in shaping identifications, subjectivations, inclusions and exclusions, economies and global political projects. Including single authored and edited volumes, it offers a dedicated space which brings together research from across the academic disciplines. The series provides a valuable and accessible resource for researchers, students, teachers, teacher trainers, textbook authors and educational media designers interested in critical and contextualising approaches to the media used in education.

More information about this series at
http://www.palgrave.com/gp/series/15151

Barbara Christophe • Peter Gautschi
Robert Thorp
Editors

The Cold War in the Classroom

International Perspectives on Textbooks and Memory Practices

Editors
Barbara Christophe
Georg Eckert Institute for International
Textbook Research
Member of the Leibniz Association
Brunswick, Germany

Peter Gautschi
Institute for History Education and
Memory Cultures
University of Teacher Education Lucerne
Lucerne, Switzerland

Robert Thorp
University of Stockholm
Stockholm, Sweden

The University of Newcastle
Newcastle, NSW, Australia

Palgrave Studies in Educational Media
ISBN 978-3-030-11998-0   ISBN 978-3-030-11999-7   (eBook)
https://doi.org/10.1007/978-3-030-11999-7

© The Editor(s) (if applicable) and The Author(s) 2019 This book is an open access publication
Open Access   This book is licensed under the terms of the Creative Commons Attribution 4.0 International License (http://creativecommons.org/licenses/by/4.0/), which permits use, sharing, adaptation, distribution and reproduction in any medium or format, as long as you give appropriate credit to the original author(s) and the source, provide a link to the Creative Commons licence and indicate if changes were made.
The images or other third party material in this book are included in the book's Creative Commons licence, unless indicated otherwise in a credit line to the material. If material is not included in the book's Creative Commons licence and your intended use is not permitted by statutory regulation or exceeds the permitted use, you will need to obtain permission directly from the copyright holder.
The use of general descriptive names, registered names, trademarks, service marks, etc. in this publication does not imply, even in the absence of a specific statement, that such names are exempt from the relevant protective laws and regulations and therefore free for general use.
The publisher, the authors and the editors are safe to assume that the advice and information in this book are believed to be true and accurate at the date of publication. Neither the publisher nor the authors or the editors give a warranty, express or implied, with respect to the material contained herein or for any errors or omissions that may have been made. The publisher remains neutral with regard to jurisdictional claims in published maps and institutional affiliations.

Cover illustration: © EyeEm / Alamy

This Palgrave Macmillan imprint is published by the registered company Springer Nature Switzerland AG.
The registered company address is: Gewerbestrasse 11, 6330 Cham, Switzerland

Foreword

There is no education without some form of media. The field of educational media is a growing area of interest in education, as educational policy papers on the 'digital agenda', the rapid expansion of media sections in national and international educational research associations, and the range of academic books on media in education show. Educational media are crucial to producing knowledge and shaping educational practices. Conflicts over the contents of textbooks and curricula, widely discussed in the daily news, illustrate how many different stakeholders are invested in sharing their particular understandings of our (shared) past, the current society and potential imagined futures with the younger generation. Policymakers, politicians and activists regard educational media as important tools which not only foster young people's media skills and world knowledge, but which also shape which ways of living are considered desirable or even legible. Textbooks and other educational media are deeply embedded in the socio-political contexts in which they are developed and used. Given this context, alongside the emerging interest in digital technology in education, the *Palgrave Studies in Educational Media* series takes stock of current research on educational media by focusing on three issues:

First, today's vibrant and dynamic research and scholarship on technology stems from a broad range of disciplines, including sociology, history, cultural studies, memory studies, media studies and education, and also information, computer and cognitive science. Traditionally, this research has drawn on textbooks and other educational media in order to engage with specific disciplinary questions, such as device-specific reading speed or social inclusion/exclusion. Studies on educational media are only beginning to be consolidated into the kind of inter- or transdisciplinary field which can build and develop on insights generated and exchanged across disciplinary boundaries.

Second, the majority of work in this field is focused on best practices, individual learning processes, or concerns over the risks involved when young people use technology. There are still relatively few studies which attend – empirically or conceptually – to the embeddedness of educational media in contemporary cultural, social and political processes, and to the historicity of the media used in education. If we see educational media as a highly contested and thus crucially important cultural site, then we need more studies which consider media in their contexts, and which take a carefully critical or generative approach to societal concerns.

Third, current work emerging in this field has turned its attention to computers and other digital technologies. Yet looking at today's educational practices, it is clear that (i) they are by no means predominantly digital, and simultaneously (ii) 'post-digital' practices abound in which the digital is no longer seen as new or innovative, but is integrated with other materials in daily teaching and learning. The potentials and risks of digital education emit a fascination for politicians, journalists and others concerned with the future of education, and are undoubtedly important to consider. Empirical observations of education around the globe, however, demonstrate the reach and visibility of a broad range of media (textbooks, blackboards, LEGO™, etc.), as well as the post-digital blending of digital and non-digital media in contemporary educational settings.

Palgrave Studies in Educational Media aims to address these three issues in an integrated manner. The series offers a dedicated space which brings together research from across the academic disciplines, encouraging dialogue within the emerging space of educational media studies. It showcases both empirical and theoretical work on educational media which understands these media as a site of cultural contestation and socio-political force. The focus lies primarily on schools, across the school subjects. The series is interested in both local and global perspectives, in order to explore how educational media are entangled with broader debates about continuity and change in today's society, about classroom practices, inclusions and exclusions, identifications, subjectivations, economies and global political projects.

We are delighted to present this fourth book in the series, on the interplay of educational media and memory practices in the classroom when teaching the history of the Cold War. Increasingly used as a label to cover the whole period between 1945 and 1989, the Cold War is now – as the thirtieth anniversary of the fall of the Berlin Wall approaches – an increasingly institutionalised issue. Numerous handbooks and journals are dedicated to the topic; specialised research institutes and museums are opening up around the world, bringing global perspectives to the period. This institutionalisation goes hand in hand with increased awareness of the contested nature of the subject, with lively debates opening up in both scholarly and public spaces: Global perspectives have become more prominent; there is a strong awareness that not only has the East collapsed, but there is also uncertainty as to what the West stands for and indeed whether it remains a useful concept.

The Cold War in the Classroom: International Perspectives on Textbooks and Memory Practices explores how the memory of the Cold War, the story of the confrontation between East and West that was once crucial for the articulation of political identities all over the world, is negotiated in history textbooks, teacher narratives and history classrooms. It brings together perspectives from Africa, Asia, Europe and Latin America. The volume not only introduces new approaches to the field of educational media studies by orienting to the uptake of textbook discourse in classroom practice, and by embedding the analysis of textbook discourse in its socio-economic and political contexts; it also enriches memory studies by shifting attention from the rather more settled memories of the two World Wars to the still very much disputed memory of the Cold War. It does so by concentrating not only on the representation but also on the appropriation of mediated memory, and finally by introducing the social space of the school as a fertile but still under-researched location for memory studies.

Brunswick, Germany
November 2018

Eckhardt Fuchs
Felicitas Macgilchrist

Preface

It is always the case that many more people are involved in the creation of a book than the table of contents can depict, and indeed this book is no exception to the rule. Authors are important, but they are not alone in their endeavours. This book is the result of a three-year international project on 'Teaching the Cold War: Memory Practices in the Classroom', funded by the Leibniz Association.

It is an elaborate procedure via which project proposals are designed and negotiated in today's academia, a world increasingly dependent on third-party funding. Sometimes one is required to describe one's ideas and plans within a meticulous word limit. I was highly fortunate in that I did not have to navigate these mires alone. I am indebted to Eckhardt Fuchs, Simone Lässig and Inga Niehaus, who with their usual aplomb were sources of great support during this process.

Research proposals are one thing; inspiring ideas another. The idea for this project and thus also for this book was first voiced at my breakfast table by its 'spiritual father', my husband, Bernard Christophe. Back then, we were musing as to why studies on memory cultures and history teaching focus so often and almost exclusively on National Socialism, a topic that nowadays is only rarely subject to differing interpretations. While Bernard did not have an answer to this question, he did point out that a different topic, the Cold War, was indeed the fulcrum of lively debate in many societies. Thus the project was born, and my thanks go to him.

Our research, however, was not limited to the Cold War itself, but to how the Cold War is taught in schools. In Germany, Sweden and Switzerland we spent hours pelting teachers with questions, and eventually penetrated their sacred territory, the classroom, with video cameras. We extend our sincere thanks to all these teachers, who allowed us insights into their work with an openness that is by no means self-evident. However, no matter how cooperative teachers may be, data collection in schools is always a troublesome thing to do with bureaucratic hurdles to overcome and permits from ministries, head teachers and parents to obtain. The authors of this book are very much indebted to Kathrin Zehr and Nora Zimmermann who did a great job in supporting us with all this and in conducting field research in German and Swiss schools.

We all know that the road from project to publication can be long and rocky. This applies in particular to projects like this, involving researchers not only from different national academic cultures but also from different academic disciplines. Peter Gautschi, Markus Furrer, Nora Zimmermann and Nadine Ritzer from Switzerland, and also Robert Thorp from Sweden, are historians or history didactics experts. Eva Fischer and I from Germany are social scientists. The thread of communication between them remained smooth and unbroken, which is also thanks to Katharina Baier, who coordinated the project with efficiency and sensitivity. To her too we express our gratitude.

It is generally good academic practice to discuss the initial results of a project with others before publishing them, and indeed this is something we did with enthusiasm. In this regard we are indebted to all those who asked us shrewd and critical questions, thus contributing valuably to more precisely defining and clarifying our findings. Special thanks go to the students of Karina Korostelina at Georg Mason University in Washington, D. C., the staff and guests of Christian F. Ostermann at the Woodrow Wilson Center in Washington, to Francisco Ramirez and his colleagues at Stanford University, and to the colleagues of Manish Jain at Jawaharlal Nehru University and Ambedkhar University, Delhi. It was during this tour that we gained the interesting, if not unexpected, insight that the discussions we held in Delhi were the most lively and productive of all, something perhaps not insignificant given that the most interesting debates in Cold War research tend to be those addressing the so-called Third World. Useful feedback was also given by students participating in international summer schools I organised in Georgia and Tajikistan. They proved the general rule that those new to the field sometimes find the most interesting patterns in material with which others may already be too familiar.

Finally, when the data has been collected, the results discussed and the papers written; that is, when a book is – from the authors' point of view – more-or-less complete, it is then that the editing begins, and for this we are grateful to Wendy Anne Kopisch, who with linguistic subtlety and human tact ensured the texts were in a reader-friendly English without anyone feeling that they had failed to master this global language. Thanks also go to Tilly Nevin, who assisted Wendy during a summer internship, and to Meyrick Payne, who helped with the proof-reading. Finally, we extend our gratitude to Eleanor Christie and Rebecca Wyde at Palgrave Macmillan for their support, as well as to two anonymous reviewers, who in the first stages of manuscript preparation offered valuable advice and suggestions.

Brunswick, Germany Barbara Christophe
May 2019

Acknowledgments

The editors gratefully acknowledge a generous grant from the Leibniz Association Open Access Monograph Publishing Fund, from the Georg Eckert Institute for International Textbook Research, and from the University of Teacher Education Lucerne, which supported the open access version of this book.

Contents

1 Introduction: The Cold War in the Classroom International Perspectives on Textbooks and Memory Practices 1
Barbara Christophe

Part I Textbook Memories 13

2 Textbook Memories of the Cold War: Introduction to Part One 15
Barbara Christophe

3 Manufacturing Coherence: How American Textbooks Incorporate Diverse Perspectives on the Origins of the Cold War 23
Eva Fischer

4 Between Radical Shifts and Persistent Uncertainties: The Cold War in Russian History Textbooks 51
Alexander Khodnev

5 The Emergence of a Multipolar World: Decentring the
   Cold War in Chinese History Textbooks   75
   Lisa Dyson

6 Americans and Russians as Representatives of 'Us' and
   'Them': Contemporary Swedish School History Textbooks
   and their Portrayals of the Central Characters of the Cold
   War   107
   Anders Persson

7 Images and Imaginings of the Cold War – with a Focus on
   the Swiss View   137
   Markus Furrer

8 Between Non-human and Individual Agents: The
   Attribution of Agency in Chapters on the Cold War in
   Flemish History Textbooks   159
   Karel Van Nieuwenhuyse

9 The Cold War and the Polish Question   183
   Joanna Wojdon

10 The Cold War in South African History Textbooks   207
   Linda Chisholm and David Fig

11 Dictatorship and the Cold War in Official Chilean
   History Textbooks   221
   Teresa Oteíza and Claudia Castro

Part II Teachers' Memories   249

12 Teachers' Memories and the Cold War: Introduction to Part II   251
Robert Thorp and Barbara Christophe

13 Ambivalence and the Illusion of Hegemony   259
Barbara Christophe

14 1968 in German-speaking Switzerland: Controversies and Interpretations 289
Nadine Ritzer

15 Reconciling Opposing Discourses: Narrating and Teaching the Cold War in an East-German Classroom 317
Eva Fischer

Part III Memory Practices in the Classroom   345

16 Introduction to Part Three: Memory Practices in the Classroom 347
Peter Gautschi, Barbara Christophe, and Robert Thorp

17 Selecting, Stretching and Missing the Frame: Making Sense of the Cold War in German and Swiss History Classrooms 361
Barbara Christophe

18 Learning from Others: Considerations within History
    Didactics on Introducing the Cold War in Lessons in
    Germany, Sweden and Switzerland   393
    Peter Gautschi and Hans Utz

19 Pedagogical Entanglements and the Cold War: A
    Comparative Study on Opening History Lessons on the
    Cold War in Sweden and Switzerland   423
    Robert Thorp

Index   449

Notes on Contributors

Claudia Castro is a social anthropologist with a master's degree in linguistics. Her research interests include social and critical discourse analysis and academic writing in higher education. She is currently working on the following two projects: *The Language of Appraisal in Spanish: Description and Systematization of Linguistic Resources to Build Intersubjectivity* (Heads: Teresa Oteíza and Claudio Pinuer), and *Project of Research, Development and Innovation of Academic Literacy Competences* (Head: Federico Navarro). She is also Professor of Discourse Analysis at the Alberto Hurtado University, Santiago, Chile.

Linda Chisholm is Professor at the Centre for Education Rights and Transformation of the Education Faculty at the University of Johannesburg, South Africa. She has published widely on the historical, contemporary and comparative aspects of education policy and curriculum in South Africa and the region. Her most recent book, *Between Worlds: German Missionaries and the Transition from Mission to Bantu Education*, was published by Wits Press in 2017. She is currently preparing her next book, *Teacher Preparation in South Africa: Past, Present and Future Perspectives,* for publication with Emerald Press.

Barbara Christophe is a Senior Research Fellow and coordinator of the Memory Cultures Research Forum at the Georg Eckert Institute for

International Textbook Research in Brunswick, Germany. She received her PhD from the University of Bremen in 1996 with a sociological study of current issues in Lithuania, and her *Habilitation* at the European University Viadrina in Frankfurt/Oder with an ethnographic study of corruption in Georgia. Her recent publications include a special issue of the Journal of Educational Media, Memory, and Society, edited together with Felicitas Macgilchrist and Alexandra Binnenkade, on *Memory Practices and History Education 7*, no. 2 (2015); edited with Kerstin Schwedes and Sophie Friedl, *Schulbuch und Erster Weltkrieg. Kulturwissenschaftliche Analysen und geschichtsdidaktische Überlegungen* (Göttingen: Vandenhoeck & Ruprecht, 2015); and, with Christoph Kohl and Heike Liebau, *Geschichte als Ressource. Politische Dimensionen historischer Authentizität* (Berlin: Klaus Scharz Verlag, 2017).

Lisa Dyson is an independent scholar based in Washington, DC. She earned her master's in Asian Studies from Georgetown University's School of Foreign Service. Her thesis, *The Korean War in Contemporary China: How and Why the Korean War is Remembered as a Victory*, examined how the Korean War is interpreted in textbooks and museums to legitimate Communist Party rule and create the state's preferred national image. She has also taught at local schools in Shanxi, China, at the high school and university level.

David Fig is an independent researcher on energy and the environment. He has a PhD in international relations from the London School of Economics. He has a background in popular and worker education, and contributed a chapter to a progressive final-year history textbook in the late 1980s. He is a research associate of both the Chair in BioEconomy at the University of Cape Town and of the Society, Work and Politics Institute at the University of the Witwatersrand, Johannesburg. He is also a fellow of the Transnational Institute in Amsterdam.

Eva Fischer was a research assistant and a research associate at the Georg Eckert Institute for International Textbook Research in Brunswick, Germany, from 2015 to 2018, where she worked on the projects *Teaching the Cold War – Memory Practices in the Classroom* and *Worldviews – The*

World in Textbooks. In the context of the Cold War project, she conducted research on current perspectives on the Cold War by East-German history teachers and on the representation of the beginning of the Cold War in recent US history textbooks. She holds an MA in National and Transnational Studies from the University of Münster and a BA in English and American Studies and German Literature from the University of Freiburg. She currently lives in Oldenburg, Germany, and is programme director for foreign languages and culture at the *Volkshochschule* in Delmenhorst.

Markus Furrer has been professor of contemporary history at the University of Teacher Education Lucerne (PH Luzern) since 2003. After receiving his doctorate from the University of Fribourg, he worked as a history teacher (1992-2003) and as vice-rector (1996-2001) at a teacher training college in Lucerne. He joined the University of Fribourg in 1998 as a part-time lecturer and held a position there as a covering professor from 2003 to 2006. His principal fields of research are European and Swiss contemporary history, with a focus on politics, culture and social history and on the communication of history to the public. His publications include 'Marignano für die Schule? Das Dilemma mit Geschichtsbildern im Geschichtsunterricht', *Didactica Historica* 1 (2015), 63-68; and (edited with K. Messmer) *Handbuch Zeitgeschichte im Geschichtsunterricht* (Schwalbach am Taunus: Wochenschau, 2013). He received his *Habilitation* from the University of Fribourg, Switzerland, with *Die Nation im Schulbuch - zwischen Überhöhung und Verdrängung: Leitbilder der Schweizer Nationalgeschichte in Schweizer Geschichtslehrmitteln der Nachkriegszeit und Gegenwart*. Hanover: Hahn, 2004.

Peter Gautschi is Professor of History Didactics at the University of Teacher Education, Lucerne, Head of the Lucerne Institute for History Education and Memory Cultures, and Honorary Professor at the University of Teacher Education, Freiburg. He is the author of two monographs on history education: *Geschichte lehren. Lernwege und Lernsituationen für Jugendliche* (Lehrmittelverlag des Kantons Aargau, 2015) and *Guter Geschichtsunterricht: Grundlagen, Erkenntnisse, Hinweise* (Schwalbach/Ts.: Wochenschau Verlag, 2011). He is also co-editor of the

Zeitschrift für Didaktik der Gesellschaftswissenschaften, and of several edited volumes: most recently, with Armin Rempfler, Barbara Sommer Häller and Markus Wilhelm, *Aneignungspraktiken an ausserschulischen Lernorten* (Münster: LIT, 2018); *Remembering and Recounting the Cold War – Commonly Shared History?* (Schwalbach/Ts.: Wochenschau Verlag, 2017); *Der Beitrag von Schulen und Hochschulen zu Erinnerungskulturen* (Schwalbach/Ts.: Wochenschau Verlag, 2014); *Shoa und Schule. Lehren und Lernen im 21. Jahrhundert* (Zurich: Chronos, 2013) and *Die Schweiz und die Shoa - Von Kontroversen zu neuen Fragen* (Zurich: Chronos, 2012), and with Daniel V. Moser, Kurt Reusser and Pit Wiher, *Geschichtsunterricht heute. Eine empirische Analyse ausgewählter Aspekte* (Bern: h.e.p. verlag ag., 2007).

Alexander Khodnev is Professor and Chair of the World History Department, Yaroslavl State Pedagogical University, Russia. His research interests include the history of the League of Nations and other international organisations, modern interdisciplinary didactics, and problems of history teaching, historical memory and public history. He is the author of several book chapters and articles in national and international journals. His recent publications include 'The Culture of the Cold War Memory in Modern Russia, 1991-2015' in: *Remembering and Recounting of the Cold War: Commonly Shared History?* (2017), 'Populäre Geschichtsmagazine in Russland. Ein Medium in geschichtskulturellen Wandel' in *Populäre Geschichtsmagazine in internationaler Perspektive* (2016), 'Le centenaire de la Première Guerre mondiale en Russie: la mémoire de la coopération francorusse' in *Revue Russe* (2016), and 'L'idee de la Société des Nations dans les projects de la fin de la Premiere Guerre mondiale' in: *France – Russie, 1914-1918: de l'alliance a la cooperation* (2015). He is a member of the Academic Advisory Board of the International Society for History Didactics, and Core Author at Public History Weekly.

Karel Van Nieuwenhuyse is Associate Professor of History Didactics at the Faculty of Arts, University of Leuven, Belgium. His main research interests relate to history education and the perspective of the present, the use of sources, students' historical narratives and their connections with their identities, historical representations of the colonial past, and the teaching of intercultural communication. He has published in several international journals such as the *London Review of Education*, *Historical Encounters*, and the *McGill Journal of Education*.

Teresa Oteíza is Associate Professor and Director of the Doctorate Program in Linguistics at the Pontifical Catholic University of Chile. Her interests include the areas of social discourse analysis, educational linguistics and systemic functional linguistics. She is currently working with Claudio Pinuer on the project *The Language of Appraisal in Spanish: Description and Systematization of Linguistic Resources to Build Intersubjectivity*. She published the book *El discurso pedagógico de la historia: Un análisis lingüístico sobre la construcción ideológica de la historia de Chile (1970-2001)* in 2006, and *En (re)construcción: Discurso, identidad y nación en los manuales escolares de historia y de ciencias sociales*, (ed. with Derrin Pinto) in 2011. Her forthcoming book, *What to Remember, What to Teach: Human Rights Violations in Chile's Recent Past and the Pedagogical Discourse of History*, will be published by Equinox.

Anders Persson holds a PhD in history education and works as a senior lecturer at Dalarna University, Sweden. Persson's research concerns both historical and pedagogical aspects of history as a school subject. In his doctoral thesis he explores upper primary teachers' experiences of a new outcome-based Swedish curriculum plan. The theoretical framework is inspired by existential philosophy, primarily as formulated in the works of Martin Heidegger and Hannah Arendt. Persson has also examined exercises, grading and textbooks within a history school context. His research focuses on the question of the existential potential of history as a school subject.

Nadine Ritzer is a lecturer in history and history didactics at the University of Teacher Education, Bern, Switzerland. She has taught at all primary school levels. She is a member of the board of the Swiss German Society of History Didactics (*Deutschschweizerische Gesellschaft für Geschichtsdiaktik*) and of the editorial committees of *Forschungswerkstatt Geschichtsdidaktik* (Workshop of History Didactics) and *Didactica*

Historica. Her main focus in her research and teaching is on teaching and learning history, cultural history, and on Cold War Studies. Her PhD about the Cold War in Swiss Schools (*Der Kalte Krieg in den Schweizer Schulen. Eine kulturgeschichtliche Analyse*) was published in 2015.

Robert Thorp is a senior lecturer at the Department of Education at Stockholm University in Sweden and a lecturer at the School of Education at the University of Newcastle, Australia. He obtained his doctorate from Umeå University, Sweden, and is an internationally active researcher. His research specialises in the relationship between the individual, society and history with an emphasis on how history shapes our contemporary perceptions, but also how these perceptions affect our relationship with the past. He has a special interest in how historical consciousness can be understood as a descriptive, analytical and normative concept. His other research interests are educational media, classroom studies, and teachers' relationships with history, with a special focus on Cold War history. Robert Thorp's latest book is *Uses of History in History Education* (Umeå, 2016). He has also published *Historical Consciousness, Historical Media, and History Education* (Umeå, 2014).

Hans Utz is affiliated with the University of Teacher Education, Lucerne. Before his retirement, he was a lecturer at the University of Teacher Education in Northwestern Switzerland, and a teacher and school principal at the Gymnasium Oberwil (Basel-Landschaft). He writes history teaching materials and conducts research on regional history. He has co-authored the textbooks *Weltgeschichte* (Zurich: Orell Füssli, 2014, 2015, 2017), *Geschichte der Neuzeit* (Zurich: Lehrmittelverlag Zurich, 2014), *Zeitreise* (Baar: Klett und Balmer, 2016-2018). On regional history, he has published *A Footnote of History* (Liestal: Kantonsverlag BL, 2015), and *The Wehrlifondskinder* (Liestal: Kantonsverlag BL, 2018).

Joanna Wojdon is Associate Professor at the Institute of History, University of Wrocław, Poland. She has been a Fulbright scholar (2014, Loyola University Chicago) and Kościuszko Foundation alumna (2003, Immigration History Research Center, Minneapolis, Minnesota; 2018 Hoover Institution, Palo Alto, California), a visiting professor at Hebrew

University, Jerusalem (2010/11), board member of the Polish American Historical Association and of the International Society for History Didactics, where she is also managing editor of the *International Journal of Research on History Didactics, History Education, and History Culture. Yearbook of the International Society for History Didactics* (JHEC). Her principal fields of research are the history of the Polish ethnic group in the United States, propaganda in education, and public history. Her publications include: *White and Red Umbrella. The Polish American Congress in the Cold War Era (1944-1988)* (Saint Helena, CA: Helena History Press, 2015); *Textbooks as Propaganda: Poland under Communist Rule (1944-1989)* (Abingdon/New York: Routledge, 2018), and 'Public History and Education', in *A Companion to Public History*, ed. D. Dean (Hoboken, NJ: Wiley, 2018).

List of Figures

Fig. 6.1	Swedish textbook depictions of the USA and the USSR (Holmén 2006, 237)	111
Fig. 9.1	A poster presenting the Marshall Plan as a dairy cow (Source: Izdebscy et al. 2015, 53)	201
Fig. 11.1	Representation of actors, events, processes and situations in historical discourses	228
Fig. 11.2	System of APPRECIATON for analysing events, processes and situations (Oteíza and Pinuer 2012; Oteíza 2017a)	230
Fig. 11.3	Evaluative prosody of power and conflict of main historical entities	242
Fig. 11.4	Evaluative prosody of fear from a temporal perspective	242
Fig. 17.1	Cartoon entitled 'Tour du Monde: Tandem oder Einrad?' by Jean Leffel. From German textbook: *Menschen in Zeit und Raum 9*, Edition for Lower Saxony, 113 (Zurich: Schulbuch Verlag plus AG, 2012)	364
Fig. 17.2	Cartoon entitled 'Entwurf fur ein Siegerdenkmal' or 'Draft of A Memorial to the Victors', published in Schweizer Illustrierte (11 April 1945). Reproduced here from the German textbook: *Entdecken und Verstehen 3*, Edition for Lower Saxony, 99 (Berlin: Cornelsen, 2010)	365
Fig. 18.1	Table of the Scheme of Changes over Time and of Development Contexts (Gautschi 2012, 97); Lower Saxony (♦), Saxony-Anhalt (O), Sweden (●), Switzerland (X)	396

Fig. 18.2	Table of Evaluation of the Thematisation of Human Action in Social Practice in Four Introductory Lessons on the Cold War; Lower Saxony (♦), Saxony-Anhalt (O), Sweden (●), Switzerland (X)	398
Fig. 18.3	Table of Evaluation of Principles and Methods of Acquiring Historical Knowledge in Four Introductory Lessons on the Cold War; Lower Saxony (♦), Saxony-Anhalt (O), Sweden (●), Switzerland (X)	399
Fig. 18.4	Table of a Common 'Schematic Narrative Template' and Different 'Specific Narrative Templates' in Four Introductory Lessons on the Cold War	401
Fig. 18.5	Table of Presentation of the Form of Teaching: Profile of the Swiss Lesson in Coding per Minutes (in brackets: teaching forms not occurring here)	405
Fig. 18.6	Table of Presentation of the Form of Teaching in Five Minute Coding: 'Task-based' (black), 'Presenting' (white) and 'Dialogue-oriented' (grey) Forms	405
Fig. 18.7	Table Ensuring Stimulating, Engaging and Appropriate Learning Opportunities: Lower Saxony (♦), Saxony-Anhalt (O), Sweden (●), Switzerland (X)	407
Fig. 18.8	Table Ensuring a Classroom Environment Conductive to Learning: Lower Saxony (♦), Saxony-Anhalt (O), Sweden (●), Switzerland (X)	408
Fig. 18.9	Table of Visualisation of the Presentation Concepts according to Barricelli on a Timeline in the Four Lessons	411
Fig. 18.10	Structure and Process Model of Historical Learning	413
Fig. 18.11	Table of Evaluation of the Use of History Teaching; Lower Saxony (♦), Saxony-Anhalt (O), Sweden (●), Switzerland (X)	415
Fig. 18.12	Table of Overall Evaluation of the Lessons after Points; Lower Saxony (♦), Saxony-Anhalt (O), Sweden (●), Switzerland (X)	416

List of Tables

Table 4.1	Number of pages allocated to each topic	56
Table 5.1	Table showing the share of the text devoted to domestic and international history and to political, economic, and cultural history in the three textbooks combined	80
Table 5.2	Table showing the most salient divisions found in the international history of the Cold War. That is, a chapter on economic developments in capitalist countries after WWII would show a division of East vs. West, whereas the growth of the non-aligned movement would show a division of North vs. South	81
Table 6.1	Table Showing an Overview of the Main Chronological, Geographical and Content-related Points of Focus in the Four Textbooks under Examination	113
Table 6.2	Table Showing the Treatment of the Cold War in the Four Textbooks Examined	113
Table 8.1	Overview of the Main Chronological, Geographical and Content-related Points of Focus in Four Textbooks	167
Table 8.2	The Treatment of the Cold War in the Four Textbooks	168
Table 9.1	Table Showing Number of Pages devoted to the Cold War and its Various Aspects in Polish Secondary School Textbooks. The results for each textbook do not sum up to 100% because more than one issue may be discussed on one page	189

List of Tables

Table 11.1	Historical, social and educational changes and their impact on History textbooks	225
Table 11.2	Attitudinal meanings in relation to entities appraised in the field of history	227
Table 13.1	Table comparing East and West German teachers' responses to a text	269
Table 13.2	How teachers from Switzerland react to a text	274
Table 13.3	Table comparing the responses of teachers from the different countries to a text	277
Table 18.1	Table of the Teaching Forms of the Four Analysed Lessons in Comparison	406
Table 18.2	Table of Beginning a Lesson, according to Gerhard Schneider (2008)	409
Table 18.3	Table of Presentation Concepts according to Barricelli	410

1

Introduction: The Cold War in the Classroom International Perspectives on Textbooks and Memory Practices

Barbara Christophe

Recalling the past has been described as an 'unnatural act', involving as it does a constant oscillation between two opposing but equally indispensable modes of defining the relation between times past and times present (Wineburg 1999). Similarities as well as differences are highlighted in one moment and rendered invisible in another. Complementing as much as constraining each other, these two approaches create familiarity *and* strangeness, proximity *and* distance in an almost paradoxical manner. Both have their own merits. While the vague idea of sharing a common identity with those who preceded us in time awakens our interest in the past, grasping the differences between the way we feel, think and act and the way people of former times did so enables us to understand the contingency of our own perceptions of and performances in the world (Wineburg 1999, 490).

B. Christophe (✉)
Georg Eckert Institute for International Textbook Research,
Member of the Leibniz Association, Brunswick, Germany
e-mail: christophe@gei.de

What appears to be the normal if somewhat ambitious script for most of our encounters with the past turns into a rather complex matter when it comes to calibrating the relationship between the Cold War past and the post-Cold War present. We are faced with at least two challenges. On the one hand, we have competing definitions of the present moment as the indispensable starting point for our reconstructions of the past. On the other, we have multiple ways of establishing a link between what is now and what was then. Some observers perceived 9/11 as the trigger moment of a new fundamental clash, a 'long war' between the West and Islam, the new antagonist that has replaced the former East (Buzan 2006). For others, Russia's annexation of Crimea in 2014 signalled a return to the familiar constellation of polarised conflict between East and West (Legvold 2014; Ciolan 2016). At the same time, various commentators have repeatedly invoked the end of the Cold War since 1990. While the East-West rivalry was seen to have abated through a sweeping and glorious victory of the West in the 1990s, recent discourses herald the eclipse of the same West in the light of mounting tensions between Europe and the USA (Kimmage 2013; Wright 2017). Without doubt, current claims of an insurmountable abyss separating the days of the Cold War from our present times has gained in plausibility with the less-than-predictable policies of President Trump towards Russia. The complex realities of today's world in which the current leader of the USA ponders publicly about accepting Russia's take-over of Crimea one moment while commanding air strikes in Syria and thus risking a military confrontation with the same Russia the next (Rutland 2017), could not contrast more sharply with the ritualised and predictable opposition between the former superpowers that dominated international politics from 1947 to 1990.

Memory theory teaches us that present moments always leave their imprint on the many different and ultimately contingent ways in which the past can be reconstructed. The current situation of uncertainty and unpredictability therefore could not but provoke a controversy on how to make sense of the Cold War. Indeed, contrary to claims according to which the end of the East-West rivalry and the opening of Soviet archives would lead to a lessening of controversies (Nehring 2012), we observe a multiplication of debates. It is not only that traditionalist, revisionist and post-revisionist frames, which either blame the USSR, the USA or both for having caused the conflict, still vie for hegemony (Lundestad 2014); the question as to whether the second half of the 20th century has been shaped more profoundly by the East-West or the North-South conflict has also triggered hot debate (Iriye 2013). On a more fundamental level, we even hear the argument that the USA and the USSR, both of which tried to change the outlook of the world according to their own images (Westad 2000; Engerman 2010; Duara 2011) shared several crucial features despite the ritualised stand-off they were staging. Finally, historians are in dispute about the true nature of the Cold War. While some point to the ever-present fear of dying in a nuclear war as the defining moment (Nehring 2012), others identify the social welfare state as a by-product of the conflict (Kaelble 2011).

The authors of this book do not engage directly in these debates but rather aim to analyse empirically to what extent practices of remembering the Cold War in history textbooks and in the social space of the history classroom are informed by the various viewpoints and positions circulating in academic and public discourses. This agenda results from conceptual decisions taken on four levels.

First, approaching the Cold War from an angle informed by *memory studies* and raising the question of how its unavoidably selective and thus political image is produced nowadays, the volume simultaneously addresses – and moves beyond – recent trends in Cold War studies. While historians have shown an increased interest in the cultural dimension of the Cold War as a phenomenon of the past for some time, looking at the roles played by different media as well as networks of people and organisations in reproducing the binary oppositions on which the conflict was based (Sanders 2000, Vowinckel et al. 2012), only scant and unsystematic attention (Lowe/Joel 2012, Jarausch et al. 2017) has been paid to processes of negotiating its meaning in the present. At the same time, memory studies have been largely preoccupied with exploring the more settled memory of the Second World War or the Holocaust. According to the authors of this book, shifting the focus to a more contested issue like the Cold War makes it simultaneously more compelling and rewarding to investigate which of the manifold events of the past are referred to in concrete acts of remembering.

Second, in dealing with *practices* of remembering the Cold War in their manifold forms and diverse facets, the authors of this book intend to bridge practice theory and memory studies. Although practice theory is a rather heterogeneous field stretching from classics like Giddens and Bourdieu to actor-network theories, two crucial ideas serve as a common denominator among various approaches. Practices are not only perceived to be a hinge between the situated actions of concrete individuals and the cultural structures that imbue these actions with a certain dose of predictability without fully determining them (Pentzold 2015); they are also seen as being based on practical knowledge that usually remains implicit, thus allowing for a certain degree of vagueness and ambivalence (Reckwitz 2003). Applying these assumptions to the study of social processes of negotiating the meaning of the Cold War, we emphasise that individual acts of remembering are shaped by collectively shared patterns of ascribing meaning to selected facts of the past considered relevant to today's memory. At the same time, however, we also admit that these patterns are embodied in usually rather polysemic texts, artefacts or performances (Sturken 1997, Sandage 1993), which do not have a life of their own beyond being reiterated, recollected and at times reshaped or reconfigured by concrete individuals (Olick/Robinson 1998, 111; Feindt et al. 2014, 30). Instead of reifying the difference between individual and collective memory, which ultimately constitutes two ways of looking at the same thing, we focus on disentangling the many different factors that play out in the concrete, situated acts of recalling the past that we call memory practices. We moreover construe these memory practices as activities that, to a certain extent, are a matter of sheer routine. We thus claim that our encounters with the past are not only shaped by conscious decisions regarding what to remember and what to forget; they are also driven by the silent work of common-sense assumptions and the binary oppositions these support. Conceiving of memory practices as based to a large degree on implicit knowledge, we thus attend to the messiness and ambivalence deemed characteristic of practices in general (Goodnough 2008), and of practices of recalling the Cold War past in particular, given not only the disputes around that period but also the postmodern trend towards chaotic, fragmentary and free-floating memories (Huyssen 1995).

Third, all authors have chosen to analyse social practices of negotiating the meaning of the Cold War in the institutional field (Schudson 1992) of the school, focusing on textbooks, teachers and students. Observing memory practices through these analytical lenses comes with several advantages. History textbooks are a mass medium for the dissemination of officially approved images of history and, at the same time, mirrors of societal controversies surrounding sensitive issues (Klerides 2010; Macgilchrist 2015). They mingle and blend myriads of discursive threads which connect them with the wider social environment (Binnenkade 2015). Situated at the boundaries between politics, history scholarship and pedagogy, they reflect curricular demands as well as scientific and pedagogic standards. They respond to market requirements and to political debates. History teachers are members of a state elite specialised in conveying official interpretations, while, at the same time, each teacher carries a unique autobiographical memory (Christophe 2012; Umetbaeva 2015). Like their students, they read newspapers and novels, watch films, browse the internet and talk with family and friends, thus bringing numerous mediated memories into the interactional space of the classroom. As the addressees of contradictory expectations, pupils are required to reproduce interpretative knowledge and, at the same time, develop interpretative autonomy (Spär/Sperisen 2010). Furthermore, they are not only future citizens who are supposed to adopt officially sanctioned knowledge; they are also the offspring of families and social milieus with their own potentially diverging memories (Welzer/Moller/Tschuggnall 2002). Textbook discourse, teacher-talk and classroom practice are thus firmly embedded in a wide range of social relations stretching far beyond them. The insights to be gained from their analysis can therefore be expected to be relevant for a broader social context. Being entangled in structural ambivalences, they can moreover be assumed to produce the ambivalence and contingency which practice theory is especially well equipped to address.

At the same time, a focus on the school proves illuminating when examining current trends in the field of memory research. Some of our authors respond to the increased interest in the generational transmission of memory (Palmberger 2016) by either analysing textbooks from a diachronic perspective or by exploring how the meaning of the past is negotiated between teachers and students as members of different generations with particular common-sense assumptions and exposure to varying media discourses. Most of the contributions resonate well with the new focus within memory research on conflict and contestation (Schwartz 2016). Some give special emphasis to ambivalences in textbooks in order to detect cracks and fissures in mnemonic hegemonies. Others approach the classroom as a social space where unresolved mnemonic disputes, often hidden behind vague phrases (Ryan 2011), are likely to bubble to the surface when students, as newcomers to their respective memory cultures, have not yet fully internalised the social rules of navigating precarious issues relating to the past.

Fourth, approaching the history classroom with a focus on memory practices, most authors move beyond analyses of learning and teaching practices. Whereas previous studies have been primarily interested in practices *of* history education, exploring which teaching strategies would be most effective in producing desired learning outcomes or asking how one can help students best master historical thinking (Wineburg 2001; Van Drie & Van Boxtel 2008), the majority of contributions to this volume look into memory practices *in* history education. The focus is not on history as a discipline, requiring certain ways of doing and saying, but rather on history education as a setting in which we can closely observe how teachers and students 'do memory' (Macgilchrist et al. 2015) and engage with the past. Emphasis is given to decisions taken on the level of content rather than teaching or learning strategies. We want to know which facts attract the attention of teachers and students and which are ignored by them. We explore which interpretations are guarded and which are rejected or simply sidelined. Attending to all these choices, we are interested in the political (Sturken 2008, 74) and not in the didactic implications that follow from them. Approaching the history classroom from the memory practices angle and thus emphasising the role of implicit knowledge and routines in our dealings with the past, we also introduce new aspects into a debate that has so far been mainly focussed on historical consciousness (Seixas 2004). While this term seems to imply that teachers and students are as a rule highly reflective when they 'do' history, the contributions to this book show that doing history is essentially not much different from doing memory. Neither can avoid taking a stance, and neither can escape being informed by social discourses with all their common-sense assumptions and categorisations which are, as a rule, not objects of conscious reflection and are thus all the more powerful.

The volume is divided into three sections, which (i) look at interpretations of the Cold War offered in textbooks, (ii) draw on teachers' understanding of textbooks and (iii) analyse how textbooks, teachers and students interact with one another in the setting of the history classroom. The chapters in the first section investigate to what extent narratives conveyed in educational media reproduce, destabilise or creatively appropriate current discourses in historiography and politics. Taking into account the particular challenges faced by practices of remembering the Cold War in times of unstable political identities, most chapters also emphasise the ambivalences and tensions built into these narratives as well as the strategies designed to deal with them. Based on interviews and observational data, the contributions to the second and third sections not only ask how teachers and students position themselves towards social discourses; they also explore how ways of remembering the Cold War can be informed by situational dynamics between interviewer and interviewee or by the expectations placed on teachers and students alike. Despite these variations in the breadth and depth of their empirical basis, and despite the peculiarity of the analytical questions they raise, all contributions share one crucial feature: All focus on rendering explicit what is often only implied in written texts or in verbal statements.

In terms of geographical scope, studies on textbooks, teacher-talk and classroom interaction in Germany, Sweden and Switzerland form the core of the book. These three countries not only happened to be at the focus of the international research projects on which the volume is based; all of them assumed diverging roles during the Cold War past. While Germany was divided into two states, each at the frontline of the Cold War and thus closely involved in the respective political and/or military alliances, Sweden and Switzerland demonstrated two varieties of neutral policy. In the case of Switzerland this followed a more pragmatic and calculated course, at the same time affirming western values (Wenger and Nuenlist 2008), while the Swedish variant followed the moral pledge for a 'Third Way' (Aselius 2005; Browning 2007). Against this backdrop, the contributions to this volume explore how these different constellations of the past inform memory practices in the present.

Case studies focusing exclusively on textbooks further enrich the comparative angle. They treat the USA and Russia as the main protagonists of the conflict, as well as Poland and Belgium as countries located on different sides of the iron curtain. They further analyse textbooks from China as the new aspiring hegemonic power, and Cold-War narratives from Chile and South Africa, both of which were part of the so-called former 'Third World'. To sum up, the chapters of this book provide rich descriptions of specific acts of recalling the contested Cold War past in the social space of the school. Covering a broad range of cultural contexts and applying a diverse set of methodological strategies, they map the dividing lines in and between memory cultures in the crisis-driven and volatile age of our present in which mnemonic consensus is clearly an issue of the past – if indeed it has ever existed at all. The authors point to varying degrees of ambivalence, vagueness and contradictions in the inescapably political textbook narratives understood to be echoes of societal and academic controversies. Authors focussing on teachers and the history classroom show how unresolved political issues create tensions and dilemmas in history education. They render visible how teachers struggle to handle these challenges by pretending that what they do is 'just history'. Obfuscating the political that is inherent to all memory practices, they produce the illusion that the history in which they are engaged is all about addressing the past with a reflexive and disciplined approach.

Bibliography

Aselius, Gunnar. 2005. 'Swedish Strategic Culture after 1945'. *Cooperation and Conflict* 40, no. 1: 25–44.

Binnenkade, Alexandra. 2015. 'Doing Memory: Teaching as a Discursive Node'. *Journal of Educational Media, Memory, and Society* 7, no. 2: 29–43.

Browning, Christopher. 2007. 'Branding Nordicity: Models, Identity and the Decline of Exceptionalism.' *Cooperation and Conflict* 42, no. 1: 27–51.

Buzan, Barry. 2006. 'Will the Global War on Terrorism be the New Cold War?' *International Affairs* 82, no. 6: 1101–1118.

Christophe, Barbara. 2012. 'Verhandlungen über den Sozialismus. Geschichtslehrer als Schnittstelle zwischen individuellem und kollektivem Gedächtnis'. *Eckert. Beiträge*, no. 1. http://repository.gei.de/handle/11428/102 (last accessed 13 May 2019).

Ciolan, Ionela Maria. 2016. 'The Role of the "New Cold War" Concept in Constructing Russia's Great Power Narrative'. *CES Working Papers* 8, no. 4. Centre for European Studies, Alexandru Ioan Cuza University: 625–647.

Duara, Prasjenit. 2011. 'The Cold War as a Historical Period: An Interpretive Essay'. *Journal of Global History* 6, no. 3: 457–480.

Engerman, David. 2010. 'Ideology and the Origin of the Cold War'. In *The Cambridge History of the Cold War. Volume I.: Origins,* edited by Melvyn P. Leffler and Odd Arne Westad, 20–43. Cambridge: Cambridge University Press.

Goodnough, Karen. 2008. 'Dealing with Messiness and Uncertainty in Practitioner Research: The Nature of Participatory Action Research'. *Canadian Journal of Education* 31, no. 2: 431–458.

Huyssen A. 1995. *Twilight Memories: Marking Time in a Culture of Amnesia.* New York: Routledge.

Jarausch, Konrad H., Christian F. Ostermann and Andreas Etges, eds. 2017. *The Cold War: Historiography, Memory, Representation.* Berlin: de Gruyter.

Kaelble, Hartmut. 2011. *Kalter Krieg und Wohlfahrtsstaat. Europa 1945-1989.* München: C. H. Beck.

Klerides, Eleftherios. 2010. 'Imagining the Textbook: Textbooks as Discourse and Genre', *Journal of Educational Media, Memory, and Society* 2, no. 1: 31–54.

Legvold, Robert. 2014. 'Managing the New Cold War'. *Foreign Affairs* 93, no. 4: 74–84.

Lundestad, Geir. 2014. 'The Cold War in Europe, 1945-1949. Some Old and New Theories about the Cold War'. In *East, West, North, South. International Relations since 1945.* London/New York: Sage.

Macgilchrist, Felicitas. 2015. 'Geschichte Und Dissens: Diskursives Ringen Um Demokratie in Der Schulbuchproduktion'. In *Erziehungswissenschaftliche Diskursforschung: Empirische Analysen zu Bildungs- und Erziehungsverhältnissen,* edited by Susann Fegter, Fabian Kessl, Antje Langer, Marion Ott, Daniela Rothe and Daniel Wrana. Wiesbaden: VS Verlag für Sozialwissenschaften. https://doi.org/10.1007/978-3-531-18738-9_10

Nehring, Holger. 2012. 'What Was the Cold War?' *The English Historical Review* 127, no. 527: 920–949. https://doi.org/10.1093/ehr/ces176

Palmberger, Monika. 2016. *How Generations Remember. Conflicting Histories and Shared Memories in Post-War- Bosnia and Herzegovina*. London: Palgrave.

Pentzold, Christian. 2015. 'Praxistheoretische Prinzipien, Traditionen und Perspektiven kulturalistischer Kommunikations- und Medienforschung'. *Medien & Kommunikationswissenschaft* 63, no. 2: 229–245.

Reckwitz, Andreas. 2003. 'Towards a Theory of Social Practices'. *European Journal of Social Theory* 5: 245–265.

Rutland, Peter. 2017. 'Trump, Putin and the Future of US-Russian Relations'. *Slavic Review* 71: 541–556.

Sandage, Scott A. 1993. 'A Marble House Divided: The Lincoln Memorial, the Civil Rights Movement, and the Politics of Memory, 1939-1963'. *Journal of American History* 80, no. 1: 135–167.

Sanders, Frances Stonor. 2000. *The Cultural Cold War: The CIA and the World of Arts and Letters*. New York: New press.

Schudson M. 1992. *Watergate in American Memory: How We Remember, Forget, and Reconstruct the Past*. New York: Basic Books.

Schwartz, Barry. 2016. 'Rethinking the Concept of Collective Memory', in *Routledge International Handbook of Memory Studies*, edited by Anna Lisa Tota and Trever Hagen, 9–20. London/New York: Routledge.

Seixas, Peter, ed. 2004. *Theorizing Historical Consciousness*. Toronto: University of Toronto Press.

Sturken, Marita. 1997. *Tangled Memories: The Vietnam War, The Aids Epidemic, and the Politics of Remembering*. Berkeley: University of California Press.

Sturken, Marita. 2008. 'Memory, Consumerism and Media: Reflections on the Emergence of the Field'. *Memory Studies* 1, no. 1.

Umetbaeva, Damira. 2015. 'Paradoxes of Hegemonic Discourse in Post-Soviet Kyrgyzstan: History Textbooks' and History Teachers' Attitudes towards the Soviet Past'. *Central Asian Affairs* 2, no. 3: 287–306.

Van Drie, Janet and Carla Van Boxtel. 2008. 'Historical Reasoning: Towards a Framework for Analyzing Students' Reasoning about the Past'. *Educational Psychology Review* 20, no. 2: 87–110.

Vowinckel, Annette, Marcus M. Payk and Thomas Lindenberger, eds. 2012. *Cold War Cultures. Perspectives on Eastern and Western European Societies*. New York/Oxford: Berghahn Books.

Welzer, Harald, Sabine Moller and Karoline Tschuggnall. 2002. *'Opa war kein Nazi'. Nationalsozialismus und Holocaust im Familiengedächtnis*. Frankfurt a. M: Fischer Taschenbuch Verlag.

Wenger, Andreas and Christian Nuenlist. 2008. 'A "Special Case" between Independence and Interdependence: Cold War Studies and Cold War Politics in Post-Cold War Switzerland'. *Cold War History* 8, no. 2: 213–240.

Westad, Odd Arne. 2000. 'The New International History of the Cold War: Three Possible Paradigms'. *Diplomatic History* 24, no. 4: 551–565.

Wineburg, Sam. 2001. *Historical Thinking and other Unnatural Acts: Charting the Future of Teaching the Past*. Philadelphia: Temple University Press.

Wright, Thomas. 2017. *A Post-American Europe and the Future of US-Strategy*, Washington: Brookings/Robert Bosch Foundation.

Open Access This chapter is licensed under the terms of the Creative Commons Attribution 4.0 International License (http://creativecommons.org/licenses/by/4.0/), which permits use, sharing, adaptation, distribution and reproduction in any medium or format, as long as you give appropriate credit to the original author(s) and the source, provide a link to the Creative Commons licence and indicate if changes were made.

The images or other third party material in this chapter are included in the chapter's Creative Commons licence, unless indicated otherwise in a credit line to the material. If material is not included in the chapter's Creative Commons licence and your intended use is not permitted by statutory regulation or exceeds the permitted use, you will need to obtain permission directly from the copyright holder.

Part I

Textbook Memories

Part I

2

Textbook Memories of the Cold War: Introduction to Part One

Barbara Christophe

Making the case for history textbooks as valuable sources for memory practices (Christophe and Schwedes 2018), appears to be rather like charging an open door. Textbook and memory research share many assumptions and raise similar questions. Both claim that reconstructions of the past are contingent on interests and beliefs in the present; both seek to unpack the – at times rather complex – relations between times past and times present. History textbooks, which have been cogently described as 'weapons of mass instruction' (Ingrao 2009), play a vital role in sustaining mnemonic hegemonies. Selecting what counts as relevant (school) knowledge from a vast plethora of historical facts, they take part in setting the limits of what can be legitimately said (Apple 2000). Powerfully reproducing and imposing on us the categorical distinctions we tend to draw in our mediated encounters with the past, they influence what can pass for common sense.

B. Christophe (✉)
Georg Eckert Institute for International Textbook Research,
Member of the Leibniz Association, Brunswick, Germany
e-mail: christophe@gei.de

At the same time, we can distinguish between two different approaches in textbook research. Some conceive of history textbooks as the 'autobiographies of nations' (Jacobmeyer 1998), as powerful instruments for crafting a broad social consensus on how to make sense of the past. Other researchers argue that textbooks are objects of fierce struggle between competing political groups over the construction of a common-sense reality (Apple 2000). They point to the many cracks and fissures that enter textbook narratives in the course of attempts to merge different positions and to speak to different constituencies (Klerides 2010). Both camps agree, however, that history textbooks do not convey neutral knowledge, but rather participate in the construction of what Raymond Williams (1961) has called the 'selective tradition'.

Although the arguments presented so far might appear as banal truisms, they have in fact met with fierce criticism. It has been argued that textbooks are far too boring, confusing and misleading (Tyson-Bernstein 1988) to shape the minds of students. Textbook stories are said to be too predictable to be interesting, focusing exclusively on challenges successfully mastered and hardships overcome (Loewen 2007). Studies on 'textbookese' (Crismore 1984) have shown how one proposition after the other is made without rendering visible who is speaking. Researchers have criticised textbook authors for tending to speak with an anonymous but highly authoritative voice, assuming the role of 'truth giver' (Crismore 1984, 292), or a 'surveyor' (Myskow 2017) of uncontested insights. They have pointed out that the reader is ascribed the rather passive and uncomfortable position of one who is to listen but not speak back as there is nobody to argue with (Coffin 2009). Finally, scholars claim that the discursive construction of 'disinterested impartiality' (Myskow 2017, 4) and the 'appearance of neutrality' (Coffin 2009, 396) clearly comes with the risk of losing the interest of the potential reader who is known to appreciate passionate authors taking stances (Commager 1966). Although some authors (Klerides 2010; Gautschi 2010) have emphasised that textbooks have seen significant changes in recent years, especially when it comes to encouraging students to pass their own judgements, they have also noticed that there is still room for further improvement. If the chapters in this section nevertheless analyse history textbooks

2 Textbook Memories of the Cold War: Introduction to Part One

as sources for the reconstruction of memory practices, they do so because they share two core assumptions, the validity of which is not affected by the compelling critique referred to above.

Firstly, even textbooks failing to persuade their readers of the propositions they make may be effective in normalising certain distinctions, systems of categorisation, and modes of structuring a story. As tiny subtleties usually pass unnoticed and enter our minds below the radar of conscious control, they may have the greatest impact on meaning-making (Christophe 2014). We thus – literally – have to take the textbook at its word (Ott 2014). Translating these considerations into carefully designed research strategies, the contributions to this section arrive at intriguing insights.

In her analysis of current Chinese textbooks, Lisa Dyson shows how meaning-making already takes place in the table of contents. Presenting the readers with three chapters on politics, economics, and culture, each of which spans the whole of the 20th century, the authors signal that they consider chronological turning-points in general, and the beginning and end of the Cold War in particular, less worthy of attention than the emergence of a truly multi-polar world with China as one of its dominating poles.

Teresa Oteíza and Claudia Castro point out how textbooks from Chile focus exclusively on American fears and concerns when addressing the Cuban revolution or the electoral victory of Salvador Allende. The emotions of other actors are not even mentioned; we learn nothing, for instance, about the hope felt by left-wing parties at these historic moments. As a result, the reader is powerfully instructed to empathise with the USA.

Linda Chisholm and David Fig explain how the predominant use of the passive voice in South African textbooks contributes to constructing the image of Africa and Africans as helpless victims of rival superpowers. However, they also point out that, conversely, the same textbooks completely ignore the influence of international factors on bringing down apartheid and ascribing agency exclusively to local resistance fighters.

Working on US-American textbooks, Eva Fischer also pays particular attention to micro-analysis. In one telling example she deconstructs a sentence stating that 'although' they were 'also' communist, Soviets were influenced by security concerns. She renders visible how the conjunction 'although' encompasses two simultaneous functions: On the one hand, it silently undermines the revisionist claim that the Soviets were fearful by implying that communists had no security concerns. On the other hand, it remains sufficiently vague about the precise relationship between being communist and having security concerns.

Focusing on current Swedish textbooks, Anders Persson describes in detail how students are instructed to judge Soviets critically and to identify with the Americans. While the former are portrayed as a faceless mass of people generally deprived of any agency, the latter are introduced as progressive and skilful individuals, as creative artists or inventive industrialists who seize any opportunity to grow.

Joanna Wojdon demonstrates how Polish textbooks always describe the USA in a favourable light, either by omitting negative aspects like the so-called witch-hunt in the McCarthy era or by focusing on solutions found to problems such as racism without examining in detail the injustices that were their root causes.

Karel Van Nieuwenhuyse elucidates how Belgian textbooks at times implicitly pass moral judgements by their choice of words. As an example he provides a close analysis of a sentence stating that the GDR was *forced* to become a Soviet ally while the FRG *chose* its attachment to the West. In addition, he unveils how textbook authors construct Western values as the natural standard by which to judge societies all over the world.

Secondly, history textbooks not only tell us which historical interpretations enjoy dominance; in various ways they also provide us with insights into controversies. At times, ambivalence or non-coherence in texts points to what critical educationalist Michael Apple has called the 'politics of incorporation' (Apple 2000), which aims at stabilising hegemony by simultaneously giving space to and taming the voices of formerly excluded minorities. Elsewhere, vagueness caters to the need to avoid open conflict over unresolved issues of the past. Finally, in some cases significant discrepancies between textbooks published by different publishing houses remind us of unresolved societal disputes. The chapters in this section provide illustrative examples of all three variants.

2 Textbook Memories of the Cold War: Introduction to Part One 19

Eva Fischer provides a detailed analysis of how American textbooks include revisionist approaches towards the Cold War by admitting, for example, that the USA pursued rather egoistic goals with its Marshall Plan. At the same time she points out that only watered-down versions of these arguments are incorporated in order to ensure that they would not destabilise the traditional positive self-image.

Writing on Russian textbooks, Alexander Khodnev reveals that their portrayals of the Cold War remain somewhat disparate. The four most widely used textbooks differ significantly, not only with regard to how much space they allocate to the so-called Third World or to cultural aspects; even when it comes to core issues such as the blame for the conflict we see a broad range of different positions. While some authors admit that there is no clear-cut answer to this question, others blame the iron fist brandished by the Americans at all opponents to their hegemonic plans.

Anders Persson points to significant differences in the portrayals of the USA offered by different Swedish textbooks. While most books describe the Western superpower in rather traditional terms as the epitome of freedom and success, as a country to which people migrated in pursuit of happiness, one mentions how women, the poor, slaves and natives were disenfranchised and how the Civil War between North and South claimed more victims than all other wars in which the USA has participated.

Karel van Nieuwenhuyse shows that Belgian textbooks differ with regard to the homogeneity they ascribe to the Eastern bloc. While some authors dedicate space to counter-voices only from within the Western camp, others focus on dissent in the Eastern camp as well.

Joanna Wojdon identifies tensions in portrayals of Winston Churchill in Polish textbooks. While Churchill is described as the first Western politician to notice the aggressiveness of the Soviet Union, he is also introduced as an outspoken critic of the transfer of German territories to Poland. However, as Wojdon argues, in the eyes of Polish textbook authors, Poland gained more from the end of cooperation between the Western powers and the USSR than it suffered from the same Western powers striking an alliance with the former war enemy Germany.

Markus Furrer reconstructs four powerful and potentially contradictory images that dominate Swiss textbook narratives of the Cold War. Switzerland is portrayed (i) as overwhelmed by anti-communist hysteria,

(ii) as a potential victim of a nuclear war, (iii) as a social space in which the economy boomed and a democratic consociation took firm root, and (iv) as a society that suffered from the iron curtain.

Finally, textbooks lend themselves particularly well to international comparison. With the global expansion of the nation-state and the school as one of its core institutions, textbooks have literally travelled the world (Christophe 2014), performing more-or-less the same instructional functions across spaces and places. The contributions to this section offer intriguing and at times surprising findings on similarities as well as differences between textbook narratives of the Cold War.

Whereas post-apartheid textbooks in South Africa seem to constitute the exception, portraying the USSR in a more favourable light, Chinese and Chilean textbook authors appear to agree on the insignificance of the Soviet Union, which is given only scant attention and moreover characterised as a failing, and thus negligible, state and social system. In fact, Chinese textbooks, like some Russian and the majority of Polish textbooks, do not give much priority to the Cold War at all. Snippets of information on the conflict are scattered over several chapters, all of which span the whole period from 1945 to the present day under shifting titles.

US-American and Russian textbooks resemble each other in one structural aspect. Both are ready to retract part of the blame they formerly placed on the 'other', the ideological rival during the Cold War, but stop short of criticising the national 'self'. Russian textbooks avoid the term 'occupation', for instance, when they deal with Cold War relations between the USSR and Eastern Europe, and US textbooks never mention capitalism as being behind the American interest in penetrating European markets with the help of the Marshall Plan.

With regard to the attribution of agency, textbooks from Poland and Sweden share one crucial aspect. Both feature active citizens only when writing about the extended West; in the extended East only politicians, primarily great white men, are presented as capable of having agency.

To sum up, the contributions to this section offer us intriguing insights into textbook discourses on the Cold War in different societies and, at the same time, present us with innovative methodological suggestions on how to analyse textbooks as manifestations of situated memory practices.

References

Apple, Michael. 2000. *Official Knowledge: Democratic Education in a Conservative Age*. New York: Routledge.

Christophe, Barbara. 2014. *Kulturwissenschaftliche Schulbuchforschung: Trends, Ergebnisse, Potentiale*. Eckert.Working Papers 6.

Christophe, Barbara and Kerstin Schwedes. 2018. 'Between Persistent Differences and Vagueness: Textbook Narratives about the First World War'. In *The Long End of the First World War*, edited by Katrin Bromber, Katharina Lange, Heike Liebau and Anorthe Wetzel, 209–234. Frankfurt a. M.: Campus.

Coffin, Caroline. 2009. *Historical Discourse. The Language of Time, Cause and Evaluation*. London: Continuum.

Commager, H. 1966. *The Nature and Study of History*. Columbus, Ohio: Charles E. Merrill.

Crismore, Avon. 1984. 'The Rhetoric of Textbooks: Metadiscourse'. *Journal of Curriculum Studies* 16, no. 3: 279–296.

Gautschi, Peter. 2010. Anforderungen an heutige und künftige Schulgeschichtsbücher. *Beiträge zur Lehrerinnen- und Lehrerbildung* 28: 125–137.

Ingrao, Charles. 2009. 'Weapons of Mass Instruction: Schoolbook and Democratisation in Multiethnic Central Europe'. *Journal of Educational Media, Memory, and Society* 1, no. 1: 180–189.

Jacobmeyer, Wolfgang. 1998. 'Das Schulgeschichtsbuch – Gedächtnis der Gesellschaft oder Autobiographie der Nation?' *Geschichte, Politik und ihre Didaktik* 26: 26–35.

Klerides, Eleftherios. 2010. 'Imagining the Textbook: Textbooks as Discourse and Genre'. *Journal of Educational Media, Memory, and Society* 2, no. 1: 31–54.

Loewen, James. 2007. *Lies my Teacher Told Me: Everything your American History Textbook Got Wrong*. New York: New press.

Myskow, Gordon. 2017. 'Surveying the Historical Landscape: The Evaluative Voice of the Textbook'. *Functional Linguistics* 4, no. 7: 1–15.

Ott, Christine. 2014. 'Das Schulbuch beim Wort nehmen. Linguistische Methodik in der Schulbuchforschung'. In *Methodologie und Methoden der Schulbuch- und Lehrmittelforschung*, edited by Petr Knecht, Eva Mattes, Sylvia Schütze and Bente Aamotsbakken, 254–263. Bad Heilbrunn: Klinkhardt.

Tyson-Bernstein, Harriet. 1988. *A Conspiracy of Good Intentions: America's Textbook Fiasco*. Washington: Council for Basic Education.

Williams, Raymond. 1961. *The Long Revolution*. London: Chatto and Windus.

Open Access This chapter is licensed under the terms of the Creative Commons Attribution 4.0 International License (http://creativecommons.org/licenses/by/4.0/), which permits use, sharing, adaptation, distribution and reproduction in any medium or format, as long as you give appropriate credit to the original author(s) and the source, provide a link to the Creative Commons licence and indicate if changes were made.

The images or other third party material in this chapter are included in the chapter's Creative Commons licence, unless indicated otherwise in a credit line to the material. If material is not included in the chapter's Creative Commons licence and your intended use is not permitted by statutory regulation or exceeds the permitted use, you will need to obtain permission directly from the copyright holder.

3

Manufacturing Coherence: How American Textbooks Incorporate Diverse Perspectives on the Origins of the Cold War

Eva Fischer

Introduction

In 2010, the Texan State Board of Education, conservative by majority, voted in favour of changing the social studies curriculum standards. As well as mandating changes that would downplay numerous socio-political issues, board members demanded a more positive representation of US-style capitalism as a 'free enterprise system' and a stronger emphasis on the Soviet Union's aggressiveness during the Cold War. They viewed their actions as a fight 'for … our nation's future' (McKinley 2010; NBC News 2010).[1]

Interpretations of the Cold War are interwoven with political and cultural values, and attached to notions of national identity. While this is true of many countries and societies (see Lowe and Joel 2013) it is the US where the concepts of 'freedom', 'progress' and 'exceptionalism', in the sense of superiority, have fed most strongly into a national master narrative (Foner 1999; Barton and Levstik 2009, 166–182; Pease 2007;

E. Fischer (✉)
Independent Researcher, Oldenburg, Germany

© The Author(s) 2019
B. Christophe et al. (eds.), *The Cold War in the Classroom*, Palgrave Studies in Educational Media, https://doi.org/10.1007/978-3-030-11999-7_3

Paul 2014). During the Cold War, the US represented itself as the leader of the free world and defender against an evil, backward Soviet Union (Pease 2007). Revisionist and post-revisionist interpretations of the Cold War have challenged this master narrative, yet alternative views have not provided any widely accepted frameworks for redefining American history and identity (ibid., 112).

The academic debates around the Cold War pose a special challenge to US history textbooks. A medium of particular socio-political concern (Höhne 2002; Klerides 2010), they are expected both to provide accurate information and to construct coherent, identity-providing national narratives (Schissler 2009, 203–226) that satisfy a diverse audience of school boards, schools, activists, and lobby groups. This chapter explores representations of the contested era of the Cold War in major contemporary US history textbooks published between 2007 and 2012. I will focus on depictions of the origins of the conflict, an area of particular controversy. I restrict my investigation to textbooks for American history, which cover the Cold War in more detail than those on world history.

My first consideration was the extent to which contemporary textbooks have adopted alternative accounts. My first finding was that the representation of the origins of the Cold War in history textbooks by the three major US publishers Pearson, McGraw-Hill, and Holt McDougal/Houghton Mifflin Harcourt (American Textbook Council 2016) is anything but uniform. There are textbooks such as Glencoe/McGraw-Hill's *The American Journey* (Appleby, Brinkley and McPherson 2007) for middle schools, which represents a purely traditionalist narrative. At the other end of the spectrum we find, for example, Pearson's text-heavy, 'advanced'[2] high-school textbook *The American People* (Nash and Jeffrey 2009), which explicitly locates US history within an international context, provides extensive discussion of both the Soviet and the US stances in the Cold War, and also focuses on the Third World. A large number of textbooks, however, seem to have adopted a middle ground between traditionalist and non-traditionalist interpretations, for example Glencoe/McGraw Hill's *The American Vision* (Appleby et al. 2007), Pearson's *America: Past and Present* (Divine et al. 2007), as well as Holt McDougal/Houghton Mifflin Harcourt's *United States History* (2012) and *The Americans* (Danzer et al. 2012).

Given the dominance of this middle course, I will focus on two high-school textbooks that combine traditionalist and non-traditionalist views:

Glencoe/McGraw Hill's *The American Vision* (Appleby et al. 2007) and Holt McDougal/Houghton Mifflin Harcourt's *The Americans* (Danzer et al. 2012). This specific focus allows me to encompass macro-textual strategies, broad argumentative patterns and linguistic realisations at micro-level (Martin and Wodak 2003, 1). By looking, for example, at sentence construction and word choice in context, I undertake what John Issitt has described as breaking down the elements of textbooks in order to refute the widely-held assumption of their bland neutrality and reveal how they 'share in the production of a hegemony of ideas' (Issitt 2004, 689). My analysis will also attend to methods of presentation, to the use of primary sources as well as exercises and graphs, and to what is *not* said (Issitt 690). Analysing how the textbooks incorporate various interpretative patterns and create ostensible common-sense assumptions (Baier, Christophe and Zehr 2014), I wish to explore the degree of public acceptance of alternative accounts of the Cold War as manifested in the textbooks as reflections of what society has deemed desirable for students to learn.

Joseph Moreau has demonstrated that US textbooks have integrated alternative narrative elements either by making them fit traditional narrative structures, as was the case when African-American history was introduced through the themes of 'freedom' and 'progress', or by physically separating them from the main text, as exemplified in sidebars containing Southern interpretations of the Civil War (Moreau 2003). I argue that these strategies are also central to the representation of divergent perspectives on the Cold War and its major actors. In *The American Vision*, revisionist and post-revisionist elements are incorporated, in a watered-down version, into the master narrative. In *The Americans*, the principle of physical distinction of alternative narratives makes it possible to relegate revisionist interpretations to the background. At one point, however, as we will discuss, revisionist elements creep into the core narrative.

My findings give rise to multi-layered implications. The co-existence of multiple interpretative patterns supports the assumption that modern textbooks mirror debates rather than telling coherent stories (Lachmann and Mitchell 2014). At the same time, the textbooks reveal a reluctance to lend revisionist accounts of the Cold War the same credibility as traditionalist and post-revisionist interpretations and to renounce an unbrokenly positive national self-image. This indicates that non-traditionalist views have become acceptable and integrated only to a point where they do not challenge the national master narrative too explicitly, which is in line with what Michael Apple (1990, 25–26) describes as 'attempts at rebuilding hegemonic control'. As perspectives of less powerful groups are incorporated under the umbrella of hegemonic discourse, the dominance of that discourse in and through textbooks 'is partly maintained [...] through compromise and the process of "mentioning"', which leaves the major ideological framework largely untouched.[3] The fact that revisionist elements do enter the core narrative at certain points, however, indicates that 'progressive echoes' (ibid., 26) in textbooks are becoming louder.

Traditionalist, Revisionist and Post-Revisionist Interpretations of Selected Cold War Events

According to traditionalist Western interpretations of the origins of the Cold War, a backward and aggressive Soviet Union was solely responsible for the outbreak of the conflict, whereas the supposedly progressive US was to be perceived as the defender of freedom and democracy.[4] While the Soviet Union, according to this view, established puppet states in Eastern Europe and was intent on undermining liberal democracy, the US implemented a policy of containment to oppose Soviet expansion. According to liberal or orthodox arguments, the US had aspired to return to a position of isolationism after the Second World War, but in the face of the Soviet threat accepted the role of Western leader in a global struggle against communist dictatorship. For traditionalists, the Marshall Plan and the formation of NATO, in which the US consolidated its new role, sprang from altruistic and defence-related motives. Bodies such as the UN are viewed as emphasising America's will to international cooperation.

Revisionist interpretations, on the other hand, see the US as a capitalist aggressor provoking a weakened Soviet Union which longed for security after the experience of war. The Soviet Union, according to this view, found itself in a position of defence against an expansionist US, which had long since begun to restrict Soviet influence (Lundestad 2014, 11). The Marshall Plan is considered part of an American expansionist agenda, primarily motivated by economic interests.[5] Multilateral institutions are viewed as means to increase American power (Kolko and Kolko 1972). Western rhetoric, including the metaphor of the Iron Curtain, is seen as having further contributed to the conflict (Williams and Appleman 1972, 159–260; 269–270; Medhurst, Ivie and Wander 1997).

Post-revisionist views on the Cold War and its origins exist in diverse forms. Adopting revisionist arguments to varying degrees, post-revisionists focus on the role of (mis)perceptions and the diversity of motives. Pointing out how both superpowers contributed to the outbreak of the Cold War, they argue either that the conflict was inevitable and neither side can be held responsible, or that both sides are equally to blame (Lundestad 2014, 11–12).

The American Vision (Appleby et al. 2007) and *The Americans* (Danzer et al. 2012)

Both these textbooks devote around 22 percent of their content to the Cold War,[6] covering political as well as social and/or cultural aspects. While both have sections entitled 'Origins of the Cold War', however, they differ in their definitions of these 'origins': In *The Americans*, this section of eight pages includes, among other things, the formation of NATO and the Marshall Plan. In *The American Vision*, these two issues are discussed in the subsequent section 'The Early Cold War Years'. The section on the 'Origins of the Cold War' is therefore only five pages long. As my analysis will show, the organisation of topics contributes to their interpretation.

The Origins of the Cold War in *The American Vision* (Appleby et al. 2007)

The American Vision makes revisionist and post-revisionist perspectives on the beginnings of the Cold War compatible with the overall master narrative. It does so by rendering the latter the basis for selectivity: While lending credibility to the idea that the Soviet Union was a victim motivated by true convictions and fears, the chapter 'Origins of the Cold War' does not include the converse argument that the US was a capitalist aggressor. Instead, it combines the more lenient reassessment of the Soviet Union with a positive (traditionalist) self-image. This strategy partly relies on the organisation of topics: The chapter focuses on the general beliefs and concerns held by each side and on differences between the two. Many specific events, such as the Marshall Plan and the formation of NATO, are not covered before the chapter 'The Early Cold War Years', which recreates a traditionalist interpretative framework.

(Post-)Revisionist and Traditionalist Elements in the Chapter 'Origins of the Cold War'

The chapter 'Origins of the Cold War' begins by describing how the 'clash of interests' between the US and the Soviet Union after the Second World War 'led to an era of confrontation and competition' that 'became known as the Cold War' (778). A purely traditionalist account would continue to construct this clash as one between communist dictatorship and capitalist democracy. This textbook, however, contrasts 'Soviet security concerns' with 'American economic concerns' (779). These headings may raise expectations of a post-revisionist account in which both superpowers pursued their self-interested preoccupations. The heading 'Soviet Security Concerns' is prone to a revisionist reading implying that the Soviet Union was weak. As we shall see, however, this expectation is only partly fulfilled.

The section under this heading represents the Soviet side of the conflict. It lends legitimacy to the Soviets' suspicion of capitalist nations while simultaneously exonerating these nations of blame:

> (1)[7] As the war ended, Soviet leaders became concerned about security. (2) The Soviets wanted to keep Germany weak and make sure that the countries between Germany and the Soviet Union were under Soviet control. (3) Although security concerns influenced their thinking, Soviet leaders were also Communists. (4) They believed that communism was a superior economic system that would eventually replace capitalism and that the Soviet Union should encourage communism in other nations. (5) Soviet

leaders also accepted Lenin's theory that capitalist countries eventually would try to destroy communism. (6) This made Soviet leaders suspicious of capitalist nations. (Appleby et al. 2007, 779)

Despite traditionalist elements, this passage contains several revisionist aspects: it explains 'Soviet control' over other countries in terms of the Soviet need for security (1-2), it represents the Soviet ambition of spreading the communist system as based on true conviction (4), and it asserts that the Soviet Union felt threatened by capitalism (5). In addition, the text refrains from explicitly judging communism.

At the same time, the text avoids placing blame on the US. The issue of 'Soviet security concerns' leads to the implicit question as to why the Soviets mistrusted capitalist nations (6). The highly ambivalent (Baier, Christophe and Zehr 2014) sentence 3 is particularly relevant here: The conjunction 'although' can be read as creating a contradiction between being concerned about security and being communist, as if communists should not, or do not usually have, security concerns. The sentence, however, can also be interpreted as claiming that security concerns were not the sole factors behind Soviet thinking, but that communism was also of influence. The precise relationship between the two driving forces remains unclear: Did security concerns and communism go hand in hand or contradict each other? Which was more important? By keeping this relationship ambiguous, the text manages to represent the perceived capitalist threat as a merely theoretical construct: Because Soviet leaders 'accepted Lenin's theory that capitalist countries eventually would try to destroy communism' (5), they were 'made … suspicious of capitalist nations' (6). While making an effort to rationalise Soviet thinking, the text thus precludes the idea that Soviet security concerns had anything to do with specific action on the part of the US.

The contrasting representation of the American perspective under the heading 'American economic concerns' complements the picture:

(7) While Soviet leaders focused on securing their borders, American leaders focused on economic problems. (8) Many American officials believed that the Depression had caused World War II. (9) Without it, Hitler would never have come to power, and Japan would not have wanted

to expand its empire. (10) American advisers also thought the Depression had been overly severe because countries cut back on trade. (11) They believed that when nations seal themselves off economically, it forces them to go to war to get the resources they need. (12) By 1945, President Roosevelt and his advisers were convinced that economic growth was the key to world peace. (13) They wanted to promote economic growth by increasing world trade. (14) Similar reasoning convinced American leaders to promote democracy and free enterprise. (15) They believed that democratic government with protection for people's rights made countries more stable and peaceful. (16) They also thought that the free enterprise system [...] was the best route to prosperity. (Appleby et al. 2007, 779)

On the surface, the text places the US on an equal footing with the Soviet Union: In a manner similar to that of the previous passage, it explains what Americans 'believed' (8, 11, 15), 'thought' (10, 16) and were 'convinced' of (12) without explicitly positioning itself towards their principles and conclusions. Both passages present the respective way of thinking as based on economic rather than moral considerations: The Soviets thought communism a 'superior economic system' that should therefore be 'encourage[d]' 'in other nations' (5). The Americans, who 'believed that the Depression had caused World War II' (8), promoted democracy not so much as a value in its own right but as part of an economically based solution to conflict. The passages consistently speak of 'leaders' (3, 5, 6, 7, 14), 'officials' (8) or 'advisers' (10, 12) rather than of the people. Taken together, the paragraphs thus suggest that each superpower had reason to believe itself in the right and, consequently, to act as it did. In this sense, the text makes a strong post-revisionist statement.

It also, however, upholds the idea of American moral superiority. While raising the expectation of a revisionist or post-revisionist interpretation, the heading 'American economic concerns' turns out to be ambiguous: These 'concerns' do not refer to matters of self-interest, but rather to more general problems of the time which the US was supposedly trying to solve via an economic approach. The text thus plays with a revisionist catchword explicated in an unexpected way. Given this reinterpretation of the concept 'economic concerns', sentence 7 in particular portrays the Americans in a more altruistic light than the Soviets.

3 Manufacturing Coherence: How American Textbooks... 31

The chapter continues to present the relationship between the two sides in the same fashion: While upholding the idea of different perspectives, each with its own legitimacy, the text depicts the US as more altruistic. Regarding the Potsdam Conference in 1945, for example, it asserts:

> (17) Truman was now convinced that German industry was critical. (18) Unless Germany's economy was allowed to revive, the rest of Europe would never recover, and the German people might turn to Communism out of desperation. (19) Stalin and his advisers were equally convinced that they needed reparations from Germany. (20) The war had devastated their economy [...]. (21) Truman [...] suggested that the Soviets take reparations from their zone [...]. (22) Stalin opposed this idea since the Soviet zone was mostly agricultural. (23) It could not have provided all of the reparations [...]. (24) At Potsdam, Truman learned that the atomic bomb had been successfully tested, and he told Stalin about the test. (25) Stalin suspected Truman was trying to bully him into a deal and that the Americans were trying to limit reparations to keep the Soviets weak. (Appleby et al. 2007, 781)

Contrasting the opposing camps, this passage, on the one hand, depicts them as 'equally convinced' (19) of their concerns and positions, and provides reasons for both sides' lines of argumentation (17–23). In the case of the Soviet Union, it does so by drawing again on the revisionist idea that the country was a victim of the Second World War (20, 25). Without judging either side, the passage also portrays the communication regarding the testing of the atomic bomb as an honest misunderstanding (24–25), which is characteristic of a post-revisionist perspective. While the US appears to be primarily concerned with Europe's wellbeing, however, Soviet interests seem egocentric, as they only relate to the payment of reparations to the Soviet Union.

As demonstrated, the text as a whole employs post-revisionist perspectives both in the equal apportioning of blame to each side and in the non-apportioning of guilt. It also adopts revisionist elements in pointing out the Soviet Union's precarious position after the war. The acceptance of alternative views, however, seems to end where such views might question the idea of US altruism, as the direct comparison of

American with Soviet reasoning indicates. The notion that the Soviet Union was not purely egocentric consequently only occurs in parts of the chapter where the Soviet Union is not directly contrasted with the US. The reader is informed, for example, that Soviet troops 'liberated Poland from German control' in 1944 (779), and that the so-called satellite nations were 'not under direct Soviet control' (782).

The early Cold War largely appears as an inevitable conflict. 'Over the next few years', we are told, 'arguments about reparations and economic policy in Germany increased tensions between the United States and the Soviet Union. These arguments became one of the major causes of the Cold War' (780). Similarly, 'the Potsdam conference marked yet another increase in tensions between the Soviets and the Americans, further paving the way for the Cold War' (782). These post-revisionist assessments are possible because they do not generally contradict the notion of American moral superiority.

In one instance, the post-revisionist perspective creates a degree of tension with the concept of American altruism. Next to a half-page photograph of a little boy holding a pair of shoes donated through the American Red Cross we find the assertion that '[t]he fate of [German] refugees became enmeshed in the growing power struggle between the United States and the Soviet Union' (780). This assessment mirrors a recent shift in historiographical debate about German victimhood (Kleßmann 2010). It implies that the superpowers cared more about their dispute as such than about countries and people, rendering them both egocentric. The information that the shoes were given to the boy by the American Red Cross, on the other hand, counters the suggestion of blame assigned to the US by representing the Americans as caring.

Partly characterised by the absence of critique on US actions, the chapter 'Origins of the Cold War' upholds central aspects of the American master narrative. I argue that the inclusion of non-traditionalist elements is also possible because subjects of debate whose alternative interpretation would necessarily cast the US in a less favourable light, such as the Marshall Plan, find themselves removed to the chapter 'The Early Cold War Years'.

Traditionalist Framework in the Chapter 'The Early Cold War Years'

This chapter follows that on the 'Origins of the Cold War' and realigns the narrative to a traditionalist framework. It introduces ideas that clearly oppose the previous mode of representation and resumes and develops traditionalist elements from the previous chapter, thus creating a degree of narrative continuity.

A text box at the beginning summarises the main idea as follows: 'As the Cold War began, the United States struggled to oppose Communist aggression in Europe and Asia through political, economic, and military measures' (783). This traditionalist introduction places the US in a position of defence while representing communism, and thus the Soviet Union, as the aggressor. While the previous chapter portrayed the developing conflict between the superpowers as inevitable, the Soviet Union now clearly becomes the scapegoat. Whereas the newly introduced notion of communist aggression is in conflict with the previously established concept of Soviet victimhood, the similarly new idea of the defensive US does not immediately contradict earlier depictions, as the overall image remains positive.

The chapter continues with paragraphs about major Cold War events, such as the Marshall Plan, the formation of NATO, and the Suez crisis. I will analyse the discussion of the Marshall Plan to illustrate the chapter's mode of representation.

The passage begins with a description of the poverty, starvation and political chaos prevailing in Western Europe after the end of the war. It then explains how Secretary of State George C. Marshall proposed the Marshall Plan, 'which would give European nations American aid to rebuild their economies' and was 'essential to containment' (785). This is followed by Marshall's famous assertion that the Plan was 'not directed against any country or doctrine' (ibid.). The core text continues:

> (26) The Soviet Union and its satellite nations rejected the offer. (27) Instead, the Soviets developed their own economic program. (28) This action further separated Europe into competing regions. (29) The Marshall Plan pumped billions of dollars [*sic*] worth of supplies, machinery and

food into Western Europe. (30) Western Europe's recovery weakened the appeal of communism and opened new markets for trade (Appleby et al. 2007, 785).

Portraying the Americans as the saviours of Western Europe, this passage ties in with the positive image of the US. The revisionist view, according to which the Marshall Plan was primarily designed to serve US economic interests, is hinted at in the last part of sentence 30 but simultaneously at least partially refuted: The position of the statement at the very end of the paragraph allows a reading in which the opening of new markets is a consequence or side effect rather than a motive. Even if we were to interpret it as a motive, the previously established idea that the US believed in global trade as a route to peace does not make its actions appear primarily selfish.

The representation of the Soviet Union complements the traditionalist image. First, the text does not clarify why the Soviet Union 'and its satellite nations' rejected the ostensibly generous offer (26). This is clearly in contrast with the previous chapter's efforts to explain why accepting America's offer to make reparations did not make sense from a Soviet perspective. Here it is claimed that the Soviets' actions in developing their own economic program 'further separated Europe into competing camps' (27). In traditionalist fashion, the Soviet Union is thus blamed for the growing conflict.

A facilitating factor of this purely traditionalist representation of the Marshall Plan is its inclusion in the textbook chapter on the 'Early Cold War Years' rather than in the 'Origins of the Cold War'. In light of the chapter's scene-setting, which puts forward the claim that 'the United States struggled to oppose Communist aggression in Europe and Asia' (783), the Marshall Plan is effectively construed as a necessary measure for saving the world. Had it been treated in the chapter on the 'Origins of the Cold War', there may have been an implication that the Marshall Plan lay at, or was among, the roots of the conflict.

While *The American Vision*'s chapter on the 'Origins of the Cold War' includes revisionist and post-revisionist perspectives, particularly on the Soviet Union, the chapter 'The Early Cold War Years' leads the overall account back into a traditionalist narrative. Considered as a whole, the two chapters thus draw an ambivalent picture of the Soviet Union while representing the US in a relatively coherent, positive way. A depiction of German refugees as the ultimate victims of the Cold War indicates how international historiographical discourse has also found its way into US textbook narratives. The purely traditionalist representation of crucial events such as the Marshall Plan is partly enabled by the chapters' thematic structure and organisation.

The Origins of the Cold War in Holt McDougal/Houghton Mifflin Harcourt's *The Americans*

Unlike *The American Vision*, the textbook *The Americans* covers all crucial events of the early Cold War in the chapter 'The Origins of the Cold War'. My analysis will demonstrate how the chapter simultaneously includes and marginalises revisionist interpretations by employing the strategy of physical separation: The main text consists of a post-revisionist and a traditionalist part, while revisionist interpretations are relegated to side boxes and graphs. There is one instance, however, in which fissures appear in the core narrative and revisionist elements enter; ambiguity ensues.

The Post-Revisionist and Traditionalist Framework

The first half of the chapter's core text is characterised by a post-revisionist framework. This begins on the first page; a personal story revolves around the encounter of US and Soviet soldiers at the Elbe River in Germany at the end of the Second World War. The section ends with the following assessment:

> (31) The Soviet and U.S. soldiers believed that their encounter would serve as a symbol of peace. (32) Unfortunately, such hopes were soon dashed. (33) After World War II, the United States and the Soviet Union emerged as rival superpowers, each strong enough to greatly influence world events (Danzer et al. 2012, 808).

This passage can be read as post-revisionist in a multiple sense. First, it puts the Soviet Union and the US grammatically and semantically in equal, or parallel, positions. Sentence 32 evaluates the end of hope for peace as negative but refrains from assigning guilt. The claim that the US and the Soviet Union 'emerged' as rival superpowers contributes to the idea of a dynamic of inevitability (33). The remainder of sentence 33 contrastingly implies that the Soviet Union and the US are both to blame for the unfortunate outbreak of the Cold War, as 'each' superpower was 'strong enough to […] influence world events'.

On the next page, the text reinforces the idea that both sides were equally to blame for the Cold War and that their conflict formed a counterpart to the concept of 'peace'. After contrasting 'Soviet communism' with 'the capitalist American system' (809) and describing the mutual Soviet-American suspicion, it elaborates on the relationship between the superpowers, the concept of peace, and the UN:

> (34) [H]opes for world peace were high at the end of the war. (35) The most visible symbol of these hopes was the United Nations (UN). (36) On April 25, 1945, the representatives of 50 nations met in San Francisco to establish this new peacekeeping body. […] (37) Ironically, even though the UN was intended to promote peace, it soon became an arena in which the two superpowers competed. (38) Both the United States and the Soviet Union used the UN as a forum to spread their influence over others (Danzer et al. 2012, 809).

The first part of this passage addresses the concepts of 'hope' and 'peace' in connection with the institution of the UN as such (34-36). Proceeding from this basis, the text constructs the United States and the Soviet Union as the combined destroyers of general hopes for peace, who misused the UN as a competitive 'arena' and as a 'forum to spread their influence over others' (37-38). Depicting both superpowers as egocentric and greedy for power, the text places equal blame on each.

In contrast, the second half of the chapter represents a largely traditionalist account of the origins of the Cold War. This is apparent in the individual portrayals of the superpowers and depictions that set them in relation to each other. One primary example is the representation

3 Manufacturing Coherence: How American Textbooks... 37

of America's establishment of its containment policy. The text, while indirectly blaming the Soviet Union for the implementation of this policy, minimises American responsibility:

> (39) Stalin installed communist governments in Albania, Bulgaria, Czechoslovakia, Hungary, Romania, and Poland. (40) These countries became known as satellite nations, countries dominated by the Soviet Union. (41) In early 1946, Stalin gave a speech announcing that communism and capitalism were incompatible – and that another war was inevitable.
>
> (42) Faced with the Soviet threat, American officials decided it was time, in Truman's words, to stop 'babying the Soviets.' (43) In February 1946, George F. Kennan, an American diplomat in Moscow, proposed a policy of containment. (44) By containment he meant taking measures to prevent any extension of communist rule in other countries. (45) This policy began to guide the Truman administration's foreign policy (Danzer et al. 2012, 811).

These two paragraphs portray the superpowers in traditionalist Western terms. First, the Soviet Union is depicted as 'dominat[ing]' other countries (39-40). Using the metaphor of 'satellite nations' (40), the first paragraph upholds the idea of Eastern European puppet states that were entirely subject to the Soviet Union. Linking the paragraphs, the phrase '[f]aced with the Soviet threat' (42) interprets Stalin's speech (41) as an immediate threat requiring a counter-reaction from the US. While the Soviet Union is assigned the role of aggressor, the US becomes the defender who 'prevent[ed] any extension of communist rule' (44). The image of a generally benign US receives further support from the text's citation of the decision by American officials 'to stop "babying the Soviets"' (42). While marked as a quotation, this statement is not questioned and is thus depicted as describing the situation accurately. It suggests that the US had been disproportionately soft and patient in the past but had finally reached the end of its tether; that the Soviet Union, through its provocative behaviour, had exhausted its generous chances and that the US now intended to meet the Soviets on equal terms. The text obscures US responsibility and initiative not only in relation to the initial establishment of the policy of containment, but also with reference to its further implementation: The final sentence, '[t]his policy began to guide the Truman administration's foreign policy' (45), constructs the policy itself as the active subject by which the Truman administration is passively led. Putting American government policy, and by extension the government itself, in the position of an object, this depiction implies that the US could not have changed the course of events. The text thus holds the Soviet Union responsible for the US policy of containment in the sense that its behaviour rendered it necessary and inevitable.

The strategy of indirectly blaming the Soviet Union for the growing tensions is continued in the text's depiction of the Iron Curtain, which follows on from the passage above. The insertion of a primary source plays a major role here:

> (46) Europe was now divided into two political regions, a mostly democratic Western Europe and a communist Eastern Europe. (47) In March 1946, Winston Churchill travelled to the United States and gave a speech that described the situation in Europe.
>
> (48) A shadow has fallen upon the scenes so lately lighted by the Allied victory. ... From Stettin in the Baltic to Trieste in the Adriatic, an iron curtain has descended across the Continent. Behind it lie all the capitals of the ancient states of Central and Eastern Europe. ... all these famous cities and the populations around them lie in ... the Soviet sphere, and all are subject in one form or another, not only to Soviet influence but to a very high and ... increasing measure of control from Moscow.
>
> (49) The phrase 'iron curtain' came to stand for the division of Europe. (50) When Stalin heard about the speech, he declared in no uncertain terms that Churchill's words were a 'call to war' (Danzer et al. 2012, 811).

The text begins by constructing the difference between East and West traditionally in terms of 'democracy' versus 'communism' as mutually exclusive concepts (46). The traditionalist view is upheld in the citation of Churchill's speech, which portrays the Soviet Union as a highly influential and controlling power (48). The contextualisation of the quotation further supports the construction of Soviet responsibility and the concealing of Western acts of aggression. First, the speech by Churchill is said to have 'described the situation in Europe' rather than having contributed to it (47). This idea is reinforced by the affirmation that '[t]he phrase "iron curtain" came to stand for the division of Europe' (49), which implies endorsement of the phrase as a fitting term to describe the situation. Unlike Stalin's speech in the section analysed above, which was represented as a 'threat' that provoked an American counter-reaction (41), Churchill's speech does not appear to have intensified the conflict between East and West, but to have merely put it into words. The text thus deviates from the (post-)revisionist notion that the speech, and Western rhetoric in general, fuelled the conflict. Moreover, the quotation marks around the term 'a call to war' in sentence 50 indicate that Stalin's interpretation of the speech as an act of aggression was subjective and inaccurate. At the same time, the phrase 'in no uncertain terms' reinforces the image of a hostile Soviet Union unwilling to compromise. By implying that Stalin, perhaps deliberately, misinterpreted Churchill's words, the passage thus ultimately blames the Soviet Union for the outbreak of the Cold War.

The core text continues its traditionalist storyline in many ways. For instance, it describes the Truman Doctrine as 'essential to keeping Soviet influence from spreading' (812). In the section about the Berlin Airlift, a photograph of children looking up at an approaching aircraft covers half a page (813), reinforcing the concept of American heroism. In the following section, I aim to demonstrate how the textbook systematically relegates revisionist elements to the background. I will also analyse an instance in which they appear to become prominent.

The Inclusion and Exclusion of Revisionist Views

I argue that the minimisation of revisionist views in the representation of the origins of the Cold War in *The Americans* takes place by three means: Either these views are rendered invisible, or they are kept separate from the core narration, or they are included in the core narration but weakened by means of ambiguity.

Rendering Revisionist Elements Invisible: The Representation of NATO

The representation of the formation of NATO is an example of the first form of minimisation: A revisionist primary source is adopted, but does not become visible as such, as it is embedded in a traditionalist story. The beginning of the relevant paragraph reads as follows:

> (51) The Berlin blockade increased Western European fear of Soviet aggression. (52) As a result, ten Western European nations [...] joined with the United States and Canada on April 4, 1949, to form a defensive military alliance called the North Atlantic Treaty Organization (NATO). (53) For the first time in its history, the United States had entered into a military alliance with other nations during peacetime. (54) The Cold War had ended any hope of a return to U.S. isolationism (Danzer et al. 2012, 814).

Next to the text, a cartoon by Edwin Marcus depicts the US, France, Britain, Canada, Norway, Belgium, the Netherlands and Luxembourg as hats on a stand. The hats of the first three countries are large and at the bottom (the US being the lowest and largest), whereas the latter five are smaller and on top. The caption reads:

> (55) This cartoon depicts the nations that signed the North Atlantic Pact, which created NATO in 1949. The nations, shown as hats, are arranged in a pyramid to show the bigger countries on the bottom supporting the smaller, weaker nations on top (Danzer et al. 2012, 814).

The traditionalist narrative in the core text is constructed on two levels. Depicting the creation of NATO as a 'result' of 'Soviet aggression' and thus as an act of 'defense' (51-52), the text places the Soviet Union in the role of the aggressor and the West in the role of the defender. Sentence 54 further suggests that American involvement in world affairs was altruistic in general, as the US had actually hoped to 'return' to 'isolationism'; this reading mirrors the so-called liberal or orthodox interpretation. Complementing the positive image of the US, the cartoon and its description reinforce the concept of an altruistic West under US leadership, which was 'supporting [...] smaller, weaker nations' (55).

Ironically, this editorial cartoon from 1949 was originally intended to criticise power relations within NATO; that is, its origins are rather revisionist. Its original caption – 'Another pyramid party' – is to be found only in the index of the textbook. Consulting the website of the Library of Congress, I found that the caption 'refers to the parties held to promote pyramid investment clubs – gambling investment schemes then popular in New York', and that the cartoon may 'suggest that, as in the pyramid clubs, some members of NATO will profit far more than others' (Library of Congress 2018). The textbook thus re-interprets a primary source critical of the US to render it compatible with a traditionalist perspective on the Cold War.

Keeping the Revisionist Interpretation Separate from the Core Text: The Representation of the Marshall Plan

In the case of the Marshall Plan, revisionist views are not rendered invisible altogether, but are kept separate from the core text. The main text introduces the topic via a detailed description of the horrific socio-economic situation in Western Europe after the World War, when 'most factories had been bombed or looted', while '[m]illions of people were living in refugee camps', and a bitterly cold winter had caused starvation and water and fuel shortages (Danzer et al. 2012, 812). This description, which resembles that in *The American Vision*, provides the basis for a traditionalist account of American actions and their consequences:

> (56) In June 1947, Secretary of State George Marshall proposed that the United States provide aid to all European nations that needed it, saying that this move was directed 'not against any country or doctrine but against hunger, poverty, desperation, and chaos.' The Marshall Plan revived European hopes. Over the next four years, 16 countries received some 13 billion dollars in aid. By 1952, Western Europe was flourishing (Danzer et al. 2012, 812).

The passage is accompanied by a photograph showing how American goods are loaded, presumably onto a ship, as well as a graph showing the amount of US aid, quantified in millions of dollars, that went to the individual countries. These elements go to create a clear depiction of the US as an altruistic saviour. While the core text provides a traditionalist account, the revisionist view is relegated to literally sidelined – or marginalised – information, in a smaller font, headed 'background'. In contrast to the main text, this section emphasises the Marshall Plan's economic benefits to the US:

> (57) The Marshall Plan also benefited the United States. (58) To supply Europe with goods, American farms and factories raised production levels. (59) As a result, the American economy continued its wartime boom.

Physically relegating this information to the 'background' allows the text to subtly include a revisionist element in the core narrative. The label 'background' implies that the information is of secondary relevance.

Weakening Revisionist Elements in the Core Narrative: The Representation of the Soviet Union

I will now look at the only instance, according to my reading, in which the main text incorporates revisionist views on the origins of the Cold War. It occurs in a short subsection headed 'Tension Mounts', which is located between the post-revisionist and the traditionalist parts of the core text. The technique of incorporating revisionist elements creates ambiguity, as these elements are interwoven with traditionalist ideas. This happens with respect to both the US and the Soviet Union:

> (60) Stalin's refusal to allow free elections in Poland convinced Truman that U.S. and Soviet aims were deeply at odds. (61) Truman's goal in demanding free elections was to spread democracy to nations that had been under Nazi rule. […] (62) Truman also felt that the United States had a large economic stake in spreading democracy and free trade across the globe. (63) U.S. industry boomed during the war, making the United States the economic leader of the world. (64) To continue growing, American businesses wanted access to raw materials in Eastern Europe, and they wanted to be able to sell goods to Eastern European countries.

(65) *Soviets Tighten Their Grip on Eastern Europe.* (66) The Soviet Union had also emerged from the war as a nation of enormous economic and military strength. (67) However, unlike the United States, the Soviet Union had suffered heavy devastation on its own soil. (68) Soviet deaths from the war have been estimated at 20 million, half of whom were civilians. (69) As a result, the Soviets felt justified in their claim to Eastern Europe. (70) By dominating this region, the Soviets felt they could stop future invasions from the west (Danzer et al. 2012, 810).

The first passage commences with a traditionalist representation of a freedom-loving US and an undemocratic Soviet Union (60–61). In sentences 62 to 64, the positive image of the US is countered by arguments that, in revisionist fashion, emphasise America's economic self-interests. The relationship between the concept of 'democracy' and economic benefits is highly ambiguous here. While they stem from opposing perspectives on the US, sentence 62 constructs them as essentially a single entity, or two sides of a coin. The text thus indicates that the spread of democracy was related to US economic growth, but it does not explain the nature of this relationship. One possible reading is that democracy equals capitalism, which would again reinforce traditionalist arguments. While employing revisionist elements, the passage thus neglects to fully develop them.

In the second passage, a similar phenomenon can be observed with regard to the Soviet Union. On the one hand, the Soviet Union is depicted from a revisionist perspective as a victim of the Second World War, having 'suffered heavy devastation' and lost millions of civilians (67). Emphasising that this condition was 'unlike [that in] the United States' (67), the text creates a contrast to Soviet 'economic and military strength' (66) and implies that the Soviet Union was no rival for the US on an equal footing. The text also gives reasons for the Soviets' 'claim to Eastern Europe' (69) and, by mentioning potential 'future invasions from the west' (70), evokes the revisionist image of an aggressive West and a defensive Soviet Union. At the same time, however, the text refrains from taking a clear position: The verb 'felt' (69, 70) emphasises the subjectivity of the Soviet view, implying that the latter might have wrongly believed that they could prevent invasions by claiming power over Eastern Europe. Whether this error came about because they had chosen the wrong measures or because such a threat had not existed in the first place, remains unclear. At the end of the paragraph, the Soviet Union is back in its role as a 'dominating' power (70). This also corresponds with the paragraph's heading, 'Soviets Tighten Their Grip on Eastern Europe' (65), which is reminiscent of traditionalist catchphrases. Ambiguity thus helps here to conceal the contrast that emerges through the employment of revisionist elements intertwined with traditionalist ones.

The conflict, however, remains visible, and re-emerges in the exercises at the bottom of the page, which ask students to identify which aims 'involved economic growth of the United States', and which 'Soviet aims involved self-protection' (810). This task is clearly in conflict with the traditionalist part of the book that follows it.

We have thus seen that the main text of *The Americans*' chapter on 'The Origins of the Cold War' is divided into a post-revisionist part, covering general ideological differences and the formation of the UN, and a traditionalist part covering issues such as the Marshall Plan, the Truman Doctrine, the Berlin Airlift, and the formation of NATO. Revisionist elements can be found both in relation to the US and the Soviet Union. While some are rendered invisible or occur as separate background information, others enter the core narrative but are kept ambivalent.

Conclusion

My analysis has shown that two major US history textbooks apply to the Cold War some of the strategies of incorporation and separation that have been deployed for other controversial issues in American history textbooks in the past. Both textbooks examined here contain post-revisionist and traditionalist perspectives.

Their simultaneous use of various interpretative patterns mirrors academic debate, specifically a lack of consensus over Cold War history: We find, for example, traditionalist perspectives and elements of revisionist interpretations of the Marshall Plan, traditionalist, revisionist and post-revisionist views on American and Soviet goals, a post-revisionist account of the UN, a liberal-traditionalist view on the formation of

NATO accompanied by a revisionist cartoon, and revisionist headings for non-revisionist paragraphs, alongside frequent combinations of different forms of post-revisionism.

The textbooks do not, however, grant equal status to the various patterns of interpretation. At the core of this seems to be a reluctance to openly criticise the US. While both traditionalist and post-revisionist views are treated as valid frameworks for interpretation, there is a tendency to employ post-revisionism in a way that conserves a positive national self-image. Meanwhile, revisionist perspectives are mitigated, pushed into the background, and/or omitted in direct comparisons between the US and the Soviet Union. While a purely negative image of the Soviet Union thus seems to be in decline, the positive image of the US still finds strong narrative support.

These findings argue against the assumption that questions of guilt and responsibility are no longer an important issue in current historiographical discourse, and that historiography has left behind the argumentative patterns of the Cold War era.[8] The concept of the Cold War as a 'good war' that resulted in American triumph, a notion John Wiener (2012) describes as a failed project of conservative US memory politics, seems to have a stronger basis than generally assumed (cf. Schrecker 2004). While low visitor numbers at Cold War memorials and museums (Wiener 2012) might suggest otherwise, history textbook narratives – and what they construe as common sense – make evident to this day the traces of 'American Cold War Culture'[9] in historical discourse.

Individual instances of revisionist elements entering the core narrative in the textbook *The Americans* suggest that we are nonetheless dealing with a fragile, ever-shifting construct. Whereas some critics from the world of education bemoan increasingly incoherent storylines in US history textbooks (see Ravitch 2004), we might regard the crumbling of the core master narrative as a sign of alternative perspectives becoming more accepted and thus of what Apple (1990, 26) might call a 'victor[y] in the politics of official knowledge'. The instance of a discourse of German victimhood in *The American Vision* further proves that the internationalisation of academia has an impact on the way national history is told. As the role of the US in the twenty-first century is changing and US history is increasingly studied from inter- and transnational perspectives, the long-term response of history textbooks to the associated challenges and necessary amendments to the traditional master narrative remains to be observed.

Notes

1. The quotation cites a member of the conservative faction on the Texas State Board of Education.
2. The Advanced Placement (AP) Program was created by the American College Board and offers college-level courses to high-school students.
3. In the argument referenced here, Apple draws on Tyson-Bernstein (1988, 18–19).
4. Here and in the following I refer to the useful summaries provided by Lundestad 2014, 8–34 and Byrd 2009, 88–90.
5. This line of argumentation can be found, for example, in Cox and Kennedy-Pipe 2005, 97–134.
6. In Appleby et al. 2007, this amounts to 234 of 1039 pages (excluding the appendix); in Danzer et al. 2012, the figure is 246 of 1123 pages.
7. The numbers in parentheses are added by the author for purposes of reader orientation.
8. This argument is brought forward, among others, by Jarausch, Ostermann and Etges (2017, 1–18; 4).
9. This term was coined by Stephen Whitfield (1991).

Bibliography

List of Textbooks Cited

Appleby, Joyce, Alan Brinkley and James M. McPherson. 2007. *The American Journey*. Glencoe/McGraw Hill.

Appleby, Joyce, Alan Brinkley, Albert S. Broussard, James M. McPherson and Donald A. Ritchie. 2007. *The American Vision*. Glencoe McGraw Hill.

Danzer, Gerald A., J. Jorge Klor de Alva, Larry S. Krieger, Louis E. Wilson and Nancy Woloch. 2012. *The Americans*. Holt McDougal/Houghton Mifflin Harcourt.

Deverell, William Francis and Deborah Gray White, eds. 2012. *United States History*. Orlando, Fla.: Holt McDougal/Houghton Mifflin Harcourt.

Divine, Robert A; T. H. Breen, George M. Fredrickson, R. Hal Williams, Ariela J. Gross, H. W. Brands. 2007. *America: Past and Present*, 8th edition. Pearson/Longman.

Nash, Gary B. and Julie Roy Jeffrey, eds. 2009. *The American People: Creating a Nation and a Society*. VangoBooks/Pearson Education.

Other Primary Sources

Library of Congress. 2018. Image of Cartoon by Edwin Marcus (1949), *Another Pyramid Party*. Retrieved from the Library of Congress website: https://www.loc.gov/pictures/item/2016683485/ (accessed 15 November 2018).

McKinley, James C. 2010. 'Texas Conservatives Win Curriculum Change. Published in *The New York Times*, 12 March 2010. http://www.nytimes.com/2010/03/13/education/13texas.html (accessed 4 October 2015).

'Texas Ready for Textbook Showdown'. NBC News, 19 May 2010. http://www.nbcnews.com/id/37220562/ns/us_news-life/t/texas-ready-textbook-showdown/#.VdR4ZUaQa1Q (accessed 4 October 2015).

Further References

American Textbook Council. 2016. 'Widely Adopted History Textbooks'. http://historytextbooks.net/adopted.htm (accessed 28 April 2019).

Apple, Michael. 1990. 'The Text and Cultural Politics'. *The Journal of Education and Thought (JET)* 24 (3a). Special Edition: *Embattled Books: The State of the Text*: 17–33.

Baier, Katharina, Barbara Christophe and Kathrin Zehr. 2014. 'Schulbücher als Seismographen für Diskursive Brüche: Ein neuer Ansatz in der Kulturwissenschaftlichen Schulbuchforschung dargestellt am Beispiel der Analyse von Schulbucherzählungen über den Kalten Krieg.' In: *Eckert. Working Papers* 4. http://repository.gei.de/bitstream/handle/11428/139/861817958_2016_A.pdf (accessed 18 December 2016)

Barton, Keith C. and Linda S. Levstik. 2009. *Teaching History for the Common Good*. New York: Routledge.

Byrd, Peter. 2009. 'The Cold War'. In *The Concise Oxford Dictionary of Politics*, edited by Iain McLean and Alistair McMillan. 3rd edition. Oxford: Oxford University Press.

Cox, Michael and Caroline Kennedy-Pipe. 2005. 'The Tragedy of American Diplomacy? Rethinking the Marshall Plan'. *Journal of Cold War Studies* 7, no. 1 (Winter): 97–134.

Foner, Eric. 1999. *The Story of American Freedom*. New York: Norton.

Höhne, Thomas. 2002. *Schulbuchwissen: Umrisse einer Wissens- und Medientheorie*. Frankfurt a. M.: Johann Wolfgang Goethe-Universität.

Issitt, John. 2004. 'Reflections on the Study of Textbooks'. *History of Education* 33, no. 6 (November): 683–696.

Jarausch, Konrad H., Christian F. Ostermann and Andreas Etges, eds. 2017. *The Cold War: Historiography, Memory, Representation*. De Gruyter.

Kleßmann, Christoph. 2010. '1945: Welthistorische Zäsur und "Stunde Null"'. Version 1:0. *Docupedia-Zeitgeschichte*, 15 October 2010. http://docupedia.de/zg/1945 (accessed 20 October 2016).

Klerides, Eleftherios. 2010. 'Imagining the Textbook: Textbooks as Discourse and Genre'. *Journal of Educational Media, Memory and Society* 2, no. 1: 31–54.

Kolko, Gabriel and Joyce Kolko. 1972. *The Limits of Power: The World and United States Foreign Policy, 1945-1954*. New York: Harper & Row.

Lachmann, Richard and Lacy Mitchell. 2014. 'The Changing Face of War in Textbooks: Depictions of World War II and Vietnam, 1970-2009'. *Sociology of Education* 87, no. 3: 188–203.

Lowe, David and Tony Joel, eds. 2013. *Remembering the Cold War: Global Contests and National Stories*. (Remembering the Modern World.) Abingdon/New York: Routledge.

Lundestad, Geir. 2014. 'The Cold War in Europe, 1945-1949: Some Old and New Theories about the Cold War'. In *East, West, North, South: International Relations since 1945*, edited by Geir Lundestad. London: SAGE.

Martin, J. R. and Ruth Wodak. 2003. *Re/reading the Past: Critical and Functional Perspectives on Time and Value*. Amsterdam/Philadelphia: John Benjamins.

Medhurst, Martin J., Robert L. Ivie, Philip Wander and Robert L. Scott, eds. 1997. *Cold War Rhetoric: Strategy, Metaphor, and Ideology*. East Lansing, Mich.: Michigan State University Press.

Moreau, Joseph. 2003. *Schoolbook Nation: Conflicts over American History Textbooks from the Civil War to the Present*. Michigan: Ann Arbor.

Paul, Heike. 2014. *The Myths that Made America: An Introduction to American Studies*. Bielefeld: transcript:.

Pease, Donald E. 2007. 'Exceptionalism'. In *Keywords for American Studies*, edited by Bruce Burgett and Glenn Hendler. New York: New York University Press.

Ravitch, Diane. 2004. *A Consumer's Guide to Highschool History Textbooks.* Thomas B. Fordham Institute. http://files.eric.ed.gov/fulltext/ED485529.pdf, (accessed 30 March 2017).

Schissler, Hanna. 2009. 'Navigating a Globalizing World: Thoughts on Textbook Analysis, Teaching, and Learning'. *Educational Media, Memory and Society* 1, no. 1: 203–26.

Schrecker, Ellen. 2004. *Cold War Triumphalism: The Misuse of History after the Fall of Communism.* New York et al.: New Press.

Tyson-Bernstein, Harriet. 1988. *A Conspiracy of Good Intentions: America's Textbook Fiasco.* Washington: The Council for Basic Education.

Whitfield, Stephen. 1991. *American Cold War Culture.* Baltimore et al.: Johns Hopkins Univ. Press.

Wiener, John. 2012. *How We Forgot the Cold War: A Historical Journey across America.* Berkeley: University of California Press.

Williams, William Appleman. 1972 [1959]. *The Tragedy of American Diplomacy.* Second rev. ed. New York: Dell.

Open Access This chapter is licensed under the terms of the Creative Commons Attribution 4.0 International License (http://creativecommons.org/licenses/by/4.0/), which permits use, sharing, adaptation, distribution and reproduction in any medium or format, as long as you give appropriate credit to the original author(s) and the source, provide a link to the Creative Commons licence and indicate if changes were made.

The images or other third party material in this chapter are included in the chapter's Creative Commons licence, unless indicated otherwise in a credit line to the material. If material is not included in the chapter's Creative Commons licence and your intended use is not permitted by statutory regulation or exceeds the permitted use, you will need to obtain permission directly from the copyright holder.

4

Between Radical Shifts and Persistent Uncertainties: The Cold War in Russian History Textbooks

Alexander Khodnev

Remembering and teaching the Cold War proves a tough challenge to anyone working within the Russian context. Since 1991, hegemonic discourse on the question of who is to blame for the Cold War has experienced three radical shifts. Whereas during the Soviet era the Americans had been portrayed as the main culprits, the first half of the 1990s witnessed the emergence of a more critical attitude towards the USSR, increasingly perceived as aggressive. Despite a dominant trend towards a perspective on history and history teaching emphasising patriotic values, current historiography remains somewhat vague when it comes to the Cold War. Against the backdrop of these shifts and the uncertainties they foster, this chapter compares Cold War narratives in the four most widely used history textbooks in Russia. Focussing on how authors ascribe responsibility for the escalation of the conflict, on differences and similarities between textbooks, and on inconsistencies within each textbook, I proceed in four steps: Firstly I summarise the curricular requirements

---

A. Khodnev (✉)
World History Department, Yaroslavl State Pedagogical University, Yaroslavl, Russia
e-mail: khodnev@yandex.ru

and provide a brief overview of these textbooks, paying particular attention to the authors themselves and how each imposes their own structure upon the history of the Cold War. I then examine portraits of the USA and the USSR in narratives on the origins of the conflict, its main crises, and the history of decolonisation.

Marc Ferro stressed that images of history live in our hearts from childhood (Ferro 1992, 8). It is difficult to define the role of school history textbooks in the construction of these images, which can remain with us, if unquestioned, for the rest of our lives. In the last 25 years in Russia, the circumstances within which historical memories are constructed have altered, however, with the change in the global outlook after the dissolution of the Soviet Union in 1991. How the history of the Cold War is interpreted and taught plays a key role in prompting changes in how memory is constructed. The Soviet view, in the second half of the twentieth century, was that its former ally, the United States, was responsible for causing the Cold War. Yet the term 'New Thinking', coined at the end of the 1980s, suggested both the consideration of universal values and the interdependence of countries, and many Soviet people began to adopt a more pro-Western euphoria. The turn of the twenty-first century saw Russia's search to consolidate its identity and national interests in order to become a great power, a successor to the Soviet Union. This cultural environment might have had, and may continue to have, a direct or, more often, indirect impact on Russian historiography and the teaching of Cold War history in schools.

Reforms and State Educational Standards in History and Historiography

According to a long-established tradition, there are two main options for teaching history in the Russian school curriculum: either the course 'History of Russia' or 'World History'. The former is allocated more hours by the curriculum than the latter. This can be explained by the demands placed upon teachers by the Federal State Educational Standard (FSES), which makes its mission to educate future citizens of Russia and patriots. The teaching of history is complicated by the introduction of two different educational standards, FSES-2004 and FSES-2010. The main difference between them is a concentric system, which recommends students study all history from grades 5 to 9, as a linear, uninterrupted course, and then the same periods again from grades 10 to 11, this time in greater depth. While FSES-2004 required twentieth-century history to be included in the curriculum for both grades 9 and 11, the new 2010 standard stipulates history be taught at grade 10 only. In the school year 2016/2017, the new standards for history teaching were used in grades 5 to 6, while the old standard from 2004 was still applied to grades 7 and 11.

The debate on history teaching in schools became even more heated in 2013, when the 'Historical and Cultural Standard' (*Istoriko-Kulturny Standart*) was issued by a group of educators and scholars. This document sought to instigate the discussion of the most disputed and controversial issues in history education between academic historians and the teaching community. Since the group was formed, the authors have also written school textbooks together. The 'Historical and Cultural Standard' includes a significant supplement, an 'Exemplary List of Difficult Questions of Russian History', with no less than 31 controversial issues, more than half of which pertain to the history of Russia in the twentieth century. Article 23 of the document declares that 'assessing the role of the USSR in the outbreak of the Cold War' is one of the most 'difficult questions' (Istoriko-Kulturny Standart 2013, 49), this conclusion being reached after some 25 years of intensive investigations into precisely this question.

The list of critical questions, complaints and suggestions from school teachers and specialists in the field of history teaching shows that teachers are concerned about the current disparity between teaching hours available within the school curriculum for Russian history as compared to World History, and also by the increasingly reduced hours allocated to the history of other countries. At congresses of history educators, teachers also spoke of their concerns about students developing neither a global outlook nor values which are important in an open and multicultural world. Ironically, the State Standard demands these qualities and students must answer questions on the topic of multiculturalism during the Universal State Exam in History (Strelova 2013, 183).

The first version of the 'Historical and Cultural Standard' comprised seven sections, each consisting of a short introduction, table of contents, a wordlist combining the basic concepts and terms of the section, personalities, and a list of events set out chronologically. The distribution of material across these sections showed that Section 6, 'Apogee and the Crisis of the Soviet System (1945-early 1980s)', oddly includes only a small number of concepts and terms (with 45, it takes third place when the sections are ranked accordingly), the fewest mentions of names from all seven sections (with 32, it ranks second to last), and few events and dates (in sixth place, with only 47). Based on these indicators, the section 'Formation and Evolution of the Soviet System' is clearly in the lead, along with 'The Great Patriotic War of 1941-1945' (Akul'shin and Grebenkin 2013, 11). Further, the detailing of historical material and dates reaching back to the early centuries of Russian history dramatically outweighs information provided on more recent periods. This increases yet more the difficulties involved in teaching the second half of the twentieth century and thus the Cold War.

A study of the Cold War by Russian historians in the 1990s took the question of responsibility for the conflict to a new level. In the Soviet period, the weight of responsibility for its origins was placed on the United States. American historiography, particularly the works of American revisionist and post-revisionist historians, influenced Russian as well as European historiography between 1980 and the end of the 1990s (Zubok and Pechatnov 2003, 144), also inspiring the beginnings of Russian revisionist historiography. However, in Russia the revisionist interpretation was associated with historians who blamed the Russians rather than the American leaders for causing the Cold War, more often accusing Stalin and his close circle of being at fault for the increasing tension in relations with former allies between 1945 and 1946.

Another trend in Russian historiography in the 2000s concerns the transition from seeing the Cold War as a complex process to analysing its inherent contradictions on both sides. This trend emphasises how the Kremlin lacked a clear plan for the post-war period, particularly regarding a long-term strategy for developing relations with the United States. Because of this uncertainty, it is maintained, the USA saw a threat in the actions of the USSR and adopted a strategy of containing the Soviet Union's power after the Second World War (ibid., 147-148).

While the 'Historical and Cultural Standard' did not put an end to the debate on interpretations of the Cold War, it at least avoided exacerbating disputes between historians on key issues. Its wording almost completely avoids ideological assessments and its interpretations are reduced to a minimum. For example, the genesis of the Cold War is described in the following neutral expressions that record only historical facts and processes: 'The Beginning of the Cold War', 'The Truman Doctrine', 'The Marshall Plan' and 'The Formation of a Divided World' (Istoriko-Kulturny Standart 2013, 40). There are no set standards for World History.

General Profile of the Texts

We chose four widely used textbooks for the study, for eleventh grade and the last year of secondary school, covering the history of the twentieth and the beginning of the twenty-first century. The first textbook (Chubar'yan et al. 2011) is the work of a team of famous Moscow historians: Alexander, scholar and expert on the foreign policy of Russia and the USSR, Alexander A. Danilov, author of many textbooks on the history of Russia over the last 25 years in cooperation with a specialist in history teaching methods, and Lyudmila N. Aleksashkina, author of the methodological questions and exercises in the textbook. The authors of the second book are experts from St. Petersburg: Historian Oleg Yu. Plenkov is a specialist in German history with a focus on the National Socialist period, and Tatyana P. Andreevskaya is a well-known expert in pedagogical approaches to history. Oleg V. Volobuev, author of the third book, is a well-known textbook author working in Moscow, combining the talents of the researcher and the didactics expert. Nikita V. Zagladin and Yuri A. Petrov, who wrote the fourth textbook, are well-known historians and, at the same time, have authored school textbooks for twenty years. Petrov is also the Director of the Institute of Russian History of the Russian Academy of Sciences. These names are renowned among both teachers and the wider Russian public in connection with the world of history and history teaching.

Table 4.1 Number of pages allocated to each topic

	Volobuev	Plenkov	Zagladin	Chubar'yan
Total:	70 (31%)	93 (28%)	80 (18%)	53 (18%)
National issues	11 (16%)	5 (5.4%)	41 (51%)	30 (57%)
International issues	50 (71.1%)	67 (72%)	20 (25%)	15 (28%)
Economy	0	13 (14%)	4 (5)	4 (7.5%)
Culture	6 (8.6%)	8 (8.6%)	12 (15)	4 (7.5%)
Everyday life	3 (4.3%)	0	3 (4%)	0

There are differences in approach to the material in the textbooks for the Russian History course and its World History counterpart. In the textbook for World History by Oleg Plenkov, Tatyana Andreevskaya and Sergei Shevchenko, the Cold War occupies a large number of pages. The peculiarity of this text is that the authors pay more attention than other textbooks to confrontations on a global scale in 'third world' countries of Asia, Africa and Latin America during the Cold War period, perhaps due to the affiliation of the editor. Associating the 'third world' with Asia and Africa is a Russian tradition, and Myasnikov is a specialist on the history of China, one of the key countries in the 'third world' story of the twentieth century told in Russian textbooks. For this reason it is understandable that some sections of the textbook describe the 'establishment of the communist regime' in China, the Korean War of 1950 to 1953, the confrontation of the two superpowers in Indochina, and other events related to this topic. The text emphasises the confrontation between powers on a global scale during the Cold War in all parts of the world. Key concepts are widely used: 'The Third World', 'Global Opposition in Asia', 'Decolonisation of Africa' and 'Authoritarianism and Democracy in Latin America'. However, the histories of Western and Eastern Europe, as well as of America, are allocated more space in the book than other parts of the world.

The textbook by Nikita V. Zagladin and Yuri A. Petrov, *Istoriya* (History), is intended for eleventh grade of secondary school. The text is designed to convey the history of Russia and the world in the twentieth and twenty-first centuries, and so the authors include information about cultural issues and changes to economic life as well as significant international events. However, the text lacks accounts of everyday life. By volume, it is the largest of the texts selected for analysis. Cold War conflicts are dealt with in paragraph 36. The authors emphasise the bipolar nature of the post-war world, with the USA's growing power and the increased authority of the USSR, whose army dominated Eurasia. Soviet troops controlled much of Central and Eastern Europe, North Iran, Manchuria and North Korea (Zagladin and Petrov 2014, 267).

In the textbook authored primarily by Oleg V. Volobuev there is no specific chapter dedicated to the 'Cold War'. Material on the history of the conflict is placed in Chapter 4: 'The World in the Second Half of the Twentieth and the Beginning of the Twenty-First Century', with two paragraphs of section 17, 'Post-war Organization of the World: International Relations from 1945 to the Beginning of the 1970s' (8 pages) and section 18, 'International Relations 1970s-1980s' and 'The End of the Cold War' (9 pages). The history of the Cold War is 'scattered' within other paragraphs, such as on the 'Social and Political Development of the West', 'Socialist Countries and Features of their Development', and 'Countries of Asia, Africa and Latin America in the Second Half of the Twentieth Century'. Aleksandr O. Chubar'yan's textbook, on the other hand, clearly seeks to reveal more about national Russian matters than global problems during the Cold War. Chubar'yan does, however, have a chapter dedicated to the Cold War story.

Ultimately, Russian history textbooks still bear the legacy of the Soviet era. The authors dedicate much space in the textbooks to political events at the expense of culture, economics and, especially, everyday life in the past.

The Origins of the Cold War

In the textbook by Plenkov et al. the question of which country was to blame for the origins of the Cold War still goes unanswered. While earlier Soviet historians believed that it was the US that unleashed the conflict, the most objective view, according to these authors, is that of common responsibility of both the USSR and the US (Plenkov et al. 2011, 136). Two reasons are given: the different interests of the United States and the Soviet Union, and the developing mistrust between the two countries.

Oleg V. Volobuev's text book states that the beginning of the Cold War is associated with the split of the world – primarily on the part of the USA – into warring blocs. In this version of post-war events, entitled 'Соединенные Штаты Америки вышли из Второй мировой войны самой сильной в экономическом и военном отношении державой. США, по словам президента Г. Трумана, способны были показать «железный кулак» всякому, кто воспротивился бы их мировому господству', the USA withdrew from the Second World War as the most economically powerful entity and could therefore 'show an iron fist' to anyone who opposed their plans for world domination (Volobuev 2012, 149). According to this interpretation, the USSR sought to ensure peace, restore its collapsed economy, and create a bloc of friendly states to secure its borders. In addition, the authors ascribe to Stalin the desire to achieve the traditional foreign policy goals of the Russian Empire, on the basis of increasing the power and authority of the USSR in the international arena. The reasons for these goals are not explored by the textbook authors.

Zagladin and Petrov's textbook states that the Cold War was caused by a 'clash of national state interests', which was 'aggravated by profound differences in economic and socio-political development in the dominant values'[1] (Zagladin and Petrov 2014, 267). The authors implicitly suggest that both superpowers had their own reasons for the confrontation and are thus both guilty of rivalry. Equally, they argue that:

> The prestige of the USSR has become stronger; its influence in the international arena has increased. However, the Soviet leadership could not use all this to ensure the peaceful development of the country. The Soviet Union was involved in a 'cold war' with its former allies.[2]

The scholar A. O. Chubar'yan was a direct participant in most conferences and projects that changed Russian historiographical approaches to the Cold War between 1990 and the 2000s. In Chapter 8 of *Istoriya Rossii*, Chubar'yan explains the beginning of the debates taking place at the end of the Second World War and the creation of a new world order, including the growing displeasure in Moscow at the 'delay in opening a second front' against Germany. At the same time, he points out that the old ideological confrontation between the 'socialist Soviet Union and the capitalist states lessened during the war'. The disagreement between these powers concerned the fate of the countries of Eastern Europe. The leadership of the USSR wanted to see them 'socialist', and the United States, Britain and France hoped to keep them under their own influence (Chubar'yan et al. 2011, 193). The fate of Germany was another source of tension. While in the Soviet zone a policy of supporting pro-communist forces was followed, in the Western zone of Germany 'events developed in the opposite direction. The old political parties were restored' (ibid. 2011, 194). This textbook portrayal is not fully correct, however: West German political parties were not merely the old political parties restored, but were certainly at least re-conceived, especially those to the right of the middle. According to Chubar'yan, as of the end of 1945 there were clashes between allies who accused each other of failing to fulfil their obligations. While the question of responsibility, for him, is answered, as the guilt of both the USSR and the United States is clear, Chubar'yan points to certain events and actions which seemingly contradict each country's foreign policy aims.

These different interpretations of the origin of the Cold War show that in all four textbooks the authors place the blame on both sides of the conflict. The traditional Soviet interpretation blames the United States. No texts criticise the Soviet Union regarding the events of the Cold War according to a revisionist line of interpretation which was popular in the 1990s. These revisionist historians called for another interpretation, and thus a change in the Russian historiographical tradition, suggesting that the blame for the Cold War beginnings lay with the USSR. In Western historiography, on the contrary, the revisionism label is used when blame is placed on the USA. The coverage of the principal international and domestic events of the epoch is extensive. The textbooks pay a great deal of attention to various aspects of domestic and international politics, with very little information about everyday life. On the whole, it must be said that the history of the Cold War (1946-1989) is not the key era for fostering identity construction in Russian school textbooks; this role rather falls to depictions of the 'Great Patriotic War' (1941–1945).

Narratives of Cold War Crises

One might imagine that Cold War crises would be central to the general narrative about this global confrontation. The Cold War played out in such a way that the main participants, the USSR and the US, did not utilise direct military operations, which threatened the use of nuclear weapons. Superpowers had to demonstrate their strength and influence in crises through actions that substituted direct military activity and, as victory or defeat in such a crisis was nevertheless comparable in importance to a victory in a real military clash, the memory of the crises must, according to the logic of military history, endure. Russian historians Aleksandr S. Seniavskii and Elena S. Seniavskaya stress:

> After a war has ended, it persists in the memory of many – its immediate participants, its contemporaries, and the direct offspring of those forced to experience the extremities of war. Where war is an event of significance to the social organism, its memory is preserved both in individual and in collective consciousness and may be reinforced in the official (ideological, political, etc.) discourse across several post-war generations (Seniavskii and Seniavskaya 2010, 54).

The Cold War, it seems, did not leave a long and preserved collective memory. It was a war in which Russia was defeated. Russian textbooks show the events of the Cold War generally in a neutral style, without reinforcing the official ideological and political discourse, and their authors avoid thorough details and analysis. They even omit certain crises, treating these as insignificant.

Plenkov and colleagues state that the Cold War was accompanied by a series of regional conflicts, most caused by ideological struggle and geopolitical confrontation between the two superpowers USSR and USA. In 160 conflicts between 1945 and 2000, 7.2 million soldiers were killed. According to the author, this is comparable to the number of victims of the First World War, which they place at 8.4 million (Plenkov et al. 2011, 135). They also cover, in a short phrase, the uprising in Hungary in 1956, including a photograph of these events. At the same time we are told that Romania achieved the withdrawal of Soviet troops from its territory in 1958 (ibid., 140).

The CSSR in 1968 is the first serious conflict to be mentioned in the textbook by Plenkov et al. Using the phrase 'The Prague Spring', the textbook relates how a group of reformers, led by Alexander Dubček, set out to remodel socialism. In Moscow this was perceived as a threat to what the Soviets considered socialism. In August 1968, under the pretext of 'protecting socialism' and 'the integrity of the socialist community', the troops of the Warsaw Pact entered Czechoslovakia: 'The attempt of the population of Czechoslovakia to repel the invasion by success failed' (ibid., 141).

On page 142 readers are informed about the Berlin crisis of 1948 and 1949. Apparently the authors considered this crisis less serious than the Prague Spring, the Berlin crisis being referred to as 'one of the first crises of the Cold War'. The authors present as its cause the attempt of the Western allies to carry out monetary reform in West Berlin. In the view of the leaders of the USSR, this step was considered a departure from the agreements concerning Berlin, and Moscow decided to organise a blockade of West Berlin. It is a story about the unsuccessful sanctions applied by the USSR against the population of Berlin. Western vehicles were not allowed to travel to West Berlin either by rail or by road. In order to communicate with the Western sectors of Berlin, the European countries established an effective airlift in which American and British aircraft successfully supplied the population with food. The blockade ended within a year. According to the authors of this text, the USSR came out worse in this conflict, now publicly perceived in a negative light because of its actions. In geopolitical terms, the blockade led to the unification of the Western zones of occupation and to the creation of the Federal Republic of Germany, as well as the emergence of NATO in 1949 (ibid., 142).

This textbook displays noticeably new attitudes to Western science and includes newly accessed documents from archives. This is a more recent trend, indicating that Russian textbook authors are trying to include different historiographical approaches. For example, an excerpt from a book by modern American historian Kathrin Weathersby about the role of the USSR in the war in Korea is provided as a source (ibid., 163). The textbook also utilises a clear method of avoiding a country-specific presentation of material, which prevailed in Soviet times at the expense of muting any problematic aspects that might interrupt the master narrative. The authors used the following headings: 'Confrontation in the

Arab World and the Problem of Israel during the Cold War', 'Decolonisation of Africa', 'Latin America between Authoritarianism and Democracy', and other headings with which they organise the material on a problem-related basis. The end of the chapter sums up the history of the Cold War as follows:

- The Cold War has become an important factor in the developments of post-war decades,
- The events of the Cold War affected various nations,
- History had never before known an ideological confrontation of this kind,
- The confrontation of the Cold War was due to differences in the social systems of the West and the East and was almost inevitable,
- The peak of confrontation occurred in the first post-war decade, while the confrontation itself continued,
- Rivalry and different approaches to solving world problems remained between the United States and Russia after the end of the Cold War (ibid., 185).

Such rivalry the author considers 'a natural process of political development', however, further claiming that 'the rivalry relations will continue in the future, but it is not at all necessary that they should take the character of militant ideological confrontation, as in the days of the Cold War' (ibid., 185).

Insurrections and conflicts against the domination of the USSR in the Eastern Bloc are not fully represented in this textbook. While there is information about the uprising in Hungary and the crises in the GDR, none is given about the Polish crises. Here again we see the features of the above-mentioned neutral style, which, of course, is associated with a common patriotic narrative: that the government of the USSR sought to protect the country's security during the Cold War and avoided mistakes. Consequently, according to Plenkov et al., some details of the events of the Cold War can be omitted as it ended without victory for the Soviet Union.

In the textbook authored by Oleg Volobuev, in paragraph 15 of Chapter 4, 'The World in the Second Half of the Twentieth to the

4 Between Radical Shifts and Persistent Uncertainties: The Cold... 63

Beginning of the Twenty-first Century', the authors examine the history of socialist countries and features of their development after the Second World War. In fact, this chapter tells the story of the Cold War. It is in this context that the main crises in this region are mentioned. The authors emphasise that divided Germany has more than once been an arena for serious conflicts. The first conflict examined by the authors is related to the events of 1948 and the Soviet blockade of the 'transport routes leading from the Western zones of occupation to the Western sectors of Berlin' (Volobuev 2012, 132). This conflict is explained by the fact that the stream of depreciated bank notes 'flowed from the western zones into the Soviet zone because of the monetary reform'. In the Soviet zone there was the threat of economic chaos (ibid., 132). We can see in this interpretation the desire of the authors to explain the blockade of West Berlin between 1948 and 1949 not as a political confrontation, but as a conflict that arose due to economic reasons.

The next crisis arose in the GDR in 1953. The authors state that, after Stalin's death, disturbances began here that grew into an uprising against the pro-Soviet regime (ibid., 132). The authors again seek the cause of the crisis in the economic state of the GDR: 'This was the Germans' response to the decline in their standard of living', while in the FRG, they state, thanks to the reforms, 'the situation ha[d] improved' (ibid., 132). The communist elite failed to suppress the opposition and Soviet troops entered Berlin. However, according to the authors, the GDR increasingly lost the competition with living standards in the FRG, and, in 1961, the border between West and East Berlin was closed. In August 1961 the Berlin Wall was built: 'This construction became a symbol of the Cold War and the split of the German nation' (ibid., 133).

Further on in the textbook, the authors analyse the crisis in Poland and the uprising in Hungary in 1956. In accordance with a long tradition, they are referred to as 'events', a common term used both in historiography and many textbooks. The authors discuss the call of the Soviet leader Nikita S. Khrushchev to establish socialism in Eastern Europe in accordance with national characteristics, a desire he expressed at the Twentieth Congress of the CPSU. Unexpectedly for the Soviet leadership, the condemnation of the old policy in Eastern Europe and Stalinism had outgrown the denial of 'socialist gains' and communist ideology (ibid., 133).

In Poland, a general strike began, which, according to the authors, was suppressed thanks to the policies of Vladislav Gomulka. In 1956, Poland succeeded in repressing further Soviet control. In Hungary, the communist leadership was less able to overcome Stalinism, and the people began an uprising. In November 1956, the uprising in Hungary was suppressed with the help of Soviet troops. The head of the rebellious government, Imre Nagy, was executed, and power passed into the hands of János Kádár (Volobuev 2012, 133-134).

The textbook authors subsequently interpret in detail the events of 1968 in Czechoslovakia. The general conclusion of this section differs significantly from earlier interpretations of the history of the socialist countries, the events being considered undoubtedly positive. The authors draw attention to the fact that, in the countries of Eastern Europe, communist governments came to power with the support of the USSR. Despite some successes in the development of the economy, leadership policies for these socialist countries led to acute sociopolitical crises. The power of the communist governments in these countries was preserved only thanks to the intervention of the USSR (ibid., 136). This conclusion comes close to describing events accurately, but it does not say that these socialist countries were occupied by the Soviets.

According to the textbook by Zagladin and Petrov, the most serious issue developing in the late 1940s was the question of Germany's place in Europe. Zagladin believes that each side in the Cold War fought for the resources and potential of Germany. This textbook provides brief information about the Berlin crisis of 1948 to 1949, stressing that, despite the critical nature of the conflict and the willingness of both sides to move towards an open military confrontation, 'the Berlin crisis was resolved peacefully, but the solution of the German question – the creation of a unified, neutral and democratic Germany – was frozen for many years' (Zagladin and Petrov 2014, 270). This idea of an unresolved German 'question' is common in recent Russian history textbooks.

The authors also analyse the main events of the Cold War in Asia. The text includes information about a clash in China, the victory of the CCP and the formation of the PRC, the war in Korea from 1950 to 1953, and the Vietnam War. The authors call the Caribbean Crisis of 1962 'the most critical conflict of the Cold War' (ibid., 273). The settlement came about, according to the authors, 'thanks to the restraint and prudence shown by President John F. Kennedy and the Soviet leader Nikita S. Khrushchev. Soviet missiles that caused an aggravation were shipped from Cuba, the United States abolished the naval blockade of Cuba, and the USA promised to respect its sovereignty and to remove missiles from Turkey targeted at the USSR' (ibid., 273). The Caribbean Crisis of 1962, known in the West as the Cuban Missile Crisis or the October Crisis, is present in all the history textbooks used. In the Plenkov et al. textbook the Cuban Missile Crisis and the increased danger of military confrontation it brought is explored over two pages (Plenkov et al. 2011, 220). Chubar'yan's textbook also treats the crisis, the authors arguing that the reason behind the behaviour of the Soviet leadership was to use Cuba to exacerbate issues in the USA: 'The existence of a socialist Cuba pushed the Soviet leaders to use this country to create difficulties for the United States'[3] (Chubar'yan et al. 2011, 200).

Zagladin's textbook examines in detail the events occurring in Eastern Europe, which was in the 'orbit of the USSR', during this period and mentions all serious conflicts and crises. Separate pages are devoted to the conflict between the People's Republic of China (PRC) and the USSR in the 1960s (Zagladin and Petrov 2014, 280-283).

Chubar'yan's textbook applies a chronological approach to the distribution of historical facts. In Chapter 8, the principal stages of the history of the Cold War are delineated: the origin, the 'split of Europe', the crises of the Cold War between 1950 and 1960, and detente. The Berlin crisis of 1948 is portrayed as the main crisis during the post-war period, from which the authors explore the remaining events of the East-West conflict: the creation of Germany and the GDR, the emergence of NATO, the Warsaw Pact, and Comecon (CMEA) (Chubar'yan et al. 2011, 196). The authors of the text connect the causes of the Berlin crisis of 1948 with the closure of checkpoints leading to West Berlin by the Soviets. The authors neither mention monetary reform in West Germany, nor do they include the economic reasons for the crisis and monetary reform which are mentioned (again 'neutrally') in Plenkov's and Volobiev's textbooks. The closing of Berlin checkpoints by the Soviets goes unexplained.

In Chubary'yan's text the author pays particular attention to the close relationship between foreign confrontation and the repressive domestic policy in the Soviet Union during the Cold War crisis. Anti-Western sentiment grew and accusations against citizens and artists who seemed to 'worship' the West mounted. At the same time: 'Similar processes related to the repression of dissidents, criticism of communism and the Soviet Union occurred in the United States and Western European countries[4] (ibid., 197).

According to the authors, the United States outstripped other countries in its reaction to anyone sympathetic towards the Soviet Union or communism in general, with anti-communist hysteria leading to a 'witch-hunt'. In the United States, even those merely suspected of sympathy for the communists were persecuted (197). However, the term McCarthyism is not mentioned in the textbook. We find more details about McCarthyism in the Volobuev textbook, which argues that, during the presidency of D. Eisenhower in the United States in the early 1950s, rumours of a pro-Soviet communist conspiracy spread, fuelled by Soviet support for the American Communists and the success of Soviet intelligence. However, the 'witch-hunt' discredited the American political system and Senator McCarthy's commission was terminated in 1954 (Volobuev 2012, 120).

The crises in Central and Eastern Europe – Hungary in 1956, the aggravation of the situation in the district of Berlin, and the Czechoslovakian crisis of 1968 – are all covered in relative detail in this chapter of the textbook. However, a large amount of space is also allocated to the 'big' crises of the Cold War, such as the Caribbean Crisis and the conflict in the Middle East (198-201). The authors suggest that events occurring between 1953 and 1955 went some way towards easing the conflict between the powers, thus referring to them as 'the first detente' of the Cold War era. After the death of Stalin in 1953, they claim, dialogue opened up between the opposing sides. As a result, an agreement was signed to end the war in Korea, the Berlin meeting was held in 1954, and in 1955 Soviet troops withdrew from Austria. However, the authors conclude this argument with the statement that the 'first discharge' did not put an end to the more general conflict (Chubar'yan et al. 2011, 198).

We can therefore see a broad selection of facts and arguments in these textbooks. For those in modern Russia who support one unified version of history and a single explanatory narrative for schoolchildren, recent textbooks will be disappointing. While the liberalisation of history, the emergence of new interpretations of the past, and discussions among historians are all developments which can be easily reversed, it is to be hoped that open debate and multiple perspectives in the field of history education cannot be completely suppressed; at least, that the memory of more liberal times will endure.

Decolonisation and the Cold War in Russian Textbooks

The USSR pursued a policy of 'proletarian solidarity' with other countries striving for national liberation in the context of decolonisation. Vladislav Zubok argues that between 1950 and 1960 the Soviet people felt pride in the USSR's foreign policy in this regard. For example, Khrushchev's course toward internationalism and sympathy for the national liberation struggles of the peoples of Asia and Africa found sincere and wide support among many people in the Soviet Union. Soviet people also sympathised with radical change in Egypt, Syria, Iraq and Algeria, as well as with the peoples of Asian countries such as India, Burma and Indonesia. At the same time, such a policy was consistent with optimistic and romantic sentiment in the educated ranks of Soviet society (Zubok 2011, 264).

The Cuban Revolution was particularly important for people in the USSR in the early 1960s. Cuba gave the Soviet people, it seems, hope that a real revolution could happen without major casualties. Thanks to Cuba, Soviet foreign policy received an injection of revolutionary romanticism. In Soviet society, a craze for anything Cuban began, which endured even beyond the Caribbean Missile Crisis. When, in the spring of 1963, Fidel Castro paid a visit to the USSR, he was greeted everywhere by enthusiastic crowds (ibid., 264). All these processes affected the teaching of history, with new scientific centres founded for the study of decolonisation and new pages written for textbooks (Khodnev 2014, 180-181).

In the textbook by Plenkov and colleagues, a separate paragraph is devoted to the decolonisation of Africa. The very term 'decolonisation' is new in Russian school textbooks. Previously, to describe one of the most important processes of the twentieth century, the Marxist expressions 'the collapse of the colonial system' or 'the destruction of colonial empires' had been broadly employed in their Russian equivalents. The authors apply a socio-geographic approach when presenting the facts, choosing to arrange the material of the text not according to the problems of decolonisation, but in terms of geographical region: 'Far East', 'Indochina', 'North', 'Tropical' and 'South Africa'. The textbook reports that, for a short period at the turn of the 1950s and 1960s, several dozens of independent states appeared in Africa, although in 1945 only three remained: South Africa, Liberia and Egypt. By 1975, the last Portuguese colonies of Angola and Mozambique were granted independence (Plenkov et al. 2011, 163).

Without explaining the reasons for such rapid decolonisation, the textbook lists the problems of the newly independent states in some detail. However, the influence of the Cold War remains the focus of the text, which emphasises that 'the West supported some odious regimes in Africa because they opposed the spread of communist ideology'.[5] The US guaranteed support for the dictators of these regimes, the textbook continues, acting not in the interests of the people but rather pursuing their own targets as well as tribal and foreign interests (ibid., 164). At the same time, according to the authors, the USSR helped these young states to break free of any remaining dependence on the former metropolises. This prompted many young African countries to choose the Soviet model of development, whereupon they received aid from Moscow. Further on, the text explores the history of decolonisation in two specific countries: Ghana and Algeria. The choice is telling: Ghana was probably one of the first independent countries in Africa to declare socialist reforms, and a protracted anti-colonial war began in Algeria.

The textbook also covers the problems of the postcolonial era. The authors note that only a few of the African states (Botswana, Cameroon, Congo, Gabon and Kenya) 'improved their standard of living', and that 28 of the 45 countries were among the most backward countries in the world in the UN classification (ibid.,168). Countries that chose a socialist model of development failed to achieve their goals. However, according to the authors' interpretation, the countries that chose the capitalist market model also found that their elected path of development brought its own difficulties, particularly with high unemployment levels[6] (ibid., 168). It should be said that many of the assessments the authors make in this part of the paragraph are outdated and much is changing in modern Africa. It will not be easy to answer the question of the influence of the Cold War on decolonisation, since one of the main factors in the rapid completion of this process is not set out in the text of the paragraph, but in an additional passage from the work of the Norwegian anthropologist T. Eriksen (ibid., 172). Eriksen mentions that the Soviet Union and the United States, rivals in the Cold War, both supported the process of decolonisation. Perhaps the authors were hoping that students would think and discover this argument for themselves.

In Volobuev's textbook, the main cause of decolonisation is the outcome of the Second World War and the weakening of ties between the colonial possessions of Britain, the Netherlands, France and the metropolises. According to the authors, after the war the peoples of Indochina, Burma and Indonesia resisted the return of former European masters (ibid., 137). The textbook also explores India's independence under the questionable heading 'Western Orientation in South Asia' (ibid., 140-139); the course of reform has actually changed several times in independent India. Another distinguishing feature of this textbook is its portrayal of the influence of Islam on Asia and Africa. The author of this part of the text finds reasons for the strengthening of Islam in processes of Westernisation and the establishment of Western (largely American) values and standards of life. For many, Islam constitutes a form of 'protection' from the Western influence. The author considers the Iranian revolution the beginning of the spread of Islamism in 1979 (Volobuev 2012, 141-142).

A small paragraph, 35, is devoted to 'The Fall of the World Colonial System' in Zagladin's textbook. The main reasons given for the collapse of these colonial empires include the strengthening of the Soviet Union's influence in the international arena, as desired by the USSR leadership, who even drew links between the liberation of the colonies and the disintegration of NATO, which included the leading colonial powers (Zagladin and Petrov 2014, 261). Peoples struggling for national independence, it states, could also rely on China, where the revolution succeeded in 1949. The textbook also emphasises the role of the United Nations, which gave international legal support for countries to decolonise (ibid., 261), evidenced with facts: Between 1958 and 1974, the USSR delivered arms to the value of 55 million dollars to Angola (ibid., 262). The same text claims that, despite its desire for allies in the Afro-Asian world, the USSR did not have sufficient opportunities to create modern industries in these newly liberated countries, disappointing both the leaders of the latter and the Soviet authorities (ibid., 264).

In the 'academic' textbook by Chubar'yan there is no specific section devoted to decolonisation, possibly because the book focuses on conflicts experienced by the USSR and Russia in the twentieth century: the confrontation between the USA and the USSR, and crises and conflicts in which the USSR participated. However, twentieth-century history is neither clear nor complete without this context, which renders this omission particularly troubling. For example, the authors state that the USSR intervened in the process of decolonisation relating to the conflict in the Middle East in 1956 by condemning the war against Egypt, in which Britain and France were participating. In the authors' opinion, events in Egypt evidenced the desire of the peoples of Asia and Africa to rid themselves of the pressure from their ex-colonisers. The Cold War continued, according to the authors, not least because the USSR and the USA sought to 'spread the positions of socialism and capitalism in Asia, Africa and Latin America' (Chubar'yan et al. 2011, 199).

This analysis shows that, while decolonisation was one of the most significant processes of twentieth-century history, this subject is overshadowed in the historical memory of many Russians. Modern textbook authors are not inclined to support the romanticism of the generation of the 1960s and to admire the feats of the peoples of Asia and Africa in crushing the colonial empires. The Soviet Union's role in this process appears from the pages of the textbooks as contradictory and inconsistent. Students can pose questions: if assistance was provided, why did it not lead 'third world' countries onto the road of progress? The texts confirm two features of the modern view of history in Russia: a lack of in-depth and complete scientific studies of decolonisation, and the tendency to build on the positive example of Russia's history in the era of the Great Patriotic War of 1941 to 1945.

Conclusion

In the case of Russia over the last 25 years, with changes in world outlook after the dissolution of the Soviet Union in 1991, ways of constructing historical memory have shifted at least three times. This cultural environment might have had a direct – or, more often, indirect – impact on Russian historiography and the teaching of history, particularly the Cold War at school. The multiple interpretations of the origins of the Cold War show that many authors actually place the blame for the conflict on both the United States and the Soviet Union. The traditional Soviet interpretation of the origins of the Cold War, which lays the blame on the United States, is reproduced in one text. The revisionist school of thought in the Russian historiographical tradition instead locates responsibility for the beginning of the Cold War with the USSR. Yet in none of these textbooks can we see revisionist interpretations, which would criticise the Soviet Union as was popular in the 1990s.

While the textbooks pay attention to various aspects of domestic and international politics, there is very little information about daily life in any of the books. It seems that neither the authors nor the specialists in pedagogical approaches to history have a clear solution to the question of how to select content for modern school textbooks, what should be included in the Russian history course material, and what should be taught in the more general courses. We can also identify changes in the use of key terminology: The modern Russian history textbooks categorically do not recognise the occupation of Eastern Europe by the USSR from 1945 to 1989, and when describing the relations of the USSR with the countries of Eastern Europe, the terms 'Support of Communists in Eastern Europe', 'Support for the USSR', 'Soviet influence' and 'Deployment of Troops for the Defence of Socialism' are used most frequently.

It is interesting to note another linguistic feature of educational literature on the history of the Cold War: In all teaching texts and in school curricula, the term 'Cold War' is written in inverted commas, probably an indirect comment on the geopolitical context in which the term was first coined by Bernard Baruch, advisor to the US president and Cold War enemy, in 1947, borrowing the phrase from George Orwell.

In spite of the fact that the authors of these textbooks seek to write in neutral tones, a patriotic master narrative dominates in modern history textbooks in Russia. The new Federal State Educational Standards directly require schools to mould students into patriotic citizens through the teaching of history. At the same time, and especially in the context of the Cold War, it cannot be said that the authors of modern history textbooks in Russia avoid acute social issues altogether; indeed, they portray serious crises of the Cold War as well as errors made by the Soviet leadership. In addition, the 'Historical and Cultural Standard' has failed to bring about a consensus on the interpretation of the history of Russia in the twentieth century. While all textbooks are different, each is affected by the individual authors who contribute to them, and their evaluations of Cold War events as well as their respective selection of facts vary greatly. However, the principle of including ready-made 'lessons of the past' in these textbooks remains. Ultimately, it must be said that portrayals of the Cold War are not paramount in the processes of identity construction engaged in by textbooks: The history of the 'Great Patriotic War' (1941-1945) is evidently considered more essential.

Notes

1. 'Столкновение национально-государственных интересов усугублялось глубокими различиями в экономическом и общественно-политическом развитиии, в господствующих системах ценностей'
2. Укрепился авторитет СССР, возросло его влияние на международной арене. Однако советское руководство не смогло использовать все это для обеспечения мирного, спокойного развития страны. Советский Союз оказался вовлечен в "холодную войну" со своими бывшими союзниками (Zagladin and Petrov 2014, 232).
3. 'Существование социалистической Кубы подтолкнуло советских лидеров к тому, чтобы использовать эту страну для создания трудностей для США' (Chubar'yan et al., 2011, 200)

4. 'Схожие процессы, связанные с репрессиями против инакомыслящих, критикой коммунизма и Советского Союза, происходили в США и странах Западной Европы' (Chubar'yan et al., 2011, 197)
5. 'Запад поддерживал в Африке некоторые одиозные режимы, поскольку те выступали против распространения коммунистической идеологии' (Plenkov et al., 2011, 164).
6. 'так как здесь сильно сказывался низкий уровень работников'

Bibliography

List of Textbooks cited

Chubar'yan, A. O., A. A. Danilov, E. I. Pivovar and L. N. Aleksashkina. 2011. *Istoriya Rossii, XX – nachalo XXI veka. 11 klass: uchebnik dlya obshcheobrazovat. Uchrezhdenij* Moscow: Prosveshchenie.

Plenkov, O. Yu., T. P. Andreevskaya and S. V. Shevchenko. 2011. *Vseobshchaya istoriya: 11 klass: uchebnik dlya uchashchihsya obshcheobrazovatel'nyh uchrezhdenij, pod obshchej red. akad. RAN V.S. Myasnikova.* Moscow: Ventana-Graf.

Volobuev, V. O. 2012. *Istoriya: Vseobshchaya istoriya. Bazovyj i uglublyonnyj urovni. 11 kl.: uchebni.* Moscow: Drofa.

Zagladin, N. V. and Yu. A. Petrov. 2014. *Istoriya. Konec XIX – nachalo XXI veka: uchebnik dlya 11 klassa obshcheobrazovatel'nyh uchrezhdenij.* Moscow: OOO Russkoe slovo – uchebnik.

Further References

Istoriko-kulturny standart. 2013. Moscow.

Akul'shin, P. V. and I. N. Grebenkin. 2013. 'Istoriko-kul'turnyj standart: koncepciya, rekomendacii, soderzhanie'. *Vestnik ryazanskogo gosudarstvennogo universiteta im. S.A. Esenina* 4, no. 41: 7–15.

Ferro, Marc. 1992. *Kak rasskazyvayut istoriyu detyam v raznykh stranakh mira.* Moscow: Vyshsya shkola.

Khodnev, A. 2014. 'The History of Colonialism and Decolonization in the Russian Educational Curriculum and the Changes to History Didactics'. *International Society for History Didactics Yearbook* 35: 177–191.

Seniavskii, A. S. and E. S. Seniavskaya. 2010. 'The Historical Memory of Twentieth Century Wars as an Arena of Ideological, Political, and Psychological Confrontation'. *Russian Studies in History* 49, no. 1: 53–91.

Strelova, O. Yu. 2013. 'Dva s'ezda uchitelej istorii v god rossijskoj istorii'. In *Kul'tura, nauka, obrazovanie: problemy i perspektivy. Materialy II Vserossijskoj nauchno-prakticheskoj konferencii*, edited by A.V. Korichko, 182–187. Nizhnevartovsk: Nizhnevartovskij gosudarstvennyj universitet.

Zubok, V. M. 2011. *Neudavshayasya imperiya: Sovetskij Soyuz v holodnoj vojne ot Stalina do Gorbacheva*. Moscow: Rossijskaya politicheskaya ehnciklopediya, ROSSPEHN.

Zubok, V. and V. Pechatnov. 2003. 'Otechestvennaja istoriografiya 'kholodnoi voiny': nekotorye itogi desjatiletilya'. *Otechestvennaya istoriya* 4: 143–150.

Open Access This chapter is licensed under the terms of the Creative Commons Attribution 4.0 International License (http://creativecommons.org/licenses/by/4.0/), which permits use, sharing, adaptation, distribution and reproduction in any medium or format, as long as you give appropriate credit to the original author(s) and the source, provide a link to the Creative Commons licence and indicate if changes were made.

The images or other third party material in this chapter are included in the chapter's Creative Commons licence, unless indicated otherwise in a credit line to the material. If material is not included in the chapter's Creative Commons licence and your intended use is not permitted by statutory regulation or exceeds the permitted use, you will need to obtain permission directly from the copyright holder.

5

The Emergence of a Multipolar World: Decentring the Cold War in Chinese History Textbooks

Lisa Dyson

Introduction

In compiling a history textbook, the authors must—regardless of their own national context—make a multitude of decisions about how to interpret and present their content. The resulting accounts bear witness to how those particular authors interpret the world and their country's place in it. In the case of how current Chinese textbooks portray the Cold War, textbook authors must take into account both China's complicated past and its equally complicated present.

China held an unusual position during the Cold War. In 1949, the American-backed nationalist regime was ousted by the Chinese Communist Party (CCP), who founded the People's Republic of China (PRC) and declared solidarity with the Soviet Union. A decade later, they were at odds with Moscow. After a period of enmity with both superpowers, the USA and the USSR, Beijing achieved a working relationship with the countries of the Western camp (Chen 2001, 49–50; 2010, 182–183).

L. Dyson (✉)
Independent Researcher, Washington, DC, USA

© The Author(s) 2019
B. Christophe et al. (eds.), *The Cold War in the Classroom*, Palgrave Studies in Educational Media, https://doi.org/10.1007/978-3-030-11999-7_5

During the course of the Cold War, China oscillated between both camps, refusing to align with either, even as it was at odds with many of the non-aligned countries (Latham 2010, 266, 274–5; Yu 2013, 695). China's shifting orientation during the Cold War had global weight in that at each stage it was, and was seen as, powerful enough to tip the balance between the two superpowers and profoundly influence the global stage, even if it could never independently shape the world to the same extent as the US and USSR (Chen 2001, 2–6). The authors of Chinese history textbooks must decide how to integrate China's changing stance and significant, if secondary, role in the Cold War into their narrative of the period.

They must also address the enormous changes China has been undergoing for the past several decades, including changes to its identity. With China's ongoing economic growth, its social transformation, and its growing global influence, how to describe China as a whole is an open question. Is it socialist or capitalist? Do economic changes require a political reimagining? Is the country a developing post-colonial country or a political and economic superpower? Is it outside or inside global structures of power? The answers to these questions are as numerous as the researchers seeking to answer them. What answers, then, do the compilers of history textbooks give, considering the rich subject of the Cold War and China's complicated history during the period? With China's identity in flux, what do they say about the country, its future, and its place in the world when describing the past, and how do they integrate China's rapid change into their narrative?

Writers of Chinese textbooks are hardly the only authors confronted with a complex background when creating a national text. That this historical and social complexity is compounded with political demands is not unique to China, nor is it unexplored in the Chinese context; indeed, the influence of the Chinese government on textbooks, as through the 'patriotic education campaign', is an area of study in its own right (Wang 2012; Zhao 1998). As with textbooks the world over, the various pressures on authors, the multiple national images they seek to convey, and the need to reconcile these with a complex history, lead to texts that combine multiple narratives, perspectives, and priorities, some of which are complimentary, and some of which are not. The result is compromise, ambivalence, and contradiction, and the fault lines in the text speak to the goals that created them (Klerides 2010, 38–41).

Against the backdrop of these complicated influences, some of which reflect universal conditions and some of which are particular to the Chinese context, this chapter analyses how a set of history textbooks currently used in many Chinese classrooms narrates the Cold War (Ahn 2009, 24–5; Li 2011, 140; Müller 2011, 48). Special emphasis is given to three interrelated aspects: how the textbook authors explain the origin of this conflict, how the Cold War past is linked to the post-Cold War present, and what all this means for the image of the national Chinese Self that emerges from the textbook's accounts. I will thus assess how Chinese textbook accounts compare with ongoing global debates and controversies regarding the Cold War. Assuming that we can learn a great deal about the messages conveyed by the textbook from how the subject matter is structured and segmented, I begin by analysing the structure the textbook authors impose on the story of the Cold War. I attend particularly to the decisions made by the authors to break down the historical narrative into separate units and chapters. Referring to current debates in global historiography, I also determine how much space is allocated to actors and events that can be categorized as relevant either for the conflict between East and West or for the conflict between North and South. In a second step, I then focus on how the narrative portrays the United States, the Soviet Union, the so-called 'Third World', and China as key actors of the conflict. How coherent or ambivalent are these portraits, and how do the authors address the tension that might arise from a complicated history during which China not only changed its alliances but also its identity?

Cold War Stories of the Cold War

Early in the Cold War, China was heavily influenced by the Soviet Union and adopted the orthodox Soviet interpretation of the conflict (Yu 2013, 685–6). This interpretation attributed the Cold War to the expansionist global ambitions of the United States, and saw the Soviet Union as the leader of the peaceful, democratic camp that stood in opposition to the imperialist capitalists led by the US (Hopkins 2007, 914–15). Mao contributed the notion that between these two camps was an intermediate zone, including China, that neither superpower controlled but both hoped to influence. Later, after the Sino-Soviet split, Mao reorganised the globe into 'three worlds' (Chen 2010, 184; Yu 2013, 693–4). The Western idea of multiple 'worlds' during the Cold War divides the globe into capitalist, communist, and developing countries, the last being the 'Third World' (Tomlinson 2003, 307, 309–10). However, in the Chinese context, the divisions are different. The USA and the USSR together make up the First World because of their power and imperialism, while the other capitalist countries belong to the Second World. All other countries belong to the third, with China as their leader in fighting against the oppression of the First World (Yu 2013, 683, 693, 696). In this new conception, the Soviet Union was as much an adversary as the United States, and development, rather than class struggle, defined the different sides of the Cold War (Chen 2010, 184–5).

Both these conceptions of the Cold War appeared in Chinese history textbooks of the era. Textbooks published immediately after the founding of the PRC reflect the Soviet influence, resulting in Eurocentric and Soviet-centric texts that pitted the United States against the Soviet Union (Martin 1990, 91–2; Yu 2013, 685–8). By the mid 1950s, however, Asia, Africa, and Latin America became more prominent, and the trend continued during the 1960s and 1970s as the Sino-Soviet split developed. During this time, textbooks came to portray the world as divided along the lines of the 'three worlds', allocating more space to the 'Third World' (Croizier 1990, 158–9; Yu 2013, 693, 696). In the late 1970s, after the beginning of Deng Xiaoping's programme of reform and opening, textbooks once again shifted, placing less emphasis on class struggle, revolution, and ideology, and more on economics, reflecting the new goals of the state. At the same time, the 'Third World' began to merit less attention and textbooks focused more on the west (Croizier 1990, 167–8; Martin 1990, 102–3).

While textbook narratives reflected geopolitical divisions of the Cold War, for much of the period the Cold War itself was not actually included in the history. From the late 1950s to late 1970s, the political standards prescribed for textbooks changed faster than authors could revise the books. At the same time, many events of recent history became extremely sensitive issues due to domestic political shifts and China's tense relations with the Soviet Union and other formerly friendly countries. As a result, only the textbooks published prior to 1959 extended their narratives to the present. For much of the 1960s and 1970s, history ended with WWII or the Chinese Revolution (Croizier 1990, 161; Martin 1990, 28; Yu 2013, 686, 693, 695–6). It was not until the late 1980s that the Cold War era was once again included in textbooks (Croizier 1990, 165–6).

The Segmentation and Organisation of the Textbooks

The authors' priorities and the themes they see in history shape how the content is organised into volumes, units, and chapters. Especially when we consider the relative amount of space allocated to different actors and themes, these divisions also show how the texts compare to other histories of the period.

The set of history textbooks I examine divide the course material into three volumes by subject rather than chronology or region. Each spans ancient history to the present day, and incorporates Chinese as well as world history. The first volume is dedicated to political history, the second examines economic and social history, and the third covers the history of culture, thought, science, and technology. Overall, structuring the books by subject matter ensures that multiple aspects of history are examined, and that culture and economics find their place alongside political history. However, simply having one volume devoted to intellectual and cultural history and another to social change does not necessarily guarantee sufficient coverage of culture and everyday life, as seen in Table 5.1. This table presents the distribution of textbook contents between various topics and time periods and shows that during the Cold War, the attention given to politics far outweighs that allocated to culture and everyday life. This shift occurs largely because the third volume dedicates two chapters to political theory in China. This content enumerates the ideas of China's top leaders without delving into their content or impact on

Table 5.1 Table showing the share of the text devoted to domestic and international history and to political, economic, and cultural history in the three textbooks combined

	All Time Periods	Pre-Cold War (to 1945)	Cold War (1946-91)	Post Cold-War (after 1991)
Entire Textbook Series	329 pages	226 pages	71 pages	32 pages
Chinese History	59%	55%	67%	64%
World History	41%	45%	33%	36%
Politics and Political Ideology	40%	39%	49%	32%
Economic Policy	26%	24%	29%	36%
Culture and Everyday Life	33%	37%	22%	31%

society, focusing on elite politics rather than everyday life. This imbalance in general, and that the attention is centred on developments in state ideology in particular, underlines the textbooks' interest in China's political institutions rather than its social transformations.

Within each textbook, the content is organised into eight multi-chapter thematic units, again eschewing a purely chronological approach, and providing students with a framework for historical interpretation. Each unit deals with either Chinese history or world history, and in each case China's experience during a given period is given first, foregrounding the Chinese experience. Meanwhile, the titles and chapter divisions of the thematic units begin to demonstrate how the textbooks interpret the Cold War as a less than definitive historical period. For example, the final unit of the politics textbook covers international history from the end of WWII to the present, and is titled 'The Trend Towards Multipolarity in the Modern World Political Structure'. Of the three chapters of the unit, only the first deals with the tension between the US and the USSR that is usually portrayed as central to the Cold War. The second turns its attention to the emergence of 'multipolarity' through other countries' efforts to resist both superpowers. The final chapter sees this trend continue at the turn of the 21st century (People's Education Press 2011a, v) (All quotations from Chinese translated by the author). Combined, this method of segmenting content reveals that the bipolar rivalry of the Cold War was only one phase in a larger historical arc rather than a definitive

5 The Emergence of a Multipolar World: Decentring the Cold... 81

period in itself. The economics textbook builds on this perspective, and its final unit, which covers the same period of history, is named 'The Trend towards Globalisation in the World Economy.' One chapter deals with the post-war creation of institutions such as the World Bank and the IMF, while the other two address the growth of regional and global trade agreements that continue to develop to the present day (People's Education Press 2011b, v). In the case of culture, not even WWII is a meaningful watershed; one unit covers global art and culture from the 19th century on, and its chapters each address developments in a different artistic medium rather than being organized by time period (People's Education Press 2011c, v). Clearly, the textbooks do not see the Cold War as a sealed, singular period, and while the large trends of history are certainly shaped by it, it is insufficient to determine them.

Meanwhile, the relative importance of the East vs. West and the North vs. South divides during the Cold War in the view of the textbook authors is reflected in how much space is allocated to each, detailed in Table 5.2. Here, I examined divisions and groupings as well as conflicts. The textbooks devote a considerable amount of space to developments and relations within the blocs, especially the Western bloc, rendering this distinction necessary.

These numbers suggest the relative importance of certain Cold War actors. Clearly, North versus South conflicts and the developing world in general are given little attention. Meanwhile, despite the preponderance of attention to East and West, a closer look shows that a relatively small amount is allotted to the USSR and the Eastern bloc. Of the international coverage of the Cold War, 49 per cent concerns the Western bloc alone, while 22 per cent is about its Eastern counterpart. The remainder

Table 5.2 Table showing the most salient divisions found in the international history of the Cold War. That is, a chapter on economic developments in capitalist countries after WWII would show a division of East vs. West, whereas the growth of the non-aligned movement would show a division of North vs. South

	Overall	Politics	Economics	Culture and Everyday Life*
East vs. West	94%	90%	100%	82%
North vs. South	6%	10%	0%	15%

*A brief passage about the development of film and television avoids drawing any divisions.

deals with the two sides in conflict or divides the world into the global North and South. The chapter topics illuminate some of this discrepancy. Both the USSR and the capitalist world are allocated units on their respective economies in the 20th century, with one chapter of each dealing with the economy after WWII. However, in the unit that explores globalisation, another two chapters are given to the international economic institutions that arose in the West during the Cold War. One single chapter on the Soviet Union claims to cover the economic history of the entire communist world (People's Education Press 2011b, 88–91, 98–101, 104–10). This imbalance is also seen in the chapters about China's international relations during the Cold War, where 30 per cent of the eight pages of text are about China's relations with the West, while only eight per cent are devoted to China's dealings with the Eastern bloc. A further 26 per cent is devoted not to China's interactions with any particular country or group of countries, but to general statements regarding China's principles, intents, and achievements in its international relations. When we turn our attention to the details of the narrative, we see that the relative absence of the Soviet Union and the Eastern bloc becomes only more evident, the exact nature of Cold War divisions becomes more nuanced, and efforts to establish China's identity continue to supersede any detailed discussion of its actions.

The Narrative of the Cold War: Origins, Agency, Culpability, and Conflicts

The first description of the global Cold War in the history textbooks depicts a bilateral struggle between communist and capitalist camps marked by global tension and local wars. While no judgment is rendered there, American aggression towards other countries quickly becomes a theme, giving the United States the bulk of the blame for the Cold War (People's Education Press 2011a, 108, 117–18). The rest of the Western world is both part of and oppressed by American efforts. Meanwhile, the Soviet Union seeks hegemony of its own, remaining, however, largely passive by comparison, or simply absent. While the 'Third World' is part of the anti-hegemonic resistance, the little attention it receives focuses just as often on its good relations with China. Combined, these narratives result in the themes of hegemony and opposition that create the textbooks' particular definition of the Cold War.

The United States, Hegemony and Multipolarity

Throughout the Cold War, the behaviour of the United States is marked by a desire for global control, and in this desire lie the origins of the Cold War. Some blame for the Cold War is attributed to the other Western nations, as in describing Churchill's 1946 'Iron Curtain' speech as a 'wanton attack' on the USSR (People's Education Press 2011a, 118). However, the Western camp is always characterised as being led by the United States without specifying which other countries it encompasses, thus in no way mitigating American culpability (People's Education Press 2011a, 107, 109, 112, 118, 119). Likewise, while 'contradictions' between the two superpowers in matters of 'social system and national interest' are mentioned at the outset as causes of enmity between the US and the USSR, no further elaboration is offered. Instead, the Cold War is explained as growing from the United States' desire to dominate the world and its need to overcome the USSR in order to achieve this goal (People's Education Press 2011a, 118).

Once the Cold War has begun, it takes the form of the United States leading Western countries to 'adopt all hostile behaviour short of armed attack' towards the Soviet-led socialist countries (People's Education Press 2011a, 119). NATO and the Marshall plan are further efforts to contain the Soviet Union (People's Education Press 2011a, 119–21). Until Sino-American relations are normalised in the 1970s, the United States also directs a particular hostility towards the newly founded PRC. Because of the thematic arrangement of the textbook, it is in the context of this hostility that we first encounter the Cold War. The United States seeks to isolate the new country diplomatically and economically, interferes in its domestic politics, and occupies the Taiwan Straits, despite Chinese hopes for better relations. American involvement in both Korea and Vietnam is part of the pattern of American aggression in pursuit of hegemony and, just as importantly, it allows the United States to directly threaten China. These threats are mentioned repeatedly, twice as an aspect of Sino-American relations, and again as a reason for China's weapons and nuclear programmes. By comparison, the actual wars in Korea and Vietnam only appear once (People's Education Press 2011a, 109–10, 112–14, 120–1, 2011c, 92, 95).

However, the textbooks make clear that the Cold War is something different than just a conflict initiated by the West against the East. The United States' hegemonic ambitions are also part of its relations with other capitalist countries. The Marshall Plan's purpose is to increase American control in Europe as much as to support economic recovery, and much the same can be said of the post-war Bretton Woods system (People's Education Press 2011a, 119, 2011b, 104–5). This control does not go uncontested, and most of the agency seen from other Western countries is expressed through disagreements within the Western bloc. When France, Germany, and other European countries unify for their own security during the 'American-Soviet Cold War', it is not clear which superpower is the actual object of concern (People's Education Press 2011a, 122, 2011b, 107). By the 1960s and 1970s, Western European unity and economic strength leads them to 'start shaking off American control', and De Gaulle's challenge to American leadership in Europe confirms the divisions emerging in the Western camp (People's Education Press 2011a, 123). This pattern distances the Cold War narrative from that of a West-versus-East conflict, but rather than making the Cold War a North-versus-South conflict, it brings to mind the Chinese 'three worlds' theory with an emphasis on conflict between the First and Second Worlds.

According to these Chinese textbooks, American ambition also extends past the end of the Cold War. After the collapse of the Soviet Union, the United States 'attempts to dominate the world single-handedly' and continues to stir up trouble abroad (People's Education Press 2011a, 127). The Western countries continue to resist, as does a rising China and a renewed Russia. As a result, the trend towards a multipolar world continues its inevitable progress. However, because of American ambitions, revived conflicts, and international terrorism, the modern world remains an unsettled one. Indeed, compared to the Korean War or any other Cold

War event, NATO's bombing campaign against Yugoslavia draws as much attention and even harsher criticism for the US.[1] In this historical vision, the theme of hegemony continues to the present day, and the root cause of suffering during the Cold War does not end with the collapse of the USSR. The entire Cold War becomes just one more phase in the constant shifts in power relations (People's Education Press 2011a, 117, 120–1, 127–9).

As much as the blame for the Cold War is attributed to the United States, there are times when the text is less damning. With regard to the division of Germany, the building of the Berlin Wall, and the Cuban missile crisis, the United States is given a comparatively neutral treatment (People's Education Press 2011a, 120–1). However, the textbooks become decidedly positive when describing American popular culture and its economic growth and technological change after WWII (People's Education Press 2011b, 90, 2011c, 64, 116–18). While the United States' interactions with other countries are portrayed as exploitative, its internal development, like that of other Western countries, is given a more positive depiction. Rock and roll is vibrant and exciting, while film and television make great strides to become new forms of art as well as signs of technological progress. The development of bebop contains the only, and somewhat oblique, reference to racism in the US in the entire set of textbooks, once a major theme used to illustrate the injustice of a Cold War adversary (People's Education Press 2011c, 116–18; Yu, 2013, 689, 692). And while modernist literature and art after WWII is described as reflecting the spiritual anguish felt in the West, this anguish is attributed to the experience of social change, two World Wars, and the Great Depression. The text seems sympathetic to the desire of artists and authors to explore these emotions (People's Education Press 2011c, 107–8, 112–13). The discussion of Cold War-era culture is not connected to the Cold War itself; rather, it is about the everyday human experience and explains ongoing developments in the global cultural landscape. In this way, the textbook narrative does not present a uniform and unceasingly critical image of the United States during the Cold War, but instead shows shared cultural trends in the West. Moreover, the interest in developments in popular culture as an aspect of technological advancement is similar to that exhibited towards economic growth in general.

In the realm of economic development, the image of the United States and the West is not simply disconnected from ideas of hegemonic struggle in the political realm, but actually contradictory to them, and the two aspects must be resolved through selective emphasis and omission. While the creation of the International Monetary Fund, the World Bank, and the Bretton Woods system in general is explained as a way for the United States to control other capitalist countries after WWII, the textbook treats the functioning of these organisations positively and credits them with promoting economic development. The authors do not fault the macroeconomic ideas these organisations embody; they only criticise them for being controlled by the United States (People's Education Press 2011b, 104–5). The Marshall Plan is depicted as a similar tool of control, while the rapid post-war recovery in Europe is seen as marvellous and independent of the Plan. As a whole, the post-war economic growth of the Western world is described as 'a "golden age" of economic development' in which countries develop the welfare state and even 'stagflation' is overcome with grace (People's Education Press 2011a, 119, 2011b, 88–90). And while in a later chapter competition within the Western bloc extends into trade, the description here does little to disaggregate the western countries, except to highlight American science and technology, and the positive role of the service sector (People's Education Press 2011b, 89–90, 108). In the face of economic success, questions of hegemony and strife disappear. This shift in perspective suggests China's recent emphasis on economic development. In the midst of the Cold War, the economic history of the West becomes a positive role model for China's own development. Meanwhile, the communist bloc is marred by economic failure, becoming a negative example, and in the political realm it offers no sympathetic counterpoint to the United States.

The Disappearing Soviet Union

Neither in its actions nor in the space allotted to it does the Soviet Union occupy a significant position in the textbooks' account of the Cold War. It more often appears as a necessary counterpart to the United States or China rather than as an active player in its own right. The actions by the

5 The Emergence of a Multipolar World: Decentring the Cold... 87

Soviet Union and other Eastern European countries in the late 1940s and early 1950s, finalising the division of Europe, are, according to the textbooks, simply reactions to the United States' efforts to contain communism (People's Education Press 2011a, 119). While the USSR also appears in various world events, it is only to be overshadowed by other actors. The chapter dealing with the early diplomatic relations of the PRC describes the Soviet Union's rapid recognition of the new Chinese regime and the treaty of friendship and alliance they sign. However, the portrayals of these events focus on how they allow the PRC to avoid diplomatic isolation by the West rather than on the relationship between the two countries (People's Education Press 2011a, 109). The same chapter also deals with the 1954 Geneva conference, which was convened to negotiate peace settlements for Korea and Indochina. The USSR attends but plays no active role. Rather, the conference is defined by obstructionist Americans and Zhou Enlai's leadership (People's Education Press 2011a, 110). In fact, of all the major incidents that mark the Cold War, the USSR is only an active participant in the Cuban Missile Crisis, when it hopes that a missile installation might 'change [its] unfavourable position in the balance of nuclear power' and secure its strategic interests (People's Education Press 2011a, 121). Even this description is fairly bland. The global influence or ambitions of the USSR appear negligible at best.

With so little space dedicated to Soviet actions and motivation, it would be unlikely for a reader to attribute much of the blame for the Cold War to the USSR. However, whenever the Soviet Union is mentioned in passing, it is clear that it, like the US, is in search of hegemony during the Cold War. Beginning in the 1950s, the newly independent countries of Asia, Africa, and Latin America initiate the non-aligned movement to avoid both American and Soviet domination (People's Education Press 2011a, 124). The bilateral contest for hegemony is mentioned as a reason for the United States to seek better relations with China, and Brezhnev seeks to gain an advantage by developing Soviet heavy industry (People's Education Press 2011a, 113, 2011b, 99). This desire for hegemony establishes that although the Soviet Union is not the primary villain of the Cold War period, it is not a model to be emulated either. It still contributes to the broader pattern of hegemonic struggles that are the cause of tensions during and after the Cold War.

However, unlike the United States, the Soviet desire for hegemony is not extended towards its own camp, because its camp simply disappears. Of all the Eastern bloc countries, only the Soviet Union appears in the sections on economics, culture, and most aspects of international relations. Not only are the countries of the Eastern bloc absent from the discussion of economics and culture, but in the chapters on film and literature, all the examples from the Soviet Union predate World War II, before the Eastern bloc existed (People's Education Press 2011c, 105, 108, 117). Politically, the countries of the Warsaw Pact disappear between its founding in 1955 and the upheaval that marks its end. The sole exception is seen when the German Democratic Republic (East Germany) is founded with the support of the USSR, while any ongoing relationship between the two countries is not explored (People's Education Press 2011a, 120). The theme that the Soviet Union possesses a great power's desire for hegemony does not overwhelm its general absence from the scene.

Another way in which the Soviet Union disappears from the Cold War is in the minimal attention given to the Sino-Soviet relationship. Aside from the 1950 Sino-Soviet treaty, there are signs of early cooperation between the two countries, although the textbooks do not engage in detailed discussion. For example, the Soviet experience influences early education policy, and until the Hundred Flowers campaign, China adopts Stalin's dogmatic rejection of the theory of genetics (People's Education Press 2011b, 66, 2011c, 96). However, the eventual disintegration of the Sino-Soviet relationship is explored even less. A decade after the split, while the threat the Soviet Union poses to China factors into improved Sino-American relations, there is no mention of any intermediate steps that led to the threat in the first place (People's Education Press 2011a, 113). Khrushchev's 1956 speech criticising Stalin is presented in the context of the economic reforms he was seeking to implement, a speech that, the textbooks claim, caused 'huge reverberations inside and outside the Soviet Union' (People's Education Press 2011b, 98). What these reverberations were and whether or not China reacted to the speech remain unclear, however.

The clearest juxtaposition, if not explanation, of the changed relationship appears in the chapter about China's technological achievements. In

1957, the Soviets assist China's weapons development by sending them missiles to serve as models. Elsewhere on the same page, students learn that China developed its own atomic bomb to 'break the monopoly on nuclear weapons . . . held by the United States, the Soviet Union, and other countries', suggesting that by 1964, the country saw a threat from both superpowers (People's Education Press 2011a, 92). This double threat appears again in the end-of-chapter questions; the reasons behind it, however, are omitted. The making of the Sino-Soviet split, a subject other historians see as a major feature of China's Cold War experience and one that fundamentally changed the conflict, disappears through the cracks in the narration while the authors place much more emphasis on American actions and the Sino-American relationship (Chen 2010, 183–4; People's Education Press 2011c, 92, 95; Z. Shen and Li 2011, xvii–xviii; Xia 2008, 104–5). The reason for this inconsistency is explained in part by the internal developments of the Soviet Union.

The economy of the Soviet Union is given a chapter that parallels that dedicated to the post-war economies of the capitalist world. Unlike the glowing account in its capitalist counterpart, however, the narrative in the Soviet chapter is of repeated attempts and repeated failures to reform a stagnant economy. Impatient with the uninterrupted economic decline, Gorbachev turns to political reforms, resulting in the dissolution of the USSR (People's Education Press 2011a, 126, 2011b, 98–101). One effect of this failure is that the Soviet Union becomes less relevant than the United States for an understanding of the modern world, as the Soviet system no longer exists.

Instead, the Soviet experience is primarily useful in that it serves as a negative model for Chinese development, and as a contrast to the path charted by the CCP. The failures of the Soviet Union are rooted in its leaders' shortsightedness and insufficiently 'scientific' understanding of the conditions they face (People's Education Press 2011b, 99–100). By comparison, Chinese political theory is characterised as scientific and adapted to Chinese conditions, allowing for the country's successful economic growth (People's Education Press 2011b, 56, 98–101, 2011c, 83–4, 87–8). Even in failure, the Soviet Union serves as a foil for the actions of others.

The portrayal of the end of the Cold War reflects another way in which the compilers of the history textbooks differ from many historians in identifying themes and questions about the Cold War. Instead of distributing credit for its peaceful end, they ask who should be blamed for the dissolution of the USSR. The depiction of the Soviet flag being lowered for the last time creates a mournful sense of domestic dislocation, and the entire period is described as one of upheaval and nationalist separatism. While Soviet economic troubles began with Stalin, ultimately the blame for the country's collapse goes to Gorbachev's decision to promote 'so-called "democratisation" and "openness"', causing his reforms 'to go awry' (People's Education Press 2011a, 126, 2011b, 98–100). The reasons how and why the textbook authors frame the end of the Cold War in this way reveal yet more about the vision of the Cold War and the vision of China they present.

First, the end of the Cold War is not presented as a cause for relief, because in this presentation nothing fundamentally changes. Hegemonic ambitions and the tensions they create outlast the Cold War. Meanwhile, fears of nuclear weapons that others identify as a major source of Cold War anxiety go unmentioned (Gaddis 2005, 48–82; Walker 1995, 1658). The Chinese effort to develop nuclear weapons to defend itself against the USSR and the US constitutes one of only two sections in the textbook that describe nuclear weapons as having a place in the Cold War. The other instance is in the case of the Cuban Missile Crisis, which begins as a confrontation over nuclear missiles and nearly leads to war. However, in neither case does the textbook suggest that nuclear war might have devastated the entire world (People's Education Press 2011a, 121). There is no association between the end of the Cold War and a subsiding fear of nuclear annihilation, as no such fear, it appears, existed in the first place.

Second, China's efforts to restore its territorial integrity are important enough to merit a chapter of their own, so the breakup of the Soviet Union is the actual source of anxiety. By contrast, the sole bright point in the turbulence in Eastern Europe is the reunification of Germany, where readers are shown images of people breaking down the Berlin Wall and celebrating in front of the Reichstag building (People's Education Press 2011a, 126). When reunification with Hong Kong, Macau and Taiwan is a major goal the textbooks attribute to China, and combating separatism in Xinjiang and Tibet is a major concern of the government, the breakup of the Soviet Union naturally becomes a cautionary tale of political liberalisation.

A Hollowed Out 'Third World'

The 'Third World' has been receiving increased attention in recent Cold War studies in the global North, and appears in the 'three worlds' theory put forward by Mao where it includes the same newly independent and developing countries (Suri 2011, 5). In the Chinese textbooks it receives some attention, with roles in the broader trends of multi-polarity and, to a degree, globalisation, but also as support and background for China's Cold War accomplishments.

The texts explain the rise of the non-aligned movement among newly independent countries as part of the trend towards a multipolar world, with these countries banding together to oppose the imperialism and the hegemonic ambitions of both superpowers. Their resistance is part of the same reaction to hegemonic ambition shown by Western Europe. However, many aspects of the histories of these developing countries are thinly covered. The textbooks say that these countries came into being due to the development of national liberation movements and decolonisation; specific struggles, however, are not explored. The Vietnam War is the only war of national liberation mentioned, and it is grouped with incidents such as the division of Germany and the Cuban Missile Crisis. Vietnamese resistance to French and American forces is described as 'heroic', but otherwise the conflict is given only a single, brief paragraph (People's Education Press 2011a, 121, 124). Whereas textbooks in years past emphasised anti-imperialist struggles in the Third World to the point of excluding all other aspects of those countries' histories, that theme has dwindled as the textbook authors' priorities have changed (Martin 1990, 96–101).

Economically, the non-aligned movement has the stated goal of 'establishing a new economic world order', but no further details are given about their efforts or the economic conditions of developing countries in general, unlike the attention given to Soviet and capitalist development

(People's Education Press 2011a, 124). Instead, within the discussion of globalisation, the challenges it poses to developing countries and to China are raised in general terms, but the text suggests that good decision-making and 'reasonable countermeasures' can allow countries to overcome them and take advantage of the opportunities (People's Education Press 2011b, 103, 111–13). As with the Bretton Woods system, the principles of globalisation itself are not challenged. Instead, globalisation is presented as a positive historical trend that has been developing for centuries (People's Education Press 2011b, 103). In both the political and economic realms, actions that Third World countries take for their own purposes are hinted at in broad terms, but receive little elaboration.

Instead, newly independent and non-aligned countries most commonly appear as friends of China. They are presented as among the first with which China establishes diplomatic relations, and they are key to giving China's seat in the United Nations to the mainland government (People's Education Press 2011a, 109–10, 112–13). The Bandung Conference is portrayed as the first major meeting without representatives from a colonial power, while the countries that convened it are not necessarily portrayed as the driving force behind its success, or even its near failure. After an outside imperialist plot helps create dissension among the attendees, Zhou Enlai plays the key role in rescuing the conference from disputes and defeat (People's Education Press 2011a, 110–11). Incorporated into the chapter about the early foreign relations of the PRC, the episode serves as a diplomatic 'coming-out party' for China, with decolonised countries in attendance. Readers are also told that when the non-aligned movement took shape, China maintained good relations and cooperation with it and its members (People's Education Press 2011a, 124). Despite this friendship, the textbooks refrain from identifying China as a member of the 'Third World'. There is a hint of association when the Chinese author Lu Xun is listed as an anti-imperialist and nationalist writer alongside Rabindranath Tagore of India, Gabriel García Marquez of Columbia, and Wole Soyinka of Nigeria, but China's Cold War era arts and literature are separated into their own chapter (People's Education Press 2011c, 108). This separation is part of a broader effort by the authors to maintain distance between

China and all other factions during the Cold War, part of their process of constructing a specific identity for China.

China and its Place in the Cold War

Several aspects of China's national image and its place in the Cold War, as presented in these textbooks, have already been mentioned, hinting at the broader picture. In addition to China's distance from all sides of the Cold War, there is its desire for friendly relations on all sides, the interest in national reunification, a focus on economic growth and technology, and a comparison to other socialist countries. Further elaboration on these themes is seen in the coverage of China's foreign relations and domestic history during the Cold War. Overcoming potential incongruities, it creates an image of China that is independent, influential, and successful in pursuing its goals, yet also just, peaceful, and somewhat withdrawn in its relations with the world. China retains its socialist identity while prioritising stable institutions and market-driven economic growth.

An Independent, Successful China

The textbook portrayals of China's relationships with the West, the East, and the South during the Cold War suggest that it is not part of any side. Instead, the textbooks emphasise the degree to which China decided its own course. They make multiple explicit statements that, following the founding of the PRC, China was 'independent and acted of its own initiative' both domestically and in its foreign relations (People's Education Press 2011a, 80, 107–9, 111). Invasions, unequal treaties, foreign spheres of influence, lost territories, and payment of indemnities were a major part of China's experience in the hundred-plus years following the First Opium War in 1840. Both Sun Yat-sen and Mao Zedong characterised China as having been reduced to a 'semi-colonial country' during this period (Wang 2012, 47–69). Reiterating China's autonomy demonstrates a break from this past and establishes the end of this 'century of humiliation' as a major achievement of the CCP in establishing the PRC, a narrative found throughout official interpretations of history (Wang 2012, 100–4). In a similar vein, the reunification of Hong Kong and Macao with the mainland and progress towards reconciliation with Taiwan are further successes of the PRC and party leadership (People's Education Press 2011a, 93, 102–5, 2011c, 87).

In the wider world during the Cold War period, the textbook asserts China's growing influence and newfound national stature. This influence appears in China's participation in the conferences in Geneva in 1954 and in Bandung in 1955, and is implied when the United States in interested in rapprochement. Otherwise, until China begins participating in UN activities in the 1980s, the effects of the influence suggested by the textbooks remain unclear (People's Education Press 2011a, 108–14, 124). China's international influence is a marker of its national renewal, yet at the same time the text separates China from all factions and the conflicts of the period. This depicts China as a peaceful and upstanding nation, and avoids conflicts between China's pursuit of its ideals and the pursuit of its interests, even though it renders the discussion of China's international influence somewhat thin.

Idealism and Interests

These interests and ideals include peace and non-aggression, opposition to hegemony and imperialism, national security, reunification with lost territories, and economic development at home and abroad. In general, the ideals and the interests are presented as mutually reinforcing. China's early policy of supporting the socialist camp in foreign relations is implemented to protect peace, independence, and the successes of the revolution. The country's support of global peace and anti-hegemony are mentioned repeatedly. Meanwhile, China's noble intentions in the pursuit of peace have the distinct pragmatic advantage of creating conditions beneficial for China's development and increasing China's international stature. In turn, both developments allow it to negotiate the return of Hong Kong and Macau from a position of strength and to regain its seat in the UN, major victories for China (People's Education Press 2011a, 81, 103, 107–15, 129, 2011c, 85). While the textbook's evidence for

China's influence is perforce rather slim as it seeks to maintain the moral image of China, its account of China's successes does not suffer the same problem.

The account of the Korean War is careful to reinforce the image of a peaceful China that would only become involved in a war for justified self-defence. The description of the start of the war reads: 'In 1950, the Korean War broke out. The "United Nations Army" led by the United States crossed the "38th parallel", invading the Democratic People's Republic of Korea and drawing near to the Sino-Korean border' (People's Education Press 2011a, 120). It makes immediate national defence the motivation for China's involvement, and also obscures the North Korean invasion of the south. Eliding their ally's role in starting the war helps preserve China's wholesome intentions in joining it.

In a few instances, China could come across as less than perfectly peaceful, but the textbooks are able to justify China's actions. The textbook mentions that the People's Liberation Army ended the shelling of Jinmen Island in 1979 as part of a new policy seeking peaceful reunification with Taiwan, but when and why the shelling started is not mentioned. Moreover, Chinese people on both sides of the Taiwan straits so desire unity that these past military efforts to achieve it are quickly passed over (People's Education Press 2011a, 104). Elsewhere, China's weapons programme is discussed as part of its scientific achievements, casting the development of nuclear weapons and missiles as positive accomplishments that increased the stature of the country. In this case, however, the text is aware of the potential conflict, asking students to consider two statements evaluating the development of nuclear weapons. One criticises it on the grounds of China's needs for economic development and 'love for peace' while the other reconciles that love with weapons development on the grounds of external security threats and a declared no first-strike policy (People's Education Press 2011c, 95). On the contrary, it argues, China actually developed nuclear weapons to safeguard world peace. Neither statement casts doubt on China's status as a peaceful country, and the main text itself pairs the development of nuclear weapons with building nuclear power plants (People's Education Press 2011c, 92, 95). In both these cases, as with the Korean War, military force is put in the context of national unity and security, becoming part of the nation's achievements rather than undermining China's high ideals.

China's Socialism and Socialism beyond the Cold War

Despite the distance the text maintains between China and the Soviet Union or the socialist camp during the Cold War, it does claim a socialist identity for the PRC throughout. The victory of the communist revolution strengthens the global socialist cause. Mao launches the Cultural Revolution in an honest effort to find a Chinese path to socialist modernity, an enterprise revitalised under Deng that continues to this day (People's Education Press 2011a, 81, 98, 2011b, 54–7). Looking beyond labels, the text establishes that China is socialist in that it absorbs lessons from other socialist countries, avoiding their mistakes (People's Education Press 2011b, 93, 2011c, 84, 88). And in setting up the contrast noted above between the leadership of the USSR and China, the textbook establishes a socialist yardstick for measuring Chinese success.

By this measure, it succeeds. The textbook states that with the dissolution of the Soviet Union, 'the world wide socialist movement suffered a setback', and that China's reforms were challenged, but not defeated (People's Education Press 2011b, 56). Later, the textbook reasserts that the dissolution of the Soviet Union has not halted efforts to build socialism elsewhere, and China's efforts are clearly among these. These statements establish that socialism remains relevant even after the breakup of the Soviet Union, further diminishing the degree to which the Cold War can be seen as a contest between Communism and capitalism, instead of the result of a particular set of hegemonic ambitions. However, the socialist identity that China carries with it into the present is a remarkably flexible one, adapting to the demands of economic development and discarding the class struggle that had once been treated as central (People's Education Press 2011b, 49, 54, 93). The textbooks exhibit this shift with an interest in development rather than revolution. With that comes positive coverage of capitalist economies, as well as a history that prioritises institutions and, despite claiming that the victory of the CCP was an inspiration to revolutionary struggles around the world, is deeply suspicious of revolutionary change in China (People's Education Press 2011a, 81).

China's Domestic Politics and the Minimising of Revolution

In fact, after 1949, the text celebrates only China's institutions and economic growth, depicting the country's efforts at radical change as restricted to particular periods and as interruptions in China's proper path. The early political history of the PRC is presented as the formation of China's political bodies, including the People's Political Consultative Congress, the National People's Congress, its local counterparts, and the minority nationality autonomous areas. The official functions and genesis of each are explained, but without details of their practical implementation. Likewise, Mao Zedong and other CCP leaders are elected to high positions, but they are not shown making decisions, or trying to transform China (People's Education Press 2011a, 94–7). Economic changes happen through orderly reforms and are guided by impersonal Five Year Plans (People's Education Press 2011b, 50–1). The chapter on Mao Zedong's thought and theory is also interested in institutions and development, with Mao's real achievement lying in synthesising the collective wisdom of the party, and his theory's achievement is in adapting Marxism to the needs of China (People's Education Press 2011c, 83–5). Prior to the Cultural Revolution, there are no rapid political shifts, and prior to the Great Leap Forward, no radical change at all.

The Great Leap Forward and the Cultural Revolution are presented as the two disruptions in China's development. The Great Leap Forward is characterised by waste and chaos as 'objective laws' are ignored in a revolutionary effort to develop the economy. As a result, China experiences 'the most severe economic difficulties since the founding of the country' while no further details are provided (People's Education Press 2011b, 52). A few years later, the Cultural Revolution is presented as a catastrophe on multiple fronts, derailing education, attacking innocent scholars, officials, and party leaders, undermining social order, and throwing the economy into chaos. It is also presented largely in the passive voice, or as a force of nature outside of human agency. With great pathos the text describes how it tramples the laws and constitution of the country and prevents the governing bodies from doing their work (People's Education Press 2011a, 98, 101, 2011b, 48, 50–3, 2011c, 101). The Cultural Revolution is described as a 'calamity' or 'great catastrophe', compared to the 'mistake' of the Great Leap Forward (People's Education Press 2011b, 49, 52–3). While both disrupt the regular, well-ordered conduct of the economy, the Cultural Revolution disrupts all levels of Chinese society, and is an even greater revolutionary intrusion. Thus, it is a greater catastrophe in a history that looks to depict a narrative of steady progress and institution-building. Any support textbooks might have shown in the past for revolutionary ideology was removed several revisions ago (Müller 2011, 41–6).

Conclusions: Evaluating the Cold War

Drawing together the analysis above, we can take from it three main insights. First, from the perspective of Chinese textbook authors, the Cold War does not mark a significant turning point in the history of the twentieth century. Rather, it appears to be one of many phases in the emergence of a multipolar world. Second, the USA and the USSR are not predominantly described as representatives of opposing social systems and ideologies. They are instead shown as two powers pursuing hegemonic ambitions, with the sole difference being that the Americans were much more successful than the Soviets in the long run. Finally, referring to the dominant narrative of the emerging multipolar world order, China is primarily portrayed as a successfully modernising power on the rise. We find hardly any traces of an old narrative that would portray China as the spokesperson of the 'Third World', the role of which is consistently marginalised. However, as the main narrative is about the emergence of a multipolar and thus simultaneously more just world, China's rise appears to be not only in the interest of the nation but also in the interests of peace and stability for all.

The most important lesson to be drawn from my analysis of the Chinese textbook is that the Cold War is not seen as an ideological struggle between communism and capitalism but rather as a contest between superpowers seeking hegemony, as well as between them and the countries they attempt to control. There is little doubt that the United States bears the greatest responsibility for the Cold War, although the Soviet Union had hegemonic ambitions of its own. Likewise, there is little doubt that the Cold War was bad. The bipolar period was marked by global tension and local war. It interfered with humanity's trend towards economic integration, and China faced threats from all sides.

However, the condemnation of the Cold War lacks the force one could expect. The bipolar order is an impediment to globalisation, but globalisation in half the world carries on regardless, accompanied by shining economic growth. Pursuit of hegemony, while portrayed negatively, is not restricted to the Cold War period, and the United States maintains its ambitions and continues its interventions to this day. We see the global tension but not the nuclear fears, and only the two paragraphs about Korea and Vietnam explain the local 'hot' wars that occurred. It is after the Cold War, when NATO bombs Yugoslavia, that violence becomes a clear tool for hegemonic ambition (People's Education Press 2011a, 117, 120–1, 127). And although China suffers threats during the Cold War, it takes reasonable measures to defend itself, pushing back the American challenge in Korea unscathed and rising above the turmoil of the period. Even the failure of communism in other countries during the Cold War cannot derail China's economic growth and search for a socialist path to modernity. The larger theme of hegemonic ambition dominates the negative aspects of the Cold War, while the ongoing positive trends in history—increasing multi-polarity, globalisation, and the relevance of socialism—also existed during the era. The ways in which the Cold War is not essential to the periodisation of history reduce its sting.

How does this view towards the Cold War era compare to current debates in mainly Western historiography? The movement away from seeing the Cold War as a definitive period and the emphasis on globalisation brings to mind a thesis articulated most prominently by the historian Akira Iriye who argues that the Cold War was only one and certainly not the most important aspect of history after WWII. However, the textbooks barely engage with decolonisation and do not acknowledge the emergence of a global human and environmental rights discourse, all trends Iriye sees as being highly significant for the history of the second half of the 20th century (Iriye 2013, 16–17, 22). In acknowledging but rejecting the idea of competition between East and West, and instead focusing on hegemony exerted by both the US and the USSR, the textbook discourse seems to echo the ideas of the historian Prasenjit Duara. However, the Chinese textbooks devote more attention to American measures to dominate Western Europe and Japan, and those countries' efforts to break free, than they do to the relations between the superpowers and the developing world. In Duara's account, the industrialised West became the United States' willing 'junior partner', a pattern not seen here (Duara 2011, 461–4, 479). While the two views divide the world along similar lines of superpowers, industrialised allies, and developing countries, the tensions seen between them are different.

At the same time, the textbooks seem to display a fair amount of continuity with older interpretations. The emphasis on American ambition after WWII echoes the Soviet interpretation developed at the dawn of the Cold War, a connection not lost on at least one Chinese history teacher (C. Shen 2013, 11). Meanwhile, portraying the USSR as imperialist alongside the United States, seeing differences between the US and its allies, and defining the Third World as standing opposed to the demands of the two superpowers continues the 'three worlds' theory China developed after the Sino-Soviet split. However, in the theory's initial deployment, the struggle between the First and Third Worlds was seen as paramount, whereas the current textbooks instead explore the tensions between the First and Second and give precious little attention to the Third (Yu 2013, 693, 696). Perhaps this shift springs from the authors' changed conception of China. With its economic development, integration into the world economy, and growing political influence, it bears more comparison to the Second World, which was always defined by being comparatively well developed, and second only to the superpowers in might (Chen 2010, 184–5). Thus, they place it alongside the European Union as a force for multi-polarity, and no longer feel that it resembles the post-colonial countries of the Third World. Granted, Chinese textbooks never gave much room for the Third World to speak for itself, substituting Chinese leadership in the anti-imperialist struggle even when the Third World merited significant attention (Martin 1990, 99–102; Yu

5 The Emergence of a Multipolar World: Decentring the Cold... 101

2013, 695). Now, however, that leadership is gone, even though China's recovered independence and national development after 1949, which receive so much attention, form a quintessential post-colonial narrative. China's particular Cold War experience led it to develop its own theories about the conflict, and these theories continue to be deployed in narrating that history, even as they are adapted in response to changing ideas about national identity and China's place in the world.

As to the question of what national identity the authors convey, and how they convey it, China is shown as successful in asserting its independence, regaining lost territories, and ensuring its security while upholding its ideals of promoting peace and opposing hegemony. Sometimes, these two aspects are made to align by arguing that China's pursuit of security is in fact part of the pursuit of peace. For the Cold War period as a whole, China is shown as keeping a distance from all sides, ensuring its independence and anti-hegemonic credentials, but downplaying the interactions China had in a complicated era and rendering its influence superficial. China is resolutely socialist, focused on economic development, and well governed by its institutions. The desirability of economic growth and technological advancement are great enough that for all the criticism the United States merits, its economic success is praised, and the international institutions it established to feed its ambition are never criticised in their own right. The benefits of economic growth go unquestioned, even though the authors must create narrative disconnects to do so. Meanwhile, to maintain the narrative of development and good government within China throughout the history of the PRC, the country's efforts to revolutionise itself under Mao are presented as unfortunate interruptions, not a central goal (Chen 2001, 49–50, 72).

Moreover, because continuity and institutions, not disruption and revolution, are emphasised, the questions that might arise from China's rapid development are softened. Yes, China's growth is an economic miracle, rapidly altering people's lives and providing them with a bounty of goods, but the reforms do not require abandoning China' socialist identity. In a system that is socialist with Chinese characteristics, it is no contradiction to speak of a 'socialist market economy' (People's Education Press 2011b, 56–7, 66–7). The authors disassociate China from the developing world and emphasise its influence, but because China also opposes the desire for international control that seems to define superpowers, the text sidesteps the question of whether China is an insider or outsider in matters of global power. As to whether economic change has made political change necessary, the answer is quite the opposite. Under Gorbachev, the Soviet Union implemented political changes, but only because economic changes had failed to take hold. The very success of China's economy proves that political changes are unnecessary. The emphasis on institutions and discrediting of revolutionary politics in China does nothing to undermine this point.

The collapse of the Soviet Union as a warning for China is one way in which the history of the Cold War is used to inform the present. However, in looking for other ways in which connections are drawn between the Cold War past and the present, we see that they are all encompassing. The overarching themes that make the Cold War less central, less of a watershed event, also make the period enormously relevant to the present world. The connection is not one of cause and effect, but direct explanation. All of the essential trends of the Cold War era, including its central conflict, continue to the present day. Explaining them explains the world.

Note

1. While the account of NATO involvement in Yugoslavia leaves out the bombing of the Chinese embassy in Belgrade, this event lends the conflict particular resonance in China (Wang, 2012, 171–178)

Bibliography

List of Textbooks Cited

People's Education Press. 2011a. *Putong Gaozhong Kecheng Biaozhun Shiyan Jiaokeshu: Lishi 1 Bixiu* (Curriculum Standards for Normal Senior Secondary Schools Experimental Textbook: History 1, Required). 3rd ed. Beijing: People's Education Press.

People's Education Press. 2011b. *Putong Gaozhong Kecheng Biaozhun Shiyan Jiaokeshu: Lishi 2 Bixiu* (Curriculum Standards for Normal Senior Secondary Schools Experimental Textbook: History 2, Required). 3rd ed. Beijing: People's Education Press.

People's Education Press. 2011c. *Putong Gaozhong Kecheng Biaozhun Shiyan Jiaokeshu: Lishi 3 Bixiu* (Curriculum Standards for Normal Senior Secondary Schools Experimental Textbook: History 3, Required). 3rd ed. Beijing: People's Education Press.

Further References

Ahn, J.-Y. 2009. 'Narratives of the Korean War in Chinese High School History Textbooks'. *The Review of Korean Studies* 12, no. 1: 23–39.

Chen, J. 2001. *Mao's China and the Cold War*. Chapel Hill: University of North Carolina Press.

Chen, J. 2010. 'China and the Cold War after Mao'. In *The Cambridge History of the Cold War*. Vol. 3, edited by M. Leffler and O. A. Westad, 181–200. Cambridge/New York: Cambridge University Press.

Croizier, R. 1990. 'World History in the People's Republic of China'. *Journal of World History* 1, no. 2: 151–169.

Duara, P. 2011. 'The Cold War as a Historical Period: An Interpretive Essay'. *Journal of Global History* 6, no. 3: 457–80. https://doi.org/10.1017/S1740022811000416

Engerman, D. C. 2010. 'Social Science in the Cold War'. *Isis* 101, no. 2: 393–400. https://doi.org/10.1086/653106

Gaddis, J. L. 2005. *The Cold War: A New History*. New York: Penguin Press.

Hopkins, M. F. 2007. 'Continuing Debate and New Approaches in Cold War History'. *The Historical Journal* 50, no. 4: 913–34. https://doi.org/10.1017/S0018246X07006437

Iriye, A. 2013. 'Historicizing the Cold War'. In *The Oxford Handbook of the Cold War*. 1st ed, edited by R. H. Immerman and Goedde, 15–31. Oxford: Oxford University Press.

Klerides, E. 2010. 'Imagining the Textbook: Textbooks as Discourse and Genre'. *Journal of Educational Media, Memory & Society* 2, no. 1: 31–54.

Latham, M. E. 2010. 'The Cold War in the Third World, 1963-1975'. In *The Cambridge History of the Cold War: Volume II Crises and Détente*, 258–280. Cambridge: Cambridge University Press.

Li, F. 2011. 'New Curriculum Reform and History Textbook Compilation in Contemporary China'. In *Designing History in East Asian Textbooks: Identity Politics and Transnational Aspirations*, edited by G. Müller, 137–46. London/New York: Routledge.

Littrup, L. 1987. 'China and World History'. In *Reform and Revolution in Twentieth Century China*, edited by Y. Shaw, 16–29. Taipei: Institute of International Relations.

Martin, D. A. L. 1990. *The Making of a Sino-Marxist World View: Perceptions and Interpretations of World History in the People's Republic of China*. Armonk/New York: M.E. Sharpe.

Müller, G. 2011. 'Teaching "the Others' History" in Chinese Schools: The State, Cultural Asymmetries and Shifting Images of Europe (from 1900 to Today)'. In *Designing History in East Asian Textbooks: Identity Politics and Transnational Aspirations*, edited by G. Müller, 32–59. London; New York: Routledge.

Shen, C. 2013. 'Gaozhong Bixiu Kecheng "Liangji Shijie de Xingcheng" Jiaoxue Fenxi' (Analysis of Teaching the Senior Secondary School Curriculum "Formation of the Bipolar World Order"). *Lishi Jiaoxue* 11: 9–12.

Shen, Z., and D. Li. 2011. *After Leaning to One Side: China and Its Allies in the Cold War*. Stanford, California: Stanford University Press.

Suri, J. 2011. 'Conflict and Co-operation in the Cold War: New Directions in Contemporary Historical Research'. *Journal of Contemporary History* 46, no. 1: 5–9. https://doi.org/10.1177/0022009410383293

Tomlinson, B. R. 2003. 'What Was the Third World?' *Journal of Contemporary History* 38, no. 2: 307–321. https://doi.org/10.1177/0022009403038002135

Walker, J. S. 1995. 'The Origins of the Cold War in United States History Textbooks'. *The Journal of American History* 81, no. 4: 1652. https://doi.org/10.2307/2081654

Wang, Z. 2008. 'National Humiliation, History Education, and the Politics of Historical Memory: Patriotic Education Campaign in China'. *International Studies Quarterly* 52, no. 4: 783–806.

Wang, Z. 2012. *Never Forget National Humiliation: Historical Memory in Chinese Politics and Foreign Relations*. New York: Columbia University Press.

Xia, Y. 2008. 'The Study of Cold War International History in China: A Review of the Last Twenty Years'. *Journal of Cold War Studies* 10, no. 1: 81–115. https://doi.org/10.1162/jcws.2008.10.1.81

Yu, M. 2013. 'From Two Camps to Three Worlds: The Party Worldview in PRC Textbooks (1949–1966)'. *The China Quarterly* 215: 682–702. https://doi.org/10.1017/S0305741013001021

Zhao, S. 1998. 'A State-Led Nationalism: The Patriotic Education Campaign in Post-Tiananmen China'. *Communist and Post-Communist Studies* 31, no. 3: 287–302.

Open Access This chapter is licensed under the terms of the Creative Commons Attribution 4.0 International License (http://creativecommons.org/licenses/by/4.0/), which permits use, sharing, adaptation, distribution and reproduction in any medium or format, as long as you give appropriate credit to the original author(s) and the source, provide a link to the Creative Commons licence and indicate if changes were made.

The images or other third party material in this chapter are included in the chapter's Creative Commons licence, unless indicated otherwise in a credit line to the material. If material is not included in the chapter's Creative Commons licence and your intended use is not permitted by statutory regulation or exceeds the permitted use, you will need to obtain permission directly from the copyright holder.

6

Americans and Russians as Representatives of 'Us' and 'Them': Contemporary Swedish School History Textbooks and their Portrayals of the Central Characters of the Cold War

Anders Persson

Introduction

Focusing on the textual representation of the two main characters of the Cold War, the USA and the USSR, this chapter presents an analysis of Cold War narratives provided by five contemporary Swedish school history textbooks. The aim is to examine how Americans and Russians are constructed as representatives of 'us' and 'them'. Previous studies on Swedish history textbooks have often focused on the depiction of Sweden and Swedishness (e.g. Danielsson Malmros 2012; Spjut 2014, 2018; Gustafsson 2017), pointing usually to the dominance of nationalist narratives (see e.g. Nordgren 2006; Lozic 2010; Spjut 2014, 2018; Persson 2016) and claiming that most textbook narratives portray an unproblematised 'us'.

A. Persson (✉)
Dep. of Humanities and Media Studies, Dalarna University, Falun, Sweden
e-mail: ape@du.se

Focusing on how Swedish textbooks depict Americans and Soviets as particular 'others' (Loftsdóttir 2010; Andersson 2010), I will also examine what kind of general assumptions about historical others inform these portrayals. My analysis will be based on some conceptual distinctions introduced by Hannah Arendt (1982) and Lisa Disch (1994, 1997). The presentation of my empirical results is thus preceded by a short overview of their main ideas, a brief summary of previous studies on the topic, and a general description of the textbooks analysed.

Theoretical Framework

My theoretical approach draws on the assumption that school history provides an opportunity to promote personal growth by seeking to make use of history as a way of 'visiting' others (Arendt 1982, 1998; Persson 2016). Essentially, this perspective derives from the conviction that history might support young people in their endeavour to be and become the world (Arendt 1998, Persson 2017). This perception highlights an existential potential embedded in history as a school subject (Persson and Thorp 2017; Persson 2017).

History didactics usually refers to the concept of historical empathy when attempting to capture the moral relationship between people in the past and a present user of history (Lévesque 2008). Most often this concept has been employed by representatives of what might be called the tradition of historical thinking, in which historical empathy is normally construed as dependent on individual cognitive capacity. What is emphasised most of the time is thus the need to prevent presentism and the importance of contextualisation, of analytical distance and of scientific procedural competencies (see Blake 1998; Retz 2015).

From an Arendtian perspective, however, such demands, which highlight the necessity to bracket off personal and contemporaneous experience, might be seen as constituting an unfair call for individuals to adopt a comfortable, distanced, touristic view of historical events. From Hannah Arendt's point of view, it is not only such rational distance, but also the opportunity to involve yourself and your own human experiences that must be recognised when conveying narratives about the past (Arendt 1982; Disch 1994, 154). The past is gone; we cannot revive it. However, as humans, our being in the world is both constituted by a forgone past and by our present use of history. As present beings we thus exist in a historical and cultural weaving of human relations (Arendt 1998). Following Arendt, the study of history is thus not merely an activity where an isolated subject rationally inspects stories about the past as distanced objects. It is not even sufficient to consider how actors in the past might themselves have been operating with a rational understanding of history. A humanistic desire to recognise the motivation of other people, Arendt argues, requires not only an awareness of the other's disparity; we should also try to recognise ourselves as historical beings (Arendt 1998; ibid., 202–206).

Additionally, using the metaphor of 'go[ing] visiting' (1982, 43), Arendt also asserts the need for imagination when making judgments about other peoples' actions. She thus stresses the obligation we have to construct stories by imagining how we would have experienced and handled a situation similar to that which others have endured (Arendt 1982; Disch 1994, 157; Disch 1997, 136). In other words, as Disch puts it, 'as a visitor you think your own thoughts but in the place of somebody else' (1994, 159). Consequently, 'visiting' the 'other' does not mean that we can fully embrace others' experiences. If we do not pay attention to the otherness of others, we insensitively make ourselves at home in what should be regarded as someone else's household. Such a naïve attitude derives from the will to assimilate the experiences of another (which is impossible), according to Arendt (1982, 43) and Disch (1994, 161–162, 168; 1997, 136). Or, as Disch notes, 'Arendt suggests that there is all the difference in the world between closing your eyes to the world, claiming to see through the eyes of someone else, and attempting to visit – see with your own eyes – someone else's position' (Disch 1994, 163).

Drawing on Arendt, Disch (1994, 1997) further distinguishes between recognising the circumstances of the other that will create distance, and visiting the perspectives of the other (Disch 1994, 154): 'the work of the imagination when visiting is twofold. It distances me from the familiar *and* takes me to standpoints that are unfamiliar' (ibid., 160).

Before this backdrop, my analysis of the portrayals of Soviets and Americans in Swedish textbooks will raise three questions: (i) Are the two main characters of the Cold War constructed as possible objects of identification and deprecation? (ii) Do the depictions of their acts and experiences contain elements of recognition? (iii) Are these acts and experiences situated in a way to create a basis for understanding?

I will proceed in three steps: First, I will investigate how the origin and the development of the Russian and American societies are narrated. Who are they and where do they come from? In what sense do the textbook portrayals of Russians and Americans embrace different kinds of plurality? Second, I will explore the motives ascribed to the two peoples and their leaders: With what intentions are they assumed to act? In what way are their acts situated? Finally I will analyse what judgements are passed in terms of guilt: How, on what basis and from what location, does the textbook retroactively judge the people and the leaders of the USA and the USSR?

Results from a Previous Study

Sweden is often described as a small nation highly reliant on its international affairs. Until the independence of Finland one hundred years ago, Russia in the east and Denmark in the west have often been attributed great importance in traditional Swedish narratives. Consequently, since the second part of the 19th century it has seemed as if the narrative of a constantly threatened homeland has been rather unopposed in Swedish history textbooks (Persson 2016).

Regarding later post-war events, it seems the portrayal of a peaceful nation trapped between the eastern and western hemispheres correspondingly includes a similar connotation (Danielsson Malmros 2012, 114). Unlike Denmark and Norway, Sweden has never formally been part of the NATO alliance. For some time, the self–image of a third way, a compromise between socialism and capitalism, remained a strong trend in public historical culture (Zander 1998). Nevertheless, previous research on Swedish history textbooks has shown that the depictions of the two superpowers changed notably during the Cold War period. Based on an analysis of almost five hundred textbooks in history, geography, and social sciences published between 1930 and 2004, Holmén (2006) shows that the picture of the Soviet Union was at its most positive right after World War II. During the late 1940s the previous description of the USSR as an undeveloped country was replaced with a much more compassionate description.

6 Americans and Russians as Representatives of 'Us' and 'Them... 111

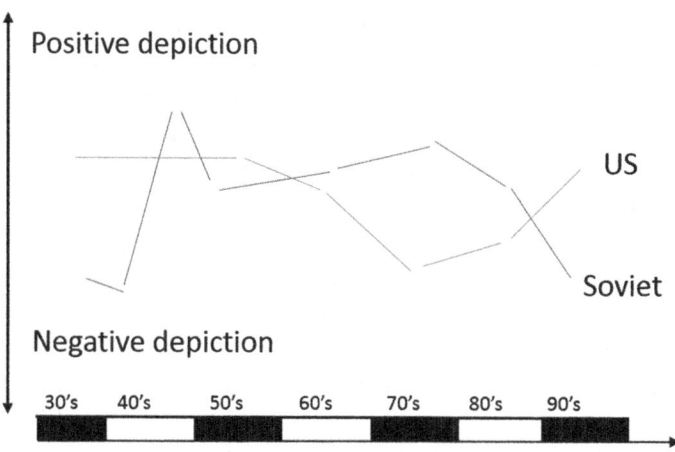

Fig. 6.1 Swedish textbook depictions of the USA and the USSR (Holmén 2006, 237)

However, already in the mid-1950s both political opinion and the textbooks were showing a much more condemning tone against the lack of democracy in the USSR. From Holmén's (2006) perspective, this is mainly explained by a wish to ensure American support during a period when Swedish military capacity was weak. Similarly, he stresses how the reinforcement of the Swedish military force led to the more US-critical approach presented in textbooks of the 1960s. Holmén notes the most anti-American stance, however, in Swedish textbooks of the more radical 1970s. These contain descriptions of social problems and betrayed ideals, and their critique in these narratives appears directed particularly at portrayals of 'underdogs', such as Native Americans and the Vietnamese.

During the 1980s, criticism was directed both towards the USA and the USSR. However, after the collapse of the latter in 1991, distancing from the Russians increased. The Centrally Planned Economy (CPE) system is described as a deficient alternative to the market economy and the undemocratic aspects of the USSR are given a prominent position in narratives published from the 1990s (Holmén 2006).

The present study was carried out more than a decade after Holmén wrote his thesis (2006). In the meantime, both the historical and political culture in Sweden and the educational system had undergone a considerable transformation. Far from the previous declaration of non-alignment and neutrality, several Swedish political parties nowadays argue for the necessity of Sweden joining NATO. At the same time, depictions of Russia in the public sphere and in mass media have become increasingly critical.

Simultaneously, since 2011 a major educational reform has been implemented within Swedish compulsory schooling. Regarding history, this policy change particularly includes a more detailed list of content knowledge, more national tests and a more explicit emphasis on disciplinary skills (Persson 2017, 7–11). Source criticism, the use of history, and other disciplinary concepts have thus permeated the new history curriculum. Several Swedish history didactics scholars have described this latter tendency as a striving towards a more academic and analytically distanced approach to history education (e.g. Persson 2017, 18–20).

Textbook Sample

Unlike many other countries, the Swedish government no longer has any control over the textbooks used in schools. Since 1991, textbook production relies on private companies and the free market. I therefore chose the best-known titles (*Utkik* 2015; *SO.S.* 2015; *PULS* 2009; *Levande Historia* 2012) from the three largest Swedish publishing houses (Gleerups, Liber and Natur & Kultur), as well as one textbook from a smaller publishing house, Sanoma: *Prio* (2016).

As we can see from the following graph, each book comprises between 222 and 390 pages of text, of which between 42 and 99 pages are devoted to the period between 1945 and 1989 or 1991. In all textbooks the majority of the content deals with international relations during this era. In most cases the East-West conflict is given about the same amount of space as North-South tensions during the period in question.

Regarding descriptions of the Cold War as such, the five books examined comprise 17–28 pages. With no exceptions, those pages largely (82–100 percent) deal with political and economic aspects of the conflict.

6 Americans and Russians as Representatives of 'Us' and 'Them...

Table 6.1 Table Showing an Overview of the Main Chronological, Geographical and Content-related Points of Focus in the Four Textbooks under Examination

	Total number of pages in text	Pages devoted to the Cold War period (1945–1989/91) vs. 1989/91–	Pages devoted to international vs. national (Swedish) affairs (in percentage)	Pages devoted to East–West gap vs. North–South gap (in percentage)	Pages devoted to politics/ economy vs. culture/ everyday life (in percentage)
PULS 2009	345 pp.	56 vs 18 pp.	76 vs 24%	31 vs 29%	82 vs 18%
Utkik 2015	343 pp.	62 vs 17 pp.	66 vs 34%	24 vs 6%	75 vs 25%
SO.S 2015	390 pp.	76 vs 18 pp.	83 vs 17%	14 vs 14%	95 vs 5%
Prio 2016	222 pp.	99 vs 67 pp.	76 vs 24%	14 vs 18% 25pp vs 32pp	76 vs 24%
Levande hist. 2012	435 pp	42 pp vs 9 pp	80% vs 20%	35 vs 16%	79 vs 21%

Table 6.2 Table Showing the Treatment of the Cold War in the Four Textbooks Examined

	Total number of pages in text	Pages devoted to the Cold War as such	Pages devoted to the Cold War (in percentage)	Pages dealing with the Cold War, devoted to international vs. national (Swedish) affairs	Pages dealing with the Cold War, devoted to politics/ economy vs. culture/ everyday life
PULS 2009	345 pp.	25 pp.	7%	64 vs 36 %	100 vs 0 %
Utkik 2015	343 pp.	30 pp.	8%	83 vs 17%	90 vs 10%
SO.S 2015	392 pp.	17 pp.	4%	88 vs 12%	94 vs 6 %
Prio 9 2016	222 pp.	28 pp.	13%	96 vs 4%	82 vs 18%
Levande historia 2012	435 pp	18 pp	4%	100 vs 0%	100 vs 0%

Results

The Origins of the USSR and the Depiction of the Russian People

While some differences are visible in the five textbooks examined, the portrayals of the Russian people and the emergence and growth of the USSR as a society show some recurring patterns. The portrayal of the pre-revolutionary years most often begins with a description of the huge gap between the rich and the poor in Tsarist Russia. The injustice is often made clear by a description of the contrast in the living conditions of different social classes, or by noting that most people were hungry despite the fertile lands and abundance of natural resources (*SO.S.*, 246–247; *PULS*, 192; *Levande Historia*, 320–324). For example, *Levande Historia* repeatedly comments on Russian hunger, illiteracy and under-development:

> Compared to Germany or France, Russia was undeveloped. Nine out of ten people lived in rural villages and subsisted on agriculture. Three out of four adults were illiterate. Crop failure and famine was common. [...] Together with poultry, cows and pigs, [the Russian peasants] tried to endure the cold of winter, when snow drifted in through thin walls and cold moisture rose from the ground (*Levande historia* 320).[1]

Although these initial narratives might contain a great deal of sympathy towards starving and oppressed farmers, they also show obvious elements of othering. Instead of intrinsically seeking to grasp their situation, the textbook portrays the serfs as 'malnourished, powerless and desperate' (*PULS*, 192).[2] This illustrates a general and frequently used depiction of ordinary Russian people as subdued, cowed and passive. The main exception in this respect can equally be found in *Levande historia*, which describes starving peasants who, despite everything, turn against 'those who took without giving anything back' (322).[3] Elsewhere, the only acts of the Russian people mentioned are related to violence. Accordingly, while readers are initially told that soldiers shouted at their officers (*Levande historia*, 324–325), they also learn that during the Civil War 'it was told that "the reds" shot all who had no calluses on the palms of their hands' (*PULS*, 197)[4] and that Lenin himself 'let his soldiers march into parliament to close it by force' (*SO.S.*, 248–249).[5]

The lack of narratives detailing positive motives for the creation of the USSR is also conspicuous when we consider how the birth and emergence of the USSR as a society is portrayed in Swedish textbooks. The few Bolsheviks are described as unwanted. Yet people are also commonly described as incapable of preventing this minority from seizing power. Madness and terror ensue (*Levande historia*, 323–327; *SO.S.*, 246–249; *PULS*, 194–195). In this book the frequency of words and phrases like 'rotting food', 'cold', 'starvation', 'strikes and demonstrations' is high (323–324). The foundation of the USSR as a state is generally described as a project of malicious leaders in a mix of determination and chaos. The origins of the USSR are thus mired in terror, murder, intolerance and backwardness by the authors of these texts.

Similar patterns shape the depiction of the Stalinist era. In *PULS* Stalin is described as 'a pathologically suspicious' and 'wary ruler' (201)[6], comparable only to Hitler and Mao. Yet even though he is obviously unpopular, Stalin is able to seize power 'after a series of ugly tricks' (*PULS*, 199).[7] The story of Stalin's rise to power is thus similar to that of the supposedly unwanted Bolsheviks. The Russian people do nothing to stop it; rather, as in *Utkik*, the reader learns of dying farmers, detention camps, executions, famine, raids and horror (218–219). Instead of describing the active resistance of the peasants, the narrative notes that anyone who refused to co-operate would find him- or herself in trouble (*SO.S.*, 259). The only notable exception in this respect seems to be the inclusion of the fact that some peasants, despite everything, resisted the Soviet central power by slaughtering their livestock and destroying their tools (*Levande historia*, 329; *PULS*, 199).

In some cases the passivity of the Russian people is related to the Soviet system as such. Comparing the USSR to Nazi Germany, some of the textbooks claim, for instance, that the Soviet communists 'wanted to make every man think in a new way. Anyone who did not fully support the party would be seen as an enemy without the right to live' (*SO.S.*, 257).[8] The Russian people are once again described primarily as powerless and oppressed sufferers. People suffered from the cold in dark apartments (*Levande historia*, 329), starving and dying in tens of millions, and yet only seldom seem to resist. Rather, the Russian people are said to be afraid (*Utkik*, 219) and forced to betray their friends and family (*SO.S.*, 260).⁹ The most detailed descriptions of Stalin's reign of terror can be found in *Levande historia,* which devotes a large amount of space to describing life in the prison camps of the Gulag:

> In the camps political prisoners were incarcerated together with criminals. Prisoners could be raped, murdered, forced to work themselves to death, or die from hunger or disease. It took strength, skill and luck to survive. [...] The feeling that no one, absolutely no one, was safe created enormous suspicion and fear that permeated all of society. Anyone could be a spy. It was easy to turn in someone you did not like, a neighbour whose room you wanted – many families were forced to share apartments – a rival, or a girl who refused to have sex (*Levande historia*, 331).¹⁰

However, the lack of opposition on the part of the Russian people is not only explained by the climate of fear. Even if both Chrustjev and Gorbachev are described as reformists in some ways (*PULS*, 305–307; *Utkik*, 266; *SO.S.*, 376–377; *Prio*, 76, 187; *Levande historia*, 383, 389, 393–392), the inefficiency and bureaucracy of the communist system, these textbooks repeatedly claim, served to pacify its citizens:

> The Soviet Union could manufacture nuclear weapons that threatened the whole world, but not enough food, clothes and homes for their own people. There were plenty of natural resources in the Soviet Union: gold, oil, coal, iron and much more. Communists exploited nature to access these riches. Then they could afford to equip the world's strongest army. But large parts of the country were poisoned by environmental degradation (*SO.S.*, 374).¹¹

In *PULS* (306)¹² it is noted that 'no one dared or wanted to take individual initiative'. Furthermore, in the textbooks stressing the environmental pollution, corruption and the inefficient and impassive system in the USSR, the citizens are often portrayed as unreceptive collaborators. In *SO.S.*, the ordinary people are even implicitly described as drunkards and thieves:

> The new leaders who came to power in the 1950s and 1960s decided that more food, clothes, homes, cars and televisions would be produced, which people needed. Then one of the Soviet Union's major weaknesses was

exposed: ordinary people were forbidden to own businesses and try to become wealthy. In the Soviet Union, it was the state that owned all companies. And it did not matter if a company went badly, the state paid the workers' wages anyway. Therefore, many employees did not feel they needed to make an effort. It was common for people to get drunk at work, or not go there at all. When the state owned the companies there were many who did not feel responsible. People stole goods and sold them. The factories and agriculture became worse the more time passed. [...] Those who dared to complain were sentenced to punishment or locked away in mental hospitals. But those who worked for the party did well. They could travel abroad, and shop in special stores with foreign goods. There you could find all the things that ordinary people lacked (*SO.S.*, 112).[13]

This allusion to Russian consumption is no exception. *Utkik* is the only textbook which does not mention this. *PULS* claims that the peasants' savings were 'often [...] spent on vodka' (192)[14] and that 'humour and vodka were the people's only consolation' (306).[15] Beyond stressing that Russians often drank at work, *SO.S.* also claims that 'in the shops there was almost nothing to buy except vodka' (*SO.S.*, 11).[16] While the narratives on the USA and Western Europe include prominent cultural figures, inventors and industrialists, virtually none of their Soviet counterparts appear in narratives on the USSR. Not only the Soviet system but also the overall picture of the Russians thus becomes distanced.

The portrayal of the Russians' miserable existence is only challenged in *Utkik*, in which descriptions of ordinary Russian people are consistently more varied. Describing Russia during the revolution, the narrative states how hungry, poor and war-weary people were actively united in the rebellion against the rich. Furthermore, this textbook is the only one to remind us that, one hundred years ago, Russia already had electricity, trams, schools and cinemas (*Utkik*, 209–10). Elsewhere, however, we are presented with a truncated portrayal of an unattractive political and economic system and a people apparently incapable of understanding their own agency. Or, as claimed under the headline 'Communism: Threat or Liberation?' in *PULS* (284), these textbooks argue that people in the East 'had never learned about democracy'.[17] It was due to this lack of knowledge, it is claimed, that the people tolerated the lack of freedom imposed upon them by the communist system.

Soviet Leaders' Motives during the Cold War

If only reconsidering the outbreak of the conflict, most of the textbooks analysed describe the Soviet leaders as playing the most active and aggressive part (*Prio*, 63–66; *PULS*, 285; *Utkik*, 256; *SO.S.*, 337), blaming them for their support of communist dictatorships in the whole of Eastern Europe. Only *Levande historia* (377) explicitly mentions that certain acts of the USSR were motivated by fear of new aggression from the West and an interest in creating a buffer zone for protection. Still, the same textbook contains phrasing that signals Soviet malice and aggression:

> In 1948 the USSR blocked the Western allies' zones of Berlin in an attempt to starve them and seize power. The Western allies – the USA, Great Britain and France – responded by having a stream of aeroplanes, an aerial bridge, fly in groceries and other goods. Stalin had to comply and the blockade ended after eleven months. The relationship between the USSR and the USA was at a record low. The American journalist Walter Lippman made the conflict known as the Cold War (*Levande historia*, 378).[18]

In some cases the textbooks seem to argue that it was the Soviet desire for expansion that led to the Cold War. One textbook even claims that 'Stalin wanted to turn the Soviet Union into the world's strongest country' (*SO.S.*, 258).[19] Most authors of these textbooks consider it important to include the consequences of these ambitions for other people. For instance, *PULS* (284) states: 'After 1948, almost all of Eastern Europe was ruled from Moscow. […] The borders were strictly guarded. Those who tried to escape were shot or locked up in prison'.[20] Although the textbook touches upon Eastern European resistance in 1989, these textbooks generally contain very few stories of resistance by Soviet citizens.

The Judgement of the USSR during the Cold War

When it comes to blame for the Cold War, the textbooks analysed varied somewhat with the different phases of the conflict. Portrayals of the 1960s often include a positive approach to the USA's actions internationally, arguing that the USA acted in response to Soviet aggression. In *Utkik* we learn how the USSR was forced to make great sacrifices during World War II, while the USA was not (254). Still the textbook argues that the policies of the USSR in Eastern Europe marked the beginning of the conflict: 'The Cold War began when the USSR introduced communism in Eastern Europe' (254).²¹

The USSR is typically described as playing the most active role, thus appearing as the guilty party when it comes to the escalation of the conflict (*PULS*, 286, 288–289; *Prio*, 63–66; *Levande Historia*, 378; *Utkik*, 253–256). In most of these cases, the Berlin blockade is typically presented as the single event that increased tensions between East and West. The textbooks also emphasise how the Soviet government made use of other countries in Eastern Europe, implicitly suggesting that it was greed driving its actions. While the American Marshall Aid Program is presented as a welcome contribution of supplies and economic support in the West, the reparations that the Soviets demanded from their European neighbours are portrayed as an extensive outflow of goods from Eastern Europe to the USSR (*PULS*, 286–287; *Prio*, 64–66; *Levande Historia*, 380, *SO.S.*, 304–305).

The textbooks level heavy criticism at the USSR for its actions in Eastern Europe. *Levande historia* states that Eastern Bloc leaders built the Berlin Wall in order to prevent people seeking freedom, and that they also, without any apparent explanation, built threatening rocket bases on Cuba (383–384). In many cases we are told how the people of Eastern Europe, despite their 'isolation', knew that their counterparts in Western democracies were much better off and in some cases tried to protest against Soviet oppression (*PULS*, 288–89; *Utkik*, 257; *SO.S.*, 178; *Prio*, 76). These aspirations came to nothing; instead we learn how Soviet tanks repeatedly quashed the 'Eastern European people's hopes for freedom' (*SO.S.*, 178).²²

This moral judgement of the USSR is also prominent in the textbook portrayals of what finally happened in Eastern Europe in 1989. *SO.S.*, states that this was the 'year of freedom and democratic revolution for Eastern Europe'²³ (*SO.S.*, 378), and in *PULS* (310) we are told how statues of Lenin, Stalin and other despised dictators in Eastern Europe were torn down. However, many of the textbooks omit the collapse of the USSR (*PULS*, 307; *Prio*, 78–83; *Levande Historia*, 391–39; *Utkik*, 276–

278). On the phenomenon that countries like Bulgaria and Albania soon re-elected communist leaders, the textbook explains: 'the communist politicians managed to retain power because there were not enough people in these countries who knew how democracy really worked' (*SO.S.*, 379).[24]

The Origins of the USA and the American People

The textbooks portrayals of the birth and progress of the USA as a nation and the Americans as a people are much more complex than those of the USSR and the Russians. However, the description of the conditions of Native Americans is worrying; they are continually referred to as 'indianer' (Indians), and descriptions of African-American history and people are equally concerning (*Levande Historia*, 276–277; *Utkik*, 122–123; *SO.S.*, 228–234). In *PULS*, it is explicitly mentioned that the Europeans took the land from people that already 'had' it (203), and the treatment of the Native Americans is even associated with ethnic cleansing (208).

In addition, however, the narrative of the birth and rise of the USA within these textbooks is (with the exception of the more particular narrative in *Utkik*) mainly one of freedom, progress and success (*SO.S.*, 228, 235–236; *PULS*, 205–206, 211–212; *Levande historia*, 202–203, 278–281). In several cases this achievement is often attributed to European immigrants. In contrast to Russians, Americans are frequently depicted as a people of innovative and diligent entrepreneurs. There are numerous examples of young, creative and strong people who are prepared to work hard (*PULS*, 206, 211; *Levande historia*, 267–269). Under the headline 'The USA became a superpower' one textbook explicitly claims that it was skilful young immigrants who made the economic success of the American nation possible (*PULS*, 209). In several cases comparisons are also explicitly made with Karl-Oskar and Kristina, two (heroic) protagonists of a well-known Swedish novel about emigration to the USA (e.g., *PULS*, 206; *Utkik*, 180). In *PULS* it is claimed, for instance, that European immigrants 'often were farmers, poor but hard working, like Karl-Oskar and Kristina' (206).[25]

Furthermore, the USA is depicted as the country of opportunity. It is said to offer most of its immigrants the right to vote, as well as religious freedom and a chance to earn much higher wages (*PULS*, 211–212; *Utkik*, 180–181; *SO.S.*, 215–217). Almost nothing, however, is mentioned about the individuals who failed or struggled to survive. Equally, the association these textbooks make between the American people and freedom extends to the creation of the nation as well. The struggle against Britain is referred to as a war of freedom. *Levande historia* even claims that the various states unanimously begged to become a part of the new attractive union (271). Similarly, *Utkik* mentions the right to life, freedom and the pursuit of happiness as the foundation of the newly liberated nation (121). While the origin of the USSR is mainly associated with chaos, violence and oppression in the textbooks analysed, the birth of the USA is related to freedom and the Declaration of Independence and Human Rights. For instance, beneath the headline 'How the USA was born', the authors of *PULS* explain the origin of the country by referring back to the Declaration of 1776. With references to its claims that 'all people are created equal', 'all power is based on the people' and that 'all laws must be approved by the people's representatives' (*PULS*, 205)[26], this text explains that the USA came to be regarded as the land of freedom on earth (for white people). In *SO.S.* the USA is even claimed to be the most democratic country in the world (227).

Likewise, when portraying the events of the early twentieth century, the narrative of economic and industrial success is highly prominent in these textbooks. *Levande historia* even argues that it was the absence of tollgates and taxes that caused an increased production of both agricultural and industrial goods: 'The United States became the country where the factories produced the most goods in the world. Lots of people found work and earned good money' (278–281).[27]

Accordingly and in most cases, descriptions of the Civil War and the roles of the North and the South in the conflict appear as unfortunate parentheses in the main success story. Here too, however, *Utkik* offers a more multifaceted description. It not only states that some loyalists were against the idea of the USA; it also ascertains that women, the poor, slaves and natives were not allowed to vote (*Utkik*, 122–123). This textbook is the only one to accentuate how the Civil War claimed more victims than all other wars in which the USA has participated since. Furthermore, the authors mention that the gap between the North and South remains visible today (*Utkik*, 161–162; *PULS*, 210). *Utkik* is also unique in the sense that it is the only textbook to deliver criticism: It asks whether the USA was really 'a country of the future' for everyone? (167)[28] or 'did everyone in the United States enjoy the "roaring twenties"?' (229).[29]

The other textbooks, however, seem to express a deep admiration for what the Americans achieved before the beginning of the Cold War. While these texts do not mention Russian or Soviet culture, there are frequent mentions of American jazz music, Hollywood (in one case described as the 'Factory of Dreams'), Walt Disney, Mickey Mouse, Donald Duck, Charlie Chaplin, and Duke Ellington (e.g., *PULS*, 213–214; *SO.S.*, 234). Furthermore, the text presents the success story of American industry during the early twentieth century, with electricity, cars, vacuum cleaners, radio and electric stoves (*PULS*, 213–214; *Utkik*, 215; *SO.S.*, 254). *PULS* uses the heading 'The land of the future' when it highlights the inventor and 'genius' Thomas Edison (211). Thanks to him, students learn, we now have both the light bulb and the steam power plant. Henry Ford is not only mentioned in relation to the invention of the assembly line principle; he is also associated with increased worker salaries (*SO.S.*, 236). Furthermore, these texts also show how – in the aftermath of the catastrophic stock market crash of 1929 – the American president cared for his people by introducing the New Deal (*SO.S.*, 255–256).

In contrast, the narrative of post-war USA is generally more complex. Here the majority of the textbooks expose social issues such as subversive youth culture, racism, and the Civil Rights Movement. In the narratives of the 1960s, the economic gap between American citizens is described as a problem (*PULS*, 216, 298–304; *Levande historia* 418–425, 232–234; *SO.S.*, 311–316; *Prio*, 72–75). Three of the textbooks mention McCarthyist policies against left-wing opponents (*PULS*, 298–302; *Prio*, 70; *Levande Historia*, 424), one book even describing McCarthyism as 'a hysterical witch hunt' (298).[30] Doubts are raised regarding democracy in the USA, claiming that the rich and their lobby organisations always sponsor the elected president (*PULS*, 304).

Unlike the critique of the Soviet system, criticism of the USA in the post-war period is mitigated by examples of how the American people chose to fight social injustices and problems. The Civil Rights Movement, the Vietnam Movement, the Green Environmental Movement, the Youth Movement and the Women's Liberation Movement are all invoked to exemplify this. The American people are thus ascribed agency and American society is described as something in which citizens can take an active part, bringing about change (e.g., *Utkik*, 273–274; *SO.S.*, 311–314; *PULS*, 301; *Prio*, 72, 75; *Levande historia*, 418–425).

USA Leaders' Motives during the Cold War

American policy is described in comparatively benevolent terms. Once again, *Utkik* offers the most detailed description, fostering identification with the individuals affected, such as its portrayal of the benefits of the Marshall Plan with a short story about a young German boy named Dieter and his struggle to survive after the Second World War (253). The Marshall Plan is described as the starting point for the rebuilding of Western Europe. And in *SO.S.* we read that 'from the ruins of the war, a new Western Europe emerged, richer than ever' (304).[31]

However, the motives of the Americans during the Cold War are not only depicted in terms of magnanimous generosity:

> In 1947, the United States government came up with an aid programme for war–torn Europe. The so-called Marshall Aid meant that Western European countries received almost $13 billion from the United States. The Americans wanted to bolster the European economy so that Europeans could afford to buy items from the United States. In addition, the Americans were afraid that poverty would encourage Western Europeans to vote for communist parties (*SO.S.*, 304).[32]

If the USSR is allegedly driven by a mad leader and an ideological determination to expand, the USA is generally associated with two other motives. Firstly, its motives are often related to a wish to prevent the expansion of communism in the world. *Levande Historia* specifies that it was Mao's victory in China in 1949 that originally motivated Truman to establish his well-known doctrine (377–378).

More often, however, American intervention into world politics is related to economic motives, a pattern already visible in explanations as to why the USA entered the First World War. While described as securing the victory of France and Great Britain and making 'the world safe for democracy' (*EPOK*, 224), the book *EPOK* also suggests that the 'real reason' is to be found in American concerns for export income (226). Likewise, *Levande historia* claims that the USA entered the war in order to guarantee future payments from European credit holders (311).

Economic motives seem to be even more explicitly articulated in the later sections of the textbook, describing later periods. *PULS*, for instance, argues that American 'economic interests are more important than the defence of the ideological ideals of democracy' (329).[33] Similarly, *Utkik* maintains that it was the defence of the free market and of American domestic corporations that dictated the international agenda of the USA during the Cold War (254).

This kind of reasoning appears most frequently where the textbooks discuss occasions on which the USA have interfered in less developed countries. *Utkik* claims that economic motives drove the USA to oppose development in Cuba after Castro's rise to power (267), and *SO.S.* describes Americans as 'worried' following Castro's success, primarily in the light of the interests of American corporations; attempts to overthrow Castro's regime thus ensued (*SO.S.*, 359). Similarly, the textbook authors explain American interference in South America with the note that 'big American companies own a lot in South America' (*SO.S.*, 365).[34] In some cases the textbooks explicitly state that the USA supported not only non-socialist but also non-democratic regimes: 'In country after country power was seized by USA-supported military regimes' (*SO.S.*, 365).[35] *PULS* even states that the American leaders regarded Latin America as its 'dairy cow' (329).[36]

Judgements of the USA during the Cold War

The textbooks portray the USA as a more-or-less reluctant participant in the Cold War, mostly describing American action around the beginning of the conflict as reactive in the sense that they felt compelled to act upon Soviet aggression (*PULS*, 216; *SO.S.*, 281; *Levande historia*, 358). Not even when the textbooks treat the aftermath of the American intervention and deployment of the nuclear bomb in Japan do we sense any critique in the narrative. The traditional narrative of how the nuclear bombs, despite everything, saved lives is prominent in the majority of the textbooks. *Levande historia*, for instance, describes the situation thus:

> On 6th August, US planes released a nuclear bomb over the Japanese city of Hiroshima. 80,000 were killed immediately, 70,000 were injured, and the entire city was turned into ashes. Three days later, an atomic bomb was also released over Nagasaki City. This was the only time that nuclear bombs have been used in warfare. Japan surrendered. World War II was over (*Levande historia*, 365).[37]

In *SO.S.* the authors even, more or less explicitly, blame Japanese suicide pilots, the latter having forced the Americans to deploy the nuclear bomb (*SO.S.*, 283). Otherwise, the event is described in an equally laconic and declarative manner as in the example above:

> At a quarter to nine on the morning of 6th August, 1945, the first atomic bomb was released over the Japanese city of Hiroshima. Three days later, an even more powerful bomb was released over Nagasaki. In only a few minutes 80,000 people died. The next day, Japan was ready to give up. World War II was over (SO.S., 283).

When dealing with later phases of the Cold War, most textbooks take a more critical stance towards American international policies. The American involvement in Vietnam receives the most negative portrayal. According to *PULS*, the USA tried to diminish 'the influence of the Soviet Union in the world' and therefore intervened in Vietnam (293). In a way similar to how the American treatment of Native Americans is described, the textbooks explicitly take sides with the Vietnamese. It is claimed that the war in South-East Asia cost the USA its hero status and popularity among young people throughout the world (*PULS*, 292–294; *Levande historia*, 386; *Prio*, 71–73; *SO.S.*, 311, 340–342; *Utkik*, 270–273). The Vietnam War 'destroyed the good reputation of the USA in the world' and made the American people realise that they had 'gone bad' (SO.S., 342).[38] Similarly, *Utkik* (270) depicts how the USA cancelled democratic elections in South Vietnam and dropped more than three times as many bombs as they released during the whole of World War

II. We are told of napalm and 2.5 million casualties. The textbook also states how Americans committed atrocities against civilians and 'sometimes burned hamlets randomly' (*Utkik*, 271).[39] In *SO.S.* we are told that American fire bombs destroyed Vietnamese peasant villages, resulting in violent protests in the USA (*SO.S.*, 342): 'For many, the United States' war in Vietnam became a symbol of how the rich world tried to crush a poor people that only wanted to live independently' (*SO.S.*, 311).[40]

As has been noted above, most of the textbooks also devote a great deal of attention to the domestic problems of the USA. The treatment of African Americans, the large economic injustices, and the recession of the 1970s are often described in a critical manner (e.g. *PULS*, 216; 298–304; *Levande historia*, 418–425; 232–234; SO.S. 311–316; *Prio*, 72–75). The struggle of the African-American community is given most space in *Levande historia*. Here six pages are devoted to describing Rosa Parks and the bus boycott of Alabama in 1955, the murder of Emmet Till, the church burnings in Montgomery, the brutal police attack against the peaceful demonstration in Birmingham of 1963 and the murder of Medger Evers later in the same year (418–423). In many cases this is contrasted with a more positive development of the domestic situation in the USA from the 1980s onwards. *PULS* tells us that 'the American economy improved' and that African Americans were able to prosper and 'work their way up in society'.[41]

Discussion

The purpose of this article has been to examine how Swedish textbooks construe Americans and Russians as representatives of 'us' and 'them'. The results that this study has yielded unveil insight as to *how* Russians and Americans are framed as objects of identification. By taking as my point of departure Lisa Disch's conceptualisation of Hannah Arendt's call to 'pay a visit', I furthermore intend to discuss *how* these two actors are textually treated as representatives of 'us and 'them'. In what respect do the depictions contain elements of recognition, and to what extent do they express the will to situate and understand the acts and experiences of these two historical players?

Regarding the portrayals of the Russian people and the Soviet Union, it seems reasonable to claim that readers of these Swedish history textbooks are offered limited opportunities to 'pay visits' in the Arendtian sense. To begin with, the character of the Russian people is repeatedly described as inexplicably passive. Most things seem to 'just happen'. No one likes the Bolsheviks, and no one wants Stalin in power, yet these entities seize power nevertheless. The situation appears terrifying and chaotic, but still the Russian people do not take action. Instead they are described as rendered passive and oppressed by the system.

Another problematic aspect is that the Russian people often appear as a homogeneous group. A great deal of what is said about the Russian person as a human being is therefore foreign and odd. Russians are described as people who are drunk at work, seeking solace in vodka. Their actions often seem motivated by malevolence and betrayal. In one case, Swedish textbook readers learn that a Russian man who was denied sex by a girl could take revenge by turning her in to the Secret Police.

Portrayals of Americans and of the USA appear to be strikingly different. Although there are also narratives of terrible oppression of Native Americans and African Americans, we also repeatedly hear stories about active, young and industrious immigrants. By references to famous brands such as Ford and Disney, well-known cultural figures such as Chaplin and Mickey Mouse, and great inventions such as the light bulb and the automobile, there should be opportunities for recognition on the part of the readers.

Furthermore, there are variations in how critical elements in the history of the USA and the USSR are presented in the textbooks studied. While an explicitly critical stance is taken in regard to the American atrocities towards African-American citizens and civilian Vietnamese, these are also connected to portrayals of how other Americans protest and try to bring about change. The Russian people, on the other hand, are portrayed as inexplicably passive objects, derived of agency, rendering the American people all the more active, reasonable and individually differentiated.

A similar difference can also be noted when the textbooks set out to explain the motives behind the actions of American and Soviet leaders during the Cold War. The USSR appears not only as the most active party in the escalation of the conflict; the motives of the Soviet leaders are rarely given any rational explanation. Apart from Stalin's hunger for more power, the reader is merely given declarative examples of how Soviet troops quash freedom-longing peoples' efforts towards democracy. In comparison, the actions of the USA appear considerably more rational in the sense that they act according to economic incentives and a logical ambition to limit the ideological influence of the USSR in other parts of the world.

Drawing on Arendt (1982, 1998) and asking to what extent the readers of these textbooks are given the opportunity to relate to these two historical actors, we can ascertain that whenever it comes to the Russians the voice of the textbook narrative is conspicuously often that of the distant beholder or tourist. The challenges that Russian people face seem to have very little in common with the situations 'we' (Swedish students) usually face. Generally speaking and beyond the particular case of the Russians, the distance is greatest when the textbook narratives implicitly indicate a moral assessment. The reader is always invited to identify with the victims of Soviet or American deeds. On the contrary, the acts of the perpetrator are rarely ever contextualised.

The perspective of the victim can in many ways be ethically appealing in a school context. The risk of this approach is, however, that it may promote a use of history where we from the vantage point of our safe contemporary world, like judging spectators, contemplate historical wrongdoings. We make no attempts at 'visiting', and the history of human atrocities thereby becomes a mere declarative description of someone else's morally condemnable acts. In the worst case scenario, the school subject of history may in this way become an activity that obstructs our younger generations from raising critical existential questions about what it means to be human.

Notes

1. 'Jämfört med Tyskland eller Frankrike var Ryssland outvecklat. Nio av tio människor bodde i byar på landet och levde av jordbruk. Tre av fyra vuxna var analfabeter. Missväxt och hunger var vanliga. [...] Tillsammans med höns, kor och svin försökte de [ryska bönderna] uthärda vinterkylan, när snön drev in genom tunna väggar och den kalla fukten steg från jordgolven' (*Levande historia*, 320).

6 Americans and Russians as Representatives of 'Us' and 'Them... 129

2. '[Bönderna] [...] blev undernärda, kraftlösa och förtvivlade' (*PULS*, 192).
3. '[...] mot dem som tog utan att ge något tillbaka' (*Levande historia*, 322).
4. 'Det sägs att "de röda" sköt alla som inte hade valkar i händerna' under inbördeskriget (*PULS*, 197).
5. 'Han [Lenin] lät sina soldater stövla in och stänga det nyvalda riksdagen med våld. Politiker som folket valt kastades ut, och Lenin blev Rysslands diktator' (*SO.S.*, 248).
6. '[Stalin]'s sjukligt misstänksam', 'likt Hitler slug envåldshärskare' (*PULS*, 201).
7. '[Stalin] [...] lyckades efter en rad fula knep'.
8. 'De [det kommunistiska Sovjetunionen och det nazistiska Tyskland] ville få varenda människa att tänka på ett helt nytt sätt. Alla som inte helt och hållet ville stödja partiet skulle ses som fiender, utan rätt att leva' (*SO.S.*, 257).
9. '[...] i den hemliga polisens tortyrkammare drevs oskylda människor att peka ut sina bästa vänner som förrädare och fiender till Sovjetunionen. Barn angav sina föräldrar, till och med Stalins släktingar greps' (*SO.S.*, 260).
10. 'I lägren blandades politiska fångar med grovt kriminella. Fångar kunde våldtas, mördas arbeta sig till döds eller dö av hunger och sjukdomar. Det krävdes såväl styrka som list och tur för att överleva [...] Känslan av att ingen, absolut ingen, gick säker skapade en enorm misstänksamhet och rädsla som genomsyrade hela samhället. Vem som helst kunde vara angivare. Det var lätt att ange någon man ogillade, en granne vars rum man ville åt – manga familjer tvingades nämligen dela lägenhet – en svartsjukerival eller en flicka som vägrat ha sex' (*Levande historia*, 331).
11. 'Sovjet kunde tillverka kärnvapen som hotade hela världen, men inte tillräckligt med mat, kläder och bostäder å sitt eget folk. Det fanns gott om naturtillgångar i Sovjetunionen: guld, olja, kol, järn och mycket annat. Kommunisterna skövlade naturen för att komma åt dessa rikedomar. Så fick de råd att utrusta världens starkaste armé. Men stora delar av landet förgiftades av miljöförstöring' (*SO.S.*, 110).
12. 'Ingen vågade eller ville ta egna initiativ' (*PULS*, 306).
13. 'De nya ledarna som kom till makten under 1950- och 60-talen bestämde att det skulle produceras mer mat, kläder, bostäder, bilar och tv-apparater. Sånt som människor behövde. Då visade sig en av Sovjetunionen

stora svagheter: För vanliga människor var det förbjudet att äga företag och försöka bli rik. I Sovjetunionen var det staten som ägde alla företag. Och det spelade ingen roll om ett företag gick dåligt, staten betalade arbetarnas löner ändå. Därför brydde sig många anställda inte om att anstränga sig. Det var vanligt att folk var fulla på jobbet, inte gick dit alls. När staten ägde företagen fanns det många som inte kände ansvar. Folk stal varor och sålde dem. Fabrikerna och jordbruken fungerade allt sämre ju längre tiden gick. [...] De som vågade klaga dömdes till straffarbete, eller låstes in på mentalsjukhus. Fast de som arbetade åt partiet hade det bra. De kunde få resa utomlands, och handla i speciella butiker med utländska varor. Där fanns allt som vanligt folk saknade' (*SO.S.*, 374–375).

14. '[...] ofta gick bondens sista pengar till vodka' (*PULS*, 192).
15. '[...] humorn och vodkan var folkets tröst och säkerhetsventil' (*PULS*, 306).
16. '[...] i affärerna fanns det nästan ingenting att köpa, förutom vodka' (*SO.S.*, 259).
17. [I stora delar av Östeuropa] 'Där hade man aldrig fått lära sig demokrati i västerländsk mening' (*PULS*, 284).
18. 'År 1948 blockerade Sovjetunionen västmakternas delar av Berlin för att försöka svälta ut området och sedan ta över. Västmakterna – USA, Storbritannien och Frankrike – svarade med att låta en ström av plan, en luftbro, flyga in livsmedel och andra varor. Stalin måste vika sig och blockaden hävdes efter elva månader. Nu var förhållandet mellan Sovjetunionen och USA bottenfruset. Konflikten blev genom den amerikanske journalisten Walter Lippman känd som *Det kalla kriget*' (*Levande historia*, 378).
19. 'Stalin ville göra Sovjet till världens starkaste land' (*SO.S.*, 10).
20. 'Efter 1948 styrdes nästan hela Östeuropa från Moskva "gränserna bevakades stenhårt", de som försökte fly stoppades eller sköts i flykten' (*PULS*, 284).
21. '[...] sedan Sovjetunionen hade infört kommunismen i Östeuropa började det kalla kriget'.
22. '[...] varje gång östeuropeiska folkens frihetsdrömmar av sovjetiska stridsvagnar' (*SO.S.*, 378).
23. '1989 blev frihetens och de demokratiska revolutionernas år för Östeuropa' (*SO.S.*, 379).

24. 'Att kommunistpolitikerna lyckades behålla makten berodde på att det inte fanns tillräckligt många människor i dessa länder som visste hur demokrati fungerade' (*SO.S.*, 379).
'Ofta var de bönder, fattiga men arbetsamma som Karls Oskar och Kristina'.
'Så föddes USA', '[...] alla människor är skapade jämlika', '[...] all makt utgå från folket, alla lagar ska godkännas av folkets representanter'.
'Ofta var de bönder, fattiga men arbetsamma som Karls Oskar och Kristina'.
'Så föddes USA', '[...] alla människor är skapade jämlika', '[...] all makt utgå från folket, alla lagar ska godkännas av folkets representanter'.
'USA blev det land där fabrikerna tillverkade mest varor i hela världen. Massor av människor fick arbete och tjänade pengar'.
'Var verkligen USA framtidslandet för alla?' (*Utkik*, 167).
'Tyckte alla i USA att det var det glada 20-talet?' (*Utkik*, 229).
'[...] ur krigets ruiner växer ett nytt Västeuropa fram, rikare än någonsin' (*SO.S.*, 304).
'År 1947 kom USAs regering med ett hjälpprogram för det krigshärjade Europa. Den så kallade Marshallhjälpen innebar att Västeuropas länder fick nästan 13 miljarder dollar av USA. Amerikanerna ville få fart på Europas ekonomi, så att européerna skulle få råd att köpa saker från USA. Dessutom var amerikanerna rädda för att fattigdomen skulle göra att västeuropéerna började rösta på kommunistiska partier' (*SO.S.*, 304).
'Ekonomiska intressen står över ideal om demokratins befriare', 'skylt på hot från kommunismen' (*PULS*, 329).
'Stora amerikanska företag äger mycket i Sydamerika' (*SO.S.*, 365).
'[...] även om de var diktatorer. I land efter land togs makten över av USA-stödda militärregimer' (*SO.S.*, 365).
'USAs mjölkko'.
'Den 6 augusti sprängdes en atombomb över den japanska staden Hiroshima. 80000 dödades omedelbart, 70000 skadades och hela staden lades i aska. Tre dagar senare sprängdes ytterligare en atombomb över staden Nagasaki. Det är första och hitintills enda gången atombomber har använts i krig. Japan kapitulerade utan villkor. Andra världskriget var slut' (*Levande Historia*, 365).

'Kvart i nio på morgonen den 6 augusti 1945 släpptes den första atombomben över den japanska staden Hiroshima. På några minuter dog 80000 människor. Tre dagar senare släpptes en ännu kraftigare bomb över staden Nagasaki. Dagen därpå var Japan berett att ge upp. Det andra världskriget var slut' (*SO.S.*, 283).

[Vietnamkriget] '[...] förstörde mycket av USAs goda rykte i världen' [...] [det amerikanska folket tvingades inse att det egna landet] 'hamnat på den "onda" sidan' (*SO.S.*, 342).

'För många unga människor blev USAs krig i Vietnam en symbol för hur den rika världen försökte krossa ett fattigt folk som bara ville leva på sitt eget sätt' (*SO.S.*, 311).

'[...] förbättrades den amerikanska ekonomin' [och de svarta lyckades utbilda sig och kunde] '[...] arbeta sig upp i samhället'.

25. 'Ofta var de bönder, fattiga men arbetsamma som Karls Oskar och Kristina'.
26. 'Så föddes USA', '[...] alla människor är skapade jämlika', '[...] all makt utgå från folket, alla lagar ska godkännas av folkets representanter'.
27. 'USA blev det land där fabrikerna tillverkade mest varor i hela världen. Massor av människor fick arbete och tjänade pengar'.
28. 'Var verkligen USA framtidslandet för alla?' (*Utkik*, 167).
29. 'Tyckte alla i USA att det var det glada 20-talet?' (*Utkik*, 229).
30. 'en hysterisk häxjakt' (*PULS*, 298).
31. '[...] ur krigets ruiner växer ett nytt Västeuropa fram, rikare än någonsin' (*SO.S.*, 304).
32. 'År 1947 kom USAs regering med ett hjälpprogram för det krigshärjade Europa. Den så kallade Marshallhjälpen innebar att Västeuropas länder fick nästan 13 miljarder dollar av USA. Amerikanerna ville få fart på Europas ekonomi, så att européerna skulle få råd att köpa saker från USA. Dessutom var amerikanerna rädda för att fattigdomen skulle göra att västeuropéerna började rösta på kommunistiska partier' (*SO.S.*, 304).
33. 'Ekonomiska intressen står över ideal om demokratins befriare', 'skylt på hot från kommunismen" (*PULS*, 329).
34. 'Stora amerikanska företag äger mycket i Sydamerika' (*SO.S.*, 365).
35. '[...] även om de var diktatorer. I land efter land togs makten över av USA-stödda militärregimer' (*SO.S.*, 365).
36. 'USAs mjölkko'.
37. 'Den 6 augusti sprängdes en atombomb över den japanska staden Hiroshima. 80000 dödades omedelbart, 70000 skadades och hela staden

lades i aska. Tre dagar senare sprängdes ytterligare en atombomb över staden Nagasaki. Det är första och hitintills enda gången atombomber har använts i krig. Japan kapitulerade utan villkor. Andra världskriget var slut' (*Levande historia*, 365).
38. [Vietnamkriget] '...förstörde mycket av USAs goda rykte i världen [...] [det amerikanska folket tvingades inse att det egna landet] hamnat på den "onda" sidan' (*SO.S.*, 342).
39. 'Eftersom man hade svårt att skilja på "fiender" och "vänner" brände man ibland byar på måfå' (*Utkik*, 271).
40. 'För många unga människor blev USAs krig i Vietnam en symbol för hur den rika världen försökte krossa ett fattigt folk som bara ville leva på sitt eget sätt' (*SO.S.*, 311).
41. '[...] förbättrades den amerikanska ekonomin [och de svarta lyckades utbilda sig och kunde]' [...] arbeta sig upp i samhället'.

Bibliography

List of Textbooks Cited

Almgren, Bengt, David Isaksson, Berndt Tallerud and Hans Thorbjörnsson. 2016. *Prio: Historia 9*. Stockholm: Sanoma utbildning AB.

Hildingson, Kai and Lars Hildingson. 2012. *Levande historia 9*. Stockholm: Natur & Kultur.

Ivansson, Elisabeth and Mattias Tordai. 2015. *SO-S: Historia Ämnesboken*. Stockholm: Liber.

Körner, Göran and Lars Lagheim. 2009. *PULS: Grundbok Historia*. Stockholm: Natur & Kultur.

Nilsson, Erik, Hans Olofsson and Rolf Uppström. 2015. *Utkik: Hi Historia 7–9*. Malmö: Gleerups.

References

Andersson, Nils. 2010. 'Intercultural Education and the Representation of the Other in History Textbooks'. In *Opening the Mind or Drawing Boundaries? History Texts in Nordic Schools*, edited by Thorsteinn Helgason and Simone Lässig, 33–60. Göttingen: V&R unipress.

Arendt, Hannah. 1982. *Lectures on Kant's Political Philosophy*. Chicago: The University of Chicago Press.
Arendt, Hannah. 1998. *Människans villkor: Vita activa*. Göteborg: Daidalos.
Blake, C. 1998. 'Empathy: A Response to Foster and Eager'. *International Journal of Social Education* 13: 25–31.
Danielsson Malmros, Ingmarie. 2012. *Det var en gång ett land: Berättelser om svenskhet i historieläroböcker och elevers föreställningsvärldar*. Diss. Lund: University of Lund, 2012.
Disch, Lisa J. 1994. *Hannah Arendt and the Limits of Philosophy*. New York: Cornell University Press.
Disch, Lisa J. 1997. '"Please Sit Down, but Don't Make Yourself at Home": Arendtian "Visting" and the Prefigurative Politics' *Hanna Arendt and The Meaning of Politics*, edited by Craig Calhoun and John McGowan. Minneapolis: University of Minneapolis Press.
Gustafsson, Jörgen. 2017. *Historielärobokens föreställningar: Påbjuden identifikation och genreförändring i den obligatoriska skolan 1870–2000*. Diss. Uppsala: University of Uppsala.
Holmén, Janne. 2006. *Den politiska läroboken: Bilden av USA och Sovjetunionen i norska, svenska och finländska läroböcker under kalla kriget*, Diss. Uppsala: University of Uppsala.
Lévesque, Stephane. 2008. *Thinking Historically: Educating Students for the Twenty-first Century*. Toronto: Buffalo.
Loftsdóttir, Kristín. 2010. 'Deconstructing the Eurocentric Perspective: Studying "Us" and the "Other" in History Books'. In *Opening the Mind or Drawing Boundaries? History Texts in Nordic Schools*, edited by Thorsteinn Helgason and Simone Lässig, 21–32. Göttingen: V&R unipress.
Lozic, Vanja. 2010. *I historiekanons skugga: Historieämne och identifikationsformering i 2000-talets mångkulturella samhälle*. Diss., Malmö: University of Lund, 2010.
Nordgren, Kenneth. 2006. *Vems är historien: Historia som medvetande, kultur och handling i det mångkulturella Sverige*. Diss. Umeå: Umeå Universitet.
Persson, Anders. 2016. 'Mormor, oönskade tyskar och en hänsynslös dansk: Några reflektioner om identifikation och mening, efter en kritisk läsning av en nyutgiven lärobok i historia för den svenska grundskolans mellanår'. In *Kulturell reproduktion i skola och nation: En vänbok till Lars Petterson*, edited by Urban Claesson and Dick Åhman, 251–268. Möklinta: Gidlunds.
Persson, Anders and Robert Thorp. 2017. 'Historieundervisningens existentialiserande potential'. *Nordidactica* 2.

Persson, Anders. 2017. *Lärartillvaro och historieundervisning: Innebörder av ett nytt uppdrag i de mätbara resultatens tid*. [History teaching in the age of performativity: Swedish upper primary school teachers' experiences of a new curriculum]. Diss. 2017. Umeå: University of Umeå.

Retz, Tyson. 2015. 'A Moderate Hermeneutical Approach to Empathy in History Education', *Educational Philosophy and Theory* 47, no. 3: 214–226.

Spjut, Lina. 2014. *Den envise bonden och Nordens fransmän: Svensk och finsk etnicitet samt nationell historieskrivning i svenska och finlandssvenska läroböcker 1866–1939*. Lic-uppsats. Umeå: Umeå universitet, 2014.

Spjut, Lina. 2018. *Att (ut)bilda ett folk: Nationell och etnisk gemenskap i Sveriges och Finlands svenskspråkiga läroböcker för folk- och grundskolan åren 1866–2016*. Diss. Örebro, Örebro universitet.

Zander, Ulf. 1998. 'Att legitimera och bli legitimerat: Historieämnet förr och nu i Sverige och annorstädes'. In *Historiedidaktiska utmaningar*, edited by Hans Albin Larsson, 32–68. Jönköping: Jönköping university press.

Open Access This chapter is licensed under the terms of the Creative Commons Attribution 4.0 International License (http://creativecommons.org/licenses/by/4.0/), which permits use, sharing, adaptation, distribution and reproduction in any medium or format, as long as you give appropriate credit to the original author(s) and the source, provide a link to the Creative Commons licence and indicate if changes were made.

The images or other third party material in this chapter are included in the chapter's Creative Commons licence, unless indicated otherwise in a credit line to the material. If material is not included in the chapter's Creative Commons licence and your intended use is not permitted by statutory regulation or exceeds the permitted use, you will need to obtain permission directly from the copyright holder.

7

Images and Imaginings of the Cold War – with a Focus on the Swiss View

Markus Furrer

Introduction

When remembering the Cold War it would be unusual to think immediately of the complex historical period between 1947 and 1991 with all its political entanglements and interdependencies. Rather, ideas associated with this period tend to be images of the atomic mushroom cloud, James Bond-esque chases, the border fortifications of the Iron Curtain, the Kremlin in Moscow, the scowling expressions of Soviet heads of state, parades and victory marches, scenarios from the Vietnam War or from mass demonstrations against the new arms resolution. These visual worlds vary strongly depending on the social origin of the individual and the generation to which the individual belongs. One's own experience and knowledge acquired early on about the period overlap with impressions from items one has read, seen and/or heard at a later stage.

M. Furrer (✉)
University of Teacher Education Lucerne, Lucerne, Lucerne, Switzerland
e-mail: markus.furrer@phlu.ch

The main argument of this chapter is that people think about the Cold War in terms of images, which vary according to the individual or collectives to which an individual belongs, as well as to age group. But as a politico-ideological, economic, technological, scientific and socio-cultural conflict, which deeply marked the everyday lives of individuals and collectives (Stöver 2007, 309–313), this event especially encourages visual thinking. Some of the images associated with the Cold War are widespread, such as the image of the Berlin Wall, which holds a dual significance as a symbol of both the division of Germany in 1961 and its reunification in 1989. 'The Fall of the Wall' simultaneously evokes an image and serves to abbreviate the narrative. Indeed the term 'Cold War' as coined by American journalist Herbert Swope[1] around 1947 implies in itself a lively pictorial imagining around a cold confrontation. The Cold War was a 'war of cultures', against the background of which entertainment was used as a weapon on both sides in West and East (Stöver 2007, 269). Contemporary media presented apocalyptic visions, which created historical imagery. The doomsday clock, for instance, suggesting a countdown, stood metaphorically for a world inches away from the abyss.

Images of history are widely used in textbooks. Here they appear as fundamental interpretations in the authors' texts as well as in the illustrations, conjuring up an imagined history in readers' minds. This approach is inspired by Walter Benjamin's philosophy of history, which has visual thinking at its core (Weigel 1997; Buchbinder 2002, 15, 75) and conceives of history as essentially reduced to a set of images (Benjamin 1980; Buchbinder 2002, 75–84). In this sense, history is always a construct, constituted in the present moment. For Benjamin, this means that we are loading a past devoid of meaning with the 'here and now' (Benjamin 1980, 701). In other words, past and present intermingle in historical narration. As building blocks of history, images are removed from their original contexts and lent meaning and significance in and by the present. Accordingly, how images might be manipulated and, consequently, how 'true' or 'false' the interpretations we make based on them are is of less concern here than the loading of historical images with relevance in and knowledge from the present (Furrer 2004, 104).

This is examined and exemplified in this chapter using the example of Swiss history textbooks and their representations of the Cold War. The question arises as to how the conflict is portrayed in the post-Cold War phase, noting that Switzerland is a special case in this context, being a Western and neutral country in which anti-communism was rampant. The Cold War ultimately led to Swiss neutrality being accepted, sometimes even appreciated, in both East and West. Switzerland decided, with a certain reluctance, to abstain from arming itself with nuclear weapons and rather focus on civil defence. No other country in the world invested so much in the construction of bunkers or civil defence facilities. Historians speak of 'total defence in a threatened small state' (Tanner 1988, 59); indeed, during the Cold War decades, Swiss society was considered to be in a 'state of emergency' (Albrecht et al. 1988), which rendered the end of the conflict a dramatic event for the Swiss self-image. Within society itself, enemy concepts had to be questioned, and the neutral small state had to reorient itself in terms of foreign policy. This new point of departure also influenced the image of the Cold War as presented in textbooks.

This chapter will thus focus on such images in textbooks. History textbooks are particularly important sources since they convey an officially sanctioned version of history (depending on their country of origin) and thus evoke specific historical images in order to be accepted and recognised. Dominant interpretations of the past find their way either intentionally or unwittingly into textbooks. But their authors also seek to reproduce official historical images, derived from research and embedded in memory culture (Furrer 2016, 280). The textbooks analysed in this chapter are aimed mainly at the secondary levels I and II in Switzerland; they were all produced and published after the Cold War and therefore reflect on the period before 'the Fall of the Wall' from a position of hindsight.

Historical images, especially when deployed in history textbooks, often allow authors to make interpretations on a macroscale by pairing the written text with illustrations or photographs. The historical image underlying the narrative becomes clearer, particularly in school history textbooks, which provide an overview of the period (Furrer, 117). As, however, they do not become historical images until they are accepted in the mind of the reader, their contours can also only be grasped through an analysis of textbook narratives. Whereas historians and social scientists explain the line of thought their narratives follow through the introduction of different theories and well-formulated arguments, when considering historical imagery in textbooks we must accept that we are mostly dealing with abbreviations (Rüsen 2008, 19) or narrative reductions. Such reductions are highly symbolic and allow readers to imagine a kind of historical painting (Furrer 2013, 221).

In the first section of this chapter, I examine theoretical approaches towards historical imagery. I then explore these approaches with particular reference to how the Cold War is taught in Swiss schools. Consequently, using examples from Swiss history textbooks, I demonstrate how such historical imagery manifests itself at the level of history teaching. The questions the chapter aims to answer always relate to changes in visual thinking and the symbolic potential of different images, particularly focussing on the imagery which recurs when textbooks treat the immediate post-war phase of the Cold War.

Theoretical Considerations on Historical Imagery

The term 'image' encompasses both an internal (image) as well as an external (picture) visual impression, so that both aspects are reflected in a single term (Boehm 2007, 11). This conceptual doubling illustrates how closely connected the visual imagination is to the form of expression and the perception of the physical image. It is thus mainly in the surplus of meaning which the image – painted or also only imagined – creates that it achieves its effect. Furthermore, since what is referred to as the 'iconic turn', scholars have also realised that knowledge becomes accessible not merely through language (Bachmann-Medick 2009, 351), but is rather shaped and produced by underlying images – a kind of visual thinking. Images actually stand for the dimension of 'showing' and are inherently strongly suggestive. Such image-active movements of thought can lead to the visual acts through which we create myths (Bachmann-Medick 2009, 352).

If imagery creates narratives, then the reverse is also true: Narratives create actual visual worlds in our imagination by providing each individual with abstract, internal historical images. These are often employed in our everyday use of language in order to refer back to memory culture and to different interpretations of historical processes. This theory focusses on the visual potency of language, which here becomes actual metaphorology, to use Hans Blumenberg's term (Boehm 2007, 44).

As historical images are thus always subject to trends and linked to the politics of history (Furrer 2013, 222), political debate focusses on the promises that narratives make to mobilise political forces and catalyse change. Thinking in images allows for the reduction of ambivalence in narratives, rendering superfluous fundamental justifications by reducing alternatives and thus easing decision-making (Rödder 2015, 298). Individuals interpret these images and search for meaning, even if this contradicts an accepted logic and evidence, in order to distinguish between fact and fiction (Hobsbawm 2002, 296).

Just as it is accessible through imagery in the present, the conflict was accessible for an audience in the forties through images and even image series, which both the movies and the spread of television in the fifties rendered possible. Thus, the Vietnam War became a 'living room war' (Paul 2004, 314). For the first time, mass media carried both a 'hot' proxy war and the Cold War into people's homes and, consequently, the general public in the US criticised American involvement in the conflict. The images transmitted on television were too horrible to not have some sort of effect on the ordinary individual.

Switzerland during and after the Cold War

According to Buomberger (2017, 20), the world was gradually slipping into the Cold War and for the Swiss people this meant an almost seamless transition from fearing National Socialism and Fascism to fearing the perceived threat of communism. The Cold War united Swiss society, creating a closed protective community which had not existed during the Second World War. The (marginal) Swiss communist party came under suspicion. Historians have argued that fierce anti-communist sentiment in Switzerland was barely less pronounced than in the McCarthyist US and that the Swiss could actually fall back on a longer tradition of anti-communism (Caillat et al. 2009). This policy lasted for the entirety of the Cold War period, even if there was a decline in the 'structure-forming' power derived from the East-West contrast (Ritzer 2015, 23). The feeling that war was imminent, and could ignite at any moment like a spark in a powder keg, was widespread in Switzerland. The early post-war period was in particular marked by two basic characteristics – the Swiss people's paralysing fear of the atomic bomb as well as the hope of better living conditions and a shared optimism about the progress of the country.

Historians also suggest that these hopes and fears in Switzerland were fed by the triangular relationship between consumption, the Cold War and consensus (Leimgruber 1992, 18–23). The economic boom made distribution issues and thus political consensus-building much easier. At the Swiss national exhibition, 'Expo', in Lausanne in 1964 the question as to how the country could survive in the event of a nuclear war was prominent. The exhibition suggested methods such as the 'concrete hedgehog' which demonstrated the people's readiness to defend themselves. In the entrance area, the organisers of the exhibition displayed steel plates perforated by gunfire to show the destructiveness of war, juxtaposed with the 'fortress Switzerland' which suggested safety and security. A permanent readiness to defend oneself was therefore encouraged, as the exhibition sought to demonstrate that the small state was able to survive on its own (Furrer, 250). Intellectuals during this period were aware of the image of a 'neurotic hedgehog' (Künzli 1964), and the writer Max Frisch and historian von Salis, among others, complained about the narrow-mindedness of society and its 'totalitarian tendencies' (Furrer, 249). Switzerland built bunkers and, with the Hungarian crises in 1956, fortification-enhancement in Switzerland thrived all the more. No European country possessed more artillery guns (Auf der Maur 2017, 99).

When analysing the Cold War it is important to both distinguish between 'structure-forming' dynamics and forms of expression as well as to look at their interactions. Obviously the political elite relied on the image of the Soviet Union as an enemy because it allowed them to practice a passive foreign policy in the shadow of the Western Alliance and simultaneously to pursue apparent autonomy through its domestic policy (Furrer, 249). Switzerland was a stowaway of NATO, as Joëlle Kuntz aptly puts it (2014, 14). For Jakob Tanner, the Cold War consolidated the Swiss myth of sovereignty (2015, 305), which resonated with the Swiss public and, in foreign policy terms, allowed the country to integrate itself into the Western sphere in economic (if not political) terms. Anti-communist sentiment had a strong impact in Switzerland: The bourgeois and the religious, amongst others, saw the core values of Western civilisation as endangered. The Cold War and anti-communism thus created cohesion within a country which, as historians have pointed out, struggled with severe social tensions (Buomberger 2017, 22), as the majority of people suddenly shared a similar world view, one which distanced Switzerland from the perceived threat by demonising an external and internal enemy. The East-West dualism turned out to be very adaptable, incorporating classical constructs from the modern and pre-modern age which systematically included or excluded certain groups of people (Imhof et al. 1996, 177). In Switzerland, for instance, anti-Slavism was on the rise, demonstrating how the issue of race was treated in the country, and, on an ideological level, communism was often associated with images of a Marxist antichrist. At the same time, images of freedom and folklore bolstered Swiss nationalism, fuelling exclusion of the 'other'. Such cultural codes created meaning and reinforced the effectiveness of anti-communist feeling in the country (Imhof et al. 1996, 177), turning it into a 'creed' (Buomberger 2017, 40 ff.).

Although the Cold War was not seen as a linear progression of events in Switzerland, this global conflict intensely and permanently impacted upon foreign and domestic policy: 'The Cold War created the optimum conditions for the merging of nation and state' (Furrer 1998, 110), rendering the end of the conflict all the more disruptive in this regard. Switzerland now had to fundamentally reorient its worldview (Furrer, 126) and thus confront its own history. Tanner and Weigel point out that each society views history in a way which it both deserves and can bear. History even becomes a causal factor in crisis-ridden phases of reorganisation as the interpretation of the past can either engender change or consolidate already existing structures and beliefs (Tanner and Weigel 2002, 20).

Central to this discourse was the question of whether Swiss neutrality, seen as a highly valuable state policy, should be maintained after the Cold War. It had only been temporarily rejected by the Communist Workers' Party in the first few post-war years, and all political camps considered it useful when making foreign policy decisions. Essentially, the Cold War shaped Switzerland's self-conception as a country in which neutrality was highly (perhaps excessively) valued. The East-West divide led to a higher value being placed on the role and function of neutral states, services certainly employed by the Soviet Union, amongst others. In Switzerland, neutrality was never associated with a neutrality of political conviction but rather with a maxim of state foreign policy. It is not, therefore, surprising that by the end of this global conflict questions as to the future political orientation of the country, including the issue of neutrality, were being raised.

Soon two camps had emerged: For one side the fixation on neutrality blocked future foreign policy actions, adding to an already negative image of an isolated, self-interested and introverted small state. Critics attacked Swiss 'neutral morality' during the Cold War (Furrer, 119f.), especially political abstinence and, at the same time, its intensive economic integration (Furrer, 126). Fearing that such a stance would prevent the development of an open-minded country, this group demanded nothing less than a redefinition of neutrality (Kreis 2004, 367–368). However, some argued that the value of neutrality as a strategy had been proven during the Cold War: Switzerland's exceptional position rendered it both capable of and also a beneficiary of a neutral stance, as a small state thus able to make full use of its sovereignty. In the context of the debate about Switzerland's position towards Europe (and the European Union) and the world (e.g., towards the UN, of which Switzerland became a member in 2002), this dispute over the value of neutrality was virulent. However, with new international and European crises from 2008 onwards the vehemence of the dispute has decreased.

Historical Imagery in Swiss History Textbooks

History textbooks that have been reprinted in new editions or published for the first time since the end of the Cold War were thus presented with the essential challenge of how to present this conflict. Significant differences become apparent when comparing them with books from the Cold War era: The latter mostly relied on a traditional interpretation of the Cold War, with imagery of a threatening Eastern superpower with its military machine. Arguments put forward in these textbooks were based on competing narratives about systems and ideologies, entirely in regards to ideas of progress. As a so-called 'neutral' state, Switzerland is generally not directly included in these narratives. The Cold War was thus considered an external event (Furrer 2016, 285). An exception occurs in the context of events between 1989 and 1991 – and only then in new narratives. These narratives are equally underpinned by pictorial thinking, for which there are a number of reasons: On the one hand, they have only limited space available for their depictions of the past, not always sufficient for an accurate historical analysis. On the other, the selection of content about the past takes place from the perspective of the present, charging these contents with the 'now' in the sense described by Walter Benjamin. In history didactics, the term 'orientation towards the present' is widely used for this purpose, in this context primarily in the sense of 'context of meaning' (Pandel 2013, 333).

This analysis focuses on representations of Switzerland during the Cold War. While textbooks from the Cold War period hardly ever directly associate Switzerland with the conflict, since the end of the bipolar divide it has increasingly been portrayed as a country with a society that was also involved. Until the end of the Cold War, Switzerland appeared as a country practically untouched by the 'Age of Catastrophe' (Hobsbawm 1994, 21), in a position to contemplate the world and Europe from the 'balcon sur l'Europe' (Pierre Béguin). For students in school, this had the peculiar effect that history generally took place outside the country (Furrer et al. 2008, 11). It was not until new history textbooks came out in the 1990s that Switzerland and its society were linked to the Cold War, primarily via anti-communism, which at the time was widespread and vehement in Switzerland. Yet here too we find exceptions to the rule: *Histoire générale* contains no reference to Switzerland at all over some 20 pages on the Cold War (*Histoire Générale* 1999, 964–984). The end of ideological antagonism brought with it a self-critical glance back at mechanisms of exclusion, defamation and setbacks within society, images of anti-communist propaganda being among the most prominent. There are, however, also other pictorial references. Why is it specifically images we are examining here? Why and how do textbooks in particular convey these? In many cases, complex historical facts are 'reduced', conveyed in a simple and mono-causal, yet highly memorable, fashion. Examining the pictorial character of these references illustrates how such portrayals are both highly selective and also target-group orientated, of only limited analytical value since the thought processes employed by historical research are barely recognisable. Images, as such, are highly conducive to the eclectic nature of many textbook portrayals. As Hans-Jürgen Pandel has put it, textbook texts tend to be enumerative rather than narrative (Pandel 2005, 37), and new teaching materials in particular tend to thus convey a selection of brief impressions of history.

If we analyse textbooks published between the 1990s and the present day, we are seeking, via images, fundamental interpretations underlying narratives on Switzerland in the Cold War. Four particular references link Switzerland and its society to the conflict: first, the image of anti-communist and hysterical Switzerland mentioned above, to be found in almost all teaching materials currently available. Threatening images also involve Switzerland in international conflicts, particularly via a widespread triangular constellation of Switzerland and its society caught between economic boom, concordance democracy and the Cold War is particularly widespread. The image of the division and reunification of the continent, including Switzerland, is also used. While, at first glance, these images appear to have been selected at random, they are underpinned by time-bound discourses that guide the textbooks.

The Image of 'Hysterical Switzerland'

The textbook *Die Schweiz und ihre Geschichte* (Switzerland and its History), designed as supplementary material for upper secondary level, deals with 'The Cold War in Switzerland?' (note the question mark). A page and a half long, the section traces the inner-societal mood, characterised by a mentality of seclusion and distance: 'Switzerland came across as a spectator at a football match, fully committed to the team from the stands, but under no circumstances willing to enter the playing field' (*Die Schweiz und ihre Geschichte* 2005, 170, all textbook translations by the author). This simile contains two essential aspects: the neutral attitude towards the outside world and the anti-communism within Switzerland, directed particularly against the Soviet-friendly Swiss 'Partei der Arbeit' (=Communist Party), and – according to critical contemporaries of the time (Jean Rudolf von Salis) was taking on ‚hysterical proportions'. The texts are supplemented by two images, a portrait of a Swiss communist, Edgar Woog (1898–1973), who described himself as a 'proud Muscovite', and a campaign placard of black rats nibbling on the white Swiss cross against a red background. The latter is from the mid-1960s, and was carried by the 'campaign against trade with the East'.[1] The textbook *Menschen in Zeit und Raum* (People through Time and Space) another example, dedicates a double page to the topic of Switzerland in the Cold War: the 'Cold War within the Country' is portrayed using the example of the 1956 Hungarian Uprising, which led to a large movement in Switzerland calling for solidarity with the insurgents and the refugees, yet also to anti-communist sentiment. One photograph, for instance, shows refugees dangerously crossing a small river marking the boundary between Hungary and Austria. Another photograph depicts a vigil held in Berne after the suppression of the uprising, demonstrating and lighting candles in solidarity (*Menschen in Zeit und Raum* 2005, 128–129). This strong involvement of Switzerland in the Cold War via anti-communism can be found today in almost all textbooks, including *Gesellschaften im Wandel* (Societies in Transition). The Cold War created a 'climate of fear' (2017, 102/03).

These references can be explained particularly well by the discourses and developments in Switzerland after the Cold War. The end of the conflict brought about a 'Jahrhundertskandal' (scandal of the century), when it became apparent in 1990 that the federal police had been registering anything that appeared 'un-Swiss' for fear of subversive tendencies. Some 900 000 people and organisations had been subject to surveillance. Intellectuals, such as the writer Max Frisch, who were themselves affected, wrote of a 'state gone bad' and dramatist and painter Friedrich Dürrenmatt coined the image of 'Switzerland as a prison in which the prisoners were also the guards. It was perhaps this scandal that opened the people's eyes to the arbitrary nature of the surveillance and also the problematic nature of the anti-communist obsession (Tanner

2015, 471). Anti-communism thus becomes a metanarrative for Switzerland in the Cold War. The textbook *Gesellschaften im Wandel* features a colour photograph of a 1990 demonstration in Berne against 'snooping Switzerland' (*Schnüffelstaat*) with protesters carrying a banner with the slogan: 'Sniff around at your own arses' (schnüffeln = spy/snoop/sniff, *Gesellschaften im Wandel* 2017, 103).

The Nuclear Threat: A Paradoxical Image

Another memorable image derives from the perception of a specific threat from the 1980s. In *Weltgeschichte im Bild* (World History in Pictures, 1990, 54–65), the idea of nuclear threat and imminent war is predominant and conveyed through imagery and photographs. In the chapter *Welt zwischen Ost und West* (The World between East and West), the topic is introduced by a quote from Arthur Koestler's book of 1978, *Janus: A Summing Up*: 'Since the day when the first atomic bomb outshone the sun over Hiroshima, mankind as a whole has had to live with the prospect of its extinction as a species'. *(Weltgeschichte im Bild* 1990, 54). The events then mentioned in the textbook all follow on from the presentation of this particular threat. One of the pictures shows an American missile silo; in another we can see the building site for launching pads in Cuba, photographed by reconnaissance aircrafts (*Weltgeschichte im Bild* 1990, 56 and 58). The Vietnam War is directly connected with the Cold War in this textbook, which focusses on the 'face of the war' as it also uses photography (*Weltgeschichte im Bild* 1990, 69). In the final chapter on the topic, explanations of the peace movement and 'peace as a goal' follow with an excursus on the law of nations. The textbook refers to the peace movement which gained strength in Switzerland in the 1980s, although it never found the same resonance as it did in the Federal Republic of Germany, against the background of the NATO Double-Track Decision, which triggered new arms dynamics and discussions. However, the textbook consistently focusses on the perceived threat to Switzerland, as well as emphasising proposed solutions to the conflict, such as the peace movement. This textbook is the only one with such a succinct approach to this area of focus. Other textbooks published between 1990 and 2000 hardly mention the nuclear threat at all (e.g. *Menschen in Zeit und Raum* 2005, 116–131). It is striking how casually images of threatening scenarios are presented in other textbooks (e.g. *Histoire générale* 1994, *Weltgeschichte* 1993). This is particularly true of material on the Cold War, which generally ignores the threat of war against Switzerland. Alternatively, a kind of controllability is suggested, such as via the image of the American SDI Program (Strategic Defense Initiative), which illustrates how 'attacking intercontinental missiles' can be intercepted and safely destroyed using space satellites (*Weltgeschichte* 1993, 290). Although the current textbook *Gesellschaften im Wandel* (2017, 99) does refer in more detail to the threat posed by nuclear weapons, the threat itself remains an abstract one. A colour photograph shows the mushroom cloud over Nagasaki; however, there is no discussion of the dangers to which humankind was exposed.

While this can be explained, it is also paradoxical. While only a few years after the end of the bipolar conflict the feeling of an immediate nuclear threat was on the wane, it is paradoxical that, even during the Cold War, despite a widespread perception of the threat, it is rarely addressed in teaching materials. On the contrary, a nuclear clash is even considered non-life threatening thanks to the Swiss army and civil defence. In the midst of the Cold War, this was a message of serenity and assurance, also conveyed in the form of images, as in the voluminous popular science work by Peter Dürrenmat, which presents a full-page black and white photograph of four fighter jets flying in formation in front of a Swiss Alpine backdrop (*Schweizer Geschichte* 1963, 705). The paradoxical way in which fear was addressed only became of interest to historiography at a later stage. Thomas Buomberger recalls a society in the hedgehog position, sheltered in underground civil defence bunkers, ready to defend itself and prepared for emergencies, indignant for and helpful towards the Hungarian rebels and refugees, but also at the mercy of a hysterical surveillance state (Buomberger, 2017). Buomberger thus presents visual worlds from the perspective of the present which had, in fact, already been shaped by imagery from the period. For example, the public were exposed to contemporary photographs of the above-mentioned 'concrete hedgehog' at the Expo in Lausanne, of the defence minister in a military aircraft (showing the readiness of the small state for war) and the Swiss population organising aid packages for the insurgents in Hungary in 1956. Others showed protest marches against trade with the East after the construction of the Berlin Wall in 1961, the defence shelters and, at the end of the Cold War in 1989/90, the demonstrations against state surveillance (the latter also targeted the army, which some wished to slaughter symbolically as a 'holy cow').

Switzerland in the Cold War between Boom and Concordance Democracy

No other Swiss textbook for lower secondary school is so strongly devoted to the subject of the Cold War, which runs as a guiding theme through the entire fourth volume of *Durch Geschichte zur Gegenwart* (1991). This book (To the Present via the Past) explains world affairs and the history of Switzerland, and provides interesting insights as to how Switzerland is embedded within the Cold War context, bringing together internal and external perceptions. The Cold War era is directly associated with the 'Swiss economic miracle' and the continued development of Swiss consensus and the concordance system, which in 1959 led to an all-party government that remained in its original constellation until 2003 (*Durch Geschichte zur Gegenwart* 1991, 69–73). This connection between the Cold War and the concordance system is also made by other textbooks. While it is a widespread idea, it has a highly associative effect, particularly where only few areas of overlap are apparent. In the Swiss history textbook *Schweizer Geschichte* (History of Switzerland, 2008, 94–98), the Cold War is presented within a Swiss context using a double-page black and white photograph of demonstrators from 1956, pushing forwards in front of the Soviet embassy in Berne, monitored and held back by Swiss law enforcement in 1950s uniforms. The image conveyed is one of an active anti-communist Swiss population protesting during the Cold War and calling for the expulsion of the Russians from Hungary: 'Down with the USSR!' (*Schweizer Geschichte* 2008, 94). This depiction is then followed in the textbook by mention of the Swiss concordance system. The Cold War thus becomes a kind of 'sub-chapter' of 'The Concordance System' (*Schweizer Geschichte* 2008, 96). The textbooks thus suggest a triangular association between 'concordance, consumerism and the Cold

War', very much in line with the vivid formula given prominence at the end of the conflict in the context of a 'special case' as presented in anniversary publications and exhibitions: a Switzerland between *Réduit* (the Swiss term for the National Redoubt, Alpine fortifications put in place during the Second World War) and Europe (see Leimgruber 1992, 23).

The Image of Division and Reunification of the Continent

The textbook *Menschen in Zeit und Raum* dedicates several pages to the Cold War, presented as *Welten im Kalten Krieg* (Worlds in the Cold War, *Menschen in Zeit und Raum* 2005, 108–133). The narrative is no longer one of competition but instead one of separation (Furrer 216, 287), which allows for two kinds of pictorial representation. On the inside front cover of this textbook, a family contemplates the remains of the Berlin wall (*Menschen in Zeit und Raum* 2005, 108/09). The idea of separation, 'An iron curtain falls' (*Menschen in Zeit und Raum* 2005, 117), recurs through imagery, becoming a major theme and means of interpretation in the narrative.

The image of a now-reunified Europe, divided after the Second World War, also embodies a meta-narrative for the Cold War in this textbook. Switzerland is also indirectly involved: solidarity with the Hungarians during the 1956 uprising is discussed in relation to Switzerland, and 'everyday life in Communist Hungary' is documented over a double page (*Menschen in Zeit und Raum* 2005, 120/21). The textbook *Gesellschaften im Wandel* (2017, 100/01) features two fictional stories about young people in East and West Berlin, who in an interview describe the everyday lives of young people in the two systems with the theme 'Two Worlds – One Friendship'. The image materials used all show the East: people queuing for bananas in front of a grocery store in 1985, and boys from the *Freie Deutsche Jugend* organisation, in action cleaning a water ditch. The division and reunification were highly significant European events, with direct relevance for the metaphor of the 'European house', given current status in the second half of the 1980s through the politics and rhetoric of Soviet party Secretary-General Mikhail Gorbachov (Kreis 2012, 577).

History textbooks mostly pick up on historico-cultural interpretations directly. Retrospective points of view of the Cold War are incorporated into their narratives and offer different methods of interpreting history. Since looking at history inevitably means connecting the past with the challenges of the future (Jeismann 2008, 34), these views find their way into textbooks and even popular science.

Conclusion

Overall, it becomes apparent that the Cold War, to use the discourse of memory culture, is both remembered and perceived on the basis of visual thinking. This is particularly the case when references to the present are made. The Cold War is an epoch which survives in the deep structures of current political and social life (Greiner 2013, 9). It is precisely because the Cold War now has such a strong effect on the present that it continues to be intensely remembered and thus achieves a specific significance in memory culture, one that – as demonstrated in this chapter – is firmly informed by visual thinking. While such image-based conceptions may tend to be judgmental and emotive, they are also highly selective and lack analytical potential (Furrer 2013, 222), rather serving to provide simple arguments.

The image-based approaches have taken the example of current Swiss history textbooks portraying Switzerland during the Cold War era. If we analyse textbooks from this period, it becomes clear how Switzerland can be woven into international events with only a few points of contact: the anti-communist hysteria and the idea of a country caught between consumption, consensus and the Cold War. Both these images are widely used, in almost all textbooks from the 1990s. Conceptions of threat also feature in retrospective portrayals, as does the image of the divided and – after 1989 – reunified continent. While these images are to be found in specific textbooks, all textbooks have clearly grown from current discourses and challenges. They offer highly selective portrayals with which to grasp and interpret the complex events of the Cold War era.

History teaching is faced with challenges in dealing with such a societally as well as politically loaded era of contemporary history. As the references to visual thinking exemplify, clear tendencies can be recognised in society and politics but also in teaching 'lessons' from history, raising the 'moral index finger'. Yet rarely do these authors point out how the past continues to impact the present, or highlight the potential of historical events, a deficit related to the function and use of history in society. The British-Australian historian Christopher Clark said in an interview that history was no schoolmaster but rather resembled the Oracle of Delphi. Indeed, image conceptions do appear to resemble an oracle, particularly in relation to the Cold War, a period remembered primarily in pictorial terms. As history now provides the only learning material at our disposal, it is important to ensure that not only educated elites have access to this knowledge by deconstructing the flood of images, analysing them as history with a specific purpose, and at the same time remaining aware of the complex structures of historical processes.

Notes

1. The term 'Cold War' had already been used by George Orwell in an essay of 1945 to describe the confrontation of the superpowers. The journalist Herbert Swope introduced the term in a speech he wrote for the American political advisor Bernard Baruch in 1947. The term was then popularised by the American journalist Walter Lippmann.
2. The Swiss Reconnaissance Service (*Schweizerische Aufklärungsdienst*, SAD) was founded in Zurich in 1947 when the onset of the Cold War appeared imminent. It became the most important organisation of the anti-communist *Geistige Landesverteidigung* (Spiritual National Defence). The activities of the SAD reached their peak at the beginning of the 1960s with campaigns against trade with the East as well as sport-related and cultural activities with communist states.

Bibliography

List of Textbooks Cited

Weltgeschichte: Vom Wiener Kongress bis zur Gegenwart. 1993. Vol. 2. J. Boesch and R. Schläpfer. Zurich: Orell Füssli.

Histoire Générale: L'époque contemporaine 1914–1990. 1999. Vol. 5. C. Bourgeois. Lausanne: Département de la Formation et de la Jeunesse du canton de Vaud.
Histoire Générale de 1919 à nos jours. 1994. G.-A. Chevallaz. Lausanne: Editions Payot.
Schweizer Geschichte. 1963. P. Dürrenmatt. Zurich: Druck- und Verlagshaus AG.
Gesellschaften im Wandel: Themenbuch 1 und 2. 2017. Zurich: Lehrmittelverlag Zurich.
Menschen in Zeit und Raum: Viele Wege – eine Welt. Erster Weltkrieg bis Globalisierung 9. 2005. Buchs: Lehrmittelverlag des Kantons Aargau.
Durch Geschichte zur Gegenwart. 1991. Vol. 4. H. Meyer and P. Schneebeli. Zurich: Lehrmittelverlag des Kantons Zürich.
Die Schweiz und ihre Geschichte: Vom Ancien Régime bis zur Gegenwart. 2005. H. Meyer, P. Felder Pierre and J.C. Wacker. Zurich: Lehrmittelverlag des Kantons Zürich.
Schweizer Geschichte 4: Zeitgeschichte seit 1945. 2008. Th. Notz et al. Berlin: Cornelsen.
Weltgeschichte im Bild 9. Buchs: Lehrmittelverlag des Kantons Aargau, 1990.

Further References

Albrecht, Peter, Andreas Gross, August E. Hohler, Peter Hug, Wolfgang Lauterburg, Thomas Schnyder, Monika Stocker-Meier, Jürg Stöcklin, Joachim Suchomski and Jakob Tanner. 1988. *Schutzraum Schweiz. Mit dem Zivilschutz zur Notstandsgesellschaft.* Berne: Zytglogge.
Auf der Maur, Jost. 2017. *Die Schweiz unter Tag. Eine Entdeckungsreise.* Basel: Echtzeit.
Bachmann-Medick, Doris. 2009. *Cultural Turns. Neuorientierungen in den Kulturwissenschaften.* Reinbek bei Hamburg: Rowohlt.
Benjamin, Walter. 1980. *Gesammelte Schriften*, Vol. 1–2. Frankfurt/Main: Suhrkamp.
Boehm, Gottfried. 2007. *Wie Bilder Sinn erzeugen. Die Macht des Zeigens.* Berlin: Berlin University Press.
Buchbinder, Sascha. 2002. *Der Wille zur Geschichte. Schweizergeschichte um 1900 – die Werke von Wilhelm Oechsli, Johannes Dierauer und Karl Dändliker.* Zurich: Chronos.
Buomberger, Thomas. 2017. *Die Schweiz im Kalten Krieg 1945–1990.* Baden: Hier und Jetzt.

Caillat, Michel, Mauro Cerutti, Jean-François Fayet and Stéphanie Roulin, eds. 2009. *Geschichte(n) des Antikommunismus in der Schweiz*. Zurich: Chronos.

Furrer, Markus. 2017. 'A View of the Cold War in the Swiss Historical Narrative'. In *Remembering and Recounting the Cold War – Commonly Shared History?*, edited by Markus Furrer and Peter Gautschi, 111–128. Schwalbach/Ts.: Wochenschau Verlag.

Furrer, Markus. 2016. 'Gebrochene Geschichten des Kalten Krieges – Narrative und der Umbruch 1989–91 in Schweizer Geschichtslehrmitteln'. In *1989 und Bildungsmedien. Beiträge zur historischen und systematischen Schulbuch- und Bildungsmedienforschung*, edited by Eva Matthes and Sylvia Schütze, 278–287. Bad Heilbrunn: Verlag Julius Klinkhardt.

Furrer, Markus. 2013. 'Geschichtsbilder in Migrationsgesellschaften'. *In Antike – Bilder – Welt. Forschungserträge internationaler Vernetzung. Elisabeth Erdmann zum 70*, edited by Charlotte Bühl-Gramer, Wolfgang Hasberg and Susanne Popp, 217–232. Schwalbach/Ts.: Wochenschau Verlag.

Furrer, Markus, Kurt Messmer, Bruno H. Weder and Béatrice Ziegler. 2008. *Die Schweiz im kurzen 20. Jahrhundert. 1914 bis 1989 – mit Blick auf die Gegenwart*. Zurich: Verlag Pestalozzianum.

Furrer, Markus. 2004. *Die Nation im Schulbuch – zwischen Überhöhung und Verdrängung. Leitbilder der Schweizer Nationalgeschichte in Schweizer Geschichtslehrmitteln der Nachkriegszeit und Gegenwart*. Hanover: Verlag Hahnsche Buchhandlung.

Furrer, Markus. 1998. 'Die Apotheose der Nation. Konkordanz und Konsens in den 1950er Jahren'. In *Die Konstruktion einer Nation. Nation und Nationalisierung in der Schweiz, 18.-20. Jahrhundert*, edited by Urs Altermatt, Catherine Bosshart-Pfluger and Albert Tanner. Zurich: Chronos.

Greiner, Bernd. 2013. *Spurensuche: Zum Erbe des Kalten Krieges. In Erbe des Kalten Krieges*, edited by Bernd Greiner, Tim B. Müller, Klaas Voss. 9–41. Hamburg: Verlag des Hamburger Instituts für Sozialforschung.

Hobsbawm, Eric. 1994. *The Age of Extremes: A History of the World, 1914–1991*. London: Michael Joseph and Pelham Books.

Hobsbawm, Eric. 2002. *Interesting Times: A Twentieth-Century Life*. London: The Penguin Press.

Imhof, Kurt, Heinz Kleger and Gaetano Romano, eds. 1996. *Wiedergeburt der geistigen Landesverteidigung: Kalter Krieg in der Schweiz. Konkordanz und Kalter Krieg. Analyse von Medienereignissen in der Schweiz der Zwischen- und Nachkriegszeit*. 173–247. Zurich: Seismo.

Jeismann, Karl-Ernst. 2008. 'Geschichtsbilder: Zeitdeutung und Zukunftsperspektive'. In: *Dossier Geschichte und Erinnerung*. Berlin: Bundeszentrale für politische Bildung, 34–47. http://www.bpb.de/geschichte/zeitgeschichte/geschichte-und-erinnerung/ (last accessed 9 February 2016).

Kreis, Georg. 2004. *Kleine Neutralitätsgeschichte der Gegenwart. Ein Inventar zum neutralitätspolitischen Diskurs in der Schweiz seit 1943*. Berne/Stuttgart/Vienna: Haupt Verlag.

Kreis, Georg. 2012. 'Das Europäische Haus'. In *Europäische Erinnerungsorte 2*, edited by Pim den Boer, Heinz Duchhardt, Georg Kreis and Wolfgang Schmale, 577–584. Munich: Oldenbourg Verlag.

Kuntz, Joëlle. 2014. *Die Schweiz – oder die Kunst der Abhängigkeit*. Zwischenruf, Zurich: Verlag Neue Zürcher Zeitung.

Künzli, Arnold. 1964. 'Die Neurose des Igels'. In *Expo 64: Trugbild der Schweiz*, edited by Walter Biel et al. 35–49. Basel: Basilius Presse.

Leimgruber, Walter. 1992. 'Die Schweiz zwischen Isolation und Integration'. In *Sonderfall? Die Schweiz zwischen Réduit und Europa*, edited by Walter Leimgruber and Gabriela Christen, 18–33. Zurich: Schweizerisches Landesmuseum.

Pandel, Hans-Jürgen. 2005. *Geschichtsunterricht nach Pisa. Kompetenzen, Bildungsstandards und Kerncurricula*. Schwalbach/Ts: Wochenschau Verlag.

Pandel, Hans-Jürgen. 2013. *Geschichtsdidaktik. Eine Theorie für die Praxis*. Schwalbach/Ts: Wochenschau Verlag.

Paul, Gerhard. 2004. *Bilder des Krieges – Krieg der Bilder. Die Visualisierung des modernen Krieges*. Zurich: Verlag Neue Zürcher Zeitung.

Ritzer, Nadine. 2015. *Der Kalte Krieg in den Schweizer Schulen*. Berne: hep Verlag.

Rödder, Andreas. 2015. *21.0. Eine kurze Geschichte der Gegenwart*. Munich: C.H. Beck.

Rüsen, Jörn. 2008. *Historische Orientierung. Über die Arbeit des Geschichtsbewusstseins, sich in der Zeit zurechtzufinden*. Schwalbach/Ts.: Wochenschau Verlag.

Stöver, Bernd. 2007. *Der Kalte Krieg. Geschichte eines radikalen Zeitalters 1947–1991*. Munich: C.H. Beck.

Tanner, Jakob. 1988. 'Totale Verteidigung im bedrohten Kleinstaat. Vom Luftschutz der Zwischenkriegszeit bis zur Zivilschutz-Konzeption 1971'. In *Schutzraum Schweiz. Mit dem Zivilschutz zur Notstandsgesellschaft*, edited by Peter Albrecht et al., 59–109. Berne: Zytglogge.

Tanner, Jakob. 2015. *Geschichte der Schweiz im 20. Jahrhundert*. Munich: C.H. Beck.

Tanner, Jakob and Sigrid Weigel. 2002. 'Gedächtnis, Geld und Gesetz in der Politik mit der Vergangenheit des Zweiten Weltkriegs und des Holocaust'. In *Gedächtnis, Geld und Gesetz. Vom Umgang mit der Vergangenheit des Zweiten Weltkrieges*, edited by Jakob Tanner and Sigrid Weigel, 7–18. Zurich: vdf Hochschulverlag an der ETH Zürich.

Weigel, Sigrid. 1997. *Entstellte Ähnlichkeit. Walter Benjamins theoretische Schreibweise*. Frankfurt/Main: Fischer.

Open Access This chapter is licensed under the terms of the Creative Commons Attribution 4.0 International License (http://creativecommons.org/licenses/by/4.0/), which permits use, sharing, adaptation, distribution and reproduction in any medium or format, as long as you give appropriate credit to the original author(s) and the source, provide a link to the Creative Commons licence and indicate if changes were made.

The images or other third party material in this chapter are included in the chapter's Creative Commons licence, unless indicated otherwise in a credit line to the material. If material is not included in the chapter's Creative Commons licence and your intended use is not permitted by statutory regulation or exceeds the permitted use, you will need to obtain permission directly from the copyright holder.

8

Between Non-human and Individual Agents: The Attribution of Agency in Chapters on the Cold War in Flemish History Textbooks

Karel Van Nieuwenhuyse

'Yes we can!' was the chant American presidential candidate Barack Obama used during his campaign of 2008, referring to the power of ordinary people to shape society and determine its direction. These words indicated that ordinary citizens are not just the passive playthings of anonymous power structures or higher powers within the Washington bureaucracy. In short, the chant, which has since become legendary, revealed the agency of ordinary people. Agency can be defined as 'the ability to act on decisions in order to bring about desired goals (whether those involve changing aspects of society or conserving them)' (Barton 2012, 132). The concept of agency is very important when thinking about society, be it in the present or past. Key questions historians ask about past societies are: Who has agency in society? Who co-determines the course of society? Who can make a difference in society? Who has the ability to bring about change over time? How do social, institutional and

K. Van Nieuwenhuyse (✉)
University of Leuven, Research Unit of History, Leuven, Belgium
e-mail: karel.vannieuwenhuyse@kuleuven.be

© The Author(s) 2019
B. Christophe et al. (eds.), *The Cold War in the Classroom*, Palgrave Studies in Educational Media, https://doi.org/10.1007/978-3-030-11999-7_8

cultural structures interact with the agency of individuals and/or groups? Over the past two centuries, historians have come up with different answers to these pressing questions (Seixas 2012).

Some historians have located agency especially in the hands of 'great men'. Thomas Carlyle's lectures *On Heroes, Hero-Worship and the Heroic in History* (1841) provide us with classic examples of this tendency. Other historians, at least in the positivist tradition, have searched for historical patterns and pointed to non-human actors, structures and comprehensive systems as agents of change or continuity, such as nations, international alliances, religious denominations or ideological systems, or they have focussed on ordinary people and/or on groups previously considered relatively powerless. Some scholars have also cast doubt on the notion of agency. The philosopher Charles Taylor (1989), for instance, relates agency to the era of modernity and the rise of individualism: In his opinion, agency cannot be a transhistorical category but rather constitutes a particular analytical lens for a particular time (modernity). Poststructuralists question the concept of agency altogether, since they consider individuals to be 'constructs mediated by and/or grounded on a social discourse beyond (way beyond) individual control' (Alcoff 1994, 103).

A pertinent and interesting critique of historians who attribute agency to nations and point to agents like 'the United States', 'the Germans' or 'the Russians' has been formulated by Tara Zahra, who writes about transnational and comparative approaches to the history of modern (Central and Eastern) Europe (2010). Zahra opposes the automatic assignment of membership within a national community and reproaches many scholars for not questioning the resonance of nationalist claims and 'imagined communities'. In this respect, she proposes the concept of 'national indifference', referring to (groups of) people expressing a complete indifference towards (belonging to) the nation. She argues:

> Even as historians assert that national groups are imagined communities, they have continued to write the history of Eastern Europe in particular with national groups in starring roles, analysing relations between 'the Czechs', 'the Germans', 'the Poles', 'the Slovenes', as though these collectives were self-evident entities. [...] It may be time, in short, to move beyond imagined communities and to consider the history of individuals who stood outside or on the margins of those communities. (Zahra 2010, 97)

Zahra emphasises the danger of using terms like 'the Americans', terms which suggest that individuals have to belong to groups and that national groups in particular are coherent social agents, opposing the homogenisation of national groups and the erasure of individual agency.

In history education, questions about and reflections on agency are also very important, not only for the students' understanding of (the course of) history, but also because of their pedagogical implications: Scholars are convinced that history education can aid pupils in developing active citizenship because it fosters agency and encourages students to see that the present is not merely determined by the past, but, on the contrary, that change and alternatives are possible, rendering civic engagement worthwhile (Harris 2011; Wilschut 2012; Wilschut et al. 2013). In this respect, however, Peck, Poyntz and Seixas argue that the focus of agency should actually be on ordinary people, so students can understand that 'if ordinary people participated actively in making the world in the past, then too, ordinary people in the present have an important potential for effecting historical change' (2011, 256). Barton agrees with this line of reasoning (2012). He argues that in order to be better prepared to think about their own role in present and future society, students need exposure to a wide range of historical actors, much wider than has traditionally been found in the school subject of history. At the same time, students need to consider the societal factors that enabled or constrained individual and group actions, as well as the diversity of perspectives and behaviours of people in the past. In line with Zahra's argument (2010), another reason to pay attention to a wide range of historical actors in history education is that this can help students consider and build their own identities. If agency is mostly attributed to nations and national groups, it seems as if a national identity is inescapable, as if students themselves do not have the agency or liberty to construct and define their own identities.

The attribution of agency also relates to the specific historical representation of the Cold War that history textbooks pass on to young people. This determines which groups are considered the main protagonists and which are rather portrayed as passive participants who do not play active roles in the conflict. In this respect, it is always important to examine how the role and agency of one's own country is represented, as well as the extent to which this agency is portrayed in a positive way; these aspects can be connected to the identity-building aims of history education.

The concept of agency in history education, and specifically how it is approached in textbooks and by teachers in their daily classroom practice, has not been examined thoroughly (Seixas 2012). Research into how history is approached in secondary schools, according to the demands of the curriculum, and into the textbooks used shows that a 'social science' vision of history as a discipline often prevails: Textbooks pay particular attention to non-human actors, large social processes and structures rather than to individuals and ordinary people (Erdmann and Hasberg 2011). This seems to indicate that structural entities possess greater capacity for agency than any individual does. As a result, students often attribute (non-human) agency to societal institutions (nations, international alliances and religious denominations) or ideas and movements (such as communism, capitalism and nationalism), assigning them human characteristics (Clark 2013; Ibid. 2014; Ibid. et al. 2011). Students consequently do not fully understand the role of agency in history; nor do they construct a balanced account of the relationship between these structural forces and the actors in historical events or fully grasp the role individuals and ordinary people can play in society.

This chapter focusses on the concept of agency as taught in history lessons in secondary schools in Flanders, whilst analysing chapters about the Cold War – meaning the state of political and military tension after the Second World War between the Soviet Union and its satellite states (the Eastern bloc) and the United States and its allies (the Western bloc) – in four history textbooks. Questions guiding my research and analysis are as follows: (1) To whom is agency ascribed and who remains a passive participant, i.e. is agency attributed especially to structures, institutions, nations, elite persons and/or ordinary men and women? Are the textbooks' 'own' country and population, Belgium and Belgians, attributed agency? And in attributing agency, do the textbook authors reflect on the concept of agency? (2) Who is held responsible for the Cold War? Whose responsibility is amplified and whose is mitigated? In this respect, with which historiographical school do the authors of each of these textbooks align themselves? (3) Do the textbooks pass moral judgment on agents and/or actions taken during the Cold War? Whose actions are constructed as being reasonable or necessary? What attitudes do the authors of these textbooks adopt towards the Western and Eastern blocs? It is difficult, perhaps impossible, to discern moral judgment; often the line between historical description and moral judgment is rather thin. Is describing Stalin as a dictator, for instance, depicting his leadership accurately or casting him in a negative light? The same question applies to the example of American 'interference' in Latin America, which will be addressed in more detail in the following.

The analysis examines the four textbooks from a comparative perspective, with a particular interest in the level of coherence within each textbook. The chapter first sketches the research context and methodology before presenting the findings.

Research Context and Methodology

In 1989, power in regards to education in Belgium was formally transferred from the national, federal level to the three Belgian 'communities': the Dutch (Flemish), French and (very small) German communities. In 1990, a new secondary-school curriculum was introduced in Flanders, the northern, Dutch-speaking part of Belgium. This curriculum is still used. The Flemish government set final objectives or standards for teaching history, delineating the minimum attainment targets that history students should achieve. In defining these standards, a deliberate choice was made not to present an extensive enumeration of the historical knowledge that students would be required to learn (Flemish Ministry of Education and Training, 2000a; ibid. 2000b). The history curriculum primarily aims to develop critical thinking skills and attitudes, namely historical consciousness. Flemish history education is characterised by a very structural approach to the past, based on the social sciences (Wils 2009): It searches for large, underlying patterns in the past. It is no coincidence that the standards, for instance, (implicitly) refer to Fernand Braudel's ideas about history. They address what Braudel calls 'medium-term' or cyclical history, focussing on empires, civilisations, the economy, and social groupings (1949). This approach to studying the past results in large, abstract narratives in which there is little room for the individual's own narrative, thoughts and actions.

An important goal of history education is the construction of a historical frame of reference in students' minds. The main frame of reference in Flemish history education is Western (especially Western European), although students are explicitly encouraged to frame historical phenomena in a broader, worldwide context. The standards require, for instance, that in each of the three stages of teaching history at secondary level, the history of at least one non-Western society is addressed. Nevertheless, the history curriculum remains oriented towards the West, suggesting that this is the most important focus of history and emphasising Europe and the Western World's slow but steady rise towards human rights, democracy and freedom (Van Nieuwenhuyse and Wils 2015).

The ways in which history education is given shape by actual classroom practice, however, is not only determined or influenced by standards; textbooks also play a role. It is important to note that the government does not regulate the production and distribution of textbooks in Flanders. Therefore, publishers have great freedom when it comes to designing their history textbooks, although they claim to base them on the curricular standards. Indeed, similar to the standards, the underlying narrative in Flemish history textbooks is a Western-oriented, liberal narrative of progress, as Bert Vanhulle has shown (2005; 2009).

This research examines the chapters on Cold War history in all Flemish history textbooks for general secondary school education for the twelfth grade, since this is when students study the post-war period. More specifically, my analysis looks at the textbooks *Historia 6* (De Deygere et al. 2009), *Storia 6* (Bekers et al. 2009), *Passages: Na de Tweede Wereldoorlog* (Draye et al. 2010), henceforth: *Passages,* and *Pionier 6* (Smeulders et al. 2014).Given the relatively small market for secondary school history textbooks, the profit and investment margins for these works are generally not very broad. This means that the authors of most textbooks are not professional (academic) historians; instead, textbooks are usually written by history teachers who take on the task on top of their teaching duties. Another consequence is that new textbooks often build on preceding versions and seldom start with a clean slate. This applies to *Historia 6* and *Storia 6*, two textbooks written by secondary school history teachers. *Passages* and *Pionier 6* are both entirely new. Whilst *Pionier* is also written by secondary school history teachers, *Passages* is the only history textbook in Flanders written and supervised by academic cultural historians; indeed, the explicit goal of the editing team was to contextualise the textbook account within academic historiography.

This study applied both a qualitative narrative content analysis and a discourse analysis to the textbooks. The narrative content analysis entailed examining the representation of the Cold War as embedded in the textbook narrative as a whole, because only as part of a whole does a specific section take on significance (Vanhulle, 2009). In order to analyse the concept of agency in each of the textbook chapters on the Cold War, I designed a coding scheme of categories of (human and non-human) agents, starting from a grounded theory approach, which relied on close reading and data analysis rather than theoretical frameworks. A distinction was made between actors who were attributed agency and entities assigned to a more passive role. I chose 'utterances' as the unit of analysis, defined as 'a phrase or a sentence that included a mention of a historical agent, or a pronoun referring to one' (Peck et al. 2011, 262). One utterance could consist of consecutive sentences if they were all about the same historical agent or entity. Searching for specific representations of the main agents and actors of the Cold War (and their presumed responsibilities), the discourse analysis focussed on the verbs used to describe the actions of both Soviets and Americans, as well as on keywords used about them.

Research Results

General (Descriptive) Findings

The Cold War is addressed in history textbooks for the twelfth grade, which deal with the post-war period. This means that, according to the textbook authors, the Cold War only began after the end of the Second World War. Historians, however, disagree on when the Cold War commenced. While many refer to the years between 1945 and 1947 as the start, others, such as the French historian André Fontaine or the Belgian historian Yvan Vanden Berghe, refer to points as early as the Russian Revolution of 1917 (2006; 2008). The textbooks *Historia* and *Storia* seem to implicitly reference this historiographical debate, since they both begin paragraphs on 'The Origin of the Cold War' with reference to 1917. At the same time, in the general introductions, the authors of both textbooks state that after the Second World War, relations between the United States and the Soviet Union worsened, resulting in an ideological battle and the beginning of the Cold War.

The four twelfth-grade textbooks under study arrange their content differently. While *Historia* and *Pionier* start from a chronological division into two main periods – 1945 to 1989 or 1991 (the period of 'the Cold War', with capitals) and 1989 and 1991 to present – *Storia* and *Passages* apply a thematic division. The former uses a rather straightforward, concrete, content-based division, starting with a chapter on the Cold War and subsequently proceeding to other themes such as European history, Belgian history, evolutions in science and technology, and different world views. The latter identifies five more abstract themes: 'war', 'labour', 'people and nation', 'nature', 'the individual'. All the textbooks start with political issues, then proceed to economics and end with socio-cultural issues. Political and economic themes occupy the lion's share of the textbook content: 91 per cent of all content in *Historia* and *Pionier*, 74 per cent in *Storia* and 60 per cent in *Passages*. Socio-cultural themes are thus addressed in much less detail, with almost no attention paid to the daily lives of ordinary people. These findings confirm what previous studies have shown about current, structurally informed approaches to the past, with influence from the social sciences, in Flemish history education, focusing on large structures rather than individuals. The international (especially Western) orientation of these textbooks is reflected when we compare the number of pages devoted to national and international issues. In each, just 13 per cent to 23 per cent of the whole is reserved for national, Belgian history. While *Historia* and *Pionier* focus especially on the East-West gap, *Passages* and *Storia* pay equal attention to both the East-West and the North-South divide. Differences among the textbooks also arise regarding the weight given to the two main time periods in the post-war era, namely 1945 to 1989 or 1991 and 1989 or 1991 to the present. While *Storia* and *Passages* (85 per cent of all content) and, to a lesser extent, *Pionier* (68 per cent of all content) mainly focus on the Cold War period, *Historia* devotes an equal amount of attention to both time periods.

Table 8.1 Overview of the Main Chronological, Geographical and Content-related Points of Focus in Four Textbooks

	Total number of pages in the twelfth-grade textbook (+ format)	Pages devoted to the Cold War period (1945–1989/91) vs. 1989/91–present	Pages devoted to international vs. national affairs (in percentage)	Pages devoted to East-West gap vs. North-South gap (in percentage)	Pages devoted to politics/economy vs. culture/everyday life (in percentage)
Historia	205 pp. (A4)	51% vs. 49%	87% vs. 13%	71% vs. 29%	91% vs. 9%
Passages	140 pp. (A4)	89% vs. 11%	86% vs. 14%	42% vs. 48%	60% vs. 40%
Pionier	345 pp. (B5)	68% vs. 32%	77% vs. 23%	75% vs. 25%	91% vs. 9%
Storia	173 pp. (A4)	85% vs. 15%	82% vs. 18%	48% vs. 52%	74% vs. 26%

The Cold War itself is also addressed on a different scale in the four textbooks, as the table shows. In general, the Cold War does not receive the most attention. While it is considered an important issue, it is nevertheless merely one among many others, such as the European unification process, the federalisation of Belgium, decolonisation, the Israeli-Palestinian conflict, environmental problems, and cultural changes in the West after 1945. All four textbooks deal with the Cold War in a purely international context. The ramifications of the Cold War in Belgium are not addressed. A telling example in this respect is the historical source included in the textbook *Storia*, which is an excerpt from the Belgian communist newspaper *De Rode Vaan*, from 4 July 1948, with the following headline: 'Spaak Signs the Bilateral Agreement that Surrenders Belgium to the Americans' (40). The article refers to the agreement that Paul-Henri Spaak, the Belgian minister for foreign affairs, signed regarding the conditions for Belgium to receive Marshall aid. The only question accompanying the source is: 'Has the Marshall Plan been received in a positive way everywhere in Europe? Discuss the reasons for your answer'. The question shows that the source has not been included to highlight the impact of the Cold War on specifically Belgium, such as the political tensions it caused between different parties. Instead, the focus is on Western Europe, illustrating a very Western and (Western) European orientation of history education in Flanders. This approach to the past is also reflected in the chapters on the Cold War: The accounts focus especially on political and economic aspects, placing far less to (almost) no emphasis on culture, especially everyday life.

An exception in this respect is the textbook *Passages* – not coincidentally written by academic cultural historians. The authors of *Passages*, and to a lesser extent those of *Pionier*, do address the influence of the Cold War on ordinary people, by including testimonies about how their lives were affected, for instance, or photographs of a nuclear attack drill in an American school in 1951. *Passages* also argues that the Cold War was fought not only on a political and economic level but also on a cultural level. Its authors elaborate, for instance, on how the Cold War affected sports and space policies.

Despite some differences, the main political and economic account of the Cold War is largely the same in all four textbooks. For the period from the 1940s to the 1950s, all textbooks address the origins of the Cold War, the American containment policy (related to the Truman Doctrine of 1947 and the Marshall Plan of 1947 to 1952), the establishment of Comecon (1949), the division of Europe and the Berlin Blockade (1948–49), the Korean War (1950–53), the establishment of the military alliances NATO (1949) and Warsaw Pact (1955), the temporary détente and co-existence policy of the 1950s, as well as the 1950s uprisings in the Eastern Bloc, at least in the GDR in 1953 and Hungary in 1956. The Polish uprising of 1956 is mentioned only in *Historia* and *Pionier*. Only *Pionier* mentions McCarthy and his 'witch hunt' in the United States in the early 1950s. The existence of Gulags in the Soviet Union is not mentioned in any of these four twelfth-grade textbooks. This is striking because all four corresponding textbooks for the eleventh grade, which cover material from around 1750 to 1945 and thus also the inter-war period, do include the Soviet Gulags.

Table 8.2 The Treatment of the Cold War in the Four Textbooks

	Total number of pages in the twelfth-grade textbook (+ format)	Pages devoted to the cold war	Pages devoted to the cold war (in percentage)	Pages dealing with the cold war, devoted to international vs. national affairs	Pages dealing with the cold war, devoted to politics/economy vs. culture/everyday life
Historia	205 pp. (A4)	14 pp.	7%	100% vs. 0%	100% vs. 0%
Passages	140 pp. (A4)	14 pp.	10%	100% vs. 0%	64% vs. 36%
Pionier	345 pp. (B5)	47 pp.	14%	100% vs. 0%	87% vs. 13%
Storia	173 pp. (A4)	17 pp.	10%	100% vs. 0%	100% vs. 0%

All textbooks, however, address the building of the Berlin Wall (1961), the Sino-Soviet split (1961), the Cuban Missile Crisis (1962), the thaw under Khrushchev, the escalation of the Vietnam War (1965 to 1973), the uprisings in the Eastern Bloc (1960s to 1970s), especially in Czechoslovakia (1968), American interference in Latin America, Asia and sub-Saharan Africa (1950s to 1980s), the Brezhnev Doctrine, the *Ostpolitik* of Willy Brandt and the SALT (1971 to 1972) and the Helsinki agreements (1975). Again, small differences emerge. *Historia*, for instance, does not mention that the removal of nuclear missiles from Turkey by the United States and NATO was part of the deal between Khrushchev and Kennedy in order for the latter to secure the withdrawal of Soviet nuclear missiles from Cuba. *Passages* is the only textbook to mention that the American nuclear missiles in Italy were also included in this deal. A marked difference arises from *Storia*'s account of American interference in different parts of the world from the 1950s onwards. While the three other textbooks clearly address this topic and provide one or more examples (from Iran, El Salvador, Chile or Guatemala), *Storia* hardly mentions American interference. In their accounts of the Cold War during the 1980s, all textbooks touch on the renewed confrontation policy, the arms race and the MAD doctrine, new uprisings (especially in Poland in 1980), the war in Afghanistan, the new détente (with Gorbachev), the fall of the Berlin Wall, the end of communism in Eastern Europe and the implosion of the Soviet Union.

Two other important phenomena and developments from the Cold War period (1945 or 1947 to 1989 or 1991), the European unification process and the expansion of the welfare state, are dealt with in all textbooks in a specific and separate (sub)chapter. The Israeli-Palestinian conflict and other developments in the Middle East are only partly framed within the Cold War context; they are also connected to global democracy, emancipation and decolonisation and, therefore, to the North-South divide as well. Decolonisation itself is addressed in a separate chapter, only tangentially connected to the Cold War context. The accounts on decolonisation in all four textbooks are rather general; they don't elaborate on one case in depth although some specific attention is paid to the decolonisation of India, the Congo, the Dutch East Indies and Ethiopia.

The Attribution of Agency throughout the Cold War

Three categories of agency and agents can be discerned in the four textbooks examined. In the first and most common category, non-human agency prevails. The textbook authors situate agency in the Cold War first and foremost in the hands of the United States and the Soviet Union rather than to people, factions, groups or institutions within each of the countries (such as secret intelligence agencies such as the KGB or CIA, the military-industrial complex or hawks in government circles). Sometimes the terms 'United States' and 'Soviet Union' seem interchangeable with 'capitalism' and 'communism', respectively, also non-human actors. *Historia*, for instance, states: 'In the opinion of the United States, communism on the march had to be contained' (25).

The second category does include human agency, here attributed, if much less frequently, to individuals from both camps in the Cold War. Above all, the agents are 'great', white men, notably the leaders of the United States and the Soviet Union, such as Truman, Eisenhower, Kennedy, Reagan, Stalin, Khrushchev and Gorbachev. *Passages* and *Storia* differ to a certain extent, because they also attribute agency to other individuals, either to the leaders of other countries (such as Tito, Castro or Thatcher) or opposition leaders (such as Lech Walesa). The roles of ordinary people are not mentioned. In this second category, there seems to be little difference in the amount of emphasis placed on human agency within both blocs.

Three of the four textbooks also attribute agency beyond the two superpowers and 'great men'. With the exception of *Historia*, all mention certain countries and groups as active agents. They mention countries belonging to one of the two camps and 'Third World' countries, as well as groups such as labourers, intellectuals, students (sometimes mentioned together, their actions characterised as protest movements), public opinion, the people, the army or political parties. Although these are mostly mentioned as passive entities, they are nevertheless attributed some agency in the context of certain events, especially towards the end of the Cold War. 'The people', for instance, along with the protest movements of students and labourers, are ascribed an important role in the fall of communism in Eastern Europe at the end of the 1980s and in the dissolution of the Soviet Union in 1991. In some cases, the stress is placed on 'multi-staged' agency: Only when approved by a superpower could a country or group start to roll out a certain policy. *Passages*, for example, writes that the vassal states of Eastern Europe dealt with their internal affairs themselves from the mid-1980s onwards once this had been approved by Gorbachev. *Storia* mentions that the communist political parties in Eastern Europe applied a specific strategy in order to seize power, but were nevertheless subject to the orders of the Soviet Union. Again, the authors of the four textbooks vary just as much for the Eastern as for the Western bloc in this third category.

In view of these three categories of agents and agency, to what extent do the twelfth-grade history textbooks represent the superpowers as homogeneous entities, and how much weight do they give to alternative voices? While *Historia* does not pay much attention to opposition within each of the power blocs, *Passages*, *Pionier* and *Storia* do. *Passages* states: 'Both power blocs were less homogeneous than they seemed at first sight' (14-15). The textbook explains, for instance, that different opinions existed within each bloc on how to deal with the opponents of the other bloc. When describing the détente after the Cuban Missile Crisis in the early 1960s, *Storia* states that not everyone in the United States was happy with this new policy (35). *Pionier* mentions that the people on both sides of the Iron Curtain disliked the new arms race at the beginning of the 1980s and organised several protests (94). Counter-voices, nevertheless, are introduced mostly in the (primary) sources accompanying the learning texts. While *Passages* presents counter voices within both camps (for instance, a Catholic priest receiving someone's confession at the shipyard of Gdansk or people in New York demonstrating against the arms race in 1961, 15), *Pionier* solely focusses on counter-voices within the Western camp. *Storia*, by contrast, does the opposite and offers only alternative voices from the Eastern bloc (46-48).

In examining the agency attributed by the textbook authors, it is important to analyse not only who is attributed agency but also who is not and even to analyse which groups are silenced in their accounts. All four textbooks' accounts of the Cold War are characterised by an abstract approach. The actual ordinary individual is almost completely ignored. In rare exceptions to this rule, he/she can be seen in a visual primary source included in the textbook, either as a passive victim of a proxy war (such as Kim Phuc in the iconic photograph showing the consequences of bombarding a Vietnamese village) or as a protester against the arms race.

Women are also completely silenced by these textbooks. Only in the learning text of one book, *Passages*, is one woman mentioned and attributed agency: Margaret Thatcher. *Storia* mentions the role of Mr and Mrs Ceaușescu in Romania (yet focusses on the husband's role) and *Pionier* notes the alleged role of Mr and Mrs Rosenberg in the espionage scandal in the United States in the 1940s and early 1950s. Neither Belgium nor any Belgians are mentioned in any textbook, and thus they are not attributed any agency. When considered in comparison with an international perspective, this might seem surprising; in the Flemish context, however, it reflects established trends. Once again, the textbooks illustrate the very (Western) European orientation of Flemish history education and the absence of attention to the learners' 'own' specific national past.

Textbook authors, furthermore, do not explicitly reflect on the concept of agency in the Cold War. They do not clearly address, for instance, to what extent ordinary people as a group and ordinary individuals were or were not passive playthings in the hands of superpowers. Nor do they instigate explicit reflection about how much agency the countries of a certain camp had vis-à-vis the superpower above them or raise questions about the relations between the people and the upper class or even within the upper class. The concept of agency itself, with all its complexities, remains below the surface of the textbooks' accounts.

Attribution of Agency and Responsibility for the Outbreak (and Continuation) of the Cold War

Another issue only implicitly touched upon by some of the textbooks is the question of responsibility for the Cold War. Since the 1950s, historians have sharply disagreed in this area. Soviet historiography, under central control, argued that responsibility lay with the West, while in the United States the 'orthodox' school blamed the Soviet Union and its expansion into Eastern Europe. In the 1960s and 1970s, however, revisionist scholars in the West started to challenge the widely accepted 'orthodox' view and considered the United States largely responsible for the Cold War. From the 1970s onwards, a third, post-revisionist school emerged among historians, which saw the Cold War as the result of predictable tensions between the United States and the Soviet Union, powers which had been suspicious of one another for many decades (Westad 2000; Vanden Berghe 2008).

First it should be stressed that none of the textbooks analysed here pay much attention to the origins of the Cold War. Each of the Flemish history textbooks spends only one to two paragraphs (half a page to one page) on this subject. Of the four textbooks, only two explicitly deal with the question of responsibility for the outbreak and continuation of the Cold War. While *Pionier* raises the question of whether or not it is possible to identify a culprit, *Storia* refers to the existing historiographical debate, stating:

> To date, historians still discuss whether or not the fear of communist expansion was justified, and to what extent Western leaders were honest in their statements. The orthodox school passes responsibility for the Cold War entirely onto the Soviet Union and its aggressive post-war politics. The United States, it says, did nothing but react appropriately and rightly. Revisionist historians, by contrast, argue that the Americans demonised the Soviet Union in order to justify their own aggressive and imperialist politics. (34)

Strangely enough, the post-revisionist school is not mentioned.

Throughout their accounts of the origin of the Cold War, all four textbooks take on a post-revisionist stance. They all refer to ideological and geopolitical tensions between the United States and the Soviet Union, as well as to the imperialist aspirations of both superpowers. Its continuation is explained as action and reaction. In other words, both the United States and the Soviet Union are ascribed responsibility, to an equal extent, for the origin (and continuation) of the Cold War. A discourse analysis affirms this finding. For instance, the textbook authors do not use specific verbs or adjectives to implicitly place blame on one of the two actors. Furthermore, the actors responsible for the outbreak of the Cold War are clearly identified as those with non-human agency. The textbooks' authors all identify the United States and the Soviet Union as the responsible parties. Only once in all four textbooks are Truman and Stalin explicitly mentioned. In all other cases, the agents are the two superpowers.

Only a few other actors are mentioned in relation to the origins and continuation of the Cold War, such as the national communist parties in Eastern Europe who held some power after the Second World War or the Western European countries who asked the Americans to help them work against Soviet expansionism. Nevertheless, according to the textbook authors, a 'multi-staged' agency was at work. First and foremost, responsibility was in the hands of the two superpowers; other actors could only (re)act with Soviet or American permission.

Moral Judgment on Agents and/or Actions during the Cold War

A further question is whether – and to what extent – any attribution of responsibility by the textbooks goes hand in hand with passing moral judgment on agents and/or actions during the Cold War. This question is not easy to answer. How should we assess statements like 'puppet regimes' to describe Eastern European governments, or the phrase 'witch hunt' to describe McCarthy's persecution of communists, the emphasis on the 'expensive' arms race or the statement (on MAD policies) that 'Both parties still went on developing ever stronger weapons'? On the one hand, these statements seem to impart moral judgments; on the other, however, they could simply be considered descriptive.

When analysing all of the chapters on the Cold War from these textbooks, we can see that the authors approach this conflict, its agents and events, for the most part in a distant, neutral tone without explicit judgement. A discourse analysis reveals no relevant results regarding specific wording. Stalin, for instance, is always mentioned by name only, without loaded adjectives. The textbooks sometimes ascribe him an authoritarian attitude ('Stalin demanded [...]'); however, the same phrasing can also be found in descriptions of Kennedy's actions during the Cuban Missile Crisis. Only in *Historia* is there one instance of clear moral judgment: In an in-depth study on the nuclear arms race during the Cold War, the author states that, with the disarmament agreements of the 1980s, 'a turn for the better' occurred (107). In *Storia*, Soviet policies are more readily criticised than American policies. Soviet interference into Eastern

European countries' internal affairs receives ample attention, for example, while American interference is hardly mentioned. Yet, for the most part, the authors of this textbook maintain a distance from the narrative; they do not show either sympathy or antipathy towards any actors in the Cold War.

Three of the textbooks nevertheless adhere to and lean on a framework of Western values and standards, albeit in a scattered and implicit way. Freedom and respect for human rights are considered important values in these textbooks, and they are portrayed as lacking in the communist bloc according to *Historia*, *Pionier* and *Storia*. *Historia* states that the GDR was forced to become a Soviet ally, while the FRG chose *Westbildung*. The right to self-determination and freedom of speech and religion is presented as hugely important in *Storia*. *Pionier* elaborates on Pope John XXIII's plea, in his encyclical *Pacem in Terris* from 1963, which calls for greater respect for human rights, freedom of religion, and dialogue. Consequently, both Soviet and American policies during that period are critically judged based on these (presumably) characteristic Western values. The judgment falls in favour of American policy, although *Pionier* also critically comments on it. Western values serve as the standard by which to judge different societies. Only *Passages* avoids a biased perspective altogether.

Conclusion and Discussion

Taking a comparative perspective, I analysed four Flemish twelfth-grade history textbooks in order to examine which groups or people are ascribed agency and responsibility for either causing or continuing the Cold War, as well as to understand to what extent the textbooks pass moral judgment. The textbooks often attribute agency to three different categories of people or entities: (1) The first and most prominent category concerned non-human agency situated in the hands of the United States and the Soviet Union, (2) the second category consisted of individuals, (3) a rather small third category consisted of certain countries, groups and 'the people' as active agents. In *Historia*, this third category received hardly any attention. The agency of ordinary people, women and Belgium itself were also mostly overlooked in all four textbooks. With the exception of *Historia*, all the textbooks recognised that both power blocs were non-homogeneous entities and that counter voices existed on both sides. Responsibility for the Cold War was unanimously dealt with in a post-revisionist manner, with the focus on ideological and geopolitical tensions between the United States and the Soviet Union and their imperialist aspirations. The analysis found that explicit moral judgment did not appear in the textbook accounts, but three of the four works nevertheless adhered to a framework of Western values and standards. Only *Passages* consistently maintained its distance from this framework.

Despite the differences between these textbooks, an important similarity emerged in terms of their approach to (agency in) the Cold War, which can be characterised as structural and informed by the social sciences. How should this attribution of agency be judged in light of the importance history education scholars ascribe to the representation of agency in (1) fostering students' complex understanding of history, (2) encouraging young people to take up societal and civic commitment and (3) contributing to young people's identity building?

Explaining past events and historical change or continuity with the necessary complexity is a very difficult matter. Analysing agency on different structural, collective and individual levels, however, allows us to have a deeper and more nuanced historical understanding of (the roles of various agents in) past events and developments. To a certain extent, the textbook authors discussed here rise to the challenge posed by such complexity. While they attribute agency to states or to 'great men', they generally pay little attention to the role of other agents. Furthermore, a reflection on the concept of agency itself is absent from the texts. This is a missed opportunity to guide students to reflect on the agents of change in history, as well as the balance between structures, collectives and individuals in creating historical change.

The authors of these four textbooks certainly illustrate the significance and effectiveness of collective action. According to them, it led to the fall of communism in Poland (the role of *Solidarnosc* in particular), the fall of the Berlin Wall and the fall of communism in general in Eastern Europe. The textbook authors also clearly show that, while collective action does not immediately produce change, it can yield results in the longer term. The elision of the importance of individual agency could have an impact on a young person's understanding of how this, too, could lead to historical change.

The emphasis on non-human agents like 'the Soviet Union' or 'the United States' in these textbooks might give students the idea, as Zahra points out, that a national identity is inescapable and they do not have the agency or liberty to construct and define their own identities (2010). An important suggestion in this respect, referring to Rogers Brubaker (2004, 12), is to analyse 'groupness' as an 'event' rather than analysing 'nations' or 'states' as historical actors (Zahra 2010, 97). This alerts students to the possibility that 'groupness' may not occur and reveals that national groups are never completely homogeneous, provoking reflections on agency on the structural, group and individual level.

Homogenisation gives rise to another problem, also related to identity building. In the four textbooks, the different blocs involved in the Cold War are mainly represented in a homogeneous way, even though some attention is paid to counter voices. Such a representation, combined with an implicit adherence to Western values and standards, carries certain risks. An 'us-versus-them' contrast can emerge between 'the West' and 'the Rest', with accompanying feelings of Western superiority. Western values and standards are judged positively and represented as being better than those of others, as previous research among Flemish students suggests (Van Nieuwenhuyse and Wils 2015). Furthermore, psychological research (in particular research into social identity theory) shows that homogenising the 'in-group' goes hand in hand with enlarging differences vis-à-vis 'out-groups', exaggerating the positive characteristics of the 'in-group' and stressing the weaknesses or shortcomings of the 'out-group' (Ford and Tonander 1998), encouraging exclusion.

It would thus be beneficial to combine the current approach (abstract, structural, with an emphasis on theory from the social sciences), which leads to a macro-historical perspective and an emphasis on non-human agents (which is certainly still valuable), with a micro-perspective focussing on the agency of ordinary individuals; this would allow for deeper and more nuanced macro-historical representations. Moreover, such a combination can support efforts to teach students to break through 'philosophical thinking' and achieve 'ironic thinking' (Egan 1997). According to the Canadian educationalist Kieran Egan, 16- to 18-year-old learners are 'philosophical thinkers': They focus on and are especially interested in 'the real truth' as a coherent system that can explain the world and reality in its entirety (1997, 104-136). Attractive systems are, for instance, religion or Marxism, which describe the world through a coherent yet strict logic but risk turning young people into rigid and authoritarian thinkers. 'Ironic thinking', Egan continues, can precisely remedy this by showing that there are always exceptions and nuance, by pointing to the unique instead of the general and by revealing the complexity of historical events and developments that cannot be understood through one simple frame (1997, 137-171). Such ironic thinking, which also includes self-conscious reflection about language use in history, contributes not only to better historical understanding but also to civic engagement and identity building. It differentiates between structures, shatters homogenisation and highlights the importance of individual and collective action on the part of ordinary people.

Bibliography

List of Textbooks Cited

Bekers, K., K. Dillen, B. Hendrickx, R. Lindemans, K. Merckx, W. Moreau, J. Philips, L. Van den Broeck, J. Van Dooren and G. Goris. 2009. *Storia 6*. Wommelgem: Van In.

De Deygere, R., W. Dupon, K. Moermans, W. Smits, C. Van der Meeren, S. Van de Perre, J. Vankeersblick and H. Van de Voorde, eds. 2009. *Historia 6*. Kapellen: Pelckmans.

Draye, G., G. Brock, H. Cools, K. Wils, eds. 2010. *Passages. Na de Tweede Wereldoorlog*. Averbode: Averbode.

Smeulders, M., I. De Leus, E. Steenackers, S. De Bock, M. Deserrano, W. Van Der Spiegel, R. Paeps, B. Reusens, eds. 2014. *Pionier 6*. Berchem: De Boeck.

Further References

Alcoff, L. 1994. 'Cultural Feminism versus Post-structuralism: The Identity Crisis in Feminist Theory'. In *Culture/Power/History: A Reader in Contemporary Social Theory*, ed. by N.B. Dirks, G.H. Eley and S.B. Ortner, 96-122. Princeton: Princeton University Press.

Barton, K. C. 2012. 'Agency, Choice and Historical Action: How History Teaching Can Help Students Think about Democratic Decision Making'. *Citizenship Teaching and Learning* 7, no. 2: 131–42.

Braudel, F. 1949. *La Méditerranée et le monde méditerranéen à l'époque de Philippe II*, 3 volumes. Paris: Armand Colin.

Brubaker, R. 2004. *Ethnicity without Groups*. Cambridge, MA: Harvard University Press.

Carlyle, T. 2010. *On Heroes, Hero-Worship and the Heroic in History*. New York: Cosimo Inc.

Clark, J. S. 2013. 'Encounters with Historical Agency: The Value of Nonfiction Graphic Novels in the Classroom'. *The History Teacher* 46, no. 4: 489–508.

Clark, J. S. 2014. 'Teaching Historical Agency: Explicitly Connecting Past and Present with Graphic Novels'. *Social Studies Research and Practice* 9, no. 3: 66–80.

Clark, J. S., C. Weber and K. C. Barton. 2011. '"African Americans Were Getting Fed Up": Choice and Inevitability in New Zealand Students' Ideas about Historical Agency'. Presentation at the annual meeting of the American Educational Research Association, New Orleans, Louisiana.

Egan, K. 1997. *The Educated Mind. How Cognitive Tools Shape Our Understanding*. Chicago: University Press.

Erdmann, E. and W. Hasberg, eds. 2011. *Facing – Mapping – Bridging Diversity: Foundation of a European Discourse on History Education*, 2 volumes. Schwalbach: Wochenschau Verlag.

Flemish Ministry of Education and Training. 2000a. 'Secundair onderwijs, derde graad ASO: uitgangspunten bij de vakgebonden eindtermen geschiedenis' [Secondary education, third stage of general education: basic principles of the history standards]. http://eindtermen.vlaanderen.be/secundair-onderwijs/derde-graad/aso/vakgebonden/geschiedenis/uitgangspunten.htm (last accessed 26 October 2016).

Flemish Ministry of Education and Training. 2000b. 'Secundair onderwijs, derde graad ASO: vakgebonden eindtermen geschiedenis' [Secondary education, third stage of general education: history standards]. http://eindtermen.vlaanderen.be/secundair-onderwijs/derde-graad/aso/vakgebonden/geschiedenis/eindtermen.htm (last accessed 26 October 2016).

Fontaine, A. 2006. *La Guerre froide 1917–1991*. In 2 volumes. Paris: Editions du Seuil.

Ford, T. E. and G. R. Tonander. 1998. 'The Role of Differentiation between Groups and Social Identity in Stereotype Formation'. *Social Psychology Quarterly* 61: 372–84.

Harris, R. 2011. 'Citizenship and History. Uncomfortable Bedfellows'. *Debates in History Teaching*, edited by I. Davies, 186–196. New York: Routledge.

Peck, C., S. Poyntz and P. Seixas. 2011. '"Agency" in Students' Narratives of Canadian History'. *The Future of the Past: Why History Education Matters*, edited by D. Shemilt and L. Perikleous, 253–280. Nicosia, Cyprus: Association for Historical Dialogue and Research.

Seixas, P. 2012. 'Historical Agency as a Problem for Researchers in History Education'. *Antíteses* 5, no. 10: 537–53.

Taylor, C. 1989. *Sources of the Self: The Making of Modern Identity*. Cambridge: Harvard University Press.

Van Nieuwenhuyse, K., Wils, K. 2015. 'Historical Narratives and National Identities: A Qualitative Study of Young Adults in Flanders'. *Belgisch Tijdschrift voor Nieuwste Geschiedenis: Journal of Belgian History* 45, no. 4: 40–72.

Vanden Berghe, Y. 2008. *De Koude Oorlog. Een nieuwe geschiedenis (1917–1991)*. Leuven: Acco.

Vanhulle, B. 2005. 'Waar gaat de geschiedenis naartoe? Mogelijkheden tot een narratieve analyse van naoorlogse Vlaamse geschiedleerboeken'. *Bijdragen tot de Eigentijdse Geschiedenis* 15: 133–75.

Vanhulle, B. 2009. 'The Path of History: Narrative Analysis of History Textbooks – A Case Study of Belgian History Textbooks (1945–2004)'. *History of Education* 38, no. 2: 263–82.

Westad, O. A., ed. 2000. *Reviewing the Cold War: Approaches, Interpretations, Theory*. Cold War Histories Series, volume 1. New York: Routledge.

Wils, K. 2009. 'The Evaporated Canon and the Overvalued Source: History Education in Belgium: An Historical Perspective'. In *National History Standards: The Problem of the Canon and the Future of Teaching History*, ed. by L. Symcox and A. Wilschut. International Review of History Education 5, 15–31. Charlotte, NC: IAP.

Wilschut, A. 2012. *Burgerschapsvorming en de maatschappijvakken*. Amsterdam-Alkmaar: Landelijk Expertisecentrum Mensen Maatschappijvakken.

Wilschut, A., Van Straaten, D., Van Riessen. 2013. *Geschiedenisdidactiek. Handboek voor de vakdocent*. Bussum: Coutinho.

Zahra, T. 2010. 'Imagined Noncommunities: National Indifference as a Category of Analysis'. *Slavic Review* 69, no. 1: 93–119.

Open Access This chapter is licensed under the terms of the Creative Commons Attribution 4.0 International License (http://creativecommons.org/licenses/by/4.0/), which permits use, sharing, adaptation, distribution and reproduction in any medium or format, as long as you give appropriate credit to the original author(s) and the source, provide a link to the Creative Commons licence and indicate if changes were made.

The images or other third party material in this chapter are included in the chapter's Creative Commons licence, unless indicated otherwise in a credit line to the material. If material is not included in the chapter's Creative Commons licence and your intended use is not permitted by statutory regulation or exceeds the permitted use, you will need to obtain permission directly from the copyright holder.

9

The Cold War and the Polish Question

Joanna Wojdon

Poland appeared to be on the 'wrong' side of the Iron Curtain. While its communist government was imposed by the Soviet Union in 1944, the Polish people supported the Western world. They expressed this opinion in the referendum of 1946 and parliamentary elections of 1947, both of which were falsified in order to prove popular acceptance of the regime (Paczkowski 2010, 182). The anti-communist guerrilla movement was active until the 1950s despite the severe persecution suffered by its supporters. Communist propaganda was used in an attempt to make the Polish people identify with the Soviet bloc, and school education became one of the Soviet Union's main tools. School textbooks from the period 1948—1989 left no doubt that the United States and Great Britain were to blame for initiating the Cold War (Wojdon 2017). However, two factors among many testify to both the durability of Polish ties to Western democracy and Poland's distance from Soviet ideology: the authority of the Catholic Church in the country and the massive numbers enrolled in the Solidarity trade union of 1980 to 1981.

J. Wojdon (✉)
Institute of History, University of Wrocław, Wrocław, Poland
e-mail: joanna.wojdon@uwr.edu.pl

© The Author(s) 2019
B. Christophe et al. (eds.), *The Cold War in the Classroom*, Palgrave Studies in Educational Media, https://doi.org/10.1007/978-3-030-11999-7_9

The same findings apply to the historiography of the Cold War. Although officially Polish historiography adopted Marxism as its theoretical basis during the General Congress of the Polish Historians in 1948 in Wrocław, and this survived as an interpretative framework until the collapse of the communist regime, some Polish historians, in Poland and in the diaspora, participated in, or at least were aware of, historiographical debates in the West (Stobiecki 2007; idem 2005). The flow of information from the West into Poland was constantly increasing with the relaxation of the passport policy of the Warsaw regime, but also due to, for example, the book distribution programme initiated by the CIA in the late 1970s (Reisch 2013, 23ff.). Foreign radio broadcasts (such as Radio Free Europe) and the independent publishing movement (beyond the control of the censorship office) broadened the audience for those alternative historical narratives. At the end of the 1980s, in larger cities, unofficial history textbooks for secondary school were illegally published and distributed as supplementary materials among pupils. However, the state struggled to the very end to hold its official monopoly on historical interpretation, by means of both school curricula and the system of textbook approval, which permitted only one textbook for each subject and grade (Wojdon 2015, 185).

Textbooks

A reinterpretation of the Cold War was one of the first changes introduced in school history textbooks after the collapse of the communist regime in 1989. Already the first textbook of 1990 (the structure of which did not change if compared to the pre-1989 edition) stated that 'the concept of the "Cold War"' is closely related with the attempts to stop the Soviet expansionism undertaken by the Western powers' (Pankowicz 1990, 195). Soviet plans for international expansion were presented in detail in these textbooks, and the authors argue that Winston Churchill's speech in Fulton in 1947 'made the world realise the communist danger' (ibid.), although it didn't start the Cold War (an interpretation which can be found in textbooks under communist control (Szcześniak 1984, 335–336)); instead, it announced that the Cold War had begun. The speech definitely ended the co-operation between the Western Powers and the Soviet Union – co-operation which had made it possible for the Soviet Union to continue its occupation of Polish territories after 1939, to subjugate Poland and to impose the communist system in East-Central Europe. A pupil might infer from the text that Churchill brought to an end the blindness of the West regarding Soviet policies and practices and that it was the Soviet Union which had started the Cold War by violating Western values, such as human rights or democracy; it just took Western leaders time to notice and articulate it.

The textbook adds, only in a final sentence, that Churchill also 'questioned our [Poland's] entitlement to the Recovered Territories[1] and the rightness of the decision of the big powers [USSR, USA, Great Britain] to resettle the German population from the territories of Poland, Czechoslovakia and Hungary' (Pankowicz 1990, 195). Altogether, however, it seems as if Poland profited more from the end of the co-operation between Stalin and the Western powers than it suffered from the Western support for German revisionism. This idea was never explicitly expressed in any textbook, but apparently it remained behind all post-1989 narratives.

The Western interpretation of the Cold War has prevailed in Polish school history textbooks, regardless of the changes in the system (and structure) of education and in school curricula. In the school year 2016 to 2017, post-Second World War history was taught in the sixth (last) grade of primary school and in the first grade of upper secondary school as a compulsory subject. In the third grade of secondary school it was optional and taught to those who chose to major in humanities. The first grade of upper secondary school therefore provided the last and most developed interpretation of the past to all schoolchildren. The aim of this chapter is to deconstruct the prevailing model of teaching the Cold War to the young generation of Poles as of 2016 and 2017 and to understand the main historiographical concepts of this conflict (traditionalist, revisionist and post-revisionist) which impact its teaching. Since a large-scale survey of the teaching practices of history teachers in Poland in 2014 proved that the textbook was their primary teaching tool, I start with a content analysis of four textbooks aimed at students in the first grade of secondary school and issued by the leading Polish publishers (Stola 2012;

Roszak and Kłaczkow 2012; Brzozowski and Szczepański 2012; Dolecki et al. 2012). The conclusions drawn from this analysis are then compared with those drawn from observing a lesson in a secondary school in Wrocław, which provides an example of real school practice. The method of approaching the Cold War within this classroom serves as a case study, illustrating a more general vision of the discipline of history as taught in Polish schools.

To begin my analysis, I look at the amount of space devoted to the Cold War and its various components within each textbook, including political (domestic and international), economic, social and cultural aspects. I then proceed to look at the interpretation of the Cold War superpowers and their allies (extended East and extended West) within each textbook, the focus on (and silencing of) particular phenomena, issues of agency and the roles of individuals on both sides of the Iron Curtain. The similarities and differences between individual textbooks are singled out.

The differences may be due to design of individual textbooks (where the publisher often has a decisive voice), to space allotted for various elements (texts, images, tasks, comments) and, to a lesser extent, to the political views of the authors[2] or to the historiographical schools they belong (for example, Dariusz Stola is both a historian and a sociologist, so he pays more attention to social processes and everyday life than other historians might). On the other hand, the similarities between textbooks are not the result of political pressure or the political affiliation of their authors. Textbooks in Poland are approved by the Ministry of Education, but the approval is based on reviews by experts in history, teaching history and the Polish language, nominated by academic and professional societies. Publishers are free to propose as many books as they wish and there is no limit on the number of textbooks available on the market. The teachers then choose textbooks for their pupils[3].

The findings from this analysis are then discussed against the historiographical models of the traditionalist, revisionist and post-revisionist interpretations of the Cold War. It should be noted, though, that in Poland the 'revisionist' model, which attributes negative moral values to the Western powers involved in the Cold War, preceded, in fact, the traditionalist Western interpretation (accusing the Soviet bloc); thus, it is hard to call it 'revisionist'. Moreover, revisionism is virtually non-existent in the current narratives taught in schools and appears only in primary sources originating from the Soviet bloc during the Cold War era. This is why in this text it is referred to as the Soviet (rather than revisionist) interpretation of the Cold War.

Elements of these models and the issues raised in textbooks were then observed during an introductory lesson on the topic of the Cold War in one of the secondary schools in Wrocław on March 14, 2016. As the teacher mentioned during one of the lessons on Cold War that followed, she was a university student between 1982 and 1987, which means that the final stage of the Cold War constitutes a part of her personal experience. One should keep in mind, however, that the atmosphere at the history department in Wrocław in the 1980s was far from the expectations of the communist regime, despite initial hardships under martial law. As my older colleagues from the department recollect it, Samizdat literature proliferated and clandestine organizations reached students with their programmes and activities.

Textbook Analysis – Structure

The Cold War is not emphasised through the structuring of school textbooks. Only one textbook (by Dariusz Stola) has a separate section entitled 'The Cold War: Europe and the world in 1945–1989', which covers the whole period both in Poland and abroad.

The authors of another textbook, Brzozowski and Szczepański, start the post-Second World War chapter with a retrospective, going back to the conferences of the Big Three in Tehran, Yalta and Potsdam, followed by a series of international events (the San Francisco conference of 1945 included). This leads up to the Berlin crisis of 1948 and the formation of the state of Israel. Only then is there an eleven-page-long chapter entitled 'The Beginning of the Cold War – The Split between East and West' (171–181). The chapter starts with a description of Stalin's policies, Churchill's speech in Fulton, the Truman Doctrine, the arms race and the two military blocs: NATO and the Warsaw Pact. It then discusses the Sovietisation of the Soviet bloc on the one hand and the European integration within the Western bloc on the other, with a clear aim to juxtapose the two processes.

Another chapter mentioning the Cold War is entitled 'The Cold War and the Main World Military Conflicts in 1945–1989' and includes the wars in Korea, Vietnam, Cambodia, Afghanistan, the Cuban Missile Crisis and the attempts at 'peaceful coexistence' (197–205). The end of the Cold War serves as an introduction to the post-1989 world, only after the post-war section has been summarised.

The third textbook, by Dolecki et al., only has a short section (one page) dealing with 'The Beginning of the Cold War' in the chapter 'Europe After WWII', and it is not clear at all from this book when the Cold War ended. Moreover, Polish issues are presented as completely separate from the rest of world history[4]. As a result, having discussed the collapse of the Soviet bloc and even the problems facing the modern world, the textbook narrative jumps back to 1944 and the communist takeover in Poland.

The fourth book analysed in this chapter, by Roszak and Kłaczkow, does not have any chapter or subchapter mentioning the 'Cold War'. It introduces the term only in a summary of the section which deals with the organisation of world politics after the Second World War and begins with the Potsdam conference and founding of the UN in San Francisco. The chapter then discusses the Truman Doctrine, the Marshall Plan and the OEEC, and it also mentions the independence of India and the beginning of the war in Indochina.

Segmenting the story of the Cold War diminishes its significance. Only in the textbook by Stola is it presented as a monumental event which shaped the world after the Second World War. In other books, the Cold War is mentioned alongside many other events which occurred during the same the period. There is thus little room left for any in-depth analysis of the Cold War and even less space in which to discuss its varying interpretations. The textbooks do not even mention that there are any historiographical debates on the Cold War. Despite the differences in structure, each textbook devotes about a hundred pages to the Cold War period and all the textbooks present a similar overall vision of the conflict, depicting the West in a positive light and taking a critical approach towards the Soviet Union and the communist regimes, which generally corresponds with the classical Western model of interpretation (Table 9.1).

Table 9.1 Table Showing Number of Pages devoted to the Cold War and its Various Aspects in Polish Secondary School Textbooks. The results for each textbook do not sum up to 100% because more than one issue may be discussed on one page

	Stola	Roszak, Kłaczkow	Brzozowski, Szczepański	Dolecki, Gutowski, Smoleński
Total:	98	124	117	112
National issues	43 (44%)	55 (44%)	56 (48%)	58 (52%)
International issues	55 (56%)	69 (56%)	61 (52%)	54 (48%)
Economy	18 (18%)	9 (7%)	6 (5%)	13 (12%)
Culture	10 (10%)	7 (6%)	8 (7%)	4 (3%)
Everyday life	17 (17%)	4 (3%)	10 (9%)	3 (3%)

Political history dominates without any doubt. In some textbooks less than ten pages are devoted to culture or everyday life in the Cold War period and as little to the economic issues. Altogether, all non-political issues occupy less than or around twenty per cent of space, with the exception of the book by Stola, where economic factors are considered alongside the political ones and discussions of everyday life and cultural issues are also integrated into the main narrative. The authors of two other textbooks (Roszak and Kłaczkow; Brzozowski and Szczepański) chose to present non-political topics (such as Stalinist propaganda, post-1968 popular culture, the space race, everyday life in the West or in the USA between the 1950s and 1970s, the Catholic Church after the Second World War) in 'infographics', occupying one or two pages. These topics are illustrated with photographs and visually separated from the rest of the chapter. The textbook by Dolecki et al. mentions these topics at the end of the chapter on 'The World after WWII: The Rivalry between the USA and USSR' which also deals with military conflicts, decolonisation and even global terrorism (on one short page which treats the subjects of both the Red Army Faction and Al-Qaida). This domination of textbooks by political history has further implications for the image of both sides of the conflict, as shown below. It is also a feature of traditionalist historiography.

Moving to the geographical aspects of textbook analysis, the history of the Eastern bloc is covered in more detail than American actions or decolonisation. The anti-regime protests in Poland in 1956, 1968, 1970, 1976, 1980, 1981 and 1988 are obviously dealt with in detail, but the

1953 uprising in Berlin, the Hungarian uprising of 1956 and the Prague Spring of 1968 are also mentioned, with a seemingly sympathetic approach in all the textbooks, and these topics are accompanied by photographs. The Soviet Gulag is not discussed in the Cold War section since the Soviet system of labour camps is discussed in the chapters of the textbooks devoted to the inter-war years. The post-Stalinist 'thaw' is addressed, also in regard to Poland, although not all the books use this term, even if they present in detail political changes in the Soviet bloc, such as the struggle for power in the Kremlin, the new Soviet leadership under Khrushchev, his criticism towards Stalin and the hopes of countries of the Soviet bloc which were epitomised in the uprisings in Berlin, Budapest and the social protests in Poland.

The United States enjoy much less attention, especially regarding their non-European policies. American internal affairs are usually only briefly mentioned. All the analysed textbooks touch on the subject of the Civil Rights Movement, although sometimes only in a few sentences. The book by Dolecki et al. is the briefest. The sentence 'In the United States people refused, en masse, military service in Vietnam' is followed by: 'Apart from the peaceful movement of Pastor Martin Luther King, who fought for equal rights for coloured members of society, the movement of Black Panthers was also founded – the leftist groups of African-American fighters who physically fought for equal rights for the black population' (289–290)[5]. This statement ends the chapter. There is no real discussion of the problems faced by African Americans. The textbook takes the traditional WASP's perspective. Other textbooks concentrate on the positive results of the movement led by Martin Luther King, who eventually convinced the US administration to promote non-discriminatory practices (Roszak and Kłaczkow 2012, 304; Stola 2012, 132). Thus, the textbooks emphasise how different countries overcame difficulties rather than the difficulties themselves. The narrative emphasises the political rather than the social or cultural. The depiction in these textbooks strengthens the positive image of the United States as a democratic country capable of solving its own problems.

Senator McCarthy does not appear in any of these textbooks. The 'red scare' is represented instead by the trial and execution of Ethel and Julius Rosenberg, Americans accused of espionage for the Soviet Union and of leaking information about the atomic bomb to the Soviet Union, thus significantly speeding up the Soviet nuclear programme.

The emphasis on the Rosenbergs instead of McCarthy corresponds with a traditionalist approach to the Cold War. The treatment of the arms race, the space race and the 'hot' conflicts of the Cold War period within these textbooks leans towards post-revisionism as the rivalry between the superpowers is presented without any moral judgments about either side involved in the conflict.

In the textbook by Stola the space race is mentioned as yet another aspect of the arms race (141). In the textbook by Dolecki et al. both are summarised on the same page (287). The portrayal of Yuri Gagarin, the first man in space, varies between the textbooks. In some he is presented just as a pilot, and his words about saving the beauty of the Earth instead of destroying it are cited (Roszak and Kłaczkow, 294), but Dolecki et al. claim that his communist views, alongside other skills, made him the first man in space. The textbook written by Roszak and Kłaczkow mentions Gagarin only briefly but devotes a special insert of two pages to give a detailed account of the moon landing (320–321). The American space programme thus looks more attractive (also thanks to the large pictures in full colour) than its Soviet counterpart, even if no explicit comments are made on this topic.

The Cuban Missile Crisis is discussed in all the textbooks, though in one only in a caption accompanying a picture of the US delegate to the UN presenting the photographs of Soviet missiles in Cuba in October 1962 (Dolecki et al., 285). Both the picture from the UN and the aerial photo of Cuba are printed in the book, alongside a tiny portrait of Fidel Castro as 'the leader of the communist Cuba in 1959–2008'. The caption also says:

> The Cuban crisis could have led to the outbreak of a nuclear war. As a response to the Soviet action, the USA announced the blockade of the island and preparations for the invasion of Cuba and for war with the Soviet Union. Khrushchev gave up and withdrew the nuclear weapons from Cuba. The USA gave up attempts to overthrow Fidel Castro.

The reasons for the Korean War are traced back to the dual occupation of Korea by the American and Soviet armies and the free elections which were to be held across the whole country yet never actually happened. The military conflict was initiated by the North, supported by the Soviet Union and China, while the South was liberated by the United Nations forces led by the Americans. It is emphasised that the two superpowers supported opposing sides of the conflict but did not openly fight with one another. As the war progressed, the United States refrained from using nuclear weapons against China in order to prevent the war turning into a worldwide conflict. Stalin's death is presented as a factor facilitating peace negotiations in 1953. The division of Korea into two states, with the totalitarian communist regime in the North founded by Kim Il-Sung, still continues today. Personal stories from the war are never included in these narratives; it is a purely political event in all the textbooks (Stola, 172–173; Brzozowski, 197–199; Dolecki et al., 278–279; Roszak and Kłaczkow, 278–279).

In the case of Vietnam, the anti-war protests and controversies in America are usually mentioned in the context of the student movement of 1968, hippies, and 'Flower Power' (and therefore as events which were not very serious), while US military intervention is justified by the doctrine of containment aimed at preventing the worldwide spread of communism (Stola, Dolecki et al.) or by the invitation from the government of South Vietnam (Roszak and Kłaczkow). Some textbooks emphasise the role of the media in adding to the negative perception of the war by the American public and repeat that the USA lost the war at home (Brzozowski and Szczepański, 201–203; Dolecki et al., 282). The disastrous results of communist rule in Vietnam, Laos and Cambodia usually follow, with an emphasis placed on the atrocities of the Khmer Rouge in Cambodia; for instance, the text is paired with illustrations of rows of skulls, victims of the regime (Stola, 175; Roszak and Kłaczkow, 280; Brzozowski, 201–203). The textbook by Andrzej Brzozowski also mentions the Soviet intervention in Afghanistan in 1979, calling it the 'Soviet Vietnam' (203–205). In the textbook by Dolecki et al. numerous other 'hot' conflicts are mentioned, but only in the form of a table with dates, parties involved and the numbers of victims in each conflict (286). Thus, these wars become statistics, with no human faces.

Decolonisation is also rarely explored in any detail, probably because it has no direct connections to Polish affairs: Poland never was a colony and never had any colonies, at least in any 'traditional', straightforward sense.[6]

This may be one reason why this topic is treated rather marginally (Techmańska 2014). The issues of colonisation and decolonisation have little impact on the image of the West in Poland. The history textbooks both corroborate and continue this opinion. In the books by Roszak and Kłaczkow and Stola, decolonisation is discussed in separate chapters (281–286, 177–181, respectively). Some textbooks give a more general overview of the process and see it as a result of the Second World War and the weakened position of colonial powers, of Japan's foreign policy which supported anti-colonialism, of the role of the UN (in which former colonies played an increasing role), of the USSR (with its anti-imperialist rhetoric) and the USA (a former colony itself) (Dolecki et al., 282; Stola, 177). Only Brzozowski and Szczepański mention the colonised peoples who wanted independence playing an active role in prompting the process and the tensions arising from the unwillingness of the colonialists and local elites to change the colonial status quo, which sometimes resulted in military conflicts (193).

As a rule, African colonies are just laid out in chronological order according to the year they gained independence (with an emphasis placed on the year 1960, 'the year of Africa') and sometimes the war in Algeria is mentioned. The book by Brzozowski and Szczepański only mentions the war in brackets: '(e.g. the civil war in Algeria lasted for a few years and ended in 1962 when the French left the colony)', while the textbook by Stola devotes a whole paragraph to this conflict. For Stola, Algeria serves as an example of an African colony with a large white population (about one fifth of all inhabitants) who opposed decolonisation. The author stresses the cruelties of the war, the death of almost half a million people and the sufferings of the civilian population. He appreciates the role of General de Gaulle, who came to an agreement with the National Liberation Front.

The apartheid system in South Africa is also sometimes part of the discussion of post-war Africa and the problems caused by a difficult co-existence of the white and black populations. India is discussed only in relation to Mahatma Gandhi and his successful policies, the text often accompanied by his portrait. The decolonisation of Indochina is usually mentioned in the context of the war in Vietnam.

The narratives on decolonisation in these textbooks generally sound as if the authors were dealing with some very distant (in space and time) affairs. They usually conclude with the presentation of difficulties experienced by the decolonised countries and their peoples, such as deteriorating living conditions, declining health statistics, poverty, military conflicts and corruption. It looks as if decolonisation brought more problems than it solved, even though the textbooks also explicitly state that the overall results were positive. The terms 'The Third World' and 'neo-colonialism' are sometimes introduced.

Such an interpretation of the processes of colonisation and decolonisation leads into a traditionalist interpretation of the Cold War. Silencing the colonialists' abuses and marginalising colonial issues helps to maintain an idealised image of the West. The dominant narrative about the situation in Western Europe in all textbooks is one which stresses the development of a consumer society and European integration. Both changes are presented in the most positive light, bringing wellbeing and overall happiness to the people. However, only the textbook by Stola uses the term 'welfare state'. It is briefly characterised in the chapter 'The Golden Age of the West' (132–139).

The textbooks all note the sexual liberation of the Western world, the spread of feminism and the acceptance of new family models, and all these topics are treated in the context of modernisation and freedom, not as posing a danger to traditional values. The Second Vatican council and other changes within the Catholic Church are often presented as a response to those challenges but no criticism is attributed to either process. Some textbooks or individual chapters are openly enthusiastic about the West, and, in general, they all present a very positive image of the 'Free World' during the Cold War.

Contrary to that within the European community, the textbooks argue that co-operation within the Soviet bloc was only superficial, forced by the Kremlin. The term Sovietisation is used in this context. Economic difficulties, lack of freedom and other daily hardships behind the Iron Curtain are stressed (with special emphasis put on Poland).

Since the textbook narratives deal predominantly with political issues, politicians are the main actors, individually or collectively. The list of individuals presented in the textbooks is rather short (probably a result of the tendency not to overload school education with names and dates). Actors are usually mentioned by surname: 'Churchill said', 'Churchill proclaimed'

(Brzozowski, 171), 'Churchill publicly stated' (Stola, 124), 'President Harry Truman proclaimed' (Stola, 124) (but also 'Truman stated' – Kłaczkow, 224), 'Marshall presented' (Roszak and Kłaczkow, 225; Dolecki et al., 259), 'Stalin introduced the regimes' (Roszak and Kłaczkow, 224), 'Stalin took care' (Dolecki et al., 258) or 'denounced the West' (Brzozowski, 171). More often than not there is no human actor and the states or nations are the subjects in the sentences: 'the Americans offered' (Stola, 124), 'the countries benefited' (Dolecki et al., 259, 'NATO expanded' (Stola, 126), 'the Soviet Union rejected' (Stola, 124), 'blocked' (Stola, 125), 'decided' (Roszak and Kłaczkow, 249), 'avoided' (Brzozowski, 171), or 'annulled treaties of alliance' (Brzozowski, 173). In the textbook by Roszak, the Soviet bloc is represented only by political leaders, while in the Western bloc the textbook refers to the general public. The (lack of) agency of the citizens of the Soviet bloc is thus reflected in the textbook's presentation.

There are hardly any negative words associated with the United States and Western world in the context of the Cold War. For example, even when Brzozowski and Szczepański present a section on the life in the United States in the 1950s through the 1970s (just one page), which deals with the American problems (the 'Red Scare' and FBI, racial discrimination and Martin Luther King, Watergate), it turns out that a solution was found for each issue, and the words are printed in bold such as 'the real leader of the West', 'economic potential', 'cultural pattern'. Terms such as 'Golden age', 'American dream', 'democracy' and 'integration' also help to build on the positive image of the West. The attitude towards Soviet activities is usually more critical.

Let us compare two sentences from the textbook by Roszak and Kłaczkow. The first sentence reads:

> In 1944–1948 Stalin imposed communist regimes in Poland, East Germany, Hungary, Romania, Bulgaria, Albania and Yugoslavia [Czechoslovakia is mentioned later]. (224)

The second sentence states that:

> In June 1947 American Secretary of State George Marshall presented a plan of economic assistance for ruined Europe. (225)

The first sentence is very short, in the form of a military order ('Stalin imposed regimes'), while the second uses analytical descriptions of American policies ('presented a plan of economic assistance') and objects ('ruined Europe') which emphasise the significance of the USA's role and their respect for Europe. Similarly, Stalin is just called Stalin while Marshall is referred to as 'American Secretary of State George Marshall'. 'Imposed' and 'regimes' are the words with negative connotations here, whilst 'assistance' carries positive connotations. The verb 'imposing' paints the Soviet Union in a negative light, a power to which the people of Poland and other countries are just passive victims. 'Presenting the plan' is only an offer to 'ruined Europe' which can be accepted or rejected – the agency is, thus, split between the participants.

The American assistance offered to Europe within the framework of the Marshall Plan is often emphasised in the Polish textbooks. Western European countries were 'systematically reconstructed' and managed to 'co-operate [...] as partners'. The refusal of Poland to participate in the Marshall Plan under Soviet pressure is (rightfully) presented as proof of Soviet dominance.

Conclusion

In narratives on the outbreak of the Cold War the traditionalist interpretation prevails. The Soviet Union is presented as a power with expansionist aims, aims the Western countries decided to work against, which led to the Cold War. The image of the USSR within these textbooks contrasts with the presentation of the positive role of the United States who supported the countries and nations threatened by the Soviets. A task in the textbook by Brzozowski and Szczepański asks pupils to 'Explain the methods the Western countries used to oppose the expansion of Communism in the world after World War II' (181).

Roszak and Kłaczkow mention the rivalry between the two blocs in their textbook, in which post-revisionist arguments can be seen, as well as in the presentation of the area of ideology and propaganda. The textbook by Stola traces the origin of the Cold War back to the debates over Soviet policy in Central Europe, which he argues was more brutal than the Western allies could tolerate. But he generally characterises the Cold War simply as a rivalry of the superpowers, without mentioning ideological issues. The superpowers each had their own interests and ambitions, and their clash was a decisive factor in the triggering the Cold War.

Lesson Observation

In the introductory lesson on the topic of the Cold War in the first grade of an upper secondary school in Wrocław, observed on 14 March 2016, I noted a post-revisionist approach towards the topic, with some inclination towards a traditional Western interpretation of the conflict.

The pupils were using the textbook by Dolecki et al. (2012), albeit only sporadically in the course of the lesson, which is not common practice at Polish schools (Choińska-Mika et al. 2014, 227), but in this case fully justified since the book does not address the origins of the Cold War satisfactorily. It approaches the topic from a traditionalist stand point and emphasises the actions of the Soviet Union which led to the Cold War, as the USA reacted to these actions. The textbook also discusses Soviet expansion in Eastern Europe, the growing influence of communist parties in France and Italy as a result of the Soviet influence, Soviet finances, the Greek civil war (as the only 'hot' conflict in Europe at that time, which was generally divided by the 'Iron Curtain') and the American doctrine of containment as a reaction to those circumstances.

The pupils had been asked to familiarise themselves with the Cold War chapter as their homework before the lesson and were expected to discuss the reading in the classroom. The teacher did not explicitly question the textbook narrative, but she used a totally different structure of the topic and introduced some elements of post-revisionist and even revisionist interpretation, but without ever naming any of them or mentioning the very existence of divergent historiographical interpretations. Thus, the textbook was only used to provide pupils (at least those who did their homework) with some background knowledge.

The topic was formulated as 'The Cold War – Its Origin, Characteristics, Problems'. Three main points of discussion were dictated by the teacher at the very beginning of the lesson: '1) The Origin of the Cold War; 2) Features and Stages of the Cold War; 3) Bipolar Image of the World and Selected International Conflicts of the Cold War Period'.

The discussion started with the definition of the term 'bipolar', as understood by the pupils, as young people and as prospective scientists (reference to physics was made). The students agreed that bipolar meant divided. Then the teacher addressed some basic facts about the sides of the conflict (USA and USSR, but also Great Britain, NATO and the Warsaw Pact), its duration (from 1946 to 1989), and the reason why it is referred to as 'cold'. The definition of the Cold War was then decided on and written down by the students in their notebooks. They wrote that the Cold War was a conflict between the capitalist (Western) world and the socialist countries allied with the Soviet Union (in the following lesson this definition was re-formulated and the Cold War was defined as the conflict between the United States and Russia of a psychological rather than military nature). As no moral judgments were attributed to either side of the conflict, the teacher's definition of the Cold War can be regarded as post-revisionist. However, as we will see, in the course of the lesson the extended East was presented in a much more critical way than the extended West.

This can be seen in the very first tasks, when the students received two primary sources (text excerpts) in order to familiarise themselves with two views on the origins of the Cold War. The first one was authored in 1948 by Julia Brystygierowa, a high-ranking officer in the Ministry of Public Security of the People's Poland (quoted in Sobańska-Bondaruk and Bogusław Lenard 1998)[7]. The other excerpt was taken from the speech of Winston Churchill in Fulton, Missouri, on the Iron Curtain. The pupils' task was to 'compare the origins of the Cold War as presented by the authors [...] Underline, what elements of the origins of the conflict the authors point to'. The texts and the questions were prepared by the teacher. They did not come from the pupils' textbooks but instead from the selection of sources for secondary school use, published in the 1990s.

Each of the sources was analysed separately, students beginning with Churchill's speech. The teacher asked: 'What reasons for breaking the co-operation between the USA and USSR does Churchill see?' Pupils referred rather to their textbook than to the source, despite a few attempts by the teacher to re-focus them on Churchill's speech. They concentrated on questioning the Polish-German border, the resettlement of the German population from Poland and also cited a fragment about 'very small [parties] in all these Eastern States of Europe, [that] have been raised to pre-eminence and power far beyond their numbers and are seeking everywhere to obtain totalitarian control'. They did not assign any moral judgment to the speech or to the speaker but simply reworded the document. It thus became an 'objective', credible source of information about the origins of the conflict rather than about the views of Churchill. The role of this text was further confirmed in the next task, which was to 'draw the Iron Curtain' according to Churchill on a map displayed on the whiteboard and to note down the countries behind the Iron Curtain.

At this moment the teacher started filling in a scheme of the Cold War with the Soviet bloc on the left and the Western countries on the right (geographically, I would prefer if the sides were changed), labelled as 'USSR and the socialist countries' and 'USA and the capitalist countries'. The names of the military blocs followed, then the political systems (police control versus democracy and planned economy versus private property). The question over Germany's place regarding the Iron Curtain was also raised. After a short discussion and quotations from Churchill on the expanding Soviet influence on Germany, the students placed the name of the country on the line that represented the curtain.

Answering the question 'And what does Brystygierowa see?', pupils interpreted the second text as a propagandist statement accusing the United Sates of being to blame for the nuclear threat posed to the whole world. The teacher chose individual students who then quoted the sentences in which Brystygierowa named the countries particularly endangered by the United States (the Soviet Union and the 'countries of people's democracy'). This time attention was paid to the nature of the speech (propaganda) and the goals of the speaker rather than to the realities described. Brystygierowa was not regarded as a trustworthy speaker but as a propagandist and manipulator.

A series of questions and answers about the Fulton speech followed: 'What is the goal of the Cold War according to Churchill?' (broadening the influence of the Western powers in the world), 'What should the West do?' (keep working together and abide by the principles of the Atlantic Charter),

'In which way? What will contain the Russians?' (only strength). The pupils were asked to evidence their replies by quoting from the speech.

A more general question over whether poverty was the reason for social unrest ('When do you think radical movements proliferate?') opened the last section of the lesson in which the teacher very briefly mentioned the post-war economic crisis and the Marshall Plan. Then she asked pupils to note down 'The origins of the Cold War. Point one: The expansion of the influences of the Soviet Union and the USA. Point two. The post-war economic crisis', statements in which no judgements are made, but instead the parallel developments on both sides of the 'Iron Curtain' are highlighted, as in a post-revisionist approach.

The last lesson task was to pick up labels with various issues related to the Cold War and place them on the scheme on the whiteboard in order to show whether they referred to one or both sides of the conflict. The teacher proposed the different labels and six pupils were appointed to complete this task. The pupils chose the arms race, military actions and intelligence or spying as the common features. Posing a threat to one's own society was a label given to the Soviet bloc while the pupils thought that the West particularly felt fear at the prospect of nuclear weapons being used. The pupils were asked to justify their choices. They mostly referred to the textbook or to their general knowledge (which they derived from spy movies, for instance) and gave examples of certain activities (such as instances of military conflicts in which both sides participated or statistics about weapon production). The classroom discussion did not result in any of the labels being moved to another place. Thus, the pupils agreed with the teacher's seeming preference for a post-revisionist interpretation of the Cold War (since they argued that most aspects developed simultaneously in the East and in the West), although this opinion was combined with more of a critical attitude towards the East than to the West (since the pupils pointed out that the Soviets persecuted their citizens and posed a nuclear threat to the rest of the world).

The teacher only added media warfare (as a common feature) and propaganda (attributed to the Soviet bloc), which corresponded with the general picture discussed above. So did a short excerpt from the opening speech of Jan Nowak-Jeziorański, the director of the Polish Section of

Radio Free Europe appointed in 1952, which the teacher played to the pupils. Nowak-Jeziorański promised that the Section would present the facts, regardless of their political beliefs. The teacher also played a short propaganda film made in Poland in order to depict Radio Free Europe in a more negative light, presenting the views of both sides involved in the conflict. The teacher again wanted the pupils to identify the differences between these two messages. However, they looked tired and were busy packing their bags (the bell rang at the end of the Nowak's speech), and so they were not able to comment on the recordings.

As a homework task, the pupils were asked to explain the terms of the Truman Doctrine and Marshall Plan and to interpret a poster presenting the Marshall Plan as a dairy cow (Fig. 9.1). The teacher did not introduce the poster in any way, and she neither mentioned that the cartoon approaches the Cold War from the perspective of someone in the East nor did she explain why she had chosen this particular image. Indeed, it did not correspond with the narrative of the Cold War presented thus far during the lesson.

Fig. 9.1 A poster presenting the Marshall Plan as a dairy cow (Source: Izdebscy et al. 2015, 53)

In the course of searching for the image myself, I found a test on the post-war world published by a teacher-training centre in Gorzów Wielkopolski (Test z historii). The test juxtaposes our poster with another one depicting the Marshall plan as a scaffold placed near a tall building with various European flags that form the wall-tiles. Apart from asking students about the symbols in and meanings of the two pictures, the test has also a question about the origin of each of the posters: It asks which one was created in the West and which one in the East (apart from the general messages of each poster, we can see that the poster with the cow on it has a caption in Czech 'Zàp. Evropa'). A similar task can be found in the 2012 state exam (*matura*): 'Explain the reasons for varying interpretations of the economic plan in the two iconographic sources'. This time the provenance of each source was clearly identified. The two sources also referred to the Marshall Plan, and one source came from the Western bloc, the other from the East: One was a (West) German poster from 1948 and the other was a cartoon drawn by Boris Yefimov, a Soviet, in 1951. Thus, the idea behind the task was not new or particularly original: The task has been used before to try to open up a new perspective on the Marshall Plan, perhaps quite a different perspective from the one primarily discussed during the lesson. Unfortunately, I was not able to see how the pupils interpreted the poster.[8]

The teacher might have intended this homework task to encourage the students to see views on the Cold War from both sides of the conflict, an attempt she'd made in showing both Brystygierowa's speech and the film on RFE to the pupils, which would bring their interpretation of the Cold War closer to a post-revisionist model (which seemed to be the teacher's own preferred model). It was difficult, however, for her to avoid a traditionalist Western approach when teaching the conflict, especially when it also corresponded with the history textbook her pupils were using and also with their general knowledge and beliefs. The main drawback of both the lesson and the textbooks I have analysed is, in my opinion, that there is still a lack of any debate on divergent historiographical interpretations of the Cold War. The discussion, if any, seems to relate only to the opinions presented in primary sources, whether from the East or West.

The selection of primary sources was supposedly intended to present the beliefs of those on both sides of the conflict, but as a matter of fact all of these sources seemed to show the Soviet bloc in a negative light, emphasising that the messages from the East could be seen as propaganda and lies and that the actions of the Soviets threatened both their own citizens and the people in the West. At the same time, no arguments which might seriously undermine an idealised image of the West were brought to pupils' attention, either by the authors of the textbook or by the teacher herself. The last cartoon, used in the homework task, could question these ideas, but could also be interpreted as yet another manipulative act on the part of the communist regime.

Using the case study of how the Cold War is taught in Poland, we can see that both teachers and textbooks emphasise a classical, positivist vision of history as a 'scientific reconstruction' of the past. Even if textbooks vary in their interpretations of the events, they seem to ignore alternative interpretations and omit any historiographical debates. Even if a teacher designs her lesson herself, does not strictly follow any textbook and uses various primary sources, she wants to teach her students 'what happened', not 'what do historians say' happened.

Notes

1. The term 'Recovered Territories' referred in the communist propaganda to the pre-war eastern and northern provinces of Germany (mostly Silesia and Pomerania) that the Big Three decided to give Poland after the Second World War. The word 'Recovered' stressed their ties with Poland in the early Middle Ages when the Polish state had been formed (10th-13th century).
2. This was more the case in the previous generation of textbooks, published at the end of the twentieth and beginning of the twenty-first century when some authors tended to justify the communist rule in Poland and provided interpretations typical for the post-communist discourse.
3. In some grades of primary school textbooks are sponsored by the state but teachers still choose the books from the set approved by the Ministry (eventually, in a few years, all primary school pupils should get their textbooks for free). In secondary school pupils (parents) pay for textbooks themselves.
4. In Poland, national and international history is combined in one subject and in one textbook, but individual sections and chapters usually deal

either with Polish or international affairs. The Cold War issues are split almost equally between Polish and international affairs.
5. '[…] lewicowych bojówek Afroamerykanów, wzywający do fizycznej walki o równouprawnie-nie czarnej społeczności Stanów Zjednoczonych' (Dolecki et al. 2012, 289–290).
6. Grzegorz Chomicki presented the Polish Galicia (Austrian partition of Poland in the 19th century) as a colony of the Austro-Hungarian Empire in his conference paper 'Galicia in the 19th century in Colonial and Post-colonial Perspective', at the Annual Conference of the International Society For History Didactics (ISHD) on *Colonialism, Decolonization and Post-colonial Historical Perspectives - Challenges for History Didactics and History Teaching in a Globalizing World* (Tutzing, Germany, 2013). Some historians claim that Poland 'colonised' Ukrainian and Belarussian territories east of its borders in the fifteenth to seventeenth centuries.
7. 'Recently, great changes have occurred in the political system both on the international and national level. The changes were caused by a fierce attack of the American imperialism which desires to submit the peoples of Europe, Asia and the whole world to the power of dollar and to enslave them economically and politically. The attack is aimed in the first place at the Soviet Union and the countries of people's democracy. The American imperialists started their attack from an attempt to threaten the world with the "nuclear war". Then they proposed the so-called Marshall Plan that cynically tries to turn Europe into an American colony.

    Further steps of the plan to subjugate Europe include crushing the struggle of the French people with the help and under pressure of the American capitalists, founding and subordinating Benelux, assembling the Western Union, preserving the fascist power in Germany with the former hitlerites in charge who act under command and according to the imperialist interests. Organising of the anti-Soviet military bloc becomes more and more apparent and unmasked'. The text comes from the selection of sources for teaching history: Sobańska-Bondaruk and Bogusław Lenard 1998, 383–385, trans. JW).
8. The task and the caricature of the Marshall Plan cow can be found on one of the Polish websites where pupils post their homework, albeit without suggested answers.

Bibliography

Textbooks Cited

Brzozowski, Andrzej and Grzegorz Szczepański. 2012. *Ku współczesności: Dzieje najnowsze 1918–2006: Podręcznik do historii dla szkół ponadgimnazjalnych – zakres podstawowy*. Warsaw: Stentor.

Dolecki, Rafał, Jędrzej Smoleński and Krzysztof Gutowski. 2012. *Po prostu historia: szkoły ponadgimnazjalne: zakres podstawowy*. Warsaw: Wydawnictwa Szkolne i Pedagogiczne.

Izdebscy, Agnieszka, Tytus Izdebscy and Barbara Furman. 2015. *Maturalne Karty Pracy (4) do historii dla liceum ogólnokształcącego i technikum. Zakres rozszerzony*. Warsaw: Nowa Era.

Roszak, Stanisław and Jarosław Kłaczkow. 2012. *Poznać przeszłość: wiek XX: Podręcznik do historii dla szkół ponadgimnazjalnych: zakres podstawowy*. 219–338. Warsaw: Nowa Era.

Stola, Dariusz. 2012. *Historia: Wiek XX: Szkoły ponadgimnazjalne: Zakres podstawowy*. 123–219. Warsaw: Wydawnictwo Szkolne PWN.

Szcześniak, Andrzej. 1984. *Historia 8. Polska i świat naszego wieku*. Warsaw: Wydawnictwa Szkolne i Pedagogiczne.

Further References

Test z historii dla klasy pierwszej szkoły ponadgimnazjalnej – Świat po II wojnie. https://womgorz.edu.pl/files/File/Doradztwo_metodyczne/Test%20z%20 historii%20-%20C5%9Awiat%20po%20II%20wojnie%20%C5% 9Bwiatowej.pdf (accessed 15 August 2018).

Choińska-Mika, Jolanta, Jakub Lorenc, Krzysztof Mrozowski, Aleksandra Oniszczuk, Jacek Staniszewski and Klaudia Starczynowska. 2014. 'Nauczyciele historii'. In *Liczą się nauczyciele: Raport o stanie edukacji 2013*, edited by Michał Federowicz, Jolanta Choińska-Mika, Dominika Walczak, Michel Sitek, Stanislaw Dylak, Jaroslaw Gorniak, Katarzyna Hall, Konarzewski, Krzysztof Konarzewski, Zbigniew Kwieciński, Grzegorz Mazurkiewicz, Maria Mendel and Magdalena Swat-Pawlica. Warsaw: IBE.

Paczkowski, Andrzej. 2010. *Spring Will Be Ours: Poland and the Poles from Occupation to Freedom*. University Park, PA: Penn State University Press.

Pankowicz, Andrzej. 1990. *Historia. Polska i świat współczesny. Podręcznik dla szkół średnich dla klasy IV liceum ogólnokształcącego oraz dla klasy III technikum i liceum zawodowego.* Warsaw: Wydawnictwa Szkolne i Pedagogiczne.

Reisch, Alfred. 2013. *Hot Books in the Cold War: The CIA-Funded Secret Western Book Distribution Program behind the Iron Curtain.* Budapest: Central European University Press.

Sobańska-Bondaruk, Melania and Stanisław Bogusław Lenard. 1998. *Wiek XX w źródłach: Wybór tekstów źródłowych z propozycjami metodycznymi dla nauczycieli historii, studentów i uczniów.* Warsaw: PWN.

Stobiecki, Rafał. 2005. *Klio na wygnaniu. Z dziejów polskiej historiografii na uchodźstwie w Wielkiej Brytanii po 1945 r.* Poznań: Wydawnictwo Poznańskie.

Stobiecki, Rafał. 2007. *Historiografia PRL. Ani dobra, ani mądra, ani piękna [...], ale skomplikowana. Studia i szkice.* Warsaw: Trio.

Techmańska, Barbara. 2014. 'Decolonization Issues in Contemporary History Textbooks for Secondary Schools in Poland'. In *Colonialism, Decolonization and Postcolonial Historical Perspectives: Challenges for History Didactics and History Teaching in a Globalizing World. Yearbook-Jahrbuch-Annales: International Society for History Didactics* 35, 137–146.

Wojdon, Joanna. 2015. 'The System of Textbook Approval in Poland under Communist Rule (1944–1989) as a Tool of Power of the Regime'. *Paedagogica Historica* 51, nos 1–2: 181–196.

Wojdon, Joanna. 2017. *Textbooks as Propaganda: Poland under Communist Rule, 1944–1989.* Abingdon/New York: Routledge.

Open Access   This chapter is licensed under the terms of the Creative Commons Attribution 4.0 International License (http://creativecommons.org/licenses/by/4.0/), which permits use, sharing, adaptation, distribution and reproduction in any medium or format, as long as you give appropriate credit to the original author(s) and the source, provide a link to the Creative Commons licence and indicate if changes were made.

The images or other third party material in this chapter are included in the chapter's Creative Commons licence, unless indicated otherwise in a credit line to the material. If material is not included in the chapter's Creative Commons licence and your intended use is not permitted by statutory regulation or exceeds the permitted use, you will need to obtain permission directly from the copyright holder.

10

The Cold War in South African History Textbooks

Linda Chisholm and David Fig

A remarkable feature of the Cold War is its coincidence with the period of apartheid in South Africa, in which it played an important role. This is evident in school textbooks, where it is a major topic in the most recent years of history. But while there is a growing body of work on the Cold War in Africa, there is a very small literature on its manifestation in South Africa and, with one exception, nothing on how school textbooks may have reinforced or challenged its main precepts.

L. Chisholm (✉)
Centre for Education Rights and Transformation, University of Johannesburg, Johannesburg, Gauteng, South Africa
e-mail: lchisholm@uj.ac.za

D. Fig
Research Associate for the Chair of Bio-Economics, University of Cape Town, Cape Town, South Africa

Society Work and Politics (SWoP) Institute, University of the Witwatersrand, Johannesburg, South Africa
e-mail: davidfig@iafrica.com

Historians of the Cold War have shown that the new wave of 'Third World' revolutions during the 1960s was central to the history of global conflict engendered by the Cold War (Halliday 1986; Westad 2007, 2017). Moscow and Washington keenly observed the moment of the formation of decolonisation movements after World War I and after the ending of formal colonisation, supported competing interests and parties. Although both were rhetorically opposed to colonialism, and held up different models of development for emulation, in practice their interventions constituted 'a continuation of colonialism through slightly different means' (Westad 2007, 5). Westad's work is helpful in showing that their approaches were both rooted in the same concept of modernity that was shared by previous generations of Europeans. Both believed in change and development as the solution to inherited colonial problems. Each promised the expansion of freedoms through different means. This literature also highlights the role of anti-colonial elites, buying into different models for various reasons including strategic and economic considerations and a sense of ideological closeness to the chosen ally. In the context of widespread poverty and inequality, as well as colonial states whose purposes were ill-suited to the visions of their new incumbents for emancipation and freedom from economic and social want, the correctness of the chosen path was legitimated both morally and politically (Westad 2007, 387).

Within the last decade, a number of studies have emerged casting new light on the Cold War in South Africa. These have been written from the perspective of the relationships forged between South Africa and its respective liberation movements with Eastern and Western powers in the struggle for democracy (Baines and Vale 2008; see for example Filatova and Davidson 2013; Houston 2008; Ndlovu 2008; Schleicher 2008; Shubin 2008b, 2008a; South African Democracy Education Trust (SADET) 2008; Wellmer 2008). They provide valuable insight into the nature, complexity and depth of the multi-faceted international relationships forged during this period by both the state and South African liberation movements in the struggle against apartheid. They also highlight the varied initiatives both to support and contest apartheid that developed outside South Africa. But how contemporary generations are being introduced to this momentous history has not been adequately explored, pointing to the need for more substantial research in this area. One exception, by Halsall and Wassermann, focuses exclusively on the place of Russia in the South African curriculum, arguing that little has changed in its treatment over time, except in so far as the fear exemplified in the apartheid-era textbooks is not evident in their latter-day successors (Halsall & Wassermann 2018, 50).

But how has the representation of the Cold War changed since 1994? In order to answer this question it is necessary in the first instance briefly to consider differences in the final year history curriculum during the late-apartheid period and after 1994. In the post-apartheid period the curriculum has been revised three times; however, these changes have not substantively altered the emphasis on the Cold War in the final year of schooling. Although textbooks of the first two iterations of post-apartheid curriculum revision could be considered (see for example Bottaro, Visser and Worden 2007; Friedman et al. 2007), those textbooks selected for closer analysis here are top of the list of provincial textbook purchases following the most recent curriculum revision (South Africa, Department of Basic Education 2019, 27–28). This means that they are among the most used textbooks in schools nationally. Two history textbooks for the final year of secondary schooling were selected. After a brief comparison of the two textbooks, this chapter will hone in on one of them (Fernandez et al. 2013; Pillay, Sikhakhane and West 2013). The approach taken here is principally descriptive, pointing out the main interpretational tendencies and omissions.

Our chapter traces the treatment of the Cold War in South African textbooks, showing how this has changed. It argues that the most significant change since the apartheid period is that the convergence of anti-communism with black liberation movements has given way to a friendlier approach towards movements for decolonisation and the East than was previously evident. In this regard, they broadly 'autobiographise' South Africa's changing positioning in international relations (Christophe and Halder 2018).

Curriculum continuities and changes pre- and post-1994

As Kallaway has pointed out, the Cold War has been a subject in both the pre-1994 as well as the post-1994 senior secondary school curriculum in the final year of schooling. Kallaway, however, is less concerned with representations of the Cold War in textbooks than with the logic, coherence, chronological sequencing and 'presentism' of the curriculum, arguing for example that failure to provide 'a comprehensive background to European and World History' leaves students ill-equipped to understand the complexities of the Cold War (Kallaway 2012, 48). Given that textbooks present the official curriculum in elaborated form, it is useful to juxtapose the 1980 and 2012 syllabi and curricula relating to the Cold War, as they inform the textbook representations examined in this chapter.

An important difference is that whereas in the pre-1994 curriculum the focus of the Cold War is within a primarily European international context, the post-1994 curriculum interlaces this history with the history of racism and resistance to racial segregation, African history and South African history. In as much as South Africa saw itself as part of the Western alliance against communism, its curricular representation of this history reflected this positioning. In a context where the victors of a post-1994 settlement had actively sought alliances with the East to promote a democratic dissolution and resolution of South Africa's racial state, the curriculum reflects this more complex positioning of the Cold War within the context of South Africa's struggle for democracy and an end to racism and racial segregation.

While the more detailed specifications in the post-1994 curriculum accord more space and content to the role of liberation movements and their choices in the Cold War, the curriculum nonetheless specifies a treatment of the Cold War as being

> characterised by conflict through proxy wars, the manipulation of more vulnerable states through extensive military and financial aid, espionage, propaganda, and rivalry over technological space and nuclear races, and sport. Besides periods of tense crisis in this bi-polar world, the Cold War deeply affected the newly independent countries in Africa and the liberation struggles in southern Africa from the 1960s until the 1990s, when the USSR was dismantled (South Africa, Department of Basic Education 2011, 25).

The curriculum requires that 'blame for the Cold War' be taught and learnt through the presentation of different interpretations and differing points of view (ibid., 25). China, Cuba and Vietnam are given as case studies. The following section on 'Independent Africa' calls for comparisons to be drawn between the experiences of the Congo as 'a tool of the Cold War' whose legacy lives on into the present and the African socialism of Tanzania. The kinds of states and leaders that emerged are specified. This section ends with the way Africa became drawn into the Cold War, using Angola as an example. Here the USSR, USA, Cuba, China and South Africa became involved militarily (ibid., 27). The curriculum requires study of the denouement of the Angolan War in the context of the ending of the Cold War and implications for international and regional relationships. How then do textbooks represent this version of history, that gives more weight to the Cold War in Africa and its relationship to decolonisation than earlier versions had done?

Representations of the Cold War in Post-apartheid Textbooks

Apartheid curricula and textbooks reflected a Cold War mentality in which the South African state was in alliance with the West. Some key points can be made about interpretations in post-apartheid curricula and textbooks. Firstly, these explicitly include the African dimension and explore the connection between the Cold War and decolonisation. Secondly, whereas the 'baddie' in the apartheid textbooks was communism, in the post-apartheid period it is the superpowers combined. While the diversity of initiatives undertaken in the US to both support and contest apartheid tends to be glossed over, a more sympathetic picture is presented in the new textbooks of the USSR as a friend and ally of liberation movements. Thirdly, however, and in the main, a Great Man theory of history prevails in the treatment of African liberation movements. Fourthly, while the active voice is dominant throughout the texts, it is consistently used when referring to the actions of superpowers and inconsistently in relation to African liberation movements. The curriculum and both the textbooks analysed seldom elaborate on why African liberation movements may have chosen one side or the other. When this occurs, it is in the context of a dependency analysis: 'Since African countries were in a state of development, they would have been tempted to accept military and economic assistance from the developed world' (Pillay et al. 2013, 116).

But there are also differences both between and within textbooks. The textbooks selected and analysed follow the curriculum quite closely. In the section on the reasons for involvement of the USA, USSR, Cuba, China and South Africa in Angola, concepts of indirect rule, non-alignment, neo-colonialism and proxy war are highlighted in one textbook, while the other emphasises key terms such as proxy, faction, pawn and zero-sum game (Fernandez et al. 2013, 123–124; Pillay et al. 2013, 116–117). Independent African states are sometimes presented as victims rather than active agents. Thus, Fernandez et al. tell students that they 'will examine how the superpowers, namely the USA and USSR, used the newly-independent African states for their own selfish reasons'. African agency is portrayed relative to the role Africans see themselves as playing on the international stage (Fernandez et al. 2013, 77). Cuba, too, is seen not as acting on its own behalf, and sometimes in conflict with the USSR, as Westad shows, but as 'intervening on behalf of the communist superpowers' (Fernandez et al. 2013, 123). The colonial dimension of the Cold War is suggested in the statement that 'the granting of independence to African countries opened up the African continent to the USA and USSR' with the aim of 'securing control over the resources, territory and people'. Moreover: 'Often a country […] existed as an extension of that superpower' (Fernandez et al. 2013, 124). In Angola, the People's Movement for the Liberation of Angola (*Movimento Popular de Libertação de Angola*, MPLA) 'was kept alive' by the support of the USSR (Fernandez et al. 2013, 128), while the anti-communist National Front (*Frente Nacional de Libertação de Angola*, FNLA) had attracted the help of the USA and of the People's Republic of China, and the National Union for the Total Independence of Angola (*União Nacional para a Independência Total de Angola*, UNITA) had received aid from the Chinese and South Africans. How Cuba came to be involved is blurred in the sentence that 'by 1963 Angolans were receiving training from Cubans' (Fernandez et al. 2013, 137). Combined with the Great Man Theory of history employed, the relationship between leaders and followers is not examined nor are the reasons for political choices made, and the subtleties of engagement and conflict among alliance partners are ignored. The textbook thus adds to African history but also simplifies it.

Pillay et al. combine the Great Man Theory of history with a narrative of heroic resistance. The Congo is also presented, as prescribed by the curriculum, as a tool of the Cold War and there is quantitatively more information on the superpowers than on the perspectives and approaches of MPLA, FNLA and UNITA (Pillay et al. 2013). Generally written in the active voice, there is a lapse when explaining how 'Tanzania came to be subjected to a one-party state' (Pillay et al. 2013, 131). However, this textbook does reveal subtleties of interpretation not present in Fernandez et al. It acknowledges, for example, that for several reasons 'Southern Africa was never a high priority on the agenda of the Soviet Union', thus also showing the shift in emphasis from the anti-communist narrative of the apartheid period to one more sensitive and alert to new historiographies on South Africa's historical relationship with Russia and the Soviet Union (Filatova 2008; Pillay et al. 2013, 378; Shubin 2008a).

Although the curriculum provides the general framework within which the textbooks are written, the textbook representations tend firstly to show some differences, such as for example in the treatment by Fernandez et al. of apartheid South Africa as independent from the Cold War, and the degree of subtlety and complexity of relationships between actors, but also some commonalities in their positioning of African liberation movements. Here too, however, the picture is not unambiguous. While the curriculum provides more information about African history and involvement in the Cold War, the approach is limited by the overwhelming emphasis on the role of leaders as great men representing differences of approach, and by the positioning of African liberation movements, not as actively choosing and shaping their involvements on the basis of assumed ideological or other commonalities, but as being tools and instruments of others. When Africans are presented as agents of their own history, as in the case of South Africa's struggle for democracy, the Cold War is invisible.

A closer examination of one of these textbooks is useful in illustrating the overall narrative and representation of the roles of the USA, USSR and South Africa during the Cold War (Pillay et al. 2013). The textbook begins and ends with this specific conflict. South Africa's involvement in the Cold

War is only really brought in at the end, suggesting that Africa somehow stood outside the conflict. The first section, on the 'Origins of the Cold War', describes the Cold War in terms of the relationship between the USA and USSR before and after the Second World War. Their ideological differences are seen as key. Thus, 'historians hold different viewpoints and interpretations about the origins of the Cold War, but […] due to ideological differences between the two superpowers tension and a mutual distrust became known as the 'Cold War'' (Pillay et al. 2013, 2). The political and economic organisation of the two societies around the two very different ideals of democracy and capitalism are also described. Reasons for the Soviet mistrust of the West and the West's mistrust of the USSR are presented. The wartime conferences of Teheran (1943), Yalta (1945) and Potsdam (1945) trace the agreements between the 'Big Three'. In a section on the creation of 'Spheres of Interest', the nature and reasons for 'the installation of Soviet-friendly regimes in satellite states' is explored, the reaction of the West is described, and the USA's subsequent policy of containment via the Truman Doctrine and Marshall Plan are spelt out. Events in Greece, Turkey and Iran 'prompted the USA into taking action to combat the spread of communism. The USA feared that the Eastern Mediterranean would also fall under communist control. They therefore adopted a policy of containment'. Consequences of the Marshall Plan and responses to it in both the USA and USSR (the formation of Cominform and Comecon) are underscored, including the debate in the USA Congress on the matter as well as sources relating to the Truman doctrine and Marshall Plan. The Berlin blockade and Western responses to it and the continuation of Berlin as a focal point of the Cold War are sketched. Kennedy's speech on 26 June 1963 is presented as a source for analysis. The formation of NATO and the Warsaw Pact are considered. Following a section on the Cuban Missile Crisis the book asks who was to blame for the Cold War and answers this question in terms of three dominant perspectives: the orthodox view, revisionist/new left perspectives and post-revisionist stances. The 'orthodox view' sees it as a result of Soviet aggression, the revisionists 'placed the blame for the start of the Cold War on the USA, rather than the Soviet Union', while the post-revisionists 'tried to show that both sides had their faults' (Pillay et al. 2013, 32). The extension of the Cold War into China and Vietnam is detailed.

10   The Cold War in South African History Textbooks   215

Between this section on the origins of the Cold War and the final section on the end of the conflict and the new world order, the textbook deals with comparative case studies of the rise of independent Africa (Congo and Tanzania), civil society protests from the 1950s to the 1970s (women's liberation, feminism and the US civil rights movement), civil resistance in South Africa from the 1970s to the 1980s, and the coming of democracy to South Africa with the processes of coming to terms with the past that this entailed. Within the section on independent Africa, the impact of internal and external factors in the form of the challenge of ethnicity, the Cold War and neo-colonialism are explored, as are the roles of the USSR, USA, Cuba, China and South Africa. Thus, 'during the Cold War both the USA and USSR attempted to increase their influence in Africa […] The USA and USSR challenged and threatened each other for political influence, trade and military bases in Africa, for example in Angola' (Pillay et al. 2013, 117).

The USA's involvement in Angola is presented as being 'to secure vital raw materials and to prevent the spread of communism' whereas the USSR 'realised that African countries were interested in projects for development and hence they concluded trading agreements, gave technical assistance and provided capital for investment and weapons' (Pillay et al. 2013, 118). A box of quotations on the reasons for the interest of the USA and USSR in Africa points overwhelmingly to 'selfish' reasons 'to preserve their own interests' and gain access to Africa's raw materials. 'Kissinger', one quotation runs, 'saw the countries and regions of the Third World in Africa only against the problem of maintaining an American-Soviet balance of power' (Pillay et al. 2013, 119). In the Angola case-study, reasons for the involvement of the USSR, USA, Cuba, China and South Africa are also provided: details are given about the USSR's military support of the MPLA (later to become the ruling party), while the USA's covert support of the rival UNITA is presented as being suspicious of 'nationalist movements with a socialist orientation'. Reagan's prioritisation of Africa when he became president in 1981 was to allow the US 'to serve as an intermediary between Angola and South Africa on the issue of Namibian independence' (Pillay et al. 2013, 127). South Africa's interest in Angola is situated squarely within its own perception of the USSR as a hostile power that threatened the region and South Africa's own control over Namibia. South Africa thus became involved in the Angolan War 'because of the threat posed to South West Africa by the MPLA's rapid expansion' (Pillay et al. 2013, 128). The devastation of the region by this multi-power influence is counterposed by a photograph of Princess Diana comforting landmine victims (129). The section ends with quotations from a smiling Nelson Mandela, the hand of Fidel Castro resting on his shoulder, about the significance of the battle of Cuito Canavale, which the South Africans lost, for the struggle for Southern African liberation (Pillay et al. 2013, 130). This battle, fought in Angola in 1988, was decisive in shifting the balance of forces in the region in favour of the Angolan army, aided by Cuba, the Soviet Union and East Germany and against UNITA, supported by the South African Defence Force.

In the following section on Civil Society Protests from the 1950s to the 1960s, the role of women's liberation and feminist movements in industrialised countries and in South Africa, as well as the US Civil Rights Movement and a case study of the Black Panther movement are highlighted. The section ends with an overview of 'The Progress Made Towards Racial Equality', with photographs of Barack Obama, Oprah Winfrey and Muhammad Ali shown to 'bear testimony to how the Civil Rights Movement has enabled some African Americans to be successful' (Pillay et al. 2013, 200). The next section on 'Civil Resistance in South Africa' is contextualised in terms of the 'Total Onslaught' South Africa saw itself as facing mainly due to communist intervention, and the 'Total Strategy' embarked upon as official policy to attempt to control resistance. The anti-apartheid struggle inside and outside South Africa is dealt with by reference to the rise and role of opposition underground, in prison and in exile, and the role and legacy of the Black Consciousness movement in South African politics. No explicit links are drawn with the Civil Rights and Black Panther movements in the United States; nor are the range of anti-apartheid initiatives in the USA referred to later on (for this history see Grant 2017). The crisis of apartheid in the 1980s details the role of internal resistance to attempted reforms of the system during the 1980s, highlighting the role of the growing trade union movement and emergence of new forms of civic mobilisation as well as the international anti-apartheid movement and its sports, consumer and cultural campaign, and boycotts. Neither the USA nor the USSR play a part in this story. Although there is substantial evidence of the role played by the West in the process, they and other international players are similarly absent from the account of the negotiations, lasting from 1990 to 1994, when democratic elections were held. Their role is only brought in right at the end, in a separate section on the end of the Cold War.

The end of the conflict is explicitly brought into play in the final section of the textbook. The specific relationship of the Cold War to South Africa is brought out firstly in South African propaganda that the country was a 'stable, civilised and indispensable member of the "free world" that opposed international communism' (Pillay et al. 2013, 377), and secondly in the support given by the Soviet Union and especially East Germany to the African National Congress (ANC). However, it also makes clear that Nelson Mandela and Oliver Tambo were not communists, despite their close relationship with the South African Communist Party (Pillay et al. 2013, 378). The narrative points to the role of international economic pressure and specifically the US Congress in imposing limited sanctions against South Africa. But there is no reference to the wider anti-apartheid campaigns in the USA. Africa is presented as having become 'caught up in the Cold War confrontation between the USA and the Soviet Union'. More detail is provided of the Cold War in southern Africa during the 1980s and the involvement of the USSR and USA in Angola, which became 'a sideshow of the Cold War' (Pillay et al. 2013, 383). The USA assured UNITA, 'to contain the spread of communism around the world and because the Angolan government was perceived to be communist', of its support 'in its attempt to overthrow the regime' (Pillay et al. 2013, 383). Source activities are again provided on the battle of Cuito Canavale, including quotations from Ronnie Kasrils, a high-ranking former member of *Umkhonto we Sizwe*, the military wing of the ANC, and by the US Secretary of State for Africa, Chester Crocker. The collapse of the Soviet Union and fall of the Berlin Wall ensured, according to the textbook, that 'the ANC could no longer rely on Soviet support, and the NP could no longer pretend to be a bulwark against the spread of communism in Africa' (Pillay et al. 2013, 387). In the context of the rise of a new world order, in which the multilateral institutions of the World Bank, IMF and WTO play an important role in a new 'global apartheid', the textbook highlights the role of Greenpeace and the potential of the BRIC countries as 'emerging economies and different forms of capitalism' (Pillay et al., 2013, 404).

Conclusion

While previous studies have paid considerable attention to representations of the history of apartheid in South Africa, both in history textbooks of the apartheid period and in more recent material, less attention has been paid to 'international history' and the links between international, African and South African history. Ironically, to place the importance of South Africa's role in the Cold War in some context, in his recent world history of the Cold War, even Westad devotes only a few cursory paragraphs to South Africa in a work of 700 pages (Westad, 2017). This chapter has attempted to address this imbalance and focus on a hitherto-neglected area of the analysis of South African history textbooks. The anti-communist bias of earlier apartheid textbooks has been replaced by, it has been argued, a friendlier approach towards the Soviet Union, while the role of the USA has by contrast been over-simplified in so far as the spectrum of actions and campaigns to illustrate US domestic contestation over apartheid is arguably inadequately represented. In addition, the portrayals of Africa and Africans has changed. Although granted greater prominence than before, and despite being made much more central to the unfolding history of the time, Africa and Africans are contradictorily seen, on the one hand, as passive victims of the superpowers and, on the other, as fighters for freedom, imbued with agency and initiative.

Bibliography

List of Textbooks Cited

Bottaro, J., P. Visser and N. Worden. 2007. *In Search of History, Grade 12: Learner's Book.* Cape Town: Oxford University Press.

Fernandez, M., L. Wills, P. McMahon, S. Pienaar, Y. Seleti and M. Jacobs. 2013. *CAPS Focus History Learner's Book Grade 12.* Cape Town: Maskew Miller Longman.

Friedman, M., C. Kros, C. Mlambo, C. Saunders, Y. Seleti and M. Jacobs. 2007. *Focus on History: Looking into the Past, Grade 12.* Cape Town: Maskew Miller.

Pillay, G., L. Sikhakhane and N. West, eds. 2013. *New Generation History Learner's Book Grade 12: FET CAPS Series*. Durban: New Generation Publishers.

Curricula

South Africa, Department of Basic Education. 2011. *Curriculum and Assessment Policy Statement Grades 10-12 History*. Pretoria: Government Printing Works.

South Africa, Department of Basic Education. 2019. *Textbook Evaluation Report of the Ministerial Task Team: Evaluation of a Broad Sample of Existing Textbooks and Learning Materials: Towards Developing a Textbook Policy that Promotes Diversity*. Pretoria: Department of Basic Education.

Further References

Baines, G. and P. Vale, eds. 2008. *Beyond the Border War: New Perspectives on Southern Africa's Late-Cold War Conflicts*. Pretoria: UNISA Press.

Christophe, B. and L. Halder. 2018. 'Concepts of the Past: Socialism'. In *The Palgrave Handbook of Textbook Studies*, edited by E. Fuchs and A. Bock. Palgrave Macmillan.

Filatova, I. 2008. 'South Africa's Soviet Connection'. *History Compass* 6, no. 2: 389–403.

Filatova, I. and A. B. Davidson. 2013. *The Hidden Thread: Russia and South Africa in the Soviet Era*. Johannesburg: Jonathan Ball Publishers.

Grant, N. 2017. *Winning our Freedoms Together: African-Americans and Apartheid 1945-1960*. Chapel Hill: University of North Carolina Press.

Halliday, F. 1986. *The Making of the Second Cold War* (2nd ed.). London: Verso.

Halsall, T. and J. Wassermann. 2018. 'A Comparative Investigation into the Representation of Russia in Apartheid and Post-apartheid Era South African History Textbooks'. *Yesterday and Today* 19: 50–65.

Houston, G. 2008. 'International Solidarity: Introduction'. In *The Road to Democracy in South Africa*, edited by the South African Democracy Education Trust, 1–39. Pretoria: UNISA Press.

Kallaway, P. 2012. 'History in Senior Secondary School CAPS 2012 and beyond: A comment'. *Yesterday and Today* 7: 23–62.

Ndlovu, S. 2008. 'The ANC and the World'. In *The Road to Democracy*, edited by the South African Democracy Education Trust, 541–571. Vol. 3: *International Solidarity*. Pretoria: UNISA Press.

Schleicher, H.-G. 2008. 'The German Democratic Republic and the South African Liberation Struggle'. In *The Road to Democracy*, edited by the South African Democracy Education Trust. Vol. 3: *International Solidarity*. Pretoria: UNISA Press.

Shubin, V. 2008a. *The Hot "Cold War": The USSR in Southern Africa*. London: Pluto Press.

Shubin, V. 2008b. 'There is no Threat from the Eastern Bloc'. In *The Road to Democracy*, edited by the South African Democracy Education Trust, 985–1065. Vol. 3: *International Solidarity*. Pretoria: UNISA Press.

South African Democracy Education Trust (SADET). 2008. *The Road to Democracy in South Africa*. Vols 1–7. Pretoria: UNISA Press.

Wellmer, G. 2008. 'A History of the Anti-Apartheid Movement in the Federal Republic of Germany'. In *The Road to Democracy in South Africa, Part 1*, edited by the South African Democracy Education Trust. Vol. 3: *International Solidarity*. Pretoria: UNISA Press.

Westad, O. A. 2007. *The Global Cold War: Third World Interventions and the Making of Our Times*. Cambridge: Cambridge University Press.

Westad, O. A. 2017. *The Cold War: A World History*. London: Allen Lane.

Open Access This chapter is licensed under the terms of the Creative Commons Attribution 4.0 International License (http://creativecommons.org/licenses/by/4.0/), which permits use, sharing, adaptation, distribution and reproduction in any medium or format, as long as you give appropriate credit to the original author(s) and the source, provide a link to the Creative Commons licence and indicate if changes were made.

The images or other third party material in this chapter are included in the chapter's Creative Commons licence, unless indicated otherwise in a credit line to the material. If material is not included in the chapter's Creative Commons licence and your intended use is not permitted by statutory regulation or exceeds the permitted use, you will need to obtain permission directly from the copyright holder.

11

Dictatorship and the Cold War in Official Chilean History Textbooks

Teresa Oteíza and Claudia Castro

Introduction

The Cold War had a significant political and social impact in the Southern Cone between the 1950s and the 1980s. As has been documented by historians, during those years almost all Latin American countries underwent military dictatorships that drastically changed the social, economic and political development of each society and shaped their history until the present (Franco & Levín 2007; Loveman 2001; Lira 2013; Hiner 2009; Stern 2006). The military dictatorships committed severe human rights violations in the region, which were even strengthened with the establishment of a state terror that was orchestrated among several national repression and intelligence organisations with the collaboration of the United States' CIA. This repressive coalition, in which Chilean, Argentinian, Brazilian, Paraguayan and Uruguayan military dictatorships were involved, was called the 'Condor Operation' (Loveman 2001). As a consequence of these dictatorships in the region, Latin American countries share national

T. Oteíza (✉) • C. Castro
Pontificia Universidad Católica de Chile, Santiago, Chile
e-mail: moteizas@uc.cl

memories of a traumatic past of human rights violations. This recent past has been historicised and recontextualised in different ways in local history textbooks and with diverse levels of hegemony regarding the competing official and alternative memories that circulate in each society.[1]

In the particular case of Chile, a violent coup d'état that overthrew the socialist government of Salvador Allende in 1973 signalled the beginning of 17 years of dictatorship led by General Augusto Pinochet (1973–1990). For the Chilean historical process and for all Latin American countries, the history of the Cold War has been a history of economic and political dependence on 'the North'. As Harmer stresses in relation to Allende's socialist Popular Unit and to Latin America as a whole, the division of the world was not between East and West, as was the case for many European countries, but rather between the global North and the global South (Harmer 2011).

As the Cold War has permeated the recent Latin American past, we believe that it is relevant to study the way by which the memory of this period is negotiated in Chilean official history textbooks, particularly how those texts address the period of dictatorships in Latin America and the role that the United States played in this process. In Chile, the traumatic recent past of a coup d'état and the human rights violations committed by Augusto Pinochet's military dictatorship is still a space of competing collective memories. The memories that coexist in Chile and that give value and explanation to a painful past can be conceptualised as key emblematic memories, as Stern (2006) has proposed. In this manner, for different sectors of Chilean society the events that began on the 11th September are remembered as (*i*) a 'salvation' from a supposed Marxist dictatorship; (*ii*) as a 'rupture' of a democratic period; (*iii*) as a 'closed box' of a past that should be forgotten; and (*iv*) as a memory of 'persecution and awakening' (Stern 2006).

This chapter pays special attention to the historical actors, events and processes identified in the textbook discourse and how they are evaluated in the construction of a historical recount of a conflictive matter regarding the recent past of the region, a past that is still open to debate. Its does so via a discourse analysis anchored in a social, ideological and socio-semiotic perspective.

History textbooks as 'official semiotic products' offer a valuable space in which to understand how a society decides to remember and teach the national and international past to new generations. In Chile, the Ministry of Education holds a contest every year, in which the main textbook publishers compete to improve upon on the official history textbook to be distributed for free in more than 90 per cent of schools 'co-existing' in the Chilean educational system; that is, schools that are subsidised or partly subsidised by the government. Consequently, in the Chilean context, the history textbook is an important pedagogical resource that is widely used by teachers and students in classes (Manghi & Badilla 2015; Oteíza & Pinuer 2016; Oteíza et al. 2015, 2018; Oteíza 2018).

For this particular chapter we analyse the latest 11th-grade history textbook published, since this is the grade level in which, in accordance with the national history curriculum, the recent national past is taught. The two units of the national history curriculum considered in this analysis are: "The Period of Structural Transformations: Chile in the Sixties and Seventies" and "The Breakdown of Democracy and the Military Dictatorship" (MINEDUC 2015).[2] The next section presents a brief account of how Chilean history textbooks have evolved in relation to the construction and legitimation of the national past in the last two decades. The third section explores the discursive analytical framework in which this work is based, followed by an analysis and discussion of the Chilean official history textbook and how it negotiates memories of the Cold War in the fourth section. The last section addresses the official construction of social processes of remembering and teaching recent past in the Chilean context.

History textbooks in Chile: Between the Dynamics of Social Change and the Official Voice of the State

Official Chilean history textbooks constitute a privileged space in which social memories are constructed and negotiated (Oteíza & Achugar 2018). These are part of a social practice that is realised discursively, for the most part using verbal and visual semiotic resources. Chilean history textbooks have been characterised by a discourse of denunciation, commemoration and victimisation based on evidence primarily collected in the official reports promoted by post-dictatorial state policies regarding human rights violations committed during Pinochet's dictatorship (Oteíza 2006, 2014).

The educational reform in Chile (1999), during the period of democratic transition after Pinochet's dictatorship (1973–1990), had a significant impact on the transformation of the history curriculum in the country (Reyes et al. 2013; Rubio 2013). As Osandón (2013) and Oteíza (2006) point out, the change in the curriculum can be seen in official textbooks, not only with regard to the topics addressed in relation to recent national history, for example the sensitive topic of human rights violations, but also in the methodology. The latter promotes a more autonomous exploration by students, requiring them to work with a variety of primary and secondary sources. Before the main educational reform of 1999, the national history of Chile ended with the promulgation of a national junta in 1973. The coup d'état and the human rights violations committed by Augusto Pinochet's dictatorship were not included as historical content in the curriculum, thus remaining absent from the official history textbooks published before 2000.

In Chile, the textbook market is conditioned by a supply and demand monopolised by the Ministry of Education, the latter being the largest customer and the authority deciding printing policies and price. While no educational establishment is actually required by law to buy and use the textbooks that the Ministry approves and distributes, the fact that these are distributed free of charge to more than 90 per cent of the country's educational establishments fundamentally determines their use (Oteíza 2006).[3]

The history curriculum, as well as history textbooks, have been influenced by the dynamics of social change regarding recent memoires of human rights violations in Chile. The publications known as the 'Rettig Report', produced and promoted by the Chilean Government's National Commission of Truth and Reconciliation (1991) and the 'Valech Report' by the National Commission on Political Imprisonment and Torture (2004 and 2011) have had a significant impact on how Chilean history textbooks portray the dictatorship and human rights violations committed by organs of state repression (Oteíza 2014). Secondary level history textbooks published in 2012 and 2013, for example, explicitly state that the 'terror campaign' against leftist parties in the country was supported economically by the United States through the CIA. Additionally, after a strong dispute between left-wing and right-wing political actors, the term 'dictatorship' was accepted as a valid label for what had previously been called the 'military government' (Oteíza & Achugar 2018). The critical changes to social and political processes in Chile and their impact on the national history curriculum and thus official history textbooks are represented in the following table.[4]

Table 11.1 Historical, social and educational changes and their impact on History textbooks

Chilean Official History Textbooks

Official documents of the Ministry of Education of Chile

Year/process	1990	1991	before 1999	1999	2004, 2011	2012–2013	2013
Historical, social and educational changes	Return to a democratic government after 17 years of A. Pinochet's Dictatorship	Chilean National Truth and Reconciliation Commission/ Rettig Report	Textbooks published before the National Educational Reform	National Educational Reform	The National Commission on Torture and Political Prison/Valech Report	Mediated national debate regarding the labels: *regime*, *government* and *dictatorship*	History Curriculum Reform
Official history textbooks				History of Chile considers a unit of a "Military Regime or Government". **Inclusion of human rights violations**. Conciliatory historical narrative of the dictatorship and of the transition to democracy	Inclusion of human rights violations. Mention of the **systematic practice of torture** upon more than 30.000 Chilean people. Historical narrative signaled by a **victimization and denounce**.	Co-existent labels of *regime*, *government* and *dictatorship* in history textbooks	Unit: "**Military Dictatorship**"

History of Chile 'ends' with the establishment of a military Junta in 1973.

Sociosemiotic and ideological discourse analysis: valuing the historical experience

We conducted a discourse analysis of history textbooks taking into consideration the lexical and grammatical resources that authors use to negotiate interpersonal and ideational meanings. We paid special attention to the ways in which historical actors, events, processes and situations are constructed in the textbook analysed. As we have pointed out in previous work (Oteíza & Pinuer 2012), the discourse of history, as a social science that seeks to comprehend the complexity of human societies from a diachronic point of view, can be seen through the key domains of causality, temporo-spatial dimension and evidentiality.

In the analysis of history discourses, these dimensions are relevant to how individual and collective historical actors build historical events and processes in a certain time and space in the past. In the following diagram, therefore, we illustrate how the 'actoral axis' is combined with the 'processual axis' in this discourse.

Our analysis employs the APPRAISAL system, developed as part of the discourse-semantic level of Systemic Functional Linguistics theory (Martin & White 2005; Oteíza & Pinuer 2012) for the analysis of the historical participants, events and processes that history textbooks deploy to negotiate the memory of the Cold War in the Chilean and Latin American recent past.

The disputes over recent national memories are ideological battles. APPRAISAL is a suitable theoretical resource that helps us to understand the evaluative character of memories as selective processes of remembering and forgetting, by which a society constructs more or less hegemonic positionings regarding the recent national and regional past of traumatic dictatorships (Stern 2006; Lira 2013; Jelin 2002; Ricoeur 2010; Wertsch 2002).

The APPRAISAL system provides a comprehensive and descriptive systematisation of the linguistic resources authors can use to construct the value of social experience (Martin & White 2005). Consequently, this analysis contributes to our understanding of the patterns of interpersonal meanings that build, in this case, a historical experience as a text unfolds. These interpersonal negotiations of meaning work in a cumulative manner in a discourse creating determinate value positions between writers and readers.

The APPRAISAL system organises interpersonal meanings into three main semantic areas: ATTITUDE, GRADUATION and ENGAGEMENT (Martin & White 2005). The area of ATTITUDE deals with feelings considered as systems of meaning socially organised as emotions (*affect*), ethics or morality (*judgement*) and aesthetic values (*appreciation*). These evaluations of ATTITUDE can be built with a positive or negative charge, which can also be portrayed as inscribed (explicit) or evoked (implicit) instances in the discourse. The organisation of these types of evaluations with regard to the discourse entities appraised is shown in Table 11.2.

The region of meaning of *affect* considers the possibility of feelings that an *emoter* directs towards or expresses in reaction to some specific emotional trigger that can be present or past. Feelings can also involve intention, rather than reaction, in relation to a stimulus that is *irrealis* rather than *realis* (Oteíza 2017a). Thus, *affect* can be classified as in/security, dis/satisfaction or un/happiness, but also as dis/inclination as desire or fear, when the stimulus is *irrealis*, as in 'the triumph of the Cuban revolution was considered by the United States as a **threat** to their interests'.[5]

The semantic domain of *judgement* pertains to the institutionalisation of feelings in terms of proposals or norms about how people should or should not behave. According to Martin and White (2005) this area of meaning can be divided into social esteem, which comprises admiration and criticism regarding values of normality, capacity and tenacity; and of social sanction, which involves praise and condemnation regarding values of veracity and propriety. An instance of an evoked positive social esteem pertaining to the capacity of president Salvador Allende, for example, can be seen in: 'Salvador Allende's rise to power, ***leader*** of the Chilean left …'.[6]

Table 11.2 Attitudinal meanings in relation to entities appraised in the field of history

Discourse entity appraised	Meanings of ATTITUDE	
Historical actors	*judgement*	*affect*
Historical events, situations and processes	*appreciation*	

The evaluative space of GRADUATION refers to the fact that expressions of attitude can be intensified or weakened, and in doing so, can construct different levels of alignment with the value positions deployed in the text (Martin & White 2005). The area or subsystem of ENGAGEMENT is considered in the framework to explore the source of attitudes; that is, to identify whether the text is relying mainly on the author's voice, constructing a monoglossic orientation or a 'single voiced' text that presents facts and ideas as taken-for-granted, and thus closing down the dialogic space; or if the authorial voice actually recognises alternative positions creating an heteroglossic space regarding specific evaluations.

For the discourse analysis we follow the main categories of *affect* and *judgement* proposed by Martin and White (2005) to examine the different regions of ATTITUDE in the discourse. Nevertheless, we incorporate the *appreciation* analytical categories offered by Oteíza and Pinuer (2012) and Oteíza (2017a, b) to better understand how historical events, situations and processes are evaluated in the history textbook. The categories of *power, impact, integrity* and *conflict* allow us to explain in a more adequate manner how the specific ideational meanings, as shown in Figure 11.1 and constructed by the authors in the historical account, are

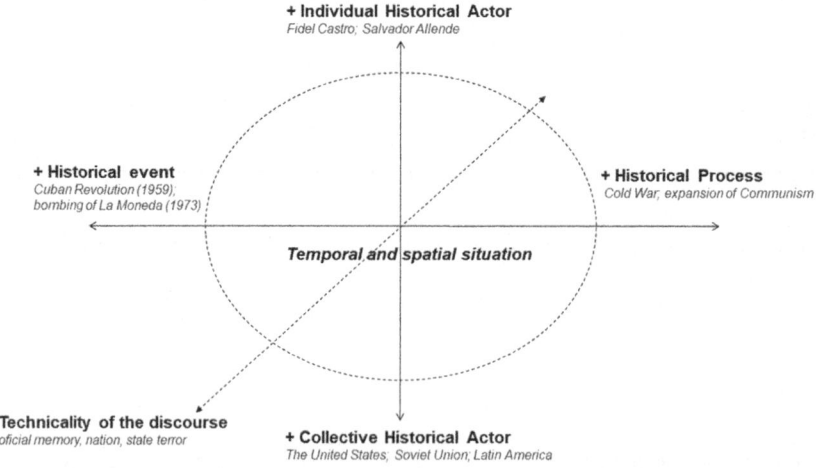

Fig. 11.1 Representation of actors, events, processes and situations in historical discourses

valued in the discourse. These four categories in combination and with different levels of negative or positive value polarity can build discourses of historical legitimation or delegitimation, as is briefly explained and illustrated by the following paragraphs.

The category of *conflict* deals with the manifestation of a social, political and/or economic tension that can be expressed with different grades of radicalism along a cline, such as in the inscribed and graduated negative evaluation of high conflict of the diplomatic relations between the military junta and the United States during Pinochet's dictatorship: 'Diplomatic relations became <u>especially</u> **tense** when the military junta reaffirmed its willingness to establish a long-term authoritarian regime'. The category of *power* is associated with the action and influence of powerful and dominant groups (Oteíza & Pinuer 2012; Oteíza 2017a, b). We can appreciate the realisation of this meaning as a high economic, military and political power enforced by the United States' intervention in Latin America, for example: 'In addition to the <u>enormous amount</u> of resources that this country assigned to operations of **sabotage** and ***political propaganda***, the dictatorships ***were promoted*** by military men trained in the US'.

Integrity refers to moral or ethical evaluations. An example of this category is the evoked positive evaluation of integrity of the historical event of Allende's election to the presidency: 'Salvador Allende's rise to power, leader of the Chilean left, ***through a democratic election…***"'. The last category of *impact* deals with the importance and social value that authors attribute to historical events, processes or situations in the discourse, such as the positive appreciation of impact regarding socialism evoked in: '<u>many</u> political organisations in the region saw socialism as ***a possibility to achieve economic growth and social development***'. These four categories of *appreciation* are shown in Figure 11.2:

We have briefly presented the framework of APPRAISAL as an analytical tool that allows us to explore how ideological positionings are constructed in a particular discursive practice through the identification of the entities appraised, of who or what is constructed in the discourse as a source of evaluation, and the type of evaluation: *judgement, affect, appreciation*. We consider evaluation as a set of values and beliefs that to a certain extent inform social practices, semiotically mediated. Many of these discursive practices circulate

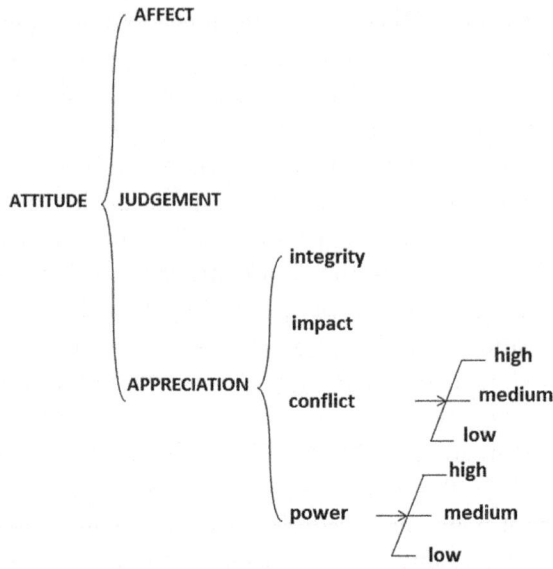

Fig. 11.2 System of APPRECIATON for analysing events, processes and situations (Oteíza and Pinuer 2012; Oteíza 2017a)

as naturalisations promoted by the interests of hegemonic and powerful groups. In this manner, 'ideologies constitute spaces of unequal distribution of semiotic resources of a community, as well as the reproduction of hegemonic and counter-hegemonic discourses' (Oteíza 2017b: 146).

In the next section we present a discursive analysis of two units of the 11th grade official history textbook published in Chile by the Ministry of Education in 2017, paying special attention to how the historical process of the Cold War is negotiated by authors in this pedagogical recontextualisation of the national and Latin American recent past.

From a Polarised Vision of East and West to an Inter-America polarisation

The selected fragments of the history textbooks analysed were part of the history units entitled: 'the period of structural transformations: Chile in the sixties and the seventies' and 'the breakdown of democracy and the military dictatorship'. The proposed general learning outcome stated in the Chilean curricula establishes the development of the two necessary skills for analysing and valuing different points of view regarding the recent national past: a) to critically analyse and compare different political views and historiographical interpretations of the past that led to the crisis of 1973 and the democratic breakdown, and b) to characterise the main features of the coup and the military dictatorship in Chile, including the systematic violation of human rights, the political violence, and the suppression of the rule of law (MINEDUC 2015:38).

The United States' longstanding relationship with Latin America as disrupted by the Cuban Revolution (1959) and the rise to power of left-wing Salvador Allende (1970)

The unit entitled 'the period of structural transformations', covers national Chilean history and how it is shaped in the local and global contexts between the 1950s and the 1980s.

The main text can be classified as a history genre in which participants, processes and events are organised in a chronological manner and in terms of a simple construction of causality. The principal participants included and evaluated with more prominence in this unit are the United States, Latin America, Cuba and world geopolitical blocs. The historical events and processes highlighted are the Cuban Revolution of 1959, the Cold War, and the propagation of communist and Marxist ideology in the region.

As mentioned above, the United States is clearly depicted as the main protagonist of this historical account. The 'country from the north' is the participant who thinks, desires, influences and worries about Latin America. The United States clearly represents here a powerful country that has both the power and the means to decide and act politically, economically and militarily across the region. It receives a positive appraisal with appreciation of great power throughout the unit. The Soviet Union is presented in a secondary role, siding with the Cuban Revolution and Fidel Castro, both representative of the threat or of the risk of the spread of Marxist ideology in the region. The Cuban Revolution plays an important role in the construction of the historical argument, as will be shown in the examples below. At the end of the unit, the United States is portrayed as partially responsible for the installation of the dictatorships in Latin America and for the brutal human rights violations that characterised these regimes.

Example 1:
In the context of the Cold War, the United States <u>intensified</u> the ***ties*** that <u>traditionally</u> **made** it **closer** to Latin America through the ***establishment of mechanisms of mutual cooperation, economic intervention and military support.*** (SM 2017: 147)

En el contexto de la Guerra Fría, Estados Unidos <u>intensificó</u> los ***vínculos*** que <u>tradicionalmente</u> lo **estrechaban** con América Latina, a través del ***establecimiento de mecanismos de cooperación mutua, intervención económica y apoyo militar.***

As *Example 1* shows, the relationship between the United States and Latin America is portrayed positively as countries that have collaborated with each other 'traditionally' and that have 'intensified' their ties in the context of the Cold War. Later in the text authors reinforce this idea of 'mutual' cooperation in which Latin America participates. However, this positive appraisal of judgment of capacity that is attributed to the United States from a monoglossic orientation renders the relationship between the two regions uneven, since it is the United States that has the power 'to intervene' economically in Latin America and give military support. Latin America as a historical participant in this narrative possesses less economic and military power and is on the receiving end of this 'support' from 'the country of the north'.

The text then emphasises how the liberal and right-wing government of Jorge Alessandri and Christian Democrat Eduardo Frei were part of this process; the close relationship with the United States underwent several important economic and social reforms. At the same time, the text states that the United States perceived the rise to power of socialist Salvador Allende, presented as part of this period of changes under the Cold War, as a threat by the United States, as illustrated in *Example 2*:

Example 2:
The rise to power of Salvador Allende, **leader** of the Chilean left, ***through a democratic election***, was interpreted by the United States as a **threat**. (SM 2017: 147)

La llegada al gobierno de Salvador Allende, ***líder*** de la izquierda chilena, ***mediante una elección democrática***, fue interpretada por Estados Unidos como una **amenaza**.

Interestingly enough, the fact that Allende was elected president of Chile has an evoked positive appraisal of integrity, 'through a democratic election', a fact not mentioned regarding the other two previously elected right-wing and centre presidents of the period, suggesting that democratic integrity is an implicit given to the two previously mentioned presidents. Allende, as 'leader of the Chilean left', is presented as an active participant evaluated with a positive judgment of political capacity. However, as a 'threat', Allende is evaluated with an inscribed negative appraisal of affect as fear by the United States, a participant portrayed by authors with the active role of being able to give opinions and to express concern in the discourse.

The Cold War is presented, as is often the case, as a polarisation in which 'global geopolitical blocs of support and rejection' sided with the United States and the Union of Soviet Socialist Republics. In this context, Latin America is portrayed as being influenced by the United States and by having a long-standing mutual relationship of cooperation. However, Salvador Allende is constructed as the source of a fear that compromises the social and political order in the region. Later in the text, the Cuban Revolution is evoked as a new economic and social opportunity for the development of the region (*Example 3*):

Example 3:
However, after the **triumph** of the Cuban revolution in 1959, many political organisations in the region saw socialism as ***an opportunity to achieve economic growth and social development***. (SM 2017: 150)

No obstante, tras el **triunfo** de la revolución cubana en 1959, muchas organizaciones políticas de la región vieron en el socialismo ***una posibilidad para lograr el crecimiento económico y el desarrollo social.***

All multilateral treaties between the United States and their allies in the region of Latin America[7] and, most of all, the economic influence of the United States over the region, were therefore in danger. The Cuban revolution implicated a new way of managing the economic and social growth that this 'Third World' needed in order to overcome poverty and its situation as underdeveloped countries. This idea is not stated outright in *Example 3* but rather implied with the use of a counter-expectative conjunction 'however', which signals a dialogic contraction.

The authors of the history unit also stress the 'mutual assistance' between the United States and Latin America. This relationship is presented with a positive evaluation of appreciation that is highly graduated by scope in time and space. It is also presented as a given situation in the region 'since the nineteenth century', and 'traditionally' by 'all' countries in Latin America that signed the Inter-American Treaty of Reciprocal Assistance and the Organization of American States (SM 2017, 150–151).

In the next section, the textbook authors address the Cuban revolution and its ideological positioning. Fidel Castro, as the leader of the 'insurrectional movement' and of the Cuban 'rebel army', is portrayed with positive evaluations of capacity in the discourse, and as a leader who took action to expropriate 'important companies, especially American ones'. This brief mention of Castro's political and economic action in Cuba is interrupted by the depiction of the political alliances in the region and the apprehension that these reforms caused in the United States, as shown in *Example 4*:

Example 4:
As a result of these measures and the progressive contact between Fidel Castro and the local Communist Party, relations between Cuba and the Soviet Union **become stronger**. On the other hand, the government of the United States, increasingly **concerned** about the course of the Cuban situation, considered **overthrowing** the newly installed regime. In December 1961, Fidel Castro declared his **adhesion** to Marxism, which ultimately defined the Cuban situation within the global context. (SM 2017: 151)

Como consecuencia de estas medidas y del progresivo contacto entre Fidel Castro y el Partido Comunista local, las relaciones entre Cuba y la Unión Soviética *se estrecharon*. Por contraparte, el gobierno de Estados Unidos, cada vez más **preocupado** por el rumbo de la situación cubana, consideró **derribar** al régimen recién instalado. En diciembre de 1961, Fidel Castro declaró su **adhesión** al marxismo, lo que terminó por definir la situación cubana dentro del contexto global.

As we perceive in *Example 4*, the text continues to portray the social and political power and influence exerted by the Cuban revolution in the region from a monoglossic authorial positioning, constructing a simple causality for the tightening of the relationship between the Soviet Union and Cuba ('as a result of these measures'). In *Example 5*, the authors change the monoglossic orientation to a heteroglossic one, introducing a negative evaluation and of appreciation giving voice to many parties and movements of the left regarding liberal democracy promoted by the north. Nevertheless, in addition to this positive appreciation of power and impact of the Cuban Revolution ('triumph'), the authors imply a negative appreciation of integrity towards these parties and movements, due to the risk that an 'armed way' represents to the rest of the region:

Example 5:
The **triumph** of the revolution in a territory <u>so close</u> to the United States and in a <u>regional context</u> of **profound** economic, social and political changes was **exemplary** for <u>many</u> parties and movements of the left, which declared their **aversion** to liberal democracy and leaned towards the ***armed way*** of access to power. (SM 2017: 151)

El **triunfo** de la revolución en un territorio <u>tan cercano</u> a Estados Unidos y en un <u>contexto regional</u> de **profundos** cambios económicos, sociales y políticos, resultó **ejemplar** para <u>muchos</u> partidos y movimientos de izquierda, los que declararon su **aversión** a la democracia liberal y se inclinaron por la ***vía armada*** de acceso al poder.

The Cuban Revolution is constructed as a 'threat' to what the United States 'desire' for the Latin American region. In *Example 5* the authors present the only instance in which the parties and movements of the left have a voice in the discourse, expressing their 'aversion' to the liberal democracy promoted by the United States with an inscribed appraisal of negative affect of unhappiness. As in previous instances in the discourse, the voice of the United States is the most prominent historical participant with the power to decide what is best for the region and, consequently, a participant 'thinking' and 'expressing its concern' in the following pages of the text. In sum, the primary historical processes in the region emphasised here stress that the Soviet Union has an ally in Latin America and that the United States considers this a 'threat to their interests', seeking to 'prevent the triumph' of socialism on the continent, as shown in the following *Example 6*:

Example 6:
The **triumph** of the Cuban revolution (1959) implied the establishment of the first allied government of the Soviet Union in America, which the United States considered a **threat** to their interests, promoting from that moment two strategies to **prevent the triumph** of socialism <u>on the rest of the continent</u>: a regional pact, the Alliance for Progress, and the establishment of the National Security Doctrine. (SM 2017: 152)

El **triunfo** de la revolución cubana (1959) implicó el establecimiento del primer gobierno aliado de la Unión Soviética en América, lo que Estados Unidos consideró una **amenaza** para sus intereses, impulsando a partir de ese momento, dos estrategias para **impedir el triunfo** del socialismo <u>en el resto del continente</u>: un pacto regional, la Alianza para el Progreso, y el establecimiento de la Doctrina de Seguridad Nacional.

The socialist and communist ideologies are evaluated with a high negative appreciation of political and social power throughout the discourse, but most of all with an inscribed and strong negative evaluation of affect- as fear that justifies the United States' military intervention in the region: 'with the aim of stopping the advance of communism in the context of the Cold War' and 'to move away the ghosts of communism".

Dictatorships in the Southern Cone: The Intervention of the United States and the Overthrow of democratic governments

The Unit entitled 'The Military Dictatorship' covers the process of 'breakdown of constitutional order' from the coup d'état in September 1973 to the return to democracy at the end of the 1980s. The processes of military dictatorship and the recovery of democracy in Chile are presented here locally as part of a series of dictatorships in Latin America, and globally as politically, economically and socially influenced by the United States. The main participants included and evaluated in the discourse are, therefore, the United States and the different administrations of the period, the dictatorial regimes in Latin America, the Chilean military junta and, to a lesser extent, the Chilean Intelligence Agency (DINA), and the groups that were opposed to the regime. The historical events and processes highlighted in the text are the rise of dictatorships in the Southern Cone, the violation of human rights, and the return to democracy. As in the previous unit, the United States is presented as an actor whose point of view is fundamental for understanding the historical development of Latin America. The feelings, opinions and interests of 'the country of the north' are central in this narrative.

At the beginning of the unit, the Latin American dictatorial regimes established in the second half of the 1960s and in the 1970s are characterised in a negative manner in terms of their lack of integrity. In addition, the discourse expresses the power these repressive regimes exerted over the populations of their countries and, primarily, over opposition groups, as shown in *Example 7*:

Example 7:
Most of these military regimes exhibited common characteristics, derived from their ascription to similar ideological trends, which sought to ***suppress*** reforms that would have led, according to them, to **internal chaos**, for which it was necessary to ***eliminate*** any kind of opposition. (SM 2017: 204)

La mayoría de estos regímenes militares presentaron características comunes, derivadas de su adscripción a similares corrientes ideológicas, que pretendían ***suprimir*** aquellas reformas que habrían llevado, según ellos, al **caos interno**, para lo cual era necesario ***eliminar*** cualquier tipo de oposición.

The discourse presents evoked appreciations about the negative integrity of the military regimes in Latin America, as well as their high power, presenting first their will to 'suppress' the reforms and then to 'eliminate' all forms of opposition. This negative evaluation is reinforced by quantification, extending that appraisal to 'most' of these regimes. On the other hand, the political and social situation of Latin American countries before the dictatorships is evaluated in an equally negative way, as conflictive. Such evaluation is sourced in the ideological standpoint of the regimes, according to which there was an 'internal chaos' provoked by an opposition that therefore had to be eliminated.

The characteristics shared by Latin American dictatorial regimes are later described using a technical lexis that informs about a series of historical processes, such as 'suppression of the Rule of Law', 'prohibition of political parties', 'use of censorship and political violence' and 'systematic human rights violations' (SM 2017: 204–205).

Despite the predominantly positive representation of the United States in these two historical units analysed, the role the US played in the advent of dictatorships in Latin America is also portrayed in a negative manner in terms of its integrity, as in the following example:

Example 8:
Most of these [dictatorships], in principle, were supported and, at times, economically sustained by the United States. In addition to the enormous amount of resources that this country assigned to operations of **sabotage** and ***political propaganda***, the dictatorships were ***promoted*** by military men trained in the U.S. Army School of the Americas, and by the introduction of the National Security Doctrine. (SM 2017: 204)

La mayoría de estas [dictaduras], en principio, fueron apoyadas y, en ocasiones, sustentadas económicamente por Estados Unidos. Además de la enorme cantidad de recursos que este país destinó a operaciones de **sabotaje** y ***propaganda política***, las dictaduras fueron ***propiciadas*** por militares formados en la Escuela de las Américas y por la introducción de la Doctrina de Seguridad Nacional.

The intervention of the United States is not only presented negatively by means of a judgment of impropriety carried out by the instances of 'sabotage' and 'political propaganda', but also highly reinforced, since this country assigned an 'enormous amount' of resources to supporting 'most of these' dictatorships. At the same time, the support the Unites States gives to the dictatorships expresses the power this country has to intervene in the political destinies of Latin American countries.

In the Chilean case, as we have seen, the US's intervention is presented as a consequence of the constant concerns and threats perceived by the latter, first regarding the Cuban revolution and then in relation to Salvador Allende's rise to power as the first democratically elected socialist government:

11 Dictatorship and the Cold War in Official Chilean History... 239

Example 9:
Avoiding the emergence in Latin America of 'another Cuba' led the United States to ***intervene*** in Chile through its intelligence agencies. At least since 1963 **it tried** ***to impede*** the election of Allende, an issue that worsened from 1970 until the military coup in 1973. (SM 2017: 205)
Evitar que surgiera en Latinoamérica "otra Cuba" llevó a Estados Unidos a ***intervenir*** en Chile a través de sus organismos de inteligencia. Al menos desde 1963 **intentaba** ***evitar*** la elección de Allende, cuestión que se agudizó desde 1970 hasta el golpe militar en 1973.

In *Example 9*, the actions taken by the United States 'to intervene' and 'to impede' express a negative evaluation of the integrity of this country. The volition of the United States is expressed by means of the verb 'tried', which is intensified as an issue that 'worsened' over time.

As the insecurity felt by the United States is presented as the main motive for its intervention, this historical account assumes a heteroglossic discursive orientation, presenting the US's perspective on the political situation of Latin America. In this vision, the Allende government is directly linked with the Cuban Revolution, which epitomises the presence of socialism in the region, read as a menace by the United States. The USSR does not appear as a participant in this historical interpretation, nor are the affects or opinions of the Chilean and Cuban governments presented (e.g. concerns about the US intervention or hopes regarding the socialist project).

The construction of the United States as the main agent in this interpretation of the Cold War period, as well as its representation as the sole *emoter* of the affections expressed ('concern', 'threat') can be particularly observed when the international relations of the Chilean regime are addressed in the text. In this regard, the affects attributed to the United States and the evaluations of judgements applied to it vary according to the specific US government in power. First, relationships are presented as positive but not entirely satisfactory for the United States during Nixon's administration, that received the military coup in Chile 'with moderate approval'. The relations then appear as conflictive due to the assassination of former chancellor Orlando Letelier and his secretary Ronni Moitt while on US territory (1976). The distance between the governments is constructed as intensified in the discourse during the Kennedy era and its change in human rights policy, as *Example 10* shows:

Example 10:
Diplomatic relations became <u>especially</u> **tense** when the military Junta reaffirmed **its willingness to establish** <u>a long-term</u> **authoritarian regime.** One of the <u>most</u> **critical** points was the **murder** in Washington of former chancellor Orlando Letelier and his secretary Ronni Moitt in September 1976, in which DINA agents *were involved*. This was a <u>clear</u> **violation** of US's security (SM 2017: 229).

Las relaciones diplomáticas se volvieron <u>especialmente</u> **tensas** cuando la junta militar reafirmó **su voluntad de establecer** un **régimen autoritario** <u>de largo plazo</u>. Uno de los puntos <u>más</u> **críticos** fue el **asesinato** en Washington del ex canciller Orlando Letelier y su secretaria Ronni Moitt en septiembre de 1976, en el que *estuvieron involucrados* agentes de la DINA, y que constituyó una <u>clara</u> **violación** a la seguridad estadounidense.

The worsening of relations is expressed in the discourse by means of resources of appreciation that express a high conflict level, reinforced by intensification: 'especially tense', 'one of the most critical points'. The historical event that explains this situation (the assassination of Orlando Letelier and Ronni Moitt) is presented as 'a clear violation of US security', which evokes a negative affect of insecurity whose *emoter* is, as in earlier instances in the discourse, the United States. This 'violation' (sharpened by the presence of the adjective 'clear'), also inscribes a negative evaluation about the integrity of the Chilean regime, represented by 'the military Junta' as a historical actor. The same negative evaluation is manifested in 'authoritarian regime', 'murder' and *'were involved'*, instances in which agents of DINA[8] are also evaluated. As a result, a contrast is presented between the United States and the Chilean regime in which the latter is evaluated negatively. Such contrast is even more evident when the text presents the Jimmy Carter government's policy with regard to human rights violations, as it is shown in *Example 11*:

Example 11:
During the government of Democrat Jimmy Carter, an international policy was applied that **privileged the respect of Human Rights** […] While diplomatic relations **improved** during Ronald Reagan administra-

tion, the **pressures** to initiate the transition to democracy continued, especially after the **crisis** of 1982 and the **social outbreak** that it provoked, which caused the State Department *to opt* for supporting the democratic opposition, extending that policy to the entire Southern Cone. (SM 2017: 229)

Bajo la presidencia del demócrata Jimmy Carter se aplicó una política internacional que **privilegió el respeto a los Derechos Humanos** […] Si bien las relaciones diplomáticas **mejoraron** con el gobierno de Ronald Reagan, las **presiones** para iniciar la transición hacia la democracia continuaron, especialmente a partir de la **crisis** de 1982 y el **estallido social** que provocó, lo que hizo que el Departamento de Estado *apostara* por apoyar a la oposición democrática, política que se extendió a todo el Cono Sur.

The international policy of the United States is presented through the measures taken by the Carter administration, in turn interpreted as a continuation of the Kennedy Amendment. This allows for the construction of a positive evaluation of the United States by means of an inscribed judgement regarding its integrity: 'privileged the respect of Human Rights'.

A contrast is then established between the relations with the Chilean regime before and after the Carter administration (manifested in the adversative conjunction 'while'). The United States began to put pressure on the Chilean regime and, over time, decided to support the democratic opposition. These instances inscribe a positive judgement on the capacity of the United States to intervene ('pressures'), as well as an affect of inclination ('opted') that expresses the will of this country to take measures regarding the politics of Chile. Such a will is not only a desire but an actual capability to decide the political fates of Latin American countries, with regard to both the rise and fall of democratic governments and dictatorial regimes. The fact that the US intervention towards the recovery of democracy is explained based on the complex social situation in Chile ('crisis') and the 'social outbreak' that this caused, contributes to the construction of a positive depicture of the international policy of the United States in the region.

The main evaluative prosodies of the analysis are presented in the following Figures:

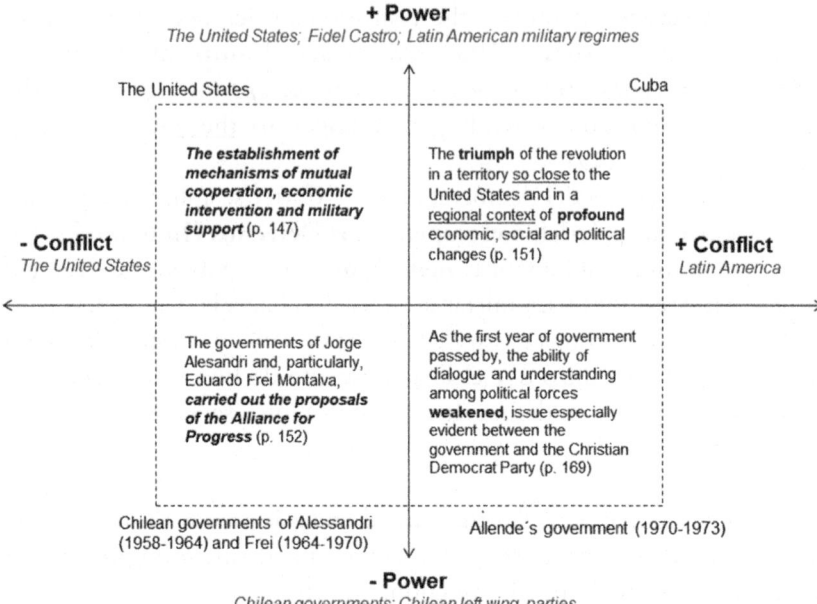

Fig. 11.3 Evaluative prosody of power and conflict of main historical entities

Historical event or process	Beginning of Cold War	Cuban Revolution	Allende's arrival to power	Coup d'état	Military dictatorship	Return to democracy
Time	1945	1959	1970	1973	1973-1989	1989
Affects of the United States	"The country of the North **tried to** reaffirm its incidence in the politics and economics of the region" (p. 150)	"The **triumph** of the Cuban revolution (...) which the United States considered a **threat** to their interests" (p. 152)	"The arrival to the government of Salvador Allende (...) was interpreted by the United States as a **threat** (147)		The United States (...) was **ambivalent** as it condemn the political actions of military men, but **praised** the government's economic management and results (p. 229)	
Actions of the United States	"mechanisms of **mutual cooperation, economic intervention and military support**" (p. 147)	"considering to **overthrowing** the newly installed regime" (p. 151)	"**tried to impede** the election of Allende, and issue that worsened from 1970 until the military coup in 1973" (p. 205)		"the State Department **to opt** for supporting the democratic opposition" (p. 229)	

Fig. 11.4 Evaluative prosody of fear from a temporal perspective

Final Remarks

History textbooks and their negotiation in the classroom play a fundamental role in the process of constructing social memories. In history textbooks authors have a tendency to portray dominant narratives that

11 Dictatorship and the Cold War in Official Chilean History... 243

express different ideological positions about the past. This is particularly evident in the reconstruction of recent national pasts, in which different contesting memories coexist. The historical period known as the Cold War has thus had an immense impact on the memory cultures of the countries involved, according to their position in the struggle and their political and social particularities.

This chapter has explored how the memory of the Cold War is currently negotiated in official Chilean history textbooks. We carried out a discourse analysis with the purpose of identifying how and which historical actors, events and processes are included and evaluated in the text. In the case of Latin America, these memories have been shaped by its geopolitical situation as a region traditionally influenced by the United States and by the series of dictatorships and human rights violations that most Latin American countries underwent in the 1970s and 1980s.

As demonstrated in the analysis, the Cold War in Latin America was experienced as a struggle between North and South rather than East and West. In the historical account presented by the history textbook analysed, the longstanding relations of cooperation and support between Latin America and the United States were disrupted by the Cuban Revolution and subsequently the election of socialist Salvador Allende in Chile, both interpreted by 'the country of the north' as a threat as they instantiated Marxist ideology in the region.

The historical construction throughout the discourse of a negative appraisal of affect as fear, provoked by the presence of Marxism, allows authors to explain and justify the measures the United States imposed on Latin America: the actions taken to undermine the Cuban regime, the attempts to prevent Allende's election, the political, economic and military support given to right-wing dictatorships across the continent, and finally the steps taken to return to democracy. At the same time, the United States is imbued with a positive appraisal of integrity, since its actions sought to maintain the security and stability of the region.

While in this historical -recount authors assign an agentive and prominent role to the United States, other historical actors are less represented in the discourse. The Soviet Union hardly appears in the text; and when it does, its inclusion is always contingent to its relationship with the Cuban Revolution as the primary counterpart of the United States in the ideological dispute over the Southern Cone. Fidel Castro plays a more active role in the narrative; however, his actions and the process of the Cuban Revolution are presented in the context of a highly conflictive situation and as a result of the poverty-stricken conditions in which most of the Cuban population lived. In the Chilean case, there are few mentions of actors such as right-wing parties, which in fact played a key role in establishing and supporting the military dictatorship. The opinions, feelings or visions of left-wing groups and parties are given even less consideration in the text.

In sum, with the discourse analysis of the actors, events and processes presented in this historical account, it is possible to appreciate how the memory of the Cold War in Latin America is constructed as a situation of political, economic and social dependency on the United States, with Chile as part of this extended process. This historical narrative of fear and conflict contributes to an interpretation of the recent Chilean traumatic past in which the dictatorship is mainly presented as the result of this dependency, blurring or minimising the role other actors played in the process. This historical positioning of an official textbook reflects a series of discussions and debates in which the Chilean society has participated over the last decades regarding the search for causes, responsibilities and explanations. The study of history textbooks, as official semiotic products that play a key role in the negotiation of memories in Chilean schools, helps us to comprehend those social debates, and in doing so identify which memories have become 'encapsulated' meanings and which memories are still open to debate in Chile and in other Latin American countries that have experienced a violent past.

Notes

1. This chapter presents findings from research grant FONDECYT 1170331 (National Funds for Science and Technology Development, Chile).
2. For studies related to history class interactions regarding the recent national pasts of dictatorships and the transmission of social and analytical

memories to new generations in the Latin American context see Achugar (2016) for the Uruguayan context, and Oteíza et al. (2015 and 2018) for the Chilean context.
3. Publishers dominating the production of school textbooks in Chile over the last decade are Santillana, Zig-Zag, SM and MN.
4. Information based on previous research on Chilean History Textbooks (Oteíza 2006, 2014).
5. Notation for the examples: **Words in bold** signal inscribed or explicit appraisals; ***words in bold and italics*** for evoked or implicit appraisals; <u>words underlined</u> signal graduation of the explicit or implicit appraisals.
6. All translations from Spanish by the author.
7. Alliance for Progress, Doctrine of National Security, Inter-American Treaty of Reciprocal Assistance (TIAR), Organization of American States (OEA).
8. DINA was the intelligence agency operating during the first four years of the Chilean dictatorship.

Bibliography

Textbook Cited

Quintana, S., S. Castillo, N. Pérez, C. Moyano and L. Thielemann. 2015. *Historia, Geografía y Ciencias Sociales.* Ministerio de Educación, Gobierno de Chile. Santiago: SM Editores.

Further References

Achugar, M. 2016. *Discursive Processes of Intergenerational Transmission of Recent History*. New York: Palgrave Macmillan.
Franco, M. and F. Levín, eds. 2007. *Historia reciente. Perspectivas y desafíos para un campo en construcción.* Buenos Aires and Barcelona: Paidós.
Harmer, T. 2011. *Allende's Chile and the Inter-American Cold War.* Chapel Hill: The University of North Carolina Press.
Hiner, H. 2009. 'Voces soterradas, violencias ignoradas. Discurso, violencia política y género en los Informes Rettig y Valech'. *Latin American Research Review* 44, no. 3: 50–74.
Jelin, E. 2002. *Los trabajos de la memoria.* Madrid: Siglo Veintiuno de España Editores, S.A.

Lira, E. 2013. Algunas reflexiones a Propósito de los 40 años del Golpe Militar en Chile y las Condiciones de la Reconciliación Política. *Psykhe* 22, no. 2: 5–18.

Loveman, B. 2001. *Chile. The Legacy of Hispanic Capitalism*. New York: Oxford University Press. Third edition.

Manghi, D. and C. Badilla. 2015. Modos Semióticos en el Discurso Pedagógico de Historia: Potencial Semiótico Para la Mediación en el Aula Escolar. *Íkala, Revista de Lenguaje y Cultura* 20, no. 2: 157–172.

Martin, J. R. and P. White. 2005. *The Language of Evaluation: Appraisal in English*. New York: Palgrave Macmillan.

Ministerio de Educación, Chile, MINEDUC. 2015. *Programa de Estudio. Historia, Geografía y Ciencias Sociales. Tercer año medio*. Retrieved from: www.curriculumenlineamineduc.cl/605/articles-30013_recurso_30_2.pdf

Oteíza, T. 2017a. 'The Appraisal Framework and Discourse Analysis'. In *The Routledge Handbook of Systemic Functional Linguistics*, edited by T. Bartlett and G. O'Grady, 457–472. London/New York: Routledge.

Oteíza, T. 2017b. Educación pública en Chile y practicas de la memoria: análisis social-ideológico del discurso e interacción en clases de historia. *Cadernos de Linguagem e Sociedade* 3: 144–174.

Oteíza, T. 2014. Intertextualidad en la recontextualización pedagógica del pasado Reciente chileno. *Discurso & Sociedad* 8, no. 1: 109–136.

Oteíza, T. 2006. *El discurso pedagógico de la historia. Un análisis lingüístico sobre la construcción ideológica de la historia de Chile (1970–2001)*. Santiago, Chile: Frasis Editores.

Oteíza, T. 2018. 'Prácticas de la memoria en clases de historia: construcción de la evidencia multimodal e intertextual del pasado reciente chileno'. *Discurso & Sociedad* 12, no. 1: 112–160.

Oteíza, T. and C. Pinuer. 2016. 'Des/legitimación de las memorias históricas: Valoración en discursos pedagógicos intermodales de enseñanza básica chilena'. *Revista signos* 49, no. 92: 377–402.

Oteíza, T, and M. Achugar. 2018. 'History Textbooks and the Construction of Dictatorship'. In *Palgrave Handbook of Textbook Studies*, edited by Eckhardt Fuchs and Annekatrin Bock, 305–318. New York: Palgrave.

Oteíza, T., R. Henríquez and V. Canelo. 2018. 'Language Resources to Negotiate Historical Thinking in History Classroom Interactions'. *Linguistics & Education* 47:1–15.

Oteíza, T., R. Henríquez and C. Pinuer. 2015. 'History Class Interactions and the Transmission of Recent Chilean Memory of Human Rights Violations'. *Journal of Educational Media, Memory, and Society* 7, no. 2: 44–67.

Oteíza, T. and C. Pinuer. 2012. 'Prosodia valorativa: construcción de eventos y procesos en el discurso de la historia'. *Discurso & Sociedad* 6, no. 2: 418–446.

Osandón, L. 2013. 'La enseñanza de la historia en la sociedad del conocimiento'. In *Enseñanza de la historia y memoria colectiva*, edited by M. Carretero, A. Rosa and M. F. González. 2nd ed., 323–346. Buenos Aires and Barcelona: Paidós.

Reyes, M. J., J. Muñoz and F. Vázquez. 2013. 'Políticas de memoria desde los discursos cotidianos: la despolitización del pasado reciente en el Chile actual'. *Psykhe* 22, no. 2: 161–173.

Ricoeur, P. 2010. *La memoria, la historia, el olvido*. Buenos Aires: Fondo de Cultura Económica.

Rubio, G. 2013. *Memoria, política y pedagogía. Los caminos hacia la enseñanza del pasado reciente en Chile*. Santiago: LOM; UMCE.

Stern, S. 2006. *Remembering Pinochet's Chile. On the Eve of London 1998*. Durkam & London: Duke University Press.

Wertsch, J. 2002. *Voices of Collective Remembering*. Cambridge: Cambridge University Press.

Open Access This chapter is licensed under the terms of the Creative Commons Attribution 4.0 International License (http://creativecommons.org/licenses/by/4.0/), which permits use, sharing, adaptation, distribution and reproduction in any medium or format, as long as you give appropriate credit to the original author(s) and the source, provide a link to the Creative Commons licence and indicate if changes were made.

The images or other third party material in this chapter are included in the chapter's Creative Commons licence, unless indicated otherwise in a credit line to the material. If material is not included in the chapter's Creative Commons licence and your intended use is not permitted by statutory regulation or exceeds the permitted use, you will need to obtain permission directly from the copyright holder.

Part II

Teachers' Memories

Part II

12

Teachers' Memories and the Cold War: Introduction to Part II

Robert Thorp and Barbara Christophe

The texts in this section of the volume address the complex and interesting question of how history teachers' personal memories and experiences of the past interact with their perceptions of historical events and a broader historical culture. Generally speaking, there are three different elements at play here that alone and combined provide a rich and challenging field for research into memory practices and history education.

History itself is a vague notion with various connotations. Academic history, often regarded as the gold standard in history education, is commonly separated from the past and memory through its focus on critical

---

R. Thorp (✉)
University of Stockholm, Stockholm, Sweden

The University of Newcastle, Newcastle, NSW, Australia
e-mail: robert.thorp@edu.su.se; robert.thorp@newcastle.edu.au

B. Christophe
Georg Eckert Institute for International Textbook Research,
Member of the Leibniz Association, Brunswick, Germany
e-mail: christophe@gei.de

methodological inquiry (Lévesque 2008; Parkes 2011; Wilschut 2012; Wineburg 2001). In this sense, academic history presupposes distance towards the past since it asks us to disregard what we cannot ground in reliable sources from it; history is regarded as the reconstruction of past events. Questions of truth, methodology and reliability become central here. Still, history also plays a central and fundamental role in the everyday perceptions we have of ourselves, of our communities and of the world at large. Accordingly, questions of identity and worldview become pivotal. It is thus not only methodological rigor and academic procedure, but also cultural aspects that heavily affect how we approach the past and history itself, as the three texts in this section will show.

History, academic and public alike, can thus be argued to share one crucial feature with memory. Both are culturally contingent, both cater to who we are and to what we perceive as meaningful at a very basic level. In this sense, all of us, including academic historians and professionally trained history teachers, can be seen as performing memory practices; that is, culturally informed ways of remembering, perceiving and making sense of the past and of history. This means that we never encounter or approach history from a neutral point of view and that history and our perceptions thereof are always contextually contingent.

With this view, you could argue that a kind of cultural self-awareness becomes central to how we approach and make sense of history, rather than whether we apply a critical methodology to the sources from the past that we have at hand. However, and this is rather crucial, much of what we know about history may be implicit and more or less taken for granted and therefore difficult to scrutinize critically, an aspect highlighted by the notion of memory practices. In this sense, history could be perceived as entangled between serious academic study, personal memories, and broader cultural and ideological aspects of the past (Thorp 2016).

If we take these aspects into account it can be argued that history education becomes a rather complex enterprise. History teachers are individuals, each with a personal relationship with history, who at the same time have been trained to approach this history with distance and scrutiny. Furthermore, history teachers are expected to comply with curricular demands and to further what could be called ideological aims whenever

12 Teachers' Memories and the Cold War: Introduction to Part II 253

they carry out their teaching. This can prove to be a rather challenging task as teachers have to navigate between what may be conflicting concerns in their profession. In addition, history carries a normative load through which we position ourselves ideologically, which may prove to be a further challenge when teaching (Persson 2017; Persson and Thorp 2017). In line with new trends in memory research, recent work in history education has highlighted these entanglements. Studies have shown how cultural contingencies affect history education and feed into how teachers and students perceive history at a very basic level (Boutonnet 2013; Persson 2017; Persson and Thorp 2017; Porat 2004; Thorp 2016; Wineburg, Mosborg, Porat and Duncan 2007; Zanazanian 2012). The three texts in this section should be regarded as a further exploration of this field.

Three Case Studies

Barbara Christophe's contribution to this section focuses on how teachers respond to ambivalence as a characteristic feature of postmodern memory cultures, the traces of which we can even find in current history textbooks. Providing a microanalysis of a textbook quotation on the origin of the Cold War from a German textbook, she shows how ambivalence is created by blending elements from rival traditions of explaining the conflict. Comparing how teachers from Germany and Switzerland read and assess this ambivalent and therefore rather typical quotation she arrives at three conclusions. First of all, teachers not only understand the same lines rather differently; they also judge them from different positions. Whereas Swiss teachers argue mostly in line with the traditionalist concept of a morally superior USA and a dictatorial Soviet Union, German teachers are much more divided among themselves, with some adhering to revisionist, others to traditionalist interpretations. Furthermore, especially among German teachers leaning towards revisionist positions, we find clear differences between those trained in former East Germany and those trained on the west side of the Wall. While West German teachers tend to express moral criticism of the USA, their East German counterparts criticise moralising views on history and normalise Soviet expansionism.

Finally, every teacher perceives his or her own interpretation of the textbook account to be the only legitimate one, thus contributing to what Christophe calls the 'illusion of hegemony', the assertion that there is one legitimate way of explaining the Cold War. Discussing her empirical findings in the light of competing theoretical considerations about the social function of ambivalence, Christophe argues that a productive engagement with ambivalence as discussed in memory studies is hampered by this illusion of hegemony.

Eva Fischer's text further explores the complex interplay and entanglement between teachers' personal experiences and professional role and focuses on how a teacher from the former GDR deals with textbook narrations about the Cold War. Guided by the question as to how people with twofold horizons of experience perceive current discourses on memory culture and how they position themselves towards those discourses, Fischer explicitly focuses on a person who, born in 1956, is old enough to have worked in the GDR and young enough to have continued her profession in reunited Germany. With recourse to methodological instruments developed by James Wertsch, Fischer analyses the stances taken by the teacher in three differently structured situational contexts: during a biographical narrative interview, a guided interview, and two video-recorded history lessons. She identifies four recurring narrative patterns mobilised by the teacher in order to build a bridge between the old narratives she grew up with in the GDR and the new narratives she feels she should use in her teaching today. The teacher (i) constructs parallels between family-related and national experiences, (ii) describes members of her family, despite their closeness to the GDR regime, as victims of national separation, (iii) narrates encounters between East and West as stories of reconciliation, and (iv) describes the West as slowly catching up with a morally superior East. The tensions and contradictions between these four narrative patterns are managed by a narrative and argumentative style which creates ambivalence and avoids the assignment of responsibility for certain actions. Fischer concludes that this teacher, who tries to narrate the story of her life in the GDR in accordance with what she perceives to be the dominant Western narrative as a sad story of separation and victimisation, enacts a kind of tacit resistance to the same Western narrative of the Cold War in class by pointing, for example, to

12 Teachers' Memories and the Cold War: Introduction to Part II 255

the moral superiority the political East enjoyed – in her eyes – over the political West.

Nadine Ritzer's study of how the broader cultural understanding of two key events of the Cold War, the Prague spring of 1968 and the Vietnam War, has evolved in Switzerland relies upon contemporary teaching journals of the period, older and modern history textbooks, and interviews with teachers. She thus does two things at the same time: She examines the subject from a position of present-day memory politics and she employs a diachronic perspective, enabling her to study discursive shifts. Ritzer's study arrives at a number of interesting results. She demonstrates that Swiss political neutrality has always leaned ideologically towards the West and that, despite several approaches showing signs of differentiation, a fundamental anti-communist consensus continues to ensure that bipolar frames of interpretation dominate textbooks. She shows that the textbooks studied do not delve deeper into the transnational significance of the year 1968, despite the fact that even contemporary witnesses point out that neither the Prague Spring nor the Vietnam War could be solely explained in terms of East-West opposition. Interestingly, the study reveals that, although the same books are generally critical of the role of the USA in the war, most of them implicitly legitimize atrocities such as the My Lai Massacre by explaining them with reference to the domino effect or the guerrilla tactics of the Vietcong. Ritzer also illustrates how the Vietnam War is regularly used in Swiss textbooks as an example of a proxy war between capitalism and communism, whilst omitting the North-South themes accentuated by recent research. Finally she elucidates how teachers regularly deviate from the textbooks' interpretation, for instance by categorising the Vietnam War as a 'third-world problem'.

Concluding Comments

Taken together, the three contributions in this section stress the importance of broader cultural, societal and situational aspects as key to understanding the complexities and challenges that go along with history education as one field where we can observe the unfolding of memory practices. The Cold War topic is shown to be heavily entangled between individuals' memories, ideological concerns, personal preferences, and broader social concerns. At the same time, the three authors render visible that culturally shared narratives as conveyed in textbooks, for instance, determine memory practices of individuals to different extents. As we have seen, teachers can chose to reproduce, to reject or to appropriate them with creativity. Furthermore, their choices can vary in differently structured situations.

References

Boutonnet, V. 2013. *Les ressources didactiques: typologie d'usages en lien avec la méthode historique et l'intervention éducative d'enseignants d'histoire au secondaire*. Montréal: Université de Montréal.

Lévesque, S. 2008. *Thinking Historically: Educating Students for the Twenty-first Century*. Toronto: Buffalo.

Parkes, R. J. 2011. *Interrupting History: Rethinking History Curriculum after 'The End of History'*. New York: Peter Lang Publishing.

Persson, A. 2017. *Lärartillvaro och historieundervisning: innebörder av ett nytt uppdrag i de mätbara resultatens tid*. Umeå: Umeå universitet.

Persson, A. and R. Thorp. 2017. 'Historieundervisningens existentialiserande potential'. *Nordidactica: Journal of Humanities and Social Science Education* 2: 59–74.

Porat, D. A. 2004. 'It's Not Written Here, but This is What Happened: Students' Cultural Comprehension of Textbook Narratives on the Israeli-Arab Conflict'. *American Educational Research Journal* 41, no. 4: 963–996.

Thorp, R. 2016. *Uses of History in History Education*. Umeå: Umeå universitet.

Wilschut, A. 2012. *Images of Time: The Role of an Historical Consciousness of Time in Learning History*. Charlotte, NC: Information Age Pub.

Wineburg, S. 2001. *Historical Thinking and other Unnatural Acts: Charting the Future of Teaching the Past*. Philadelphia: Temple University Press.

Wineburg, S., S. Mosborg, D. Porat and A. Duncan. 2007. 'Common Belief and the Cultural Curriculum: An Intergenerational Study of Historical Consciousness'. *American Educational Research Journal* 44, no. 1: 40–76 https://doi.org/10.3102/0002831206298677.

Zanazanian, P. 2012. 'Historical Consciousness and the Structuring of Group Boundaries: A Look at Two Francophone School History Teachers Regarding Quebec's Anglophone Minority'. *Curriculum Inquiry* 42, no. 2: 215–239.

Open Access This chapter is licensed under the terms of the Creative Commons Attribution 4.0 International License (http://creativecommons.org/licenses/by/4.0/), which permits use, sharing, adaptation, distribution and reproduction in any medium or format, as long as you give appropriate credit to the original author(s) and the source, provide a link to the Creative Commons licence and indicate if changes were made.

The images or other third party material in this chapter are included in the chapter's Creative Commons licence, unless indicated otherwise in a credit line to the material. If material is not included in the chapter's Creative Commons licence and your intended use is not permitted by statutory regulation or exceeds the permitted use, you will need to obtain permission directly from the copyright holder.

13

Ambivalence and the Illusion of Hegemony

Remembering the Cold War in Germany and Switzerland

Barbara Christophe

Umberto Eco once wrote, 'A text yearns for someone to help it function' (1998, 64). To him, texts are cloths woven from signs and gaps between signs. They call on us as readers to fill in these gaps. At the same time, they provide us with all of the clues we need in order to perform this task. Metaphorically speaking, Eco sees a text as a kind of roadmap showing us where, in the maze-like library of our cultural knowledge, we find the elements implied but not explicitly mentioned in the textual structure we are trying to make sense of. But what happens if these assumptions do not work? How do we, as readers, perform our guesswork when confronted with a text that gives us contradictory clues? How do we deal with ambivalent accounts?

According to insight from memory research, in the plural and fragmented societies of our time we are increasingly faced with ambivalent representations of the past (Ryan 2011). Taking this observation as a

---

B. Christophe (✉)
Georg Eckert Institute for International Textbook Research,
Member of the Leibniz Association, Brunswick, Germany
e-mail: christophe@gei.de

© The Author(s) 2019
B. Christophe et al. (eds.), *The Cold War in the Classroom*, Palgrave Studies in Educational Media, https://doi.org/10.1007/978-3-030-11999-7_13

starting point, I will explore empirically how people coming from different memory cultures – and thus presumably equipped with different cultural knowledge – engage with ambivalent historical narratives. The goal is to provide solid ground for a theoretical reflection on the functions that ambivalent representations of the past can assume. Answers given so far oscillate between the claim that ambivalence helps to stabilise hegemonic narratives by avoiding open conflict (Beattie 2008) and the argument that it may support the emergence of spaces for more complex perspectives (Sturken 1997). Positioning myself somewhere between these poles, I will argue that ambivalent accounts invite readers to produce rather diverse readings, but at the same time they create the illusion of hegemony, encouraging the assumption that there is only one privileged reading.

This argument is based on insights gained from interviews with history teachers from Germany and Switzerland, who were asked to reflect on a textbook quotation about the origin of the Cold War that I read as rather ambivalent. My thematic focus on the Cold War follows from the assumption that this historical period is a likely candidate for ambivalent portrayal, due to still-unresolved contestations and recent discursive shifts. History teachers interest me in their double function as members of memory cultures and as professionals specialised in conveying state-approved patterns of interpretation; they thus occupy a central role in the transmission of memories. Before presenting and discussing my empirical data, I will look into the diverging functions ascribed to ambivalence in different academic debates. I will moreover provide a rough sketch of the competing arguments made by historians about the origins and causes of the Cold War. Finally, I will share my own thoughts on the textbook quotation that the teachers were invited to comment on.

Ambivalence, History, Memory and History Teaching

Ambivalence is touched upon in four different academic debates, and in each one scholars arrive at a different conclusion concerning its value.

Ambivalence and the Debate about History and Memory

For Peter Novick (1999, 4), ambivalence is a typical feature of historical accounts. For him historians are likely to develop complex and ambivalent stories as they are disciplined enough to resist the temptation to focus only on historical facts that would fit best into preformed narratives. His image of the historian prone to painting pictures in many shades of grey owes a great deal to a counter-image of memory in which narratives of the past are manipulated in order to serve present needs. Ambivalence thus plays a crucial role in drawing a clear-cut line between memory and history.

Ambivalence and Hegemony in Discourse Theory

In discourse theory ambivalence is closely connected with political projects of hegemony (Reckwitz 2006). Borrowing Gramsci's definition, I understand the concept of hegemony to describe the ability of a ruling group to rule by consent, consent itself being the result of attempts by rulers to impose their interpretation of reality as the natural state of affairs upon the ruled. Vagueness can become an important tool in this attempt to rule, because it allows a variety of social actors with different agendas to rally behind the same concepts, for example *freedom* or *democracy*. Vagueness – alternatively we could speak of ambivalence – is thus deemed crucial for securing hegemony (Butler 2005, 33).

Ambivalence and Critical Discourse Analysis (CDA)

In Critical Discourse Analysis, ambivalence is understood as something that can emerge from the interplay between two features considered common to all texts (Fairclough 1989). Firstly, texts leave open gaps: Neither the relationship between the text and the world, nor the relationship between different parts of the text, can be fully spelled out. As a result, texts require readers to mobilise cultural knowledge, and thus their understanding of usual cultural constructions, in order to fill in these gaps. This knowledge, which is presupposed but not explicitly referred to by the text (understood as 'situated discourse'), derives from meta-discourses, which constitute particular ways of representing the world. Secondly, texts are seen as being inherently inter-textual themselves, an assemblage of bits and pieces from other texts, each of which may have been shaped by different meta-discourses. Studies show that intertextuality easily leads to ambivalence (Janks 1997), especially in a historical context characterized by discursive shifts when texts are expected to reflect dominant discourses both before and after certain changes.

Ambivalence and the Memory of Contested Pasts

In the field of memory studies, Marita Sturken has explored the effects of ambivalence most carefully (1997, 44–84). Taking a close look at the practices of remembering enacted by different people at the Vietnam Veterans' Memorial in Washington, Sturken claims that the memorial's most outstanding feature is its ambivalence. While for some it speaks to the heroism, honour and sacrifice of those who fought in Vietnam, for others it gives voice to the loss and pain of men who died in an unjust and shameful war. In her more theoretical remarks, Sturken credits ambivalence with the ability to resist a desire for coherence and narrative closure, which, she writes, inevitably leads to the erasure of all the details that may not fit into a neat frame. Ambivalence thus works to keep stories told about the past open and incomplete. In doing so, ambivalence preserves the political aspect of memory, which follows from the fact that memory is inherently selective, partial and contingent on decisions that could have been taken differently. Sturken's concern for the political as something valuable and important but endangered by closure and the illusion of completeness brings her close to theories of hegemony. However, her claim that ambivalence does not necessarily work to stabilise hegemony but instead keeps alive an awareness of how inherently political memory always is sets her apart from those who view ambivalence mainly as a manipulative tool in the hands of rulers.

Ambivalence and History Teaching

How should history teaching position itself towards ambivalence? Should it embrace ambivalent accounts as an indicator of complexity? Should we deliberately use narratives open to competing interpretations in order to prevent narrative closure? Should students be invited to deconstruct ambivalent narratives understood to serve the stabilisation of hegemony?

Peter Seixas (2000) has suggested we can distinguish between three different approaches towards history teaching (2000), which are not only based on different epistemological beliefs (Parkes 2009) but can also be understood as dealing differently with ambivalence. The first aims at conveying the *best story of the past* by including as many different perspectives as possible. Implicitly subscribing to the view that historical accounts are able to mirror past reality, this approach would likely result in closed narratives and a positive assessment of ambivalence as the inevitable outcome of the attempt to give voice to many different historical actors. Starting from the premise that all we have from the past are sources and artefacts as the building blocks from which historians *construct* their accounts, the second approach focuses on equipping students with the disciplinary knowledge they need to check on the robustness of competing accounts with the help of evidence inferred from sources. From this perspective, ambivalence could be viewed either as an adequate reflection of complex evidence or as the result of a 'messy' way of storytelling. The third approach aims to aid students in *deconstructing* historical accounts by rendering visible the traces of the present in narratives about the past. In all likelihood, this would also entail exploring how ambivalence serves present interests or reflects different discourses.

While these three approaches can be expected to yield different ways of dealing with ambivalence, problems may arise from combining them without being aware of the epistemological shifts involved.

Ambivalence and the Political in Stories about the Cold War

The Cold War was contested between East and West right from its start. Since the early 1960s, however, we can also observe a ritualised stand-off between two competing approaches in the West (Lundestad 2014), with traditionalists blaming the USSR for having caused the conflict and revisionists ascribing responsibility for the break-up of the wartime alliance to the United States. Both engage in a debate informed by binary oppositions. While traditionalists portray the United States as having been predominantly concerned with demobilisation in the immediate aftermath of the Second World War, revisionists point to the far-reaching expansionist agenda the United States pursued, relying upon, among other things, the Marshall Plan. While traditionalists explain the shift towards a more assertive stance in American foreign policy as a response to the tightening Soviet grip over Eastern Europe, revisionists describe Soviet policies in Eastern Europe as a defensive reaction to the global ambitions of the United States, bolstered by its atomic monopoly and overwhelming economic might. In the 1970s, Gaddis launched an attempt to combine bits and pieces from both accounts into a new narrative (1972; 1987), which later received the label 'post-revisionist'. While pointing to US policies as an important factor in aggravating the conflict, he also claimed that these policies responded to perceptions of Soviet behaviour. Instead of raising questions of guilt and responsibility, he pointed to the role of perception and misperception. He understood political decisions to be the contingent outcome of political interaction between both sides, neither of which could fully control the situation.

Recent trends in writing about the Cold War have rather added new vigour to old arguments and controversies. Shifting the focus of the debate from Europe to the so-called 'third world' and from politics to culture has lent new credibility to old revisionist arguments. Authors have thus argued, for example, that US policies of lending support to postcolonial dictatorships (Engerman 2010) or racial discrimination at home (Dudziak 2011), undermine the American claim of having defended the principles of freedom and democracy against a totalitarian

Soviet Union. We can also observe a revitalisation of traditional discourses in the writings of authors who insist on a crucial difference between an American empire based on invitation and a Soviet empire based on imposition or in the work of those who argue that the Cold War could have been avoided if not for a paranoid Stalin obsessed with world revolution (Gaddis 1997).

Mapping Ambivalence: Reading a Textbook Quotation

The rivalry between competing explanations given by historians on the origin of the Cold War has left its mark on the quotation from the textbook which we asked history teachers to comment on. We did not choose this particular quotation to serve as a catalyst in our interviews because it is representative of current textbooks in general. For us it instead resembles a 'rich point' (Agar 1994), as it appears to be particularly illustrative of a larger trend towards ambivalent representations of the past. By comparing what *is* said with what *could* have been said in the quotation, and by comparing our trigger narrative with narratives found in other textbooks, I will explain why I read the following lines as ambivalent.

> [1] At the Potsdam Conference of 1945, the USA, the USSR and Britain agreed on a specific approach to be taken towards Germany. [2] After that point, political differences determined their subsequent approaches. [3] In its sphere of influence, the USA championed democracy and economic liberalism. [4] The USSR organised a socialist sphere of influence extending as far as central Europe to meet its security concerns. [5] The Soviet army was stationed in Eastern and Southeastern European countries. [6] There, governments supported politically and economically by the Soviet Union came to power. [7] As in Poland, Czechoslovakia, Hungary, Bulgaria and Romania, a 'people's democracy' emerged in what was to become the GDR. [8] The Western powers regarded these developments as an expansion of the Soviet sphere of influence (Ebeling and Birkenfeld 2011, 190–91).[1]

To my mind, this paragraph bears not only the marks of both traditionalist and revisionist accounts, but is also open to different readings.

The systematic difference between the activities ascribed to the United States and the USSR in sentences three and four recalls the traditionalist discourse on the Cold War. While the United States 'championed democracy and economic liberalism', the USSR 'organised a socialist sphere of influence'. Difference is amplified by the particular choice of words here. While the Americans are portrayed as standing up for something and thus as supporting universal values, the Soviets are described as *organising* a sphere of influence that happened to be socialist. The word 'organising' conjures up notions of efficiency and says nothing about the values pursued. Quite the reverse; learning that the Soviets invested their efficiency in enhancing their security needs, we see them only as having followed a highly particularistic agenda. The binary opposition introduced here is intensified by sentence five. While it offers details on the deployment of Soviet troops, it keeps silent about the whereabouts of American troops, whose very existence is thus pushed to the back of the reader's mind.

However, sentence four introduces Soviet 'security concerns', a term that is regularly used as a kind of 'flagship word' (Hermanns 1982) in revisionist accounts. Ambivalence is further increased by polysemous expressions (Hermanns 1989). When sentence eight emphasises that 'the Western powers regarded these developments [in Eastern Europe] as an expansion of the Soviet sphere of influence', this can be understood in two different ways. We can read it as a caveat, reminding us that this statement does not necessarily reflect objective truth but is rather a subjective assessment by one side to the conflict. But we can also arrive at the opposite conclusion, arguing that an assessment made by those in the West appears to be particularly trustworthy.

My impression that the text seems quite ambivalent is corroborated by a comparison with alternative accounts. The traditionalist elements I have identified in the excerpt clearly pale in comparison to the following sentences from a textbook published in West Germany in 1961, during the Cold War:

[1] Soon after the end of the war, more and more tension arose between the victorious great powers, between the USSR on the one hand and the Western Allies, mainly the USA, on the other. [2] The reason was the

increasingly blatant imperialist drive of the USSR, which imposed the Bolshevist system of rule on one occupied country after another (Ebeling 1961, 259).[2]

Criticism of the Soviet Union is much more outspoken in the older text, which treats Soviet aggression as a fact beyond all doubt. Furthermore, relations within the Soviet bloc are represented differently. While the current textbook speaks about Eastern European governments that came to power with a little help from Soviet friends, the older textbook talks about Bolshevik systems of rule being imposed on them.

Comparison with a third textbook shows that revisionist discourses can also be expressed much more clearly.

> At the end of the Second World War, the Soviet Union had lost more than 20 million people and was devastated to a large extent. But the Red Army had occupied almost all of Eastern Europe and moved as far as Germany. These territories were under Soviet control and represented an increase in power. The most important goal after the war was the reconstruction of the [Soviets'] own land. In order to achieve this, the Soviet Union wanted to use German reparation payments and American credits. In the long run, the Soviet head of state, Stalin, feared a conflict with the USA and other capitalist states. The military and economic strength of the USA had contributed significantly to its victory over Nazi Germany. It was the only country among the great powers not to suffer devastation. Its factories were producing more than ever before. Unlike after the First World War, the USA firmly decided to help shape the political reordering of the world. Democracy and human rights should be established everywhere. But the Americans also wanted to secure their economic dominance, and to reach this goal they needed free access to the markets and resources of the entire world (Burkard 2010, 72).[3]

This text makes a greater effort to justify Soviet security needs by reminding the reader of the Soviet experience of the Second World War. Pointing to the military might and economic power of the United States lends more urgency to these needs. Moreover, this textbook presents the United States as not only in pursuit of the noble goal of encouraging the spread of democracy and human rights but also as motivated by the rather egoistic aim to secure access to markets and resources.

Mapping Ambivalence: Teachers Making Sense of a Textbook Quotation

Methodological Approach

How readers approach a text empirically can never be predicted by analysis of the text alone. I therefore invited nine history teachers from the former West Germany, nine from the former East[4], and ten from Switzerland to share their interpretations of the quotation discussed above with my colleagues and myself. We asked them (i) how they read the quotation, (ii) how they judged its appropriateness, and (iii) what they themselves think about the events represented in it.[5]

When talking with them about their reading, we started with rather general questions but ended by directing their attention to the aspects we found to be reflective of traditionalist, revisionist and ambivalent discourses in the text. Accordingly, we asked them to comment on (i) the activities ascribed to the United States and the USSR, (ii) the emphasis given to Soviet security needs and (iii) the accent placed on the way the Western powers perceived Soviet policies. These questions addressed the teachers in their different roles as both members of a professional group and also as participants of different memory cultures. Being asked to assess a text written by another person clearly reminded them of their daily job grading papers. The invitation to elaborate on their thoughts about the origins of the Cold War as private individuals, however, might have been perceived as interfering with the objectivity and neutrality teachers are often expected to display.

I interpret the data gathered from these interviews in three steps. Since I want to know *whether* and, if so, *how* people deal differently with an ambivalent text, I will first provide an analytical description of the teachers' answers. Since I also want to explore how (mostly) national memory cultures and textbooks influence teachers' own narratives of events, I will then conduct a cross-national comparison. And, since I am interested in the implicit or explicit stances the teachers take with regard to ambivalence, I will finally discuss the way they position themselves in relation to the different theoretical perspectives outlined in the introduction.

Analytical Description

An overwhelming majority of teachers from Germany, 15 out of 18, reads the quotation as blaming the Soviets for having triggered the Cold War. Exactly the same number of teachers argues in line with post-revisionist positions when they discuss the events the text is dealing with. According to them either both or neither of the two rival superpowers is to be held responsible. Reflecting on the quality of the text, ten teachers criticise it for being too pro-American, one denounces the same lines for being too pro-Soviet, two praise it for being well balanced, and two assess it as being appropriately pro-American.

If we compare teachers from East and West Germany, differences appear to be rather minimal at first glance. Teachers from both sides of the Iron Curtain interpret the quote as placing the blame on the USSR. Both even advance similar arguments. They speak ironically about the super-stereotype[6] of the Americans as the good guys and the Soviets as the epitome of evil[7]; they point to the disturbing silence regarding American soldiers and American spheres of influence[8]; and, finally, they criticize the authors for mixing apples and oranges by contrasting a Western commitment to democracy with an Eastern drive for expansion.[9]

However, as soon as one looks into the position from which this critique is raised, differences come into view. Our West German teachers argue very much from the position of *putting blame on the Americans* by

Table 13.1 Table comparing East and West German teachers' responses to a text

	Teachers from East Germany		Teachers from West Germany	
Interpretation of the text: Who is to blame?	No one:	1	No one:	2
	USSR:	8	USSR:	7
Assessment of the text: Who is to blame?	Too pro-US:	7	Too pro-US:	3
	Appropriately pro-US:	1	Appropriately pro-US:	1
	Too pro-Soviet:	0	Too pro-Soviet:	1
	Well balanced:	0	Well balanced:	2
	Inconclusive:	1	Inconclusive:	2
Assessment of the event: Who is to blame?	No one/both parties:	8	No one/both parties:	7
	USSR:	1	United States:	1
			USSR:	1

mentioning, for example, the harassment of leftists and communists in the West[10] or reminding us of the United States' economic agenda.[11] At the same time, the East German teachers are much more concerned with *taking away blame from the Soviets* by normalising their policies. They point out that what the Soviets did was nothing but natural, since the side that wins the war always pushes through its interests[12] and ideals,[13] imposes its own political system on others[14] and dictates its will.[15] To reframe the contrast once more: While the critical teachers from West Germany we spoke to accuse the text of not being persistent enough in its moral reasoning, the critical colleagues from East Germany we have interviewed take offence with what appears to them as an unnecessary high level of moralising.

Differences among West German teachers come to light especially when we focus on how they relate the text's emphasis on Soviet security needs and on Soviet expansionism. Diverging answers on how to account for the tension between these two statements seem to correlate with differences in the assessment of the text. Those who are very critical of the quotation because they perceive it as being one-sided and pro-American downplay the relevance attributed to Soviet security needs. Some even claim that Soviet security needs are clearly referred to as a sheer pretext.[16] For them they function as a mere excuse for further expansion. Others argue that the quotation purposefully constructs the Soviets as maniacs, crazy enough to fear even the democracy- and freedom-loving Americans.[17] Those, however, who appreciate the quotation as being relatively balanced cite the text's emphasis on Soviet security needs as the decisive factor that marks a clear-cut break from the black-and-white stories about the thoroughly evil Soviets to whom they had been exposed as children.[18]

The teachers from East Germany show different patterns of reasoning. Unlike us, their interviewers from the West who raised the question in the first place, they do not construct a morally charged opposition between having legitimate security needs and pursuing an expansionist agenda. Indeed, they are generally hesitant to make moral claims. Most of them simply state that the two motives do not exclude but rather complement each other,[19] or they argue that expansion naturally follows from security needs.[20] Others talk openly about their struggle with a question[21] that raises too many moral issues.[22] They defend the emergence of clearly demarcated spheres of influence not only as a legitimate process but also as a necessary precondition for the preservation of peace.[23]

The degree of removal of some of the East German teachers' discourse from West German standards becomes especially visible at moments during two interviews, when the West German interviewer and both East German interviewees talk past each other. One of these moments occurs in an interview with a teacher born in 1961, here referred to as Kristin Schreiber.[24] Everything begins with her claim that the emphasis the quotation gives to Soviet security needs serves an alibi function. Initially, she remains quite vague on what she actually means: 'This is an excuse for what one does; this kind of alibi function', she says, without specifying who the culprit might be, who is in need of an 'alibi, an excuse'. Only at a later point in the interview does she identify the United States as the party seeking an alibi to cover up its evil deeds. In that moment she is thinking aloud about a question that appears rather troubling to her against the backdrop of what she has previously learned to be historical facts. She tries to understand why the Western power could have perceived Soviet policies as being expansionist and why the text would give so much emphasis to this perception. She argues:

> It is a su-, a subjective thing, because, I mean it is a kind of excuse for having built the Iron Curtain, right. I mean, it is a kind of excuse: 'We wouldn't have done that if the security needs of the USSR and the expansion of their sphere of influence hadn't been so significant. We didn't actually want it at all'.[25]

By implying that the Americans built the Iron Curtain and then invented Soviet expansionism as a kind of retrospective justification, she completely inverts the version usually told in the West about the division of Europe. At the same time, Schreiber argues as if her explanation were not only the dominant one but also the one the textbook authors had in mind when writing these lines.

Something very similar happens in an interview with another East German teacher,[26] referred to here as Matthias Fürst. Asked to sum up the textbook quotation in his own words, he produces the following account:

> Okay, in principle it is about, uh, the representation of, the development of, uh, the Soviet sphere of influence. Not only the representation, but also a certain assessment, how the Western powers, how, I guess, it is also made clear, how the authors perceive this. Um, that the Soviet Union in Southern and Southeastern Europe, through their policy of occupation, which, uh, ultimately resulted from and is still resulting from the course of the war, how it was pushed into it, that such a [...] a Soviet sphere of influence was established there.[27]

Fürst also reads the text as a confirmation of something he clearly believes himself: Soviet policies in Eastern Europe were not simply an outcome of the Second World War. These policies, which led to the establishment of a 'sphere of influence', arose as a result of the Soviets being 'pushed' to do something, something they would not have done otherwise and which was not for their own sake but rather the outcome of external, rather than internal, pressures. To this teacher, such a conclusion is hardly new or surprising. Like the GDR discourses he grew up with, Fürst takes it for granted that everybody sees the Soviets as the ones who liberated Eastern Europe from the Germans, as the ones who occupied it. At the same time, the rest of the interview reveals two things clearly. First, the West German interviewer has a hard time catching up with all of the assumptions and ideas Matthias Fürst implicitly relies on without explicitly stating them. Second, as soon as the interviewer articulates her bewilderment, as soon as she reminds him – without realising it – of the discursive shift that had turned his version of historical events into a story too strange to be comprehensible, he retreats:

I: So, you just said that the Soviet Union was pushed to establish a sphere of influence [...]
MF: No, they pushed it forward, [it was] that way around.[28]

Very quickly, without further remarks, Matthias Fürst adapts to what he perceives as the dominant discourse. In his newly adopted narrative, the Soviets are no longer pushed by others; they are the ones to push. Some minutes later, another case of hastily correcting a 'mistake' occurs in the same interview. When Matthias Fürst comments on the relation the text constructs between the security needs and the expansionist drive ascribed to the Soviets, the dialogue between interviewer and interviewee again runs into trouble:

I: Now, there is also something else, if one looks at how the USSR is portrayed and its motives. [The text] says, 'it expanded its sphere of influence and it met its security concerns' [...] How (MF: Mhm) do these two things relate to one another from the perspective of the text? Are they presented as motives that can go hand in hand? Can one have security concerns and expand at the same time? Or are they motives that mutually exclude each other because one is rather defensive and the other aggressive? [...] From the perspective of the text?
MF: Well, it implies that, um, in the end it was wanted by the Eastern European countries as well.
I: Mhm [...] So there was a security concern, but it was not [...] there?
MF: For their security/no, nonsense, (I: Yes), yes. For their, um, it is about the Soviet Union (I: Yes). For their security concerns. Well, that is this cordon that they would like to have today (I: Mhm) again too, yes.[29]

Again, the misunderstanding is mainly caused by the fact that interviewer and interviewee draw on completely different background knowledge to fill in the gaps left open by the text. Whereas Matthias Fürst automatically thinks of the Eastern Europeans as the ones who had security concerns, the interviewer no less automatically identifies the Soviets as the ones concerned about their security. Interviewer and interviewee mobilise completely different stories from their cultural repertoires in order to make sense of the same lines. Again in line with GDR historiography, Mathias Fürst constructs the Eastern Europeans as the concerned beneficiaries of protection offered to them by the Soviets. The interviewer, on the contrary, draws on revisionist accounts of the Cold War, which regularly mention Soviet security concerns. In the end, however, it is again the interviewee who steps back and bows to the new hegemonic discourse with which he is confronted, because he realises the power difference between the two narratives.

Summing up, we can conclude that the quotation leads the teachers from both parts of Germany to position themselves in different ways. The teachers from Lower Saxony (West) are pretty much divided. Some read elements of revisionist accounts within, or into, the textbook lines and appreciate the quote for its balance and fairness. Others fail to see traces of revisionism and reject the same quote for being too one-sided. As we can see, it is rather differences in interpretation but not differences in evaluative standards that account for the divide in their assessments. Interestingly, the same does not apply to the teachers from Saxony-Anhalt (East). Most of these teachers project onto the quotation a sceptical and morally neutral view of a world inhabited by countries, for them understandably, invested in their own self-interest. Occasionally, we observe these teachers drawing upon moral narratives from the GDR period. However, this seems to happen exclusively in situations when the teachers being interviewed temporarily seem to lose control and react almost automatically. As soon as they recognise the bewilderment their answers have caused, they immediately withdraw from their initial position – as if they sense that they had crossed a line demarcating what may be said.

To a certain extent, the Swiss teachers we interviewed do exactly the opposite of the German teachers. Whereas the majority of German teachers read the quotation as blaming the USSR, 8 out of 10 Swiss teachers

Table 13.2 How teachers from Switzerland react to a text

	Teachers from Switzerland	
Interpretation of the text:	No one: 8	8
Who is to blame?	USSR: 2	2
Assessment of the text:	Too pro-Soviet:	5
Who is to blame?	Too cautious:	1
	Too pro-US:	2
	Well balanced:	2
	Inconclusive :	
Assessment of the event:	No one:	7
Who is to blame?	USSR:	3

come to the conclusion that neither superpower is ascribed any blame for having caused the conflict. And while only 1 out of 18 German teachers criticised the text for being too pro-Soviet, 5 out of 10 Swiss teachers do so.

In contrast to the case study of German teachers, a closer examination of the arguments put forward by the Swiss teachers does not undermine the first impression of unanimity. Most of them do not only read the quotation in line with post-revisionist accounts, as emphasising structural causes of the Cold War, but most of them also do so for similar reasons, drawing mainly on a rather general knowledge concerning human behaviour and interaction. One teacher characterises the alliance between the Soviets and the Americans during the Second World War as a marriage of convenience that could not help but break up as soon as Germany, the common enemy, was defeated.[30] Another compares the conflict to an argument between children in the 'sandbox'.[31] A third one claims, 'one always ends up with the same human drive for power and self-preservation'.[32] At the same time, these teachers have no difficulty emphasising the fundamental differences between the United States and the USSR.

From this perspective, the difference between the majority of eight teachers, who read the text as being rather neutral, and the minority of two, who read it as either blaming the Soviets[33] or being biased towards the United States,[34] begins to diminish. All of these teachers agree that the United States was in pursuit of morally superior goals compared to a USSR which they perceive as following a much more egoistic agenda; the only thing they disagree about is whether the quotation reflects this belief or not.

Something similar can be observed with regard to the assessments the Swiss teachers give to the text. On the surface we observe a variety of statements, with 5 teachers rejecting it for being too pro-Soviet, 2 embracing it as well balanced, 2 giving inconclusive answers and only 1 criticising it – as over half of the German teachers do – for being too pro-American. The teachers who accuse the textbook authors of being too cautious with regard to the USSR refer to a historical reality missed by the text. The Soviet approach in Eastern Europe, they insist, could have been described in a much more drastic and outspoken way.[35] The label 'people's democracy' to describe the Soviet-style regimes, they continue, is highly misleading, rendering invisible the pure dictatorship to which the text is actually referring.[36] Others are offended by the casual way in which the text depicts the establishment of dictatorships in the satellite states without giving voice to the oppressed Eastern European people.[37] Considering all of these omissions, which he describes as incomprehensible, one teacher even assumes that the text must have been written by a person born in the former GDR and still very much influenced by everything he or she had learned back then.[38]

Overall, the teachers who criticise the text for casting the Soviets in too positive a role, do so on the basis of the same distinction – equally upheld by the rest of their colleagues – between a morally superior United States and a morally questionable USSR. Furthermore, even the most outspoken critics of the text paint rather complex pictures of the historical reality. For example, of the group of Swiss teachers, the two individuals who draw a line of continuity between the aggression of Soviet Russia and Tsarist Russia,[39] and who portray the Soviet Union as a society never touched by the Enlightenment and thus deeply enmeshed in autocratic traditions,[40] are particularly sympathetic to the socialist idea of justice and equality.

We can learn two things from these conclusions. Firstly, anti-communist sentiment seems to be deeply internalised by all of the Swiss teachers, including those leaning towards the political left. Secondly, although they argue in line with traditionalist accounts and clearly take sides with the West in what they consider to be a conflict between Western democracy and Eastern dictatorship, the Swiss teachers also tend to talk about aspects such as social justice and equality, issues which often go unrecognised by pure traditionalists. The combination of anti-communism and a concern for complexity thus creates a position that all Swiss teachers can identify with, even if they may differ with regard to nuances.

This impression is reinforced when we look at the ways in which Swiss teachers talk about the United States. Some engage in criticism of the Western superpower, but all the Swiss teachers stop short of drawing an equal sign between the United States and the USSR. Speaking openly about the Americans having lost their image as saviours of the world, and admitting that the same Americans are now perceived as the 'policemen' of the world, mainly motivated by their interest in oil, one teacher nevertheless insists on the crucial difference between American democracy and Soviet one-party rule.[41]

In contrast to their German colleagues then, these Swiss teachers' individual narratives share many similarities. Minor discrepancies among these narratives do not refer to core beliefs or evaluative standards but rather to the degree to which these teachers read the quotation as either confirming or questioning their own beliefs. Half of the teachers appreciate the neutral treatment of both superpowers on the part of the text but simultaneously point subtly to the moral differences between them. The other half equate subtlety with caution and argues that this caution is bought at a dear price as it entails a silence in regards to what was endured by the people of Eastern Europe under the Soviet regime.

To my mind, there are two compelling insights to be gained from a comparison of the interview data: The textbook quotation triggers many different and, at times, openly contradictory reactions. At the same time, the variation we observe follows a clearly recognisable national pattern.

The most obvious contrast is probably between the 11 teachers who read the quotation as blaming both superpowers for causing the Cold War and the 17 teachers who understand it to ascribe responsibility exclusively to the Soviet Union. If we look at how the text is assessed, we can distinguish between those who appreciate it and those who reject it

Table 13.3 Table comparing the responses of teachers from the different countries to a text

		WG	EG	CH
Interpretation of the text: Who is to blame?	No one	2	1	8
	USSR	7	8	2
Assessment of the text: Who is to blame?	Too pro-US	3	7	1
	Appropriately pro-US	1	1	0
	Too pro-USSR	1	0	5
	Well balanced	2	0	2
	Inconclusive	2	1	2
Assessment of the event: Who is to blame?	No one/both	7	8	7
	USSR	1	1	3
	United States	1		

or even suspect that it was written by an ideologically brainwashed person from the East. Furthermore, among the critics, 11 teachers blame the text for being too pro-American, while six others perceive it as being too pro-Soviet. Something similar happens with the teachers who are positive towards the text. While two teachers praise it for being appropriately pro-American, 4 teachers like the text for being well balanced.

To my mind, all these differences support the thesis that the textbook quotation is indeed ambivalent, in the sense that it is open to many different readings. Teachers obviously read opposite meanings into the same lines, most vividly exemplified by the different understandings of the quotation concerning the Western powers' perception of Soviet behaviour as aggressive. All of this points to the fact, that even schools, as institutions expected to convey consensual knowledge (Höhne 2003), cannot easily reach any consensus on how to make sense of the Cold War.

However, we see considerable variation between national samples. While the Swiss sample is far more homogeneous with the majority of teachers stressing – in line with traditional accounts on the origins of the Cold War – a crucial difference between the democratic United States and the dictatorial USSR, the German sample displays strong heterogeneity. While most of the German teachers read the quotation as blaming the USSR, they tend to strongly disagree as to whether this represents an adequate reflection or a distortion of historical reality. Furthermore, since it is mainly West German teachers with these clearly diverging views, the phenomenon can hardly be explained with reference to the former divide between East and West alone. It also seems to point to the social effectiveness of textbooks, which, in the case of Germany, display rather diverse viewpoints, each mixing traditionalist, revisionist and post-revisionist accounts on the origins of the Cold War in multiple ways (Christophe 2017). In line with a theoretical argument according to which textbooks simultaneously shape and mirror societal discourses (Williams 2014), we can expect teachers to be influenced by the textbooks to which they are exposed and with which they work on a daily basis, and we can also assume that textbook authors are themselves influenced by the cultural environment they share with the teachers and students for whom they are writing.

Yet, despite the diversity of narratives offered in German textbooks, there still seem to be certain limits on what can be legitimately said. East German teachers, at least, perceive these limits, as we can see in moments when they find themselves saying something that would have been normal in GDR times but appears almost incomprehensible to the West German interviewer. It is in these moments that they seem to feel compelled to correct themselves immediately.

Discussion

As we have seen, none of the teachers interviewed gives voice to the possibility of reading different meanings into a text that has clearly enabled rather different interpretations. From interviews with these teachers, it is clear that their belief in hegemonic narratives seems to have outlived even the end of the hegemonies themselves. Although all of the teachers appear to hold different positions when discussing the textbook quotation, each seems to believe that there exists only one appropriate position from which to speak the truth.

The situation we are faced with simultaneously resembles and differs from the memory practices Marita Sturken has observed at the Vietnam Memorial (1997). Like her, we observe people drawing on competing discourses in order to fill in the gaps left open by an ambivalent representation of the past; like her, we are able to witness the emergence of many different voices on how to make sense of the past. But there is one crucial difference. While contestation and thus the political character of all memory is in the open in the case of the Vietnam War, the illusion of hegemony, which is encouraged by these teachers, still renders invisible the degree of conflict and competition extant in the study of the Cold War. We can assume that under these conditions, ambivalence does not contribute to smoothing the sharp edges of which everybody remains painfully aware; instead, ambivalence helps to circumvent the recognition of those edges.

Concerning the question of what keeps the political out of the teachers' discourses on the Cold War, epistemological beliefs about the relationship between history as events past and history as the narrative told about these events seem to play a role as well. When thinking aloud about how to assess the textbook narrative, all of the teachers refer to the complexity of historical reality sooner or later. And while they arrive at rather different conclusions, all of them perform the same kind of evaluation exercise. In the spirit of historians like Peter Novick (1999), all check whether the shape of the narrative adequately reflects what they know about the shape of historical reality; additionally, all of them seem to be convinced that this reality is accessible to them. For someone standing on this epistemological ground, history is about truth, narratives are not fully negotiable, and the political has only limited relevance for the historical.

Again, the German teachers are an exception to the general rule. The epistemological positions from which they argue appear to be much more ambivalent. Like their Swiss colleagues, they also evoke images of the historical past in order to either approve or disapprove of the textbook narrative. But, especially among the most outspoken critics of the quotation, some switch the epistemological position from which they argue and engage in the discourse-analytical enterprise of deconstruction. Instead of comparing the textbook story to an image of historical reality, there are instances when they identify absences in the narrative by scrutinising it in light of possible alternatives. From here it would be only one small step to recognise the political nature of history and memory. However, they do not take that step, perhaps because they can always fall back on the first strategy of evoking images of historical reality in order to evaluate the appropriateness of a narrative.

As we can learn from our interviews with the German teachers, shifts in epistemological assumptions can create a certain ambiguity, which may then prevent teachers from fully exhausting the potential of ambivalent representations. As long as the teachers aim to tell the most inclusive or appropriate story about the past, they embrace the ambivalent narrative as an adequate response to complexity. As soon as they aim to deconstruct stories, they criticise the same ambivalent narrative for the absences or imbalances it entails. But unless the teachers recognise that their guiding assumptions about the status of historical facts change when pursuing these two aims, the operations they perform may easily interrupt each other. History teachers seem to be stuck between two opposing epistemological positions. We may even assume that the competing demands they face require them to dwell on the shifting ground between those two poles. In the end, they hardly have a chance of attaining a third position, one that could be rather appealing in the age of increasingly plural and ambivalent memory cultures: They do not read the ambivalent text as Umberto Eco (1998) suggests, as an invitation to generate a multitude of different interpretations. To accept such an invitation would require acknowledging the political in teaching history. It would moreover involve a readiness to remove persistent limits on what can be said – limits of which some of our East German teachers remain all too aware.

Notes

1. 'Auf der Potsdamer Konferenz 1945 vereinbarten die USA, die UdSSR und Großbritannien ihre gemeinsamen Positionen im Umgang mit Deutschland. Danach bestimmten die politischen Gegensätze das weitere Vorgehen. In ihrem Machtbereich setzten sich die USA für Demokratie und wirtschaftlichen Liberalismus ein. Die UdSSR organisierte bis nach Mitteleuropa für ihr Sicherheitsbedürfnis einen sozialistischen Machtbereich. Die sowjetische Armee stand in den Ländern Ost- und Südosteuropas. Dort kamen Regierungen an die Macht, die von der Sowjetunion politisch und wirtschaftlich gestützt wurden. Neben Polen, der Tschechoslowakei, Ungarn, Bulgarien und Rumänien vollzog sich auch in der späteren DDR die Entwicklung zu einer Volksdemokratie. Die Westmächte sahen diese Vorgänge als Expansion des sowjetischen Einflussbereiches an'.
2. 'Schon bald nach Kriegsende kam es zu immer stärkeren Spannungen zwischen den siegreichen Großmächten, der UdSSR auf der einen Seite und den westlichen Alliierten, besonders den USA, auf der anderen. Der Grund war das immer unverhülltere imperialistische Streben der UdSSR, die einem von ihr besetzten Staat nach dem anderen das bolschewistische Herrschaftssystem aufzwangen'.
3. 'Am Ende des Zweiten Weltkrieges hatte die Sowjetunion mehr als 20 Millionen Kriegstote zu beklagen und war in weiten Teilen verwüstet. Doch die Rote Armee hatte fast ganz Osteuropa besetzt und war bis

nach Deutschland vorgestoßen. Diese Gebiete standen nun unter sowjetischer Kontrolle und bedeuteten einen großen Machtzuwachs. Das wichtigste Ziel nach dem Krieg war der Wiederaufbau des eigenen Landes. Dazu wollte die Sowjetunion deutsche Reparationsleistungen und amerikanische Kredite nutzen. Langfristig fürchtete der sowjetische Staatschef Stalin einen Konflikt mit den USA und anderen kapitalistischen Staaten. Die militärische und wirtschaftliche Stärke der USA hatte entscheidend zum Sieg über das nationalsozialistische Deutschland beigetragen. Als einziger der großen Staaten war das Land ohne Zerstörungen geblieben. Seine Fabriken produzierten mehr als jemals zuvor. Anders als nach dem Ersten Weltkrieg waren die USA fest entschlossen, die politische Neuordnung der Welt mitzugestalten. Demokratie und Menschenrechte sollten dabei überall durchgesetzt werden. Die Amerikaner wollten aber auch ihre wirtschaftliche Vorrangstellung sicherstellen; dazu brauchten sie den freien Zugang zu den Märkten und Rohstoffquellen der Welt'.
4. 'West German' refers here to individuals born in pre-1990 West Germany, who currently teach in states that were part of that territory; 'East German' teachers were born in the GDR and currently teach in states that were part of the former East Germany.
5. The following section is based on interviews I conducted between December 2013 and August 2014 together with my colleagues Kathrin Zehr and Nora Zimmermann. I thank them for their support not only in gathering but also in discussing and coding the data. All interviews were recorded, transcribed and rendered anonymous by giving code names to persons and places mentioned and assigning each interview a number. As a rule I cite each interview by its number, date, and the interviewee's country of origin (WG for western Germany, EG for eastern Germany and CH for Switzerland). Only in cases where I discuss answers from a single interview in more detail is the interviewee's code name mentioned. The interviews in Germany and Switzerland were conducted in German using the original quotation in German.
6. WG 8 (6 May 2014).
7. EG 1 (15 July 2014); EG 2 (15 April 2014); EG 6 (19 June 2014); WG 5 (11 February 2014); WG 9 (29 April 2014).
8. WG 1 (13 May 2014); WG 8 (6 May 2014); EG 4 (13 May 2014); EG 6 (19 June 2014).
9. WG 8 (6 May 2014); EG 7 (18 June 2014); EG 9 (26 June 2014).
10. WG 1(13 May 2014).

11. WG 5 (11 February 2014); WG 8 (6 May 2014).
12. EG 5 (19 May 2014), EG 8 (19 May 2014).
13. EG 4 (13 May 2014).
14. EG 2 (15 April 2014); EG 8 (19 May 2014).
15. EG 3(27 March 2014).
16. WG 9 (29 April 2014).
17. WG 8(6 May 2014).
18. WG 10 (15 July 2014).
19. EG 2 (15 April 2014)
20. EG 3 (27 March 2014; EG 6 (19 June 2014).
21. EG 4 (13 May 2014); EG 5 (19 May 2014); EG 8 (19 May 2014).
22. EG 6 (19 June 2014).
23. EG 5 (19 May 2014).
24. EG 6 (19 June 2014).
25. EG 6 (19 June 2014): 'Es ist eine su/ subjektive Sache, weil, ist ja auch eine Art Entschuldigung dafür, dass sie dann äh den eisernen Vorhang (I: Mhm.) errichten, ja. Also es ist ja auch eine, eine Art Entschuldigung. "Wir hätten es ja nicht gemacht, wenn das Sicherheitsbedürfnis der UdSSR und der Ausbau des Machtbereichs nicht so groß gewesen wäre. Wir wollten das ja eigentlich gar nicht'.
26. EG 7 (18 June 2014).
27. EG 7 (18 June 2014): 'Okay, na ja, es geht im Prinzip hier um die, äh die Darstellung der, der Entwicklung des äh s/ sowjetischen Machtbereichs. Nicht nur Darstellung, auch eine gewisse Wertung, wie es a) von den Westmächten, wie es, hm, denke mal, wird auch deutlich, wie es, wie es die Autoren sehen. Ähm dass also die Sowjetunion in Süd- und Südosteuropa durch ihre äh Besatzungspolitik, die durch den Kriegsverlauf letztendlich zus/ äh sich ergeben hat oder auch noch weiterhin äh ergibt, ja, dazu getrieben wurde, dass dort so eine, (...) ein sowjetischer Machtbereich aufgebaut worden ist.'
28. EG 7 (18 June 2014): I: Ähm Sie hatten gerade gesagt, dass die Sowjetunion getrieben wurde dazu, einen Machtbereich zu errichten. MF: Nee, sie haben das vorangetrieben, so rum.
29. EG 7 (18 June 2014): I: Jetzt ist ja dann noch so was, also wenn man sich anguckt, wie die UdSSR dargestellt wird und ihre Motive. Da steht: "Sie erweitert ihren Einflussbereich und sie erfüllt Sicherheitsbedürfnisse". [...] Wie (MF: Mhm.) stehen diese beiden Dinge aus Sicht des Textes miteinander in Beziehung? Werden die als Motive aufgefasst, die miteinander einhergehen können? Also man kann ein Sicherheitsbedürfnis

haben und gleichzeitig expandieren? Oder sind das Motive, die sich gegenei/ äh gegenseitig ausschließen, weil das eine defensiv ist eher und das andere aggressiv? [...] Also aus Sicht des Textes?

MF: Na ja, es impliziert, dass ähm das letztendlich durch die osteuropäischen Länder ja schon auch gewollt wurde.

I: Mhm. [...] Es gab zwar ein Sicherheitsbedürfnis, aber das war nicht [...] da?

MF: Für ihr Sicherheits. Nee, Quatsch, (I: Ja.) ja. Für ihr, äh/ Hm, es geht ja um die Sowjetunion. (I: Ja.) Für ihr Sicherheitsbedürfnis. Ähm na das ist dieser, dieser Gürtel, der/ den sie heute auch (I: Mhm.) gerne wieder hätten, ja.

30. CH 1 (1 April 2014).
31. CH 2 (1 April 2014).
32. '... und da landet man ja letztlich ja eigentlich immer beim selben menschlichen Urtrieb von Macht und Erhaltung', CH 9 (17 April 2014).
33. CH 7 (10 June 2014).
34. CH 6 (2 October 2014).
35. CH 2 (1 April 2014).
36. CH 1 (1 April 2014); CH 9 (17 April 2014).
37. CH 3 (14 May 2014); CH 4 (20 May 2014).
38. CH 3 (14 May 2014).
39. CH 2 (1 April 2014).
40. CH 10 (14 April 2014).
41. CH 1 (1 April 2014).

Bibliography

Textbooks Cited

Burkard, Dieter. 2010. *Zeitreise 3*. Edition for Lower Saxony. Stuttgart/Leipzig: Klett.

Ebeling, Hans. 1961. *Die Reise in die Vergangenheit IV: Unser Zeitalter der Revolutionen und Weltkriege*. Edition for Lower Saxony. Braunschweig: Westermann.

Ebeling, Hans, and Wolfgang Birkenfeld. 2011. *Die Reise in die Vergangenheit. Ein geschichtliches Arbeitsbuch 9/10*. Edition for Saxony-Anhalt. Braunschweig: Westermann.

Further References

Agar, M. 1994. 'The Intercultural Frame'. *International Journal of Intercultural Relations* 18, no. 2: 221–37.
Beattie, Andrew H. 2008. *Playing Politics with History: The Bundestag Inquiries into East Germany*. New York: Berghahn.
Butler, Rex. 2005. *Slavoj Zizek: Live Theory*. London: Continuum.
Christophe, Barbara. 2017. '"Eigentlich hingen ja alle mit drin". Entnazifizierung und Kalter Krieg in Deutschen Schulbüchern und in den Erzählungen von Lehrenden'. In *Das geteilte Deutschland im Schulbuch. Die Darstellung des Kalten Krieges am Beispiel Deutschlands in den (Geschichts-) Schulbüchern von 1945 bis in die Gegenwart*, edited by F. Flucke, B. Kuhn und U. Pfeil, 147–165. St. Ingbert: Röhrig Universitätsverlag.
Dudziak, Mary L. 2011. *Cold War Civil Rights: Race and the Image of American Democracy*. Princeton: Princeton University Press.
Eco, Umberto. 1998. *Lector in fabula: Die Mitarbeit der Interpretation in erzählenden Texten*, 3rd edition. Munich: Dtv.
Engerman, David. 2010. 'Ideology and the Origins of the Cold War'. In *The Cambridge History of the Cold War*. Vol. 1. Edited by Melvyn P. Leffler and Arne Odd Westad, 20–43 Cambridge: Cambridge University Press.
Fairclough, Norman. 1989. *Language and Power*. Essex: Pearson Education Limited.
Gaddis, John L. 1972. *The United States and the Origins of the Cold War, 1941–1947*. New York: Columbia University Press.
Gaddis, John L. 1987. *The Long Peace: Inquiries into the History of the Cold War*. New York: Oxford University Press.
Gaddis, John L. 1997. *We Know Now*. Oxford: Oxford University Press.
Hermanns, Fritz. 1982. 'Brisante Wörter. Zur lexikographischen Behandlung parteisprachiger Wörter und Wendungen in Wörterbüchern der deutschen Gegenwartssprache'. In *Studien zur neuhochdeutschen Lexikographie II*. Edited by Herbert Ernst Wiegand, 87–108. New York: Olms.
Hermanns, Fritz. 1989. 'Deontische Tautologien. Ein linguistischer Beitrag zur Interpretation des Godesberger Programms (1959) der Sozialdemokratischen Partei Deutschlands'. In *Politische Semantik. Bedeutungsanalytische und sprachkritische Beiträge zu politischen Sprachverwendung*. Edited by Josef Klein, 69–152. Opladen: Westdeutscher Verlag.

Höhne, Thomas. 2003. *Schulbuchwissen. Umrisse einer Wissens- und Medientheorie des Schulbuchs*. Frankfurt am Main: Universität Frankfurt Institut für Sozialpädagogie.

Janks, Hilary. 1997. 'Critical Discourse Analysis as a Research Tool'. *Discourse: Studies in the Cultural Politics of Education* 18, no. 3: 329–42.

Lundestad, Geir. 2014. 'The Cold War in Europe, 1945–1949: Some Old and New Theories about the Cold War'. In *East, West, North, South: International Relations since 1945*. London/New York: Sage Publications.

Novick, Peter. 1999. *The Holocaust and Collective Memory: The American Experience*. Boston: Bloomsbury Publishing.

Parkes, R. J. 2009. 'Teaching History as Historiography: Engaging Narrative Diversity in the Curriculum'. *International Journal of Historical Teaching, Learning and Research* 8, no. 2: 118–32.

Reckwitz, Andreas. 2006. 'Ernesto Laclau Diskurse, Hegemonien, Antagonismen'. In *Kultur. Theorien der Gegenwart*. Edited by Stephan Moebius and Dirk Quadflieg, 339–49. Wiesbaden: Verlag für Sozialwissen.

Ryan, Lorraine. 2011. 'Memory, Power and Resistance: The Anatomy of a Tripartite Relationship'. *Memory Studies* 4, no. 2: 154–89.

Seixas, Peter. 2000. 'Schweigen! Die Kinder! Or Does Postmodern History Have a Place in the Schools?' In *Knowing, Teaching, and Learning History: National and International Perspectives*. Edited by Peter Stearns, Peter Seixas and Samuel Wineburg, 19–37. New York: New York University Press.

Sturken, Marita. 1997. *Tangled Memories: The Vietnam War, the AIDS Epidemic, and the Politics of Remembering*. Berkeley: University of California Press.

Williams, James H. 2014. *(Re)Constructing Memory: School Textbooks and the Imagination of the Nation*. Rotterdam: Sense Publishers.

Open Access This chapter is licensed under the terms of the Creative Commons Attribution 4.0 International License (http://creativecommons.org/licenses/by/4.0/), which permits use, sharing, adaptation, distribution and reproduction in any medium or format, as long as you give appropriate credit to the original author(s) and the source, provide a link to the Creative Commons licence and indicate if changes were made.

The images or other third party material in this chapter are included in the chapter's Creative Commons licence, unless indicated otherwise in a credit line to the material. If material is not included in the chapter's Creative Commons licence and your intended use is not permitted by statutory regulation or exceeds the permitted use, you will need to obtain permission directly from the copyright holder.

14

1968 in German-speaking Switzerland: Controversies and Interpretations

Nadine Ritzer

'1968' has become an 'associative space of societal attributions and authorial interpretations of the self' (Frei 2008, 211). A study of the Swiss print media of the time reveals that two protests in particular had been responsible for moving public opinion in 1968, both of which relate to the Cold War to an equal extent: protests against the repression of the Prague Spring and against the war in Vietnam (Kleger 1999). Both events are distinctive in that they thoroughly destabilise bipolar constructions of the Cold War.

Reformers in the circles of Alexander Dubček and Ludvík Svoboda were fighting neither for liberalism nor for capitalism; rather, they sought a brand of socialism with a human face (Karner 2008). This is why anti-communist interpretations of the Prague Spring generally fall short. More recent studies now read the events in Prague as part of the international 68 movement and emphasise parallels between the forms of action taken and the demands made by both East and West (Frei 2008, 190–197). Similarly, the war in Vietnam and the role of the USA as an advocate of

N. Ritzer (✉)
Pädagogische Hochschule Berne, Berne, Switzerland
e-mail: nadine.ritzer@phbern.ch

© The Author(s) 2019
B. Christophe et al. (eds.), *The Cold War in the Classroom*, Palgrave Studies in Educational Media, https://doi.org/10.1007/978-3-030-11999-7_14

freedom and democracy are radically questioned. At the same time, the war in Vietnam had always been more than a mere proxy war in the East-West conflict. Many historians assume today that the North-South component was just as significant as the East-West aspect: '[...] the First Indochina War was simultaneously a colonial conflict and a Cold War confrontation', writes Fredrik Logevall (2010, 286), for instance. Others even maintain that from the 'third world' perspective there were hardly differences between the superpowers that were the USSR and the USA (Westad 2000, 564).

With this in mind, this chapter inquires as to how the Prague Spring and the Vietnam War have been and continue to be interpreted in schools in German-speaking Switzerland, based on three source types: teacher periodicals from the relevant period,[1] history textbooks from the relevant period and the present day, and teacher interviews.[2] The study design is informed by two key lines of inquiry: How homogeneous or controversial have the various interpretations negotiated in different media been and to what extent do these controversies continue? Can shifts in these interpretations be identified over the course of time?

The results of the comparative study unveil ambivalences that surprisingly recur in all analysed formats, indicating that both events were from the outset too complex to be mapped within a simplistic structure of East/West dualism.

Switzerland in the Cold War

While Switzerland assumed an officially neutral position in the Cold War, it was western-oriented in terms of ideology, economy, geography and national policy. This was not least evident in its generally anti-communist stance, shared by the population at large as well as the prominent political parties. As Kurt Imhof (1999) emphasises, anti-communism served as a societal 'basic consensus', a buttress of Helvetian identity construction and 'organising principle of political communication'. The latter also informed the school, which – in the context of the so-called 'spiritual national defence' (*Geistige Landesverteidigung*) – also sought to 'arm' its young people for the fight against communism (Ritzer 2015, 129–162). Events in Czechoslovakia in 1948 and Korean War had fuelled fear of the 'red menace'. In 1951, the Swiss Federal Council issued a secret decree on 'preserving national security', which led to some 900,000 persons being registered by the state on lists of potentially suspicious individuals. It was not until these surveillance mechanisms were unveiled in the so-called 'secret files scandal' (*Fichenaffäre*) of 1990 that the decree was revoked (Bretscher-Spindler 1997, 213; Kreis 1993). Although Switzerland was shocked and unsettled by the scandal, the resulting reinterpretation of the events of the Cold War was nevertheless slow in coming.

The Early Autumn of the Prague Spring

The violent end to the Prague Spring brought by the Warsaw Pact troops shaped the news reports in Swiss media like no other event in 1968 (Kleger 1999). Thousands of Swiss citizens, including entire school classes, took to the streets in order to protest against 'the Russians'. During a special session of the national council, Walther Hofer declared the solidarity of 'freedom-conscious Switzerland' with the 'violated' people of Czechoslovakia. Switzerland, he proclaimed, was appalled by the infringement of 'the right of self-determination of a small state and of its endeavours towards a self-defined and independent existence' (www.dodis.ch/32187, 2). Federal Council President Willy Spühler evoked an instructive lesson to the Swiss people not only to remember the value of, but also to defend, their own civil liberties. Members of parliament praised in particular the commitment and enthusiasm of young people for the flame of freedom being ignited amongst the Czechoslovakian people (www.dodis.ch/32187, 29–33). The SLZ considered it the 'serious duty of all teachers' to address these events in class (N.N., SLZ 113, 1968, 1315).

Contemporary Interpretations in the Teacher Periodicals

In July 1967, twenty Czechoslovakian teachers paid a visit to members of the Swiss Teachers' Association, who returned the visit in Czechoslovakia in the spring of 1968. This visit was intended to significantly shape initial interpretations of the Prague Spring and indeed was subject to detailed commentary in various reports following the crushing of the Prague Spring (Hänni, SLZ 113, 1968, 1299; Adam, SLZ 113, 1968, 1299–1310 and 1350–1357). These interpretations repeatedly moved beyond the bipolar structure conventionally applied to the Cold War. The reports focus on the political euphoria in the ČSSR and the cautious optimism of the host teachers: 'We felt so free, we could have been anywhere', a member of the Association described the atmosphere in Prague in the spring of 1968 (Adam, SLZ 113, 1968, 1354). The reporter emphasises the openness of the people, who were speaking – uninhibited by the recently lifted censorship of the press – of old grievances and new hopes. In these jubilant days, one teacher writes, public criticism on the part of artists and intellectuals had become a thing of possibility (Adam, SLZ 113, 1968, 1350–1357). What were perceived as the objectives of the 'Czech Revolution'? The ČSSR was in the process, thus the general theme, of 'becoming a democratic socialist state', a state with 'all civil liberties' (Adam, SLZ 113, 1301). The Swiss seemed to believe that the Czechoslovakians found themselves on the threshold of breaking through the conventional dichotomy of 'democracy' and 'socialism', and taking a third path (Adam, SLZ 113, 1968, 1299–1310 and 1350–1357; Hruby, SLZ 114, 1969, 1240–1245). Following the Warsaw Pact invasion, however, the tone of the reports changed somewhat, even in the SLZ. The dichotomous worldview dominated perceptions of the events, which were also interpreted in terms of the national master narrative of a Helvetian 'tradition of liberalisation', as the struggle of an 'enslaved people' for freedom and against Soviet communism. If the report is to be believed, the climate at universities and schools was one of denunciation, intimidation, fear and dismissal, the teachers being held responsible for the 'failure to Sovietise Eastern Europe' (N.N., SLZ 115, 1970, 1572–1575). This led to the Czechoslovakian education system being ransacked in search of 'unreliable persons' by means of 'inquisition papers', demanding all those questioned to inform against critically minded colleagues. Although, according to the SLZ, some 95 per cent of teachers refused to complete the 'inquisition papers', a 'cleansing' of professors and academic staff nevertheless took place (N.N., SLZ 115, 1970, 1572–1575; N.N., SLZ 115, 1970, 115).

The Swiss teacher periodicals took on the task of denouncing the instrumentalisation of education by these communist governments, and painted pictures of the courageous and clever resistance measures on the part of the people against the system of injustice. Particularly striking is that the teachers were usually portrayed as victims of the regime rather than as the agents and vehicles of the ruling ideology (Ritzer 2015, 85–94). The euphoria in the ČSSR in the spring of 1968 and the quest for a new form of socialism on the part of the 'reform communists' were now hardly mentioned. The protesters were considered role models in the struggle against communism due to their civil courage, working in the interests of 'spiritual national defence' (Frei, PB 62, 1968, 69). The protests in Prague or Bratislava served as a warning to the Swiss to fight to preserve their own civil liberties. Because the martyr image suited the concept of 'intellectual national defence' better than that of reformer, not only the protesters but also the reform communists, in particular Ludvík Svoboda and Alexander Dubček, were celebrated as heroes in the struggle against Soviet communism.

In Switzerland, numerous young people organised demonstrations and rallies. Many teacher teams and education authorities were critical of their political activities. One outraged teacher reported how a colleague had spoken out against young people being encouraged to demonstrate and thus being 'instrumentalised' for other people's ideals; ultimately, young people can be equally motivated to 'do completely the opposite … as in the case of the Hitler Youth'. Criticising his colleague, the teacher continues: If he, as a teacher, is no longer in a position to clearly condemn 'such a nefarious attack on human rights' and to name the 'culprits', 'if I am no longer in a position to present the judicious courage and resolute determination of the Czech people as an example of civil courage and civic duty, then I can no longer be a teacher. Then I am no more than the infamous "conveyor of facts"' (N.N., SLZ 113, 1968, 193–1194). He was not alone. Many teachers were impressed by the initiatives taken by their pupils, supporting or encouraging them to participate in protest marches (N.N., SLZ 113, 1968, 1193–1195; G.S., ScS 55, 1968, 725).[3] Blue, white and red pennants were displayed on bicycles and cars and flags were carried to demonstration marches and silent protests. During one of the largest demonstrations in Bern, hundreds of pupils – with permission from their teachers – performed a sitting strike in front of the Soviet embassy, disregarding, however, police regulations (*Schweizer Fernsehen*, 21 August 1968).

The SLZ also showed great interest in the youth demonstrations of the ČSSR, most of which were portrayed as the spearhead of the anti-communist movement. Only seldom were parallels drawn between the 1968 movements in East and West. The newsletter of the SLV declared the attempt to communise ČSSR youth a failure (N.N., SLZ 115, 1970, 1572–1575). Recent research, however, refutes this claim. The rebellion of Czech youth may have turned against Soviet Orthodox communism; not, however, against reform communism (Karner 2008, 8). Demands were also made for societal change (Frei 2008, 190–197), dramatically exceeding the hopes of many Swiss protesters for the ČSSR. It was only seldom pointed out that the young people of the ČSSR were questioning 'authorities' and criticising the education system as were young people everywhere. Although a speaker pointed to the transnational character of the 1968 protests during a demonstration, at the same time he strongly criticised the 'rebellion' in Switzerland:

> Young people in Czechoslovakia also experienced demonstrations and riots only a few months ago. And in Prague too, for the same - quite unspectacular - issues as in almost all large cities of the world. The apprentices, students and pupils who took to the streets in Prague were no more original than their counterparts in Berlin, Rome and Paris. What was unique and exemplary in Czechoslovakia, however, was that it was the young people and not only the much more experienced and mature adults who in the space of these few months had admirably taken on responsibility and self-discipline, thus achieving resistance in its most effective form (Fuchs, SLZ 113, 1968, 1195).

Some warned, however, that anti-communist reflexes could not do justice to the complexity of the conflict in the ČSSR. Even some pupils acknowledged that the 'Czechs were and wanted to remain communists, that in this case anti-communism would not have the desired effect' (G.S., ScS 55, 1968, 725). Sociologist Karl Hruby (SLZ 114, 1969, 1244) put it in plain terms at an international teacher conference in 1969: 'No one has demanded that state capitalism - in the East referred to as "socialism" - be abolished'. As suggested above, the teachers who reported of the hospitality of their ČSSR friends knew this too, albeit not without emphasising that these 'amiable people are communists who believe in an improved social order and fight for it with honesty and conviction' (Adam, SLZ 113, 1968, 1299–1310). It was the protesters themselves, and not so much the periodicals, who pointed to the ambivalent interpretations that could be applied to the events in the ČSSR: In Basel, the streets echoed with the call of 'Dubček! Svoboda!' Posters drew parallels between the violence in Prague and in Vietnam. Both American *and* Soviet 'imperialism' were given a harsh verdict: At a demonstration in Basel on 22nd August 1968, protest banners read: 'ČSSR – out with the UdSSR! Vietnam – out with the USA!' (NZZ, 22 August 1968, 4). In Zürich, too, the 'interventions' of both superpowers were denounced by the *Progressiven Mittelschüler* (progressive *Gymnasium* pupils) or the *Fortschrittliche Studentenschaft* (progressive students) (Becker 2014, 60).

The Prague Spring in the Textbooks

Although the Swiss textbooks for the most part tend to locate the Prague Spring within a bipolar world order, ambivalences are nevertheless perceptible. While a few early portrayals suggest that the Prague Spring sought not to defeat but rather to reform the socialist system, two strands of interpretative thinking were dominant in the 1970s and 1980s. It was only after the end of the Cold War that teaching materials offered a more nuanced depiction of the protagonists and their objectives, albeit retaining the fundamental narrative - in images and text alike - of the struggle of a freedom-loving people against a dictatorial Soviet communism.

A history textbook of 1968 presents interpretive elements that reappear at later intervals: The dispute between the 'Moscow-friendly communists and the innovators', it claims, was won by Alexander Dubček, who relaxed the censorship of the press. 'The elation of young people about this glimmer of liberty compelled Dubček to make further concessions.' This was not tolerated, however, by 'the Russians', who consequently ordered the Warsaw Pact forces to invade (CH-1968-Göldi, 61). According to this interpretation, the 'communists' allowed for the new liberties only under pressure; no autonomous will to reform is attributed to them. The dominance of the bipolar logic that informs such interpretations also becomes evident in references to the Brezhnev Doctrine that claim 'Russia' primarily intervened because no satellite state may be allowed to think differently. At the same time, the insurgents were portrayed as martyrs; it had been only their non-violent protest that had prevented further bloodshed. An image of young protesters around and on an army tank, with the caption 'Prague 1968: Not Afraid of Tanks' emphasises the interpretation of the conflict as a struggle between David and Goliath (CH-1968-Göldi, 61).

The history textbook published shortly after the events, *Denkwürdige Vergangenheit* (1969), briefly indicates the will to reform in the political leadership of the ČSSR. Svoboda and Dubček, the book explains, had attempted to combine the ideals of East and West; to reconcile fraternity and liberty. What exactly this meant was not explained in detail. The responsibility for the repression of the Prague Spring was attributed to the 'Kremlin powers'. Despite its abrupt ending, the textbook claims, the Prague Spring inspired hope, 'for the unanimously non-violent resistance on the part of the Czechoslovakian people bore witness as never seen before to the indestructible power of liberty and spirit. And this witness came from the communist camp' (CH-1969-Müller, 266).

Here too, non-violent protest is a model for the Swiss pupils. This author, however, unlike many articles published in the association newsletters, expressly points out that the insurgents belonged to the 'communist camp' and were not acting in opposition to communism. This interpretation destabilised the bipolar logic of 'spiritual national defence': positive political activity was even possible in the communist camp! This reading tends, however, to constitute the exception to the rule in Swiss textbooks. Portrayals from the 1970s and early 1980s retain the differential semantics of 'freedom and democracy' versus 'coercion and communism'. A widely used textbook, for example, presents a highly emotional depiction of the attempt of 'courageous men' to liberate themselves from the Soviet pressure (CH-1970-Jaggi, 306–307). Here too, the book mentions that the leaders of the protests in the ČSSR retained communism, albeit with 'as much liberty and humanity as possible'. Was the author suggesting here that most of the insurgents - unlike the leaders -

were questioning communism? Certainly, the insurgents were depicted as heroes: 'Many women are crying. The men, however, are becoming embroiled in heated debate with foreign soldiers. Their words are lost in the din from the Russian tanks. Foolhardy citizens of Prague succeed in exploding Russian tanks'. Interestingly, the author makes an alteration with regard to those responsible for ending the Prague Spring. In 1970 he had emphasised that 'powerful Russia' had not been willing to grant more liberties (CH-1970-Jaggi, 306). Another version of his history textbook, published eight years later, includes the ruling powers of the Soviet 'subordinate countries' amongst those responsible for the ČSSR invasion, rather than just 'the Russians' (CH-1978-Jaggi, 382).

It was not until the mid-1980s that these narratives shifted. At this time there was also a change in the design of history textbooks. Since the end of the 1970s, increasing numbers of sources had been used, with the intention of inspiring learners to form their own perceptions of history. The book *Zeiten Menschen Kulturen* (ZMK), published in 1985, for example, primarily features sources. The text describing the Prague Spring was reduced to a table outlining the history of events in the ČSSR since 1918, with a focus on structural differences between East and West. The production of consumer goods in the ČSSR had been neglected in favour of heavy industry, leading to a division in the Communist Party between the 'Moscow-faithful' and 'reformers'. Initially, the reformers had prevailed. Their goal had been paving their own way to socialism, 'holding on to communism, but guaranteeing civil liberties', which had been thwarted by the invasion of the 'Warsaw Pact States' (CH-1985-Ziegler, 61–63 and CH-1993-Ziegler, 61–63). Interestingly, ambivalent interpretations were inherent in the sources. Excerpts from the 'Two Thousand Words Manifesto' and the Brezhnev Doctrine were printed, along with an opinion piece by Swiss social democrat Walther Bringolf, who claimed the CPSU had had strategic reasons for hindering the 'ideological liberation' of the ČSSR from the 'corset of communist discipline'. Were the ČSSR to fall away, he argued, the 'southern flank' of the CPSU would have been open to attack, bringing about the end of the 'Soviet-Russian superpower policy towards the West' (CH-1985-Ziegler, 62 and CH-1993-Ziegler, 62). The pictorial sources, on the other hand, continue the 'David and Goliath' theme, showing soldiers or tanks in the midst of a peaceful demonstration with the caption 'Russian invasion of Czechoslovakia, 1968: Tanks against freedom fighters' (CH-1993-Ziegler, 53). Depite the juxtapositioning of contradictory interpretations of events – the economic East-West divide, the threat to communism posed by the freedom movement in the CSSR and the strategic military motives of the USSR – learners are never explicitly made aware of these differences.

After the end of the Cold War, the portrayal of the Prague Spring gained further in nuance. The history textbook *Weltgeschichte im Bild* (WiB), volume 9, 1996, was the first to point out that the Communist Party, alarmed by the level of unrest in the country, had placed itself at the 'spearheard of the movement'. Dubček sought to develop a form of communism with 'a human face' (CH-1996-Bühler, 51); indeed, as a pictorial source suggests, 'a deeply democratic society suitable for the Czechoslovakian conditions', having himself initiated the Prague Spring: 'Following a long period of police rule, terror and oppression, now better times seemed to be on the horizon'. But the USSR did not approve of this unique path, the textbook seems to suggest. Accompanied by catcalls, invading tanks of the Warsaw Pact had put an end to the Prague Spring (CH-1996-Bühler, 51). Despite the nuances in the text, the pictorial language continued the established theme.

Differences in living standards between East and West also constituted a theme in a history textbook published after the Cold War with several new issues published over twenty years without any changes to the Prague Spring narrative. The lower standard of living as compared to the West and also the monitoring of the population by the Communist Party had fomented displeasure in a number of countries. As a result, 1968 saw upheaval within the Party in the ČSSR and also various reforms. As the USSR had feared that this development could 'spread to other countries' and endanger the 'communist system of government', it intervened with the purpose of 'saving socialism', establishing a party leadership that reversed the reforms in the ČSSR (CH-2010-Meyer, 73–74). Although this textbook, still used today by some learners, does address the upheaval within the ČSSR Communist Party, the opposition between the protestors and Soviet communism – the pattern 'freedom fighters versus communist oppressors' – remains the central motif of the narrative, echoed in the pictorial source (CH-2010-Meyer, 74). Above all, the textbook fails to mention that the reforms were introduced by the communists.

The Prague Spring in Memory Construction

The teachers interviewed emphasise varying aspects of the Prague Spring: the protests against 'the Russians', the biased anti-communist interpretation of the events, and the general anti-communist feeling in Switzerland.

One teacher, here referred to as Heinz Sutter (*1943), speaks of the demonstration in Bern 'against the Russians', which led to skirmishes with the police, riots and tear gas, as the demonstrators, among them our interviewee, did not follow police instructions.[4] Protesting against the injustices in Prague and Bratislava therefore did not automatically suggest acceptance of the 'western' order. The protest against 'the Russians' was at the same time a protest against the authorities: against teachers and parents who had forbidden participation, against the government and the police, whose rules were ignored. Not only 'the Russians' were infringing upon the constitutional order; Swiss youth too, blocking the roads, choosing their own demonstration routes and ultimately protesting without permission in front of the Soviet embassy.

As I have shown, some teachers approved of their pupils' demonstrations. One (*1940) reports that his pupils, like many others, had demanded permission to demonstrate 'for Czechia', which, 'of course', was granted:

> They [the pupils, N. R.] extended breaktime, assembled and marched across the playground. They were carrying a Czechian flag and shouting 'Dubček! Svoboda! Dubček! Svoboda!' They knew about demonstrating from the news media and had been so moved by it that they wanted to take an active part themselves. It really made an impression on us.[5]

Another interviewee (*1944) reminds us that the shouts of 'Dubček and Svoboda' were for most people the call for a new, anti-communist beginning.[6] He himself, under observation by state security due to numerous trips to Eastern Europe, questioned this reading, emphasising that protesters in the ČSSR sought to re-examine, but not overcome, communism. At the same time he pointed out that 'people' certainly sympathised with some ideas of the Eastern bloc. 'One', he continued, had the feeling that 'socialism with a human face' would be an interesting model with future potential.[7]

A secondary-school teacher (Gymnasium, *1958), reports that he had heard about events in the ČSSR in the primary school and on the radio and 'simply understood that it was the evil Russians occupying a peaceful country and population against their will, and that that's a bad thing'.[8] Another teacher (*1961) mentions the many sources of information, unable to recall from whom he had heard what exactly was happening in the ČSSR. In his recollection, television images and newspaper reports are blended with explanations from his parents. His father was an officer and as a boy he had learnt that the USSR constituted a permanent threat, which influenced his understanding of the events in Prague.[9] Today, his memory of the protests is overshadowed by his memory of a new Czechoslovakian schoolmate, a refugee.

The Vietnam War in Focus

In Switzerland too, the 68 movement brought protests against the war in Vietnam onto the streets and into the lecture halls. As early as 1965, the organisation *Fortschrittliche Studentenschaft Zürich* (Progressive Students of Zurich), convened a 'teach-in' at the ETH Zurich on the conflict in Indochina, understood here as a result of colonialism and imperialism (Peter 2008, 62–73). In this sense, the Swiss critics of the Vietnam War were part of the 'counter-cultures' described by Jeremi Suri, who fought against 'imperialism' and 'fascism', thus casting doubt on the 'Cold War order' (Suri 2010, 470). In Switzerland there was a growing debate in the Vietnam War context about the forms which 'development aid' and solidarity with the 'third world' should take (Holenstein 1998, 115–125). At the same time, interdependencies between the 'Third World problem' and the Cold War led to public discourse on the Vietnam War shifted the East-West dualism into one of North and South. The result was that anti-communism decreased in credibility as a sustainable basic consensus for civil society (Imhof 1996, 26–27).

Further, the Vietnam protests were also the scene of generational conflict. Western Europe's youth questioned the policies of their political leaders and glorified the Viet Cong peasant warriers as well as Mao Zedong or Che Guevara as 'symbols for a revolution against not just political institutions, but the basic organization of society' (Suri 2010, 469). The hippies were only *one* manifestation of the 'counter-cultures' experimenting with new forms of protest in San Francisco, Prague or Zurich. Various forms of active protest such as American 'anti-Vietnam songs' and peace activists as well as demonstrations, sit-ins and 'teach-ins' are firmly anchored in the Swiss collective memory.

Despite the wide support for the protests, significant voices in Switzerland defended the Vietnam War as a necessary measure to protect against communism and condemned the protests as communist intrigue. In 1966, the Federal Political Department informed the ambassador in Washington, D. C. of an 'extreme left-wing infiltration', a torchlight procession in Bern to protest against the Vietnam War (www.dodis.ch/31167). The reporting on the war in Vietnam by the media was also criticised by Peter Sager, founder of the Swiss *Ost-Institut*, where numerous – often anti-communist – brochures on the Eastern bloc were published for readers including schools. He even considered democracy endangered; it had become impossible, he claimed, to form an objective opinion because the people were overwhelmed by the images and portrayals of Vietnam. He not only rejected the heroising of the Viet Cong as inappropriate; he also compared the war in Vietnam with World War II. Inspired by domino theory, he argued that the Americans in Vietnam must oppose communism, just as the Allied Forces had done with Hitler (Sager 1968, 82).

Contemporary Reception in Teacher Periodicals

Unlike the daily press (Imhof et al. 1999, 246–249), the teacher periodicals barely registered the war in Vietnam. No discourse relating to the war is discernible in either the SLZ or the ScS, nor did any of the association periodicals comment on the demonstrations. It was not until the USA's retreat that the SLZ addressed the topic, focusing on the humanitarian catastrophe and calling for support for the 'International Youth Aid Union' (*Internationale Vereinigung für Jugendhilfe*) to help children and young war victims in Vietnam (N.N., SLZ 120, 1975, 313). Following the communist annexation of South Vietnam, and the inclusion of the 'Boat People' in the discourse, the SLZ called once again for solidarity with those affected and loudly criticised not only the communist regime but also the 'leftist' students at the University of Bern with their provocative slogan 'No to Hirschy; yes to Giap!'[10] (Gut, SLZ 124, 1979). There was no critique of the US warfare, no question of the great western power sharing responsibility for the humanitarian crisis. It was not until 1989, in an article on Vietnam, Laos and Cambodia, that the cause and course of the war was given candid attention (Rudolf, SLZ 134, 1989, no. 9, 14). It is striking that, while the article speaks of 'efforts towards independence', there is no mention of a 'struggle against communism'. Following the author's historical overview of the colonial period, a 'Vietnamese woman' speaks of the era under French rule and the Vietnamese struggle for independence, and then describes – with precise year dates and specialist terms – how the 'cruel rule of terror' under Ngo Dinh Diem 'persecuted all "leftist suspects"', supported by the Catholic Church and the USA. She states that the American bombings began in 1965, without, however, mentioning a catalyst for these attacks. She also described the losses on the US side and the end of the war, the forced reunification, and the fact that some 2.5 million people resettled or fled the communist powers (Rudolf, SLZ 134, 1989, No. 9, 14–16). Although at the end of the narrative it was the communist North that showed its ugly face, this presentation breaks through the long-dominant reading of the war in Vietnam as a struggle between communism and capitalism. Criticism of the warring parties was expressed in the depictions of a 'contemporary witness', a popular method often used by history teaching materials.

The Vietnam War in the Textbooks

As Richard Lachmann and Lacy Mitchell (2014) have shown, the portrayal of the war in Vietnam changed dramatically in American textbooks. While the atrocities of the war were barely mentioned in the 1960s and 1970s, they were given increased attention from the 1980s. This went hand-in-hand with growing criticism of US foreign policy. US textbooks had been placing more value on 'the hellish and personal aspects of the Vietnam War' since the 1990s. Pictorial sources increasingly showed wounded or dead US soldiers, the trauma of the latter depicted in the text, while the Vietnamese victims were still only mentioned in passing. The anti-Vietnam-War protests have only seldom been mentioned until today, although attention paid to this subject is now increasing (Lachmann and Mitchell 2014).

What form does this take in the Swiss textbooks? Although the conflicts in the French colony were already escalating in the 1950s, the conflict in Indochina was ignored by most Swiss textbooks of the 1960s. Even in 1978, the subject was merely a note in the margin of one of the most widely used textbooks of German-speaking Switzerland, stating that communism, propagated by Russia and China, had spread through Indochina as had been the case in Korea. Vietnam was divided, it states, once the USA, NATO and France had deployed 'opposition troops' (CH-1978-Jaggi, 377). The first textbook to mention the war was *Denkwürdige Vergangenheit* (1969). The author, Otto Müller, dedicates a great deal of attention to the subject of human rights, as well as decolonialisation and the 'third world', unlike the authors of other textbooks (Ritzer 2015, 294–295). Müller mentions the French phase of the conflict in Indochina and the defeat of the colonial power at Dien Bien Phu. The battles ended, Müller continues, with the division of Vietnam into a communist North and 'a dreadful gulf between rich and poor in the South' (CH-1969-Müller, 261), ultimately leading to civil war. In a relatively critical manner for the time, the author notes that the USA supported a government in South Vietnam that primarily backed the interests of large landowners and not those of the desperate rice farmers. Subsequently, however, he is also careful to justify – or at least explain – US intervention, with recourse to domino theory: 'They [the Americans; N. R.] wished to prevent the communism that was ruling North Vietnam from coming to power in South Vietnam, possibly even across the whole of South-East Asia' (CH-1969-Müller, 264). No criticism of the US war strategy can be found here; indeed, a critical voice is heard for the first time in a teaching brochure of 1975, in which the author begins by describing the colonial history of Indochina and the French phase of the war in great detail. Here, he mentions both the role of the People's Republic of China in the anti-colonial freedom struggle of the 'Vietnamese Independence League' (Viet Minh) and the ambivalent role played by Ngo Dinh Diem's supporters and the Viet Cong (CH-1975-Göldi, 45–57). Here too, the struggle against communism is given as the reason for the US intervention, triggered by the Tonkin Incident. At the same time, the text repeatedly emphasises that the USA determined the course of the war events. The author harshly scorns the 'war tactics' of the Americans, such as the expulsion of thousands of civilians, the use of new weapons such as cluster bombs and firebombs, and the use of gas and defoliants. The author depicts the My Lai massacre by citing from a source, an unusual method for this author:

> The clearer it was becoming to the Americans that the Viet Cong could not be taken, the more they lost control and resorted to massacres. The best-known example is the obliteration of the My Lay village. Because the Americans believed it to be a Viet Cong stronghold, Leutenant Calley was given the order to eliminate the village and all its inhabitants. Machine guns mowed down men, women and children. No one gave a precise number; it was certainly far more than a hundred. (Excerpt from the booklet *Du und der Krieg*, quoted in: CH-1975-Göldi, 53)

Within this source, the author not only criticises the murder of women and children on the part of American soldiers; he also provides an explanation for the US atrocities. The guerrilla tactics of the Viet Cong led, he claims, the Americans to 'lose control'. A similar oscillation between naming the horrors of American warfare and putting them into proportion and context can still be perceived in textbooks published towards the end of the Cold War. In the history textbook *Weltgeschichte im Bild 9* (WiB) of 1989, for example, we read: 'Because it was impossible to differentiate between the guerrillas and ordinary farmers, the government troops burned suspicious villages to the ground with napalm bombs. In some cases, all inhabitants of a town, men women and children alike, were all killed (CH-1989-Bühler, 60). It is striking that the author speaks of 'some cases'; even the most recent of the textbooks examined insists that the US soldiers were 'at a disadvantage' due to the guerrilla warfare tactics and the good camouflage of the Viet Cong. The book sequatiously describes the actions of the US soldiers and their allies as 'retaliatory strikes' for the Viet Cong attacks, pointing out that these strikes often hit innocent civilians (CH-2005-Argast, 124).

It is still striking that criticism of the Americans, not necessarily in line with the general public opinion of the time, is usually 'hidden' within the source texts. This is also the case for the book *Weltgeschichte im Bild 9* (WiB) of 1978, which only allocated little space to the Vietnam War. The dichotomised reading of the conflict prevails: 'The Americans took up defence in South Vietnam against the communist North. They did not move from this warzone until after decades of bloodshed' (CH-1978-Allemann, 42). This book, otherwise generous with sources, depicts hardly any pictorial or textual sources at this point; the war is not addressed again until in a later chapter, 'Korea – Vietnam', with a pictorial source showing children behind barbed wire, yet without any contextualisation. The text mentioned that the war was extended due to support from the Americans and Chinese. In 1968, it continues, the USA armed 500,000 men against the 'freedom fighter Ho Chi Minh'. The war cost more than two million lives before counting the civilian losses (CH-1978-Allemann, 54). There is insufficient mention of the use of chemical weapons and the atrocities of soldiers; rather, criticism of the USA confined itself to the mild reproach that its intervention prolonged the war. Use of the term 'freedom fighter' for Ho Chi Minh could be interpreted as a quiet expression of sympathy as the term had positive connotations in the context of the Swiss 'tradition of liberation'. It remains open whether the authors considered the war necessary to suppress communism; no verdict is given in the 1985 edition, although critical nuances are perceptible in the source texts. The history textbook *Zeiten Menschen Kulturen* (ZMK) provides a table showing how the conflict had developed since the 1940s, and names the 'alleged' Tonkin Incident as the catalyst for the first US air raids over North Vietnam. Alongide textual sources of American origin – many of which came from the office of President Johnson, who pointed to the necessity of the war against communism – space is also allocated to critical voices, such as that of Ho Chi Minh, denouncing US warfare and 'murder' (CH-1985-Ziegler, 26–31), albeit in the absence of a source to support the charge of 'murder' at My Lais, for instance.

It was only in history textbooks published towards the end of the Cold War that space was allocated to a discussion of the consequences of the Vietnam War for civil society. In the new 1989 edition of *Weltgeschichte im Bild 9* (WiB), the Vietnam War was even made a key topic of the Cold War, and thus contextualised from the outset within the East-West conflict. At the same time, however, the same book also addresses – albeit implicitly – the North-South conflict that manifested itself in the war, via, for instance, depictions from the perspective of a rice farmer struggling neither for communism nor for democracy, but simply for a better life. Similarly, the authors emphasise that it was primarily the high poverty level that had moved the people of South Vietnam to support the 'National Front for the Liberation of South Vietnam' (Viet Cong). Text and images alike sketch a picture of an unequal struggle in which the highly technologized yet powerless USA ultimately surrenders to a badly equipped yet efficient Viet Cong. The consequences of the US intervention, such as destruction by napalm or Agent Orange, were now explicitly mentioned in this textbook, tellingly accusing both sides of torture and murder:

> Once it was established that not only the guerrilla fighters but also the American soldiers had tortured prisoners and killed innocent civilians, a storm of protests against the war overcame the USA. Tens of thousands took to the streets. Young men tore up their call-up papers and Vietnam veterans threw their medals of bravery on the steps of the White House (CH-1989-Bühler, 60).

Discussion of the protests against the Vietnam War was also new.

As we have seen, while the 1989 history textbook WiB addresses the North-South component of the Vietnam conflict, it locates the latter primarily within the East-West pattern. This remained the case until 1991, when the textbook *Durch Geschichte zur Gegenwart 4* (GZG) expressly discussed the Vietnam War in the chapter 'From Colonisation to the "Third World"', thus removing it from the Cold War context. This shift of emphasis led to a detailed overview of French colonialism becoming integrated into the narrative. The textbook explained that the population's siding with the Vietminh was due to the farmers' hopes for a redistribution of land (CH-1991-Meyer, 111). The atrocities of the war were portrayed in great detail; the sources provided evidence of napalm, of defoliants and massacres of civilians. Consequently, the book points out in all clarity, the perception of the American role in world politics had shifted dramatically. The former saviour from fascism and communism had now – such was increasingly public opinion – become a butcher. It is also noteworthy how the textbook has recourse to the 'David and Goliath' motif here. The authors suggest between the lines that 'little Switzerland' has far more in common with the small, yet courageous, North Vietnam than with the American giant. This becomes especially clear in an exercise asking the learners whether Switzerland, like North Vietnam, would be able to prevail against a world power (CH-1991-Meyer, 116).

The 2005 textbook, *Menschen in Zeit und Raum 9* (MZR) seemed to permanently oscillate between varying perspectives of the war, which, despite being introduced in the title as a 'proxy war', is traced in its origins back to the Vietminh struggle for independence from imperial France (CH-2005-Argast, 122–125). As soon as the book speaks of dividing the country into a 'communist and a capitalist part' (CH-2005-Argast, 122), however, the East-West dualism regains in dominance. Although learners read that Ho Chi Minh was drawn to socialist and communist ideas primarily in his desire to reform the economy and society following the effects of colonialisation, the text continues to state that the Vietminh considered the 'European forms of state' unjust, partly due to their colonialist association. Later again, however, the text claims that China and the USSR had encouraged the communist aspects of the reform. At the same time, the alliance of the USA with the 'dictatorial president' in South Vietnam is given cautious justification on the basis of domino theory and containment: 'For the USA, the government leader Diem – despite the lack of democracy in his own dealings – was a reliable ally in the battle against communism' (CH-2005-Argast, 123). MZR also discusses the devastating consequences of the war for the Vietnamese civilian population and for the American veterans. With this war, the book concludes, the USA has damaged its reputation in the world.

We can thus ascertain that the textbooks, similar to the case of the Prague Spring, reveal continuities in their interpretative patterns; however, the shifts are more dramatic than in the narrative of the protest movement in the ČSSR. As early as 1969 there were first signs of a North-South reading of the conflict, as is the case in research today; the bipolar logic being especially dominant in the 1970s. Domino theory, based on an East-West divide, is repeatedly referred to in the context of motives for the American intervention. Towards the end of the Cold War, the dominance of these dichotomous readings was to a certain extent destabilised. References to French colonialism became more explicit and discussion of social injustice became more important. However, the 1991 textbook explicity located the conflict in Indochina within the decolonisation context, thus introducing the '68 discourse' to the classroom. Yet the most recent textbook under analysis, published in 2005, still refers to the Vietnam War as a proxy war between communism and capitalism.

The US' form of warfare was criticised as early as 1975, much earlier than in the American textbooks, and often sources are used to express critique. At the same time, and still today, Swiss authors explain the atrocities committed by the USA and its allies with an apologetic description of the soldiers' desperation as a result of the Viet Cong guerilla tactics. Swiss textbooks urge the remembrance of the victims of both sides, although there are only very few images of American victims. The protests in the USA were mentioned only as of 1989, in the margins of textbook narratives, and it is these protests, criticising the 'imperialism' of the West as early as 1968, that constitute the focus of the teacher interviews.

Remembering the War in Vietnam

These teachers, for whom discussing the events of 1968 means to a large extent discussing the protests agains the war in Vietnam, strays rather far from the interpretative guidelines provided by the textbook. While many emphasise that the war in Vietnam had been a taboo subject during their studies, others recount that they had witnessed the war being taught. This does not mean that all interpretations were 'sayable' everywhere. In debates on whether and how 'contemporary history' should be addressed in history lessons, warning voices advised against 'letting oneself be defined by the events of the day, doing politics rather than history' (Ritzer 2015,

267–269). Possibly many tutors considered the Vietnam War 'too political' to be discussed in the classroom. At the end of the 1960s, a too pronounced anti-Americanism did not yet seem opportune, as the following example of a teacher examination reveals. In 1968, a teacher in training – referred to in the following as Fritz Meier – was required to discuss the Vietnam War with his pupils in front of the school inspector. In his interview this teacher said that he had heard that the sympathies of this inspector were for America. He 'came to the defence of the Vietnam War' and argued that the USA must protect the world from the communist threat. This must have impressed the inspector; Meier passed the test.[11] A different teacher, who was having difficulties finding a job on account of his refusal of military service, criticises in an interview that the Americans, and right-wing circles in Switzerland, had attempted to reduce the Vietnam war to an East-West dualism. As a self-avowed 'pacifist student', he believed 'developing countries' to have been exploited in Indochina.[12] Similarly, a different interview partner (*1950) reports that he gradually became aware that the Americans were not always the good ones and the communists not always the 'bad'.[13]

Conclusion

This chapter has sought to fulfil a twofold objective: to render visible the homogeneity of and controversies inherent in interpretations of the Prague Spring and the Vietnam War at different points in time and in different media discourses; and to examine how readings of both events have changed over time. Four key results emerge from the analysis. First, the study has shown that the willingness to address both these topics with a sophisticated awareness of nuance has diminished with time. While in the 1960s, varying readings are perceptible in the sources analysed, from the 1970s onwards the dominant interpretations were those which followed a bipolar logic, thus gaining compatibility with other prevailing Cold War discourses (Ritzer 2015). With increasing distance to the event there seems to have been a cementing of the narrative; indeed, an ideologism of the various readings.

Second, two factors inspiring change in the textbooks were identified: innovative design of the medium textbook, leading to more multiperspectivity via sources, which were sometimes contradictory in nature; and the end of the Cold War itself, which required a (if only partial) reorientation process on the part of society, to reflect the historico-cultural work that bore witness to these events of 1968. The conflict over the Vietnam War, for example, reflected historical and cultural manifestations. It was in the context of the Vietnam War debate that textbooks from 1990 onwards articulated more scathing criticism towards the Western hegemonic power that would not have been possible before. In the Prague Spring discourse, on the other hand, despite two main nuances from 1990 onwards, elements of continuity with key interpretative patterns of 'spiritual national defence' can still be observed. Third, we have seen that the debate surrounding the war in Vietnam in German-speaking Switzerland was much more controversial than that on the Prague Spring. Fourth, in the light of the present day, we can ascertain that the teachers interviewed certainly deviated from the readings prescribed by the textbooks, by locating the Vietnam War more clearly within the context of the 'Third World problem', for example. They were thus also criticising the long-dominant concepts prevailing in Switzerland of 'spiritual national defence' and the 'semantic gap' with regard to the East-West conflict.

As a whole, the analysis shows that interpretations of the Prague Spring and the Vietman War based on a bipolar understanding of the Cold War are repeatedly destabilised in all media formats examined in the study, even if the occasional clichéd idea remains even today. Interpretations of the Cold War have thus become more fluid and fragmented, as if the ideologically painted narratives have been gradually deconstructed; certainly a result of the fading concept of 'spiritual national defence' as well as the end of the Cold War itself.

Notes

1. The periodicals analysed are the *Schweizerische Lehrerzeitung* (SLZ) (with no religious affiliation) and *Schweizer Schule* (ScS), published by the Catholic Teachers' Association.

2. The study is based on interviews with 27 teachers, 17 of which were guided interviews conducted during my doctoral research on the Cold War in Swiss schools (Ritzer 2015). Ten further interviews were conducted by Nora Zimmermann for the international research project, *Teaching the Cold War – Memory Practices in the Classroom*, whom I thank for access to the data. All interviews are cited by their assigned number, date, and the interviewee's country of origin (CH for Switzerland).
3. See also interview with CH12 (24 March 2010).
4. Interview with CH13 (26 March 2010).
5. Interview with CH12 (24 March 2010).
6. Interview with CH16 (1 April 2010).
7. Interview with CH18 (1 April 2010).
8. Interview with CH03 (27 August 2014).
9. Interview with CH04 (20 November 2014).
10. In February 1973, Hirschy was to give a guest lecture at the University of Berne on the *valeur éducative* of the army. The lecture was howled down by the students (Rogger 2008, 29–31). Giáp was a leading military strategist of the Viet Minh.
11. Interview with CH19 (9 April 2010).
12. Interview with CH11 (22 March 2010).
13. Interview with CH17 (29 March 2010).

Bibliography

Sources

Textbooks

(MZR) Argast, R., A. Binnenkade, F. Boller and P. Gautschi. 2005. *Menschen in Zeit und Raum 9. Viele Wege – eine Welt. Erster Weltkrieg bis Globalisierung.* Aarau: Lehrmittelverlag des Kantons Aargau.

Göldi, H. 1968. *Die Russische Revolution.* Wattwil: Artel.

Göldi, H. 1975. *Weltgeschichte 1945 bis 1975.* Wattwil: Artel.

Jaggi, A. 1970. *Aus Welt- und Schweizergeschichte seit 1815: ein Lesebuch für die bernischen Primarschulen.* 3rd edn. Berne: Paul Haupt und Staatlicher Lehrmittelverlag.

Jaggi, A. 1978. *Von den Anfängen der Reformation bis zur Gegenwart. Welt- und Schweizergeschichte: Lehrbuch für untere Mittelschulen*. 5th edn. Berne: Paul Haupt und Staatlicher Lehrmittelverlag.
(GZG) Meyer, H. and P. Scheebeli. 1991. *Durch Geschichte zur Gegenwart 4*. Zurich: Kantonaler Lehrmittelverlag.
(GZG) Meyer, H. and P. Scheebeli. 2010. *Durch Geschichte zur Gegenwart 4*. 7th edn. Zurich: Kantonaler Lehrmittelverlag.
Müller, O. 1969. *Denkwürdige Vergangenheit. Welt- und Schweizergeschichte*. Vol. 2. Aarau: Kantonaler Lehrmittelverlag.
(WiB) Nordwestschweizerische Erziehungsdirektoren-Konferenz (1974–1978). 1978. *Weltgeschichte im Bild. Lehrmittel der Welt- und Schweizergeschichte für das 6.-9. Schuljahr*. 4 Vol. Solothurn: Lehrmittelverlag des Kantons Aargau.
(WiB) Nordwestschweizerische Erziehungsdirektoren-Konferenz (1986–1989). 1989. *Weltgeschichte im Bild. Lehrmittel der Welt- und Schweizergeschichte für das 6.-9. Schuljahr*. 4 Vol. New edn. Buchs: Lehrmittelverlag des Kantons Aargau.
(WiB) Nordwestschweizerische Erziehungsdirektoren-Konferenz. 1996. *Weltgeschichte im Bild. Lehrmittel der Welt- und Schweizergeschichte für das 6.-9. Schuljahr*. 4 Vol. 5th edn. Buchs: Lehrmittelverlag des Kantons Aargau.
(ZMK) Ziegler. P. 1985. *Zeiten, Menschen, Kulturen 9*. Zurich: Lehrmittelverlag des Kantons Zürich.
(ZMK) Ziegler, P. 1993. *Zeiten, Menschen, Kulturen 9*. Zurich: Lehrmittelverlag des Kantons Zürich.

Periodicals

Adam, H. 1968. 'Prager Tagebuch'. *SLZ* 113: 1299–1310 and 1350–1357.
Fuchs, P. 1968. 'Liebe Schülerinnen und Schüler, liebe junge Zuhörer'. *SLZ* 113: 1195.
Frei, W. 1968. 'Schulsynode des Kantons Zürich'. *Der Pädagogische Beobachter* 62: 69.
Gut, T. 1979. 'Zweimal Vietnam'. *SLZ* 124: 19.
G.S. 1968. 'Pauschalurteile sind gefährlich'. *ScS* 55: 725.
N.N. 1968a. 'Der moderne Geschichtsunterricht'. *SLZ* 113: 1315.
N.N. 1968b. 'Verlautbarung'. *SLZ* 113: 1063.
N.N. 1968c. 'Die Demonstration'. *SLZ* 113: 1193–1195.
N.N. 1970a. 'Ein geplagtes Volk'. *SLZ* 115.
N.N. 1975. 'Für die Kinder in Vietnam'. *SLZ* 120: 313.

N.N. 1970b. 'Hexenjagd an den tschechoslowakischen Universitäten und Schulen'. *SLZ* 115: 1572–1575.
Hänni, R. 1968. 'Schweizer Lehrer in der Tschechoslowakei'. *SLZ* 113: 1299.
Hruby, K. 1969. 'Politische und geistige Entwicklung eines autoritären Systems'. *SLZ* 114: 1240–1245.
Rudolf, H. 1989. 'Indochina'. *SLZ* 134, no. 9: 14–16.

Diplomatic Documents

Nationalrätliche Kommission für auswärtige Angelegenheiten, Ständerätliche Kommission für auswärtige Angelegenheiten. *Protokoll der ausserordentlichen, den Vorgängen in der Tschechoslowakei gewidmeten Sitzung vom 23.8.1968 in Bern*. https://dodis.ch/32187 (last accessed 31 May 2018).
Eidgnössisches Politisches Departement. *H. Kaufmann an die Schweizerische Botschaft in Washington: Vietnam-Demonstration der 'Jungen Sozialisten' in Bern vom 28.11.1966*. https://dodis.ch/31167 (last accessed 31 May 2018).

Further References

Kanyar Becker, H. 2014. *Prager Frühling und die Schweiz 1968–2008*. Exhibition documentation, Basel.
Bretscher-Spindler, K. 1997. *Vom heissen zum kalten Krieg: Vorgeschichte und Geschichte der Schweiz im Kalten Krieg 1943–1968*. Zurich: Orell Füssli.
Frei, N. 2008. *1968 Jugendrevolte und globaler Protest*. München: Deutscher Taschenbuch Verlag.
Holenstein, R. 1998. '"Es geht auch um die Seele unseres Volkes". Entwicklungshilfe und nationaler Konsens'. In *Dynamisierung und Umbau. Die Schweiz in den 1960er und 70er Jahren, Die Schweiz: Staat – Gesellschaft – Politik 1798–1998*, edited by M. König, G. Kreis, F. Meister and G. Romano, 115–125. Zurich: Chronos-Verlag.
Imhof, K. 1999. 'Entstabilisierung. Zukunftsverlust und Komplexitätsreduktion in der öffentlichen politischen Kommunikation der 60er Jahre'. In *Vom Kalten Krieg zur Kulturrevolution. Analyse von Medienereignissen in der Schweiz der 50er und 60er Jahre*, edited by K. Imhof, H. Kleger and R. Gaetano, 35–54. Zurich: Seismo.

Imhof, K., H. Kleger and R. Gaetano, eds. 1999. *Vom Kalten Krieg zur Kulturrevolution. Analyse von Medienereignissen in der Schweiz der 50er und 60er Jahre.* Zurich: Seismo.

Imhof, K. 1996. 'Das kurze Leben der geistigen Landesverteidigung. Von der 'Volksgemeinschaft' vor dem Krieg zum Streit über die 'Nachkriegsschweiz' im Krieg'. In *Konkordanz und Kalter Krieg. Analysen von Medienereignissen in der Schweiz der Zwischen- und Nachkriegszeit*, edited by K. Imhof, H. Kleger and R. Gaetano, 19–83. Zurich: Seismo.

Karner, S. 2008. 'Der Prager Frühling, Moskaus Entscheid zur Invasion'. *Aus Politik und Zeitgeschichte* 20: 6–18.

Kleger, H. 1999. 'Normalfall und Sonderfall: Unheimliche Stabilität bei rasanten Veränderungen 1956–1963'. In *Vom kalten Krieg zur Kulturrevolution. Analyse von Medienereignissen in der Schweiz der 50er und 60er Jahre*, edited by K. Imhof, H. Kleger and R. Gaetano, 191–234. Zurich: Seismo.

Kreis, G., ed. 1993. *Staatsschutz in der Schweiz: die Entwicklung 1935–1990. Eine multidisziplinäre Untersuchung im Auftrag des schweizerischen Bundesrates.* Berne/Stuttgart/Wien: Haupt.

Lachmann, R. and L. Mitchell. 2014. 'The Changing Face of War in Textbooks: Depictions of World War II and Vietnam, 1970–2009' *Sociology of Education* 87: 188–203.

Logevall, F. 2010. 'The Indochina Wars and the Cold War 1945–1975'. In *The Cambridge History of the Cold War. Volume II. Crises and Détente*, edited by M. P. Leffler and O. A. Westad, 281–304. Cambridge Histories Online. Cambridge: Cambridge University Press.

Peter, N. 2008. 'Wilhelm Tell, Marianne und Ho Chi-Minh – Vietnamsolidarität in den 60er Jahren'. In *Zürich 68. Kollektive Aufbrüche ins Ungewisse*, edited by E. Hebeisen, E. Joris and A. Zimmermann, 62–73. Baden: Hier und Jetzt.

Ritzer, N. 2015. *Der Kalte Krieg in den Schweizer Schulen. Eine kulturgeschichtliche Analyse.* Berne: hep.

Rogger, F. 2008. 'Holz-Affäre und Hirschy-Krawall – die 68er an der Uni Bern'. *UniPress* 137: 29–31.

Sager, P. 1968. *Berichte aus Vietnam. Tatsachen und Meinungen.* Bern: Verl. Schweizer. Ost-Institut.

Suri, J. 2010. 'Counter-Cultures: The Rebellions against the Cold War Order, 1965–1975'. In *The Cambridge History of the Cold War. Volume II. Crises and Détente*, edited by M. P. Leffler and O. A. Westad, 460–482. Cambridge Histories Online. Cambridge: Cambridge University Press.

Westad, A. O. 2000. 'The New International History of the Cold War: Three Possible Paradigms'. *Diplomatic History* 24, no. 4: 551–565.

Open Access This chapter is licensed under the terms of the Creative Commons Attribution 4.0 International License (http://creativecommons.org/licenses/by/4.0/), which permits use, sharing, adaptation, distribution and reproduction in any medium or format, as long as you give appropriate credit to the original author(s) and the source, provide a link to the Creative Commons licence and indicate if changes were made.

The images or other third party material in this chapter are included in the chapter's Creative Commons licence, unless indicated otherwise in a credit line to the material. If material is not included in the chapter's Creative Commons licence and your intended use is not permitted by statutory regulation or exceeds the permitted use, you will need to obtain permission directly from the copyright holder.

15

Reconciling Opposing Discourses: Narrating and Teaching the Cold War in an East-German Classroom

Eva Fischer

Introduction

A few years ago, a long-term study showed that German Reunification has produced highly ambivalent stances among many citizens of the former German Democratic Republic (GDR): While most Eastern Germans in their 30s view the reunification as positive and identify with the Federal Republic of Germany (FRG), they have also continued to feel connected with the GDR. Some have remained critical towards capitalism, for example, and most prefer the GDR's welfare system (Förster 2011, 144, 189 and 233; Förster 2008, 153[1]). Ambivalence also characterises academic debates about the Cold War. The downfall of the Soviet Union has destabilised binary patterns of interpretation – both in East and West – and Cold War history is discussed more controversially than ever (Erll 2011, 3). The various positions have been categorised as traditionalist, revisionist and post-revisionist. Stemming from the era of the Cold War itself, these different schools of thought used to be primarily concerned

E. Fischer (✉)
Independent Researcher, Oldenburg, Germany

with assigning responsibility for the conflict. While some argue that the question of guilt has become obsolete in the post-Cold War era (Jarausch, Ostermann and Etges 2017), others insist that it is still dominant (e.g. Lundestad 2014). The topics of debate, in any case, have broadened. They include such questions as whether the conflicts between East and West were more crucial as compared to those between North and South, and whether the fear of nuclear war or the development of the welfare state was more characteristic of the era (Iriye 2014).

While the academic community is far from reaching a consensus, history teachers from the former GDR seem to sense the presence of a traditionally western hegemonic discourse. They often do not seem to view themselves in legitimate speaker positions when interpreting the past, especially in the presence of a West German.[2] They are, as Sabine Reh has observed, under an implicit pressure to justify themselves and to express 'confessions' and 'commitments' (Reh 2003, 19, 169). Reh partly traces this back to the fact that, after Reunification, the education system of the GDR became a major target of critique in a western-dominated discourse on education that was interwoven with broader academic discourses on East German identity (transformation) (ibid., 18). As public education in the East was viewed as an emblem of a repressive political system, its teachers were believed to have been either disenfranchised or part of the regime (ibid., 111–119).[3]

On the grounds of these insights, this case study will explore an East German history teacher's 'talking' and 'doing' (Ahlrichs et al. 2015) in relation to Cold War history. I will investigate how the teacher, Julia[4], perceives and positions herself within the current discourse on the Cold War in the presence of a West German researcher, what strategies she develops to construct coherent narratives and where she (re)produces the limits of what can be said (Foucault 1969). By explicitly looking at different contexts and social situations, I acknowledge recent trends in memory studies that view memory as context-bound (Ahlrichs et al. 2015) and have replaced the 'individual' versus 'collective' dichotomy with the notion of 'entangled' memory (Feindt et al. 2014, 24–44).

Born in 1956, Julia experienced working life both before and after reunification, beginning her career in the GDR and continuing to work once her state had become part of the reunited FRG. According to Bernd Lindner, members of this 'integrated generation' are characterised by their full social integration into GDR structures. They grew up in a divided country, experienced the development of a GDR youth culture, and benefited from social reforms in the 1970s. Most of them therefore identified with their state and had a positive image of it (Lindner 2003). 'Overrun' by the collapse of the GDR, however, the 'integrated generation' is ascribed a 'twofold horizon of experience', as its members have spent much of their adulthood in the Western system (Welke 2012, 75). By focusing on a teacher from this generation, I follow Barbara Christophe's suggestion to view history teachers 'in their double function as members of memory cultures and as professionals specialised in conveying state-approved patterns of interpretation' (p. 256 of this volume; see also Chapter 17).

Thematically, I will focus on the immediate post-1945 period, the interpretation of which is relevant for memory politics in divided Germany. The GDR officially adopted the image of the 'Soviet liberators' from National Socialism (Kleßmann 2010; Müller 2008), while the FRG insisted on the concept of political defeat and accused the GDR of having upheld a totalitarian system. The GDR, in turn, presented itself as the truly anti-fascist German state in which the entire Nazi elite had been eliminated. They claimed that the Western allies, in contrast, had failed to overthrow old structures, and that the FRG was thus the immediate successor of Nazi Germany. It was only with the social movements of the 1960s that some of this criticism was in fact adopted by left-winged activists in the West, who demanded structural reforms (Kleßmann 2010).

As a hinge between World War II and the Cold War, the post-1945 period has also been a major issue of post-reunification historiographical discourse. Proving the ultimate failure of the Eastern system, the collapse of the GDR revealed the full ambivalence of the year of 1945 (ibid; Möller 1995). While official GDR interpretations of history have become obsolete, historians have put a new focus on individual experiences of German victimhood during the post-World War II period (Kleßmann 2010, 7–8). Debates about the Cold War have also renewed both traditionalist and revisionist arguments regarding the role of the superpowers during this phase (Lundestad 2014).

Looking at a variety of social situations, this study explores Julia's *repertoire* of strategies with which to create narratives about an ambiguous past. This approach requires different types of data. We audio-recorded and transcribed a biographical interview as well as a guided interview on the basis of textbook passages about the Cold War. We further video-recorded two history lessons and had them transcribed.[5] As I will outline, Julia produces different accounts of the Cold War while re-employing narrative templates (Wertsch 2002, 60–62) that interconnect political history and the personal sphere. Despite her awareness of Cold War controversies, her (re)actions imply a deep insecurity regarding the social legitimacy of her positions. However, she also engages in resistance.

Methods

The biographical interview addresses Julia as a private person, serving to access her life story. The construction and constant revision of our life stories enables us to ascribe meaning to our lives and 'to exist in the social world with a comfortable sense of being a good, socially proper, and stable person' (Linde 1993, 3). Attempting to create a sense of coherence and agency, we draw on unspoken, culture-specific supplies of expected life events and acceptable reasons for our decisions (ibid., 3, 11, 19 and 93). The life story approach is particularly promising for this case study: Since Julia is a member of the 'integrated generation', the cultural supply-kit has changed in the course of her life. Especially in the presence of a West German, she may feel required to re-adapt her story, which can provide hints at how she perceives her own position in discourse. The rather personal set-up of the biographical interview may thus not be as 'innocent' as it seems (cf. Reh 2003, 17–18). Following the recommendations by Fritz Schütze, we started the interview with an open question and asked follow-up questions only after Julia had finished speaking (Schütze 1982, 570).

The textbook-related interview addresses Julia in her professional role as a history teacher. Using a questionnaire, we specifically asked her what she thinks about selected ambivalent passages about the origins of the Cold War (cf. Baier, Christophe und Zehr 2014) and how useful she finds them for class.

The classroom, as a third social context, places Julia in a position of relative power. The more she engages in discussion and textbook work, however, the less she is in control over the course of events and elements entering from outside discourses (see Binnenkade 2015). I will therefore compare situations that vary in their forms of interaction: first, situations in which Julia talks (almost) uninterruptedly to the class; second, situations with more lively dialogues; third, a situation in which Julia interacts with both the students *and* the textbook, the latter providing an additional conveyer of narratives[6].

I will draw on Wertsch's (2002, 60–62) concepts of 'specific narratives' and 'schematic narrative templates' to interpret the data.[7] The former refers to stories that people construct in order to make sense of specific events of the past. The latter describes generalised narrative forms and patterns that underlie a range of stories. By exploring the narrative templates employed by Julia, I aim to identify continuity across the different contexts and situations.

Life Story: Connecting Political and Family History

Julia's life story is characteristic of the 'integrated generation'. She describes her childhood as 'free' and 'cheerful',[8] detailing how she went through the entire GDR school system. She was given special attention because of her father's position with the police, and received a university scholarship. As 'the first year to benefit from the social reforms', Julia and her husband could afford a flat and two children while studying.[9] Her attitude towards the GDR is ambivalent. She experienced its collapse as 'enormous'.[10] '[Y]ou had these questions in mind. What will happen? How will things continue?'[11] As a history teacher, she was 'close to a coma' by mid-November 1989, not knowing what to teach and test anymore.[12] Unlike her father, who was too old 'to fully enjoy' the new situation,[13] however, Julia adapted to life after Reunification. While continuing her career as a teacher, she read West German literature in order to learn 'what's going on on the other side'.[14] She also retrospectively denounces her education in the GDR through the public system as a form of indoctrination: Her teachers 'taught the curriculum' and 'clearly positioned' themselves.[15] At university, they studied 'two years of GDR history' with 'dates, dates, dates [about] the founding of the GDR and of the SED

[Socialist Unity Party of Germany]', all of which was 'written by followers, of course', and represented 'uncritically and heroically'.[16] Professors blocked any challenging questions, and Julia 'simply absorbed what they said'.[17] When talking about the 1970 movie *The Strawberry Statement* about student protests in the US, she provides an explanation which reads like a self-justification for why she and her university friends did not rebel more: 'We were probably too mellow, thinking "oh well, we are pretty well off"'.[18]

The division of the country is a prominent element of Julia's life story. She is the daughter of East Prussian refugees who had 'put down new roots' in her East German home town[19] while part of her mother's family had settled in the West. 'Reorientating' himself, her father became a painter and then joined the GDR police force[20], which implies a significant occupational and social advancement in the system. Because of the father's position, Julia's family was officially forbidden to maintain any contacts in the West. Since her mother's relatives lived there, this was a subject of constant tension between Julia's parents.[21]

What strategies does Julia employ to construct coherence in a life story that is characterised by division and ambivalence? Looking at two passages from the interview, I argue that she constructs her family history analogous to German history by intertwining the narrative templates of 'family and nation', 'victim' and 'reconciliation'. In the first passage, Julia talks about her father's position as a police officer and its consequences for their family life:

(1)[22] Er hat sich immer nur gewundert, dass das mit [...] der Beförderung bei ihm nicht hingehauen hat. [...] Und er schob das dann immer auf diesen Punkt [dass die Familie Kontakte in den Westen hatte] (2) Und das, denke ich, ist so ein Zeichen für diese Sa/ für diese Zeit, für das Leben, was dann in Deutschland so/ oder in der DDR so eingekästelt war (3) Dass man so nach außen keine Beziehungen pflegen durfte [...]. (4) Und wenn dann die Großmutter mal zu Besuch war, dann suchte meine Mutti einen Tag aus, wo der Vater zur Schicht war [...]. Und dann war die mal für zwei, drei Stunden da, also und dann war es das (5) Also daran, denke ich, konnte man bei uns in der Familie sehen, wie gespalten [...] das eigentlich war und wie schlimm (6) Denn so eine Familie auseinander zu reißen, das ist/ durch diese Grenze, das ist wirklich schlimm gewesen. (7) Und, und das hat man eben bei der Mutter gemerkt. (8) Und ich denke, die hat da auch so einen richtigen Lebensschmerz gehabt, die ist mit 48 Jahren verstorben. [...] (9) Ähm, puh, das ist/ gibt viele Ursachen, aber ich denke, das ist auch eine da mit, dass sie da nicht so, eben nicht glücklich [...] war.[23]

(1). He always wondered why [...] he was never promoted [...] and he always blamed it on [the fact that the family had contacts in the West]. (2) And this, I think, is indicative of those times and of that life that was so restricted in Germany, or in the GDR. (3) That you weren't allowed to have any outside contacts. [...] (4) When my grandmother was in town, my mother would pick a day when my father had shift-work, and my grandma [...] would stay with us for two, three hours and that was it. (5) From that, I think, you could see in our family how divided [...] this really was and how awful. (6) Because to tear apart a family by this border was really awful. (7) And you could see that with my mother. (8) I believe she had a really hard life. She died at the age of 48 [...] (9) There are many reasons, but I think one of them was that she just wasn't happy there.

The account merges political and family history by relying on the theme of division and a strategy of obscuring. On a linguistic level, the merge is epitomised in the phrase 'you could see in our family' (5), where the demonstrative pronoun 'das' (this) could refer to the family, the country, society and culture, or all of them. Similarly, the phrase 'to tear apart a family' (6) does not specify an agent. On the basis of this interplay, Julia describes the consequences of the division as 'awful' and 'really awful' (5–6) and even connects them to her mother's early death (7–9); again, the word 'there' in 'she just wasn't happy there' could refer either to the family or the state, thus connecting the two. Against this background, Julia employs the narrative template of 'victim' to describe how her father was being disadvantaged in his career as a result of having contacts in the West (1).

In a later passage, the father's role changes from being a victim of division to being an active obstacle of 'reconciliation', which represents another narrative template:

(10) Und dann haben wir es ja geschafft, dass sich die West- und die Ostverwandtschaft äh wieder trifft. Das war '94. (11) Da hatten wir sie dann mal am Tisch [...] dass man diesen, diesen Bruch versucht zu beheben. [...] (12) Wir hatten [meinem Vater] gesagt: 'Es kommt dein Schwager [...] und deine Schwägerin' – 'Oh nee [...]. Kann ich nicht, halte ich nicht aus'. (13) Da haben wir gesagt: 'Du, das müssen wir jetzt einfach versuchen'.[24]

(10) We managed to arrange a reunion of the Western and Eastern relatives [...] in 1994. (11) We had them all at one table [...] to try and resolve the divide [...]. (12) We had said [to my father]: 'Your brother- and sister-in-law are coming' – 'Oh, no, [...] I can't bear it'. (13) And we said: 'We just have to try'.

(14) Also mein Vater wollte das nicht einrühren. (15) Das haben wir eingerührt, einfach weil wir neugierig waren und weil wir das nicht verstehen wollten, dass sich Familien so trennen [...]. (16) Das kann ich bis heute nicht. Wenn ich mich mit jemandem zanke, dann kann das sein. Aber dann muss man irgendwo den Punkt finden [...]. (17) Und ähm das fand sich dann eben. (18) Die sind so aufeinander zu gegangen so wie Katzen und sich umschlichen und dann haben sie sich doch auf die Schultern geklopft [...]. Und da war alles gegessen, (19) da [...] konnte man sich an den Tisch setzen und in Ruhe reden und ähm, ja, und dann wurden auch so Jugenddummheiten rausgekramt. [...]. (20) Und das hätte noch mehr gebraucht davon [...]. So, aber wenigstens der Punkt, dass sie sich alle finden und sagen: 'Ja, ausgestanden. So'.[25]

(14) My father didn't want it (15). We initiated it, simply because we were curious and because we didn't want to accept that families split up like that. [...] (16). I still cannot. It might be possible if I argue with someone. But eventually you have to find a point [...] (17). And it was found then (18). They approached each other like cats, tiptoeing around each other, but finally they patted each other's shoulders. And the subject was closed (19). We were able to sit down at the table and talk calmly, and youthful follies were dug out (20). More of that would have been needed [...] but at least there was this point where everyone comes together and says: 'All right; let's put it all behind us'.

While Julia describes herself and her siblings as putting a lot of effort into re-uniting the family, their father, who 'didn't want it' (14), now appears as a defender of division. The shift in the father's role is possible because of the ambiguous interconnection of political and family history in both passages, which does not clearly assign responsibilities. The narrative here is again constructed around the theme of division, evoked by the terms 'Bruch' (break/divide) (11) and 'trennen' (split up) (15). The tensions in the family are released when finally 'everyone comes together' (20). According to Julia's narrative, the reconciliation of the family is thus intrinsically entwined with the reunification of the country.

A Textbook-Related Interview: 'Sometimes the West is as Good as the East'

The template of 'reconciliation' recurs in the context of the guided, textbook-related interview. First of all, it expresses itself in Julia's post-revisionist view of the Cold War. On the basis of a textbook passage that is ambivalent about assigning responsibility for the conflict's origins, she was asked whom she holds responsible: 'I believe each political system contributed its share by defining certain spheres of control'.[26] '[It was about] resources and also markets. Ultimately, it was about money in the economy'.[27] Distancing herself from both traditional Eastern and traditional Western narratives, Julia thus opts for a compromise position. In another instance, she reconciles the Western perspective by constructing a narrative that raises the West to the moral level of the East. While discussing a textbook excerpt about the policies and considerations of the commanders in the British and American occupation zones, the interviewer asks Julia whether she believes in a German consensus regarding the role of the Western allies. Julia replies:

> (21) Ich denke eher, das wird sehr kontrovers betrachtet. Die einen haben solche/ Es gibt doch eine Erfahrungswelt. Ähm und dann liegt es noch ähm sehr im Auge des Betrachters, auf welcher Seite der Grenze er groß geworden ist. Da gibt es überhaupt noch keinen Konsens. Da gibt es nur punktuelle Erfahrungen und äh Dinge, die man als Quellen gelesen hat

(22). Da fällt mir dieser wunderbare Film ein zum, zum, zur Rettung der Kunstwerke [...] 'Monuments Men' [...]. Da ging es doch um die Rettung der Kunstwerke, die aus ähm, die zusammengeraubt wurden, [...] und ähm dann versteckt und anschließend, ja, im Film von den Amerikanern gerettet wurden (23). Das ist aber nur eine Seite [...] (24). Es gibt eine ähnliche Geschichte für die Kunstwerke in Dresden. Da haben sie die Russen aus dem Stollen geholt [...] (25). Für mich war das höchst interessant, [...] der/ (...). Clooney [...], der erklärte die Aufgabe der amerikanischen Armee bezüglich der Rettung der deutschen Kunstwerke [...] (26). [B]in ich so groß geworden mit den Geschichten, dass von den Russen, und jetzt kommt für mich die/ es war ein Wissensgewinn [...] (27). Und wir haben ja gedacht, ach die Amis, die waren ja immer so schlecht, und das war ja alles sowieso nicht so gut, und dann ist daraus der Westen entstanden, ja (28). Ähm das, [...] da wurde in meinem Kopf auch noch mal was gerade gerückt[.][28]

(21) I think this is very controversial. [...] There are realms of experience. And then it also depends on the eye of the beholder, which side of the border one grew up on. [...] There are only selective experiences and things you read as sources. (22) I remember this beautiful movie [...] *Monuments Men* [...] about rescuing artwork that had been robbed [...] and hidden and was then rescued by the Americans, according to the movie. (23) But that is only one side. (24) There is a similar story in Dresden, [where] the Russians took [artwork] out of a mine tunnel. (25) It was extremely interesting for me how [...] [George] Clooney [...] explained the task of the American army regarding the rescue of German artwork [...]. (26) I grew up with the stories about the Russians, [so] this was new knowledge [...]. (27) And we used to think that those Americans were always so bad, and that it all wasn't good, and that the West resulted from it [...]. (28) That sorted out something in my mind[.]

Julia suggests that the different views on the Western allies are equally legitimate: She refers to differences in experience, the geographical position, the 'eye of the beholder', and the selectiveness of historical sources (21). However, she expresses great surprise over learning that the Americans were not only 'bad' (26–27) but devoted themselves to Germany just as the Russians did (26). Whereas the Russians' good deeds are a given to her, the idea of American good deeds is a 'new knowledge'. Rather than reversing her ideas of good guys and bad guys, Julia identifies good in both sides, thus constructing a narrative that can be summarised as 'sometimes the West is as good as the East'.

The Variety of Accounts in Different Classroom Situations

When teaching the Cold War in class, Julia constructs three different types of accounts that correlate with different forms of interaction. The narrative templates of her life story are developed accordingly. I will first look at two situations in which Julia speaks uninterruptedly and constructs a relatively coherent historical account. In the first lesson, she has the students discuss a cartoon depicting a horse that Franklin D. Roosevelt and Winston Churchill ride in one direction and Josef Stalin in another. Standing in front of a wall map of central Europe, Julia produces the following monologue:

(29) Und das ist […] hier die Scheidewand zwischen diesen beiden Systemen [deutet Grenze zwischen Ost- und Westeuropa an]. Für uns das hier [deutet Grenze zwischen Ost- und Westdeutschland an] […] (30) Da passiert jetzt was ganz Besonderes. (31) Wer sich nicht leiden kann und sich nicht anguckt, der spricht nicht miteinander. (32) Der zieht in Gedanken eine Grenze […]. (33) Der zieht politisch eine Grenze. (34) Der zieht eine Grenze wirtschaftlich. (35) 'Dir borge ich keinen Kuli. Du kannst mich mal. Was, du hast was vergessen? Dann sieh doch zu, wie du klarkommst. Mit dir nicht'. (36) Ich stelle mal noch ein paar Forderungen. Ich will dies, das und jenes haben. Sprich, Reparationen. […] (37) Aber dann ist es Rille. (38) Es schließt sich jetzt hier zwischen diesen beiden Teilen Deutschlands […] (39) Der eine der demokratisch geführte, und der andere der in diese Richtung geführte [deutet in Richtung Ost] […]. (40) Da schließt sich wie so ein Vorhang. […]. (41) Und wenn der Vorhang unten ist, dann sieht man nicht mehr, was auf der anderen Seite passiert. Dann hört man vielleicht noch was, aber das ist alles nur schon noch die Hälfte […]. (42) So entstehen Gerüchte, falsche Meldungen (43). Und in dem Moment: 'Na ja, bei euch ist das ja jetzt so. Bei uns so', entwickeln sich die beiden Staaten auseinander […]. (44) Hier senkt sich wie im Theater jetzt ein Vorhang. (45) Die in, in der […] sowjetischen Besatzungszone, […] wissen nicht mehr, was im Westen passiert. Und umgedreht.[29]

(29) [T]his [...] is the dividing line between these two systems [indicates line between Eastern and Western Europe]. For us, it's here [indicates line between East and West Germany] [...] (30) Something exceptional is happening here now. (31) If people don't like each other and don't see each other, they don't talk to each other. (32) They draw a mental line [...] (33) They draw a line politically. (34) They draw a line economically. (35) 'I won't lend you a pen. Go to hell. You left something at home? Don't come to me for help' [...] (36) I make a couple of demands [...] Reparations, that is [...] (37) But then I couldn't care less. (38) It's closing down now between these two parts of Germany [...] (39) The one that is democratically ruled and the other one that is ruled in this direction [points towards the East] [...] (40) It's like a curtain that is closing [...] (41) And once the curtain is down, you can no longer see what is happening on the other side. You might hear something, but only partially [...] (42) That's how rumours and false reports develop. (43) And at that moment: 'where *you* are, it's like this. Where *we* are, it's like that', the states are drifting apart [...] (44) Like in a theatre, a curtain is closing here now (45). Those [...] in the Soviet occupation zone [...] don't know what is going on in the West anymore. And vice versa.

While telling the story of German division, Julia re-applies elements of the narrative template 'nation and family' as well as the strategy of not assigning agency. The theme of division is translated into multiple metaphors. Starting out from the geo-political 'dividing line between these two systems' (29), which she physically indicates on the map, Julia first transfers the divide onto the abstract level of a 'mental line' (32). This connects the political sphere to everyday realities where people 'don't like each other', 'don't see each other' and consequently 'don't talk to each other' (31). The Cold War is thus constructed as a conflict that simultaneously takes place on a personal and political level, resembling Julia's description of the break than ran through her family and separated her Eastern and Western relatives. She continues to intertwine these spheres: The same people who draw a mental line also draw 'political' and 'economic' 'lines' (33–34). The fictitious person who demands reparations (36) is the same who 'won't lend you a pen' (35).

The intermingling of the political and personal level is epitomised in the metaphor of the curtain, borrowed from the concept of the Iron Curtain that, according to a speech by Winston Churchill from 1946, separated the Soviet sphere from the West. Julia also employs this metaphor to emphasise the idea of 'division', but she transfers it onto the level of everyday life, where 'you can no longer see what is happening on the other side' (41) and have to rely on 'rumours and false reports' (42) while developing a sense of 'us' versus 'them' (43). The emphasis of the metaphor thus shifts from the iron wall that painfully separates people to a curtain that hinders visual contact and thus encourages mutual stereotyping. The political component is only re-introduced when Julia finally refers to the two sides as 'the Soviet occupation zone' and 'the West' again (45).

Julia's curtain metaphor also moves the focus away from finding a scapegoat. By generalising the concepts of conflict and division, she supports the notion that the early Cold War was a conflict between two equals. At the end, the curtain is the actor that is 'closing' (40), forcing people in both occupation zones to become ignorant of each other (45). Once again, the blending of the spheres relies on a lack of agency. The Eastern part of Germany 'is ruled' in a particular yet not further specified way (39), 'rumours and false reports' appear to 'develop' by themselves (42), and 'the states are drifting apart' without any apparent agent (43).

In a lesson about the air strikes on Dresden in February 1945 and the aftermath, Julia draws on the notion of division and conflict to construct the Cold War as a story of reconciliation. She re-employs her 'specific narrative' about the moral standing of the Russians and the Americans:

Julia: (46) Da hat man ja in Dresden sämtliche Kunstgegenstände versucht, in Sicherheit zu bringen, indem man diese schönen Gemälde in Kisten verpackt in irgendwelche Bergwerksschächte verfrachtet hat. […] (47) Anschließend gehen die Gemälde nach Moskau zur Restauration und werden dann drei, vier Jahre später wiedergebracht und dann erst wird in Dresden eine neue Galerie der alten Meister aufgebaut. […] (48) Diese anderen Gebäude in Dresden an der Elbe, die das schöne Panorama immer ausmachen bei jeder Sendung über Dresden, die waren Zentrum, Angriffspunkt, dort war platt. Da war alles platt. […] (49) So, Dresden. Hier (ziemlich bei uns). […], auch mit dem (Herzen). […] (50) Bombardiert hat wer? Welche Fliegerverbände waren denn das? […]

Julia: (46) In Dresden they tried to secure all the works of art by putting these beautiful paintings in boxes and storing them in mine tunnels. [...] (47) Afterwards, they were taken to Moscow for restoration and returned three, four years later, and only then a new gallery of the old masters was built in Dresden. (48) The [...] buildings by the riverside [...], always shown in attractive panorama shots in television programmes about Dresden, were the centre, the point of attack. That was all flattened. (49) Here, relatively close to us, also to our hearts. (50) Who did the bombing? Which bomber squadron?

Student: (51) Die Amerikaner?

Student: (51) The Americans?

Julia: (52) Die angloamerikanischen Kriegsverbände. [...] Die [Frauenkirche] hatte so ein schickes Kreuz auf dem Altar stehen. Und das ist in dieser Bombennacht kaputtgegangen (53). Also als die Frauenkirche vor vier Jahren wieder eingeweiht wurde, haben die Amerikaner und die Briten aus Spendengeldern ein neues Kreuz dieser Art für die Frauenkirche gespendet und praktisch überreicht (54) [...]. Das ist richtig schick mit ganz vielen Edelsteinen. Also es war sehr/ Es war wirklich ein tolles [...] und wertvolles Stück. (56) Und das hat man den Dresdnern wiedergeschenkt. [...] So, die Dresdner haben sich wahnsinnig gefreut.

Julia: (52) The Anglo-American army groups. [...] (53) The Frauenkirche [Church of Our Lady] had a lovely cross on its altar, [which...] was destroyed during this night of bombing. (54) When the Frauenkirche was re-inaugurated four years ago, the Americans and the British donated a new cross of the same kind ... and formally presented it. (55) It's huge [and] [...] truly impressive, with many gemstones [...]. It was really a wonderful and valuable object. (56) And that was given back to the people of Dresden. [...] (57) The people of Dresden were delighted.[30]

The narrative template of 'reconciliation' provides the basis of this account. Just as in Julia's life story, the concept of a successfully solved conflict thus features prominently. Taking up the topic of rescued artwork, she marks the final phase of World War II as the beginning, and the present age as the end of a conflict between the Americans and British on the one hand and the people of Dresden on the other. By pointing out the merits of the new cross (55) and how delighted the people were (57), she represents the donation as a gesture that finally ended hostilities. The Cold War, as the intervening period, has thus come to a happy end.

The narrative template of reconciliation comes along with the re-employment of the idea that the Americans became as good as the Russians had always been. In the first part of the dialogue, Julia portrays the Russians as rescuers, restorers and donors of 'beautiful' and culturally significant artwork (46–47) in a city we are all fond of (49). Implicitly creating a contrast between 'us' and the Western allies, she then lets the students conclude that the Americans and British were responsible for the bombing (50–51). The two sides are reconciled when the Americans and British donate an extraordinarily 'impressive' and 'valuable' (55) cross, i.e. when they show themselves as devoted to art culture, and hence the people of Dresden, as the Russians did.

Not all of Julia's Cold War accounts in class are reconciliatory. In the following, I will analyse more interactive situations, beginning with a unit about the different political and social orders in the future occupation zones. Talking about changes in Germany after 1945, Julia first portrays the Western powers, especially the US, in a traditional Western fashion as representatives of democracy:

Julia: (58) Könnt ihr mir bitte sagen, […] in welcher Gesellschaftsstruktur die Amerikaner '45 gelebt haben? […] Was ist das für ein Land? Wer regiert? Wer hat die Regierung dahin gesetzt? Wie ist dieses Land gesellschaftlich aufgeteilt? […]

Julia: (58) Could you please tell me […] in what social order the Americans were living in 1945? […] What kind of a country is that? Who rules it? Who put the government in power? […]

Student: (59) In Demokratie.
Student: (59) [In a] democracy.
Julia: (60) Sehr schön.
Julia: (60) Very good.
[After elaborating on the roles of Britain and France, Julia writes on the blackboard: 'USA, GB, FR democracy'.]³¹

When continuing about the Western economic system, however, Julia brings in an element of an interpretation that was officially supported by the GDR:

Julia: Wer besitzt die Cola-Fabriken, die Jeans-Fabriken, Autofabriken? Wer besitzt Geschäfte? [...] [I]ch will das Prinzip wissen. [...]
Julia: (61) Who owns the Coca-Cola factories? The jeans factories? The car factories? I [...] want to know the principle. [...]
Student: (62) Ja, dem, dem die Fabrik gehört.
Student: (62) Well, whoever owns the factory.
Julia: (63) Genau. Da ist eine Privatperson der Besitzer. [...] Das ist also ein privatwirtschaftlich organisierter Staat. Man nennt das auch kapitalistisch oder imperialistisch. [...] (64) So, jetzt brauche ich hier die Mitte der Tafel. [...] (65) Und jetzt die Frage, wie ist das in der Sowjetunion [...]?
Julia: (63) [...] Exactly. A person has private ownership [...] So it's a privately organised state economy. This is also called capitalist or imperialist. (64) Alright [...] Now I have to write in the middle of the board. [For the US, Britain and France, she writes 'capitalist/imperialist (private ownership of capital goods)' on the blackboard.] Property is also privately owned by individual people. (65) And now the question is, what about the Soviet Union?³²

Mixing elements of Eastern and Western narratives, Julia produces mixed representations of Cold War actors. What is striking is her use of the term 'imperialist', a concept frequently used to describe the West in traditional

Eastern and revisionist interpretations. Casually dropping the term in as a mere synonym for 'capitalist', Julia equalises the principle of 'private ownership' with imperialism (63). She does not specify on the blackboard that this refers to the economy. Consequently, the terms 'capitalist/imperialist' can be read right underneath the term 'democratic', all of which are listed as features of the Western powers. The equalisation of 'capitalism' with the clearly negatively connoted term 'imperialism' is not clarified or discussed. Even when a student later asks 'what it says there' next to 'capitalism', Julia merely repeats 'imperialist', which the student then copies into his exercise book.[33]

The mixing of discourses with the resulting ambivalence also affects the representation of the Soviet Union. In one lesson, a student is asked to repeat some of the contents from a previous lesson at the wall map:

(66) *Student*:	Berlin. Wurde von den Sowjet/ von den, von der Sowjetunion besetzt. [...]
Student:	[...] Berlin wurde halt auch in vier Teile geschnitten sozusagen. [...]
Student:	[...] Die Briten haben den westlichen Teil besetzt. Die F/ ähm Franz/ die/
(66) *Student*:	Berlin [was] occupied by the Soviet Union. [...]
Student:	[...] Berlin was also cut into four pieces [...]
Student:	[...] The British occupied the Western part. [...] The Fre [...]
Julia	(67) Nein, die Amis.
Julia:	(67) No, the Yanks.
Student:	(68) Die Amis haben den südlichen Teil besetzt und die Sowjetunion den östlichen Teil.
Student:	(68) The Yanks occupied the southern part and the Soviet Union the Eastern part. [...]
Student:	(69) [...] Zu den politischen Problemen gehörte, dass die vier Länder aufeinander trafen. [...] Sie wollten die sozusagen Demokratie machen.
Student:	(69) [...] One of the political problems was that those four countries encountered each other [...]. They wanted to make democracy, so to speak.

Julia:	Die Sowjetunion auch?
Julia:	(70) The Soviet Union, too?
Student:	(71) Nee, die Sowjetunion nicht. Nur die Frankreich, Amerika und die britische. […]
Student:	(71) Nope, not the Soviet Union. Only France, America and the British. […]
Julia:	(72) Bei Berlin aufpassen: Es wurde tatsächlich äh hier von der Roten Armee die Befreiung ähm geschafft. Und dann erst die Einteilung, du hast das Wort 'geschnitten' benutzt, kann man ruhig sagen. Es passt da irgendwo an diese Stelle, mhm (zustimmend). Gut. So. Das ist Deutschland. Jetzt frage ich dich […] nochmal: Du hast irgendwann mal gesagt, du hast einen Ausflug gemacht in eine dieser Weststädte. Wo warst du denn?
Julia:	(72) Alright […] Careful with Berlin: Its liberation was, in fact, achieved by the Red Army. Only then was it divided […] (73) Now I'm asking you again […]: You once said that you went on a trip to one of those *Weststädte* [towns in the West]. Where did you go?[34]

The Soviet Union is portrayed with a mix of traditionalist Western interpretations and a terminology stemming from traditional Eastern discourse. Whereas Julia makes the student re-construct the democracy-dictatorship dichotomy as the major political problem (69–71), she later states that the Red Army 'achieved' the 'liberation' of Berlin (72). Representing the Soviets as liberators, she employs an essential element of official GDR narrations of the post-World War II period. This is supported by the formerly pejorative colloquial term 'Amis' (Yanks) (67), which has its origins in the post-World War II and early Cold War period (the slogan 'Ami, go home!' was upheld especially by the GDR).[35] By finally referring to certain German cities as 'those Weststädte', Julia employs another term that is based on a clear division between East and West. She thus re-creates the same 'us' versus 'them' mentality she explicitly criticises in the previously analysed lesson. Again, none of the contradictions are identified, discussed or clarified.

In the final classroom situation, Julia reconstructs former GDR discourse when interacting with the students *and* dealing with the textbook. As for post-World War II history, the textbook from the series *Entdecken und Verstehen*, published by Cornelsen, takes a traditional Western perspective on the Soviet Union (Christophe 2017). Regarding denazification in the Soviet occupation zone, it says:

> Mit der Parole von der 'Ausrottung der Überreste des Faschismus' wurden die bisherigen Eliten in Schule, Justiz, Verwaltung, Polizei und Wirtschaft radikal entmachtet und durch Sozialisten bzw. Kommunisten ersetzt. Die Kommunisten nutzten die Entnazifizierung aber auch, um politische Gegner [...] auszuschalten. So wurde die Entnazifizierung hier zum Mittel kommunistischer Herrschaftssicherung. [...] Die SED ging davon aus, dass die antifaschistische Gesinnung wichtiger sei als Fachkenntnisse [...]. Andererseits wurden bereits nach wenigen Jahren auch in der DDR viele ehemalige Fachleute wieder in staatlichen Funktionen (Polizei, Militär) eingesetzt, soweit ihnen nicht konkrete Vergehen angelastet wurden und wenn sie vor allen Dingen nur glaubhaft die 'richtige' Gesinnung zeigten (*Entdecken und Verstehen*, 25).
>
> Under the slogan 'eliminating the remnants of fascism', the elites in the school, judiciary, administration, police and economy were radically disempowered and replaced by socialists and communists. But the communists also used denazification to eliminate political opponents [...]. Denazification was thus used as a means to secure communist power. [...] The SED assumed that an anti-fascist attitude was more important than expertise [...]. On the other hand, in the GDR, too, many former experts were returned to their public offices (police, military) after only a few years as long as they were not accused of any specific misdeeds and, most importantly, if they could convincingly display the 'correct' attitude.

According to the text, denazification in the Soviet zone was flawed by communist ideology. While interacting with a student, however, Julia turns this interpretation into a 'successful denazification in the East' narrative. In the following scene, the student was asked to summarize the implementation of denazification in the Soviet zone as described in the textbook:

Student: (74) Na, Lehrer wurden entlassen und ersetzt durch Sozialisten und Kommunisten. Ähm Entnazifizierung wurde zum Mittel kommunistischer Herrschaftssicherung. Ähm es wurde klar unterschieden zwischen aktiven Nazis und Mitläufern. Äh in der DDR wurden ehemalige Fachleute äh wieder eingesetzt.

Student: (74) Well, teachers were released and replaced by socialists and communists. Denazification was used as a means to secure communist power. [...] (75) In the GDR, former experts were put back in office.
[Meanwhile, Julia writes on the blackboard: teachers released, communists take over positions.]

Julia: (76) Gut. Ihr habt mitgeschrieben. Richtig. (77) Hier ist es klar. (78) Vorhin haben wir noch gefragt, was ist in den anderen Besatzungszonen los? Was ist in den Ämtern los? (79) Wahrscheinlich, heißt es, die Amerikaner übernehmen oder die Briten oder die Franzosen. (80) Und hier ist es klipp und klar, raus mit den Nazis. (81) Und an ihre Stelle kommen alle die, die sich äh während der Nazizeit in einer kommunistischen Partei oder auch in einer sozialdemokratischen Partei engagiert haben.

Julia: (82) Good. You have all copied from the board. Right. (83) It's a clear case. (84) Earlier, we asked: what is happening in the other occupation zones? What is happening in the offices? (85) Probably, it says, the Americans took over or the British or the French. (86) And here it's clear as day: out with the Nazis. (87) And their positions are taken over by all those who were active in communist or social democratic parties during Nazi times.[36]

The student, who does not seem disturbed by the textbook account, correctly repeats its major claims. Julia, however, tacitly turns the traditional Western portrayal on its head. On an explicit level, she agrees with the student's summary ('good', 'right' [82]) and hence with the textbook account of denazification in the Soviet occupation zone. Her highly selective notes on the blackboard ('teachers released, communists take over positions'), however, provide the ground for transferring this account to match former GDR narratives. Catching merely the first and relatively neutral point of the student's summary, they ignore the aspects that mark the narrative as traditionally Western, i.e. the claims that the communists used denazification for their own purposes and that former Nazis were put back in office. This reduction of the text makes it possible for Julia to develop the contrary argument that, in East Germany, 'it's clear as day: out with the Nazis' (86). She backs this up by contrasting the situations in the East and West zones (84–86). Again, the East is constructed as the model for success against which the West is measured and with which the latter cannot compete this time, thus reversing the textbook's logic. Finally, Julia turns the communists and socialists who, according to the text, took over the positions, into communists and *social democrats* (87). This small alteration has significant consequences, as it deconstructs the idea that denazification in the East was used to eliminate political opponents.

Conclusion

This study has explored how a teacher of the 'integrated generation' relates to contemporary Cold War discourse in different contexts and situations. My analysis shows that Julia has developed a repertoire of accounts of the Cold War consisting of both individual narratives and underlying narrative templates. She employs the concept of 'reconciliation' for constructing her life story as well as for evaluating textbooks and teaching history. She thus de-politicises the historical conflict while also attributing a political component to the division within her family. This twofold process also applies to the template of the 'victim', which she uses to describe her father's situation in GDR times. While the spheres of 'family' and 'nation' become deeply intertwined, the non-assignment of agency weakens the political element: It remains obscure who is responsible for the division and thus for the victimisation.

In class, the mixing of the spheres and the non-assignment of agency recur in reconciliatory accounts of the Cold War. Other classroom situations triggered different accounts. In student-teacher dialogues, Julia constructed ambivalent images of the two major actors by combining traditional Eastern and Western patterns of interpretation. When including the traditional Western textbook as an additional authority, and thus relinquishing her own level of control to a certain extent, she resorted to former GDR narratives.

While Julia seems to have acquired some traditionally Western ideas, these instances suggest an internalisation of GDR discourse. This ambivalent condition expresses itself in narratives such as 'the West is sometimes as good as the East', in which she turns around the logic by measuring the West against the East.

The fact that Julia reinterprets narratives not by openly criticising but by tacitly altering them confirms James C. Scott's observations about resisting hegemonic ideas in social contexts with asymmetrical power-relations. According to Scott, whose subject of study was a group of Malaysian peasants in the 1970s, such resistance usually does not occur in the form of conscious and articulated revolution, but (partly) by constructing alternative narrations on the basis of shared norms (Scott 1985). Julia's acts of reinterpretation can thus be seen as a form of negotiation that avoids fuelling antagonism and hostility. This also indicates that it is still taboo to openly challenge presumably official versions of history in Germany. The instance of resorting to GDR narratives as a reaction to the textbook's one-sided view on denazification in the Soviet zone can then be read as an escape mechanism; it may result from not daring to publically deconstruct a perspective on the GDR that is considered socially dominant. The teaching of recent history thus reveals a severe lack of discussion.

The ambiguity Julia produces when dealing with the past also reveals a broader challenge that members of the 'integrated generation' face: Given that the GDR is primarily viewed as a failed dictatorial regime today, the values with which this generation grew up can no longer serve as a 'cultural supply' of acceptable means to construct a life story (Linde 1993). Instead, members of this generation are urged to adapt the images they construct of themselves to new expectations, which, however, remain vague and unspoken. In the course of this study, we have encountered traces of a considerable gap between the way in which Julia experiences and positions herself towards Cold War discourse and the way in which the students relate to it. More research on the younger generation is needed to enrich the debate and contribute to our understanding of how the legacy of the GDR and the history of the Cold War are dealt with in Germany.

Notes

1. Both publications refer to the *Sächsische Längsschnittstudie*, which has analysed the transformation of (young) Eastern Germans from GDR into FRG citizens since 1987. http://www.wiedervereinigung.de/sls/index.html (accessed 22 February 2017).
2. Cf. this and the previous sentence with Chapter 13 of this volume, by Barbara Christophe.
3. As Reh points out, some actors, such as the union *Erziehung und Wissenschaft* (Education and Science), had a more differentiated view on education in the former GDR (ibid., 112–113).
4. Real name withheld.
5. The material was collected between June and November 2014 by Kathrin Zehr, whom we would like to thank for her support. The interviews and lessons were recorded, transcribed, and rendered anonymous by giving code names to persons and places mentioned. As a rule I quote from them by indicating the file name and the location of the quote in minutes of recording as indicated in the transcription. The quotes I use in the text were translated from German by the author. The original files can be consulted at the Georg Eckert Institute in Braunschweig on the basis of respecting and guaranteeing the privacy rights of the people involved.
6. See his concept of 'cultural tool' in Wertsch 2002.
7. In his development of the concepts of 'specific narratives' and 'schematic narrative templates', Wertsch draws on MacIntyre 1984 and Propp 1968.
8. 'Ja, dieses freie Kindsein, wir haben das gelebt'.TCW_Biogr_9_SA.doc, #00:18:14-2# - #00:19:19-9#, #01:21:49-6# - #01:22:45-5#; 'Wir haben gespielt und sind da äh durch die Siedlung getobt und haben uns vergnügt.' Ibid, #00:01:41-2#-#00:04:08-3#.
9. 'Und wir hatten auf der gleichen Etage, wo mein Vater wohnte, nebenan so eine geteilte Wohnung. Die hat nur 10 Mark gekostet. […]Ach so,

wir haben fürs Kind auch noch mal 60 Mark gekriegt im Monat. Ja. Da gab es noch diese Unterstützung für Studenten mit [...] Kind. Wir waren, glaube ich, der erste Jahrgang, bei dem das da so alles mit diesen Sozialmaßnahmen dann kam.' Ibid, #00:47:05-7# - #00:49:29-5#.

10. '[...] die Wende. [...] Die war für mich enorm.' Ibid, #01:49:25-8# - #01:50:14-4#.

11. 'Na ja, vor der Wende schon, dieses 89er Jahr dann. [...] Aber, hm, [...] man hatte selber die Fragen im Hinterkopf, was wird? Und wie geht das hier alles weiter?' Ibid, #01:43:36-9# - #01:46:28-8#.

12. 'Wende und Schulsystem. Ja, das war schon hart. Ich habe am 19. November, wenn das der Montag war, eine Klassenarbeit schreiben wollen. Thema: "Die Mauer", 19. November '89. Das war also wochenlang vorher Thema. Ähm, hm. An dem Tag saßen sieben Schüler in der Klasse mit der Bild-Zeitung bewaffnet. (Laughs) Ich habe diese Klassenarbeit nicht geschrieben, aber ich war irgendwo dem Koma nahe'. Ibid, #01:32:04-0# - #01:38:02-7#.

13. 'Da gab es dann ein paar wenige Gespräche dazu, aber der ist auch '96 verstorben, also [...] er konnte das nicht mehr voll genießen.' Ibid, #00:53:21-5# - #00:55:46-3#.

14. 'Nach der Wende. Ich habe dann sämtliche Bücherläden wieder mal und immer noch und, ja, na das, das ist dann so, ja, wenn man einmal den Anstoß hat und Franziska Linkerhand gelesen hat, dann muss man auch wissen, was ist denn da in der anderen Seite los?' Ibid, #01:21:49-6#-#01:22:45-5#.

15. 'Und dann hat [die Staatsbürgerkundelehrerin] unterrichtet, was im Lehrplan steht. [...] Sie hat sich da schon klar positioniert. Auch bei den anderen Klassenlehrern so.' Ibid, #01:05:30-2# - #01:06:42-4#.

16. 'Da standen Daten, Daten, Daten, [...] ähm DDR-Gründung, ähm SED-Gründung aus der und der dann und dann das und das. So. "Lesen Sie dort und dort nach." Und das war ein Werk, was natürlich von einem der Mit/ Mitläufer, Mitmacher äh geschrieben wurde, also unkritisch. Also nur heroisch dargestellt.' Ibid, #01:17:32-7# - #01:19:24-9#.

17. 'Genau, die [Fragen] wurden abgebogen. [...] Ich habe brav das Wissen aufgesogen.' Ibid, #01:17:38-5#-#01:19:24-9#.

18. 'Ja, wenn, wenn ich dran denke, wie das in den 68er-Kreisen eigentlich war, wir haben dann hier "Blutige Erdbeeren" angeguckt und haben gestaunt, dass man sich als Studenten äh so engagieren und so aufreiben kann. [...] Ich glaube, da haben wir zum ersten Mal drüber nachge-

15 Reconciling Opposing Discourses: Narrating and Teaching... 341

dacht, ob man das mal machen sollte. [...] Aber nie ernsthaft irgendwo in eine Richtung. Da waren wir vielleicht auch schon wieder zu sanft und haben uns gesagt: "Och, es geht uns doch eigentlich ganz gut."[,].' Ibid, #01:23:54-2# - #01:25:56-8#.

19. 'Ja, und irgendwann zwischen '51 und '52 haben sich meine Eltern dann (fester) gefunden und '54 geheiratet. [...] Ja, und dann haben sie das getan, was alle taten, irgendwo die Grundlagen legen für [...] das gemeinsame Nest. Ja, und weil ähm eben diese Flüchtlingsgeschichten dahinter stecken, ist das ja so neues Wurzelsuchen oder Wurzelnbilden.' Ibid, #00:18:14-2# - #00:19:19-9#.
20. 'Und das hat sich ergeben, weil er mit seiner Familie [...] aus Ostpreußen äh geflüchtet ist. Hier dann 1945 ankam und sich praktisch neu orientieren musste.'Ibid, #00:15:24-7# - #00:19:19-9#.
21. 'Da gab es [...] so einen Befehl, wo sich die Angehörigen dieser Einrichtung von ihrer Westverwandtschaft lossagen mussten. [...] Und ich denke, deswegen ist auch die Beziehung schwer belastet gewesen.' Ibid, #00:24:05-9#-#00:27:09-0#.
22. The numbers in brackets are added by the author for the reader's orientation.
23. Ibid, #00:27:09-0# - #00:29:44-2#.
24. Ibid, #00:53:21-5# - #00:55:46-3#.
25. Ibid, #00:55:50-7# - #00:56:55-0#.
26. 'Ich denke, da hat jedes politische System seinen Teil zu beigetragen. Indem man eben bestimmte Machtbereiche abgesteckt hat und bestimmte wirtschaftliche Interessen ähm bedienen wollte'. TCW_Amb_9_SA.doc, #01:34:48-8# -#01:35:10-5#.
27. 'Rohstoffe, [...] ähm auch Märkte. [...] Letztendlich um Geld in der Wirtschaft'. Ibid, #01:35:18-7# - #01:35:30-1#.
28. Ibid, #00:44:15-1# - #00:47:12-0#.
29. 2014-11-14_Vid-L_9_SA.doc; 2014-11-14_Vid-L_9_SA.avi, #00:40:11-9# - #00:43:04-2#.
30. 2014-09-26_Vid_9_SA.doc; 2014-09-26_Vid_9_SA.avi; #00:11:06-1# -#00:14:10-8#.
31. Ibid; #00:31:49-6#-#00:34:44-3#.
32. Ibid; #00:34:48-8#-#00:36:37-0#.
33. Ibid; #00:37:47-9#-#00:37:53-6#.
34. 2014-10-24_Vid-L_9_SA_a.doc; 2014-10-24_Vid-L_9_SA_a.avi; #00:04:45-4# -#00:07:40-3#.

35. This slogan partly became popular through the song 'Ami, Go Home' by Ernst Busch, published in his *Internationale Arbeiterlieder* of 1953 (142–144). See the lyrics at *erinnerungsort: Materialien zur Kulturgeschichte*: http://www.erinnerungsort.de/Ami-2C-go-home-21-_88.html (accessed May 15, 2018).
36. 2014-10-24_Vid-L_9_SA_a.doc, #00:43:48-0# - #00:45:00-6#.

Bibliography

Textbook Cited

Entdecken und Verstehen 10. Vom Ende des Zweiten Weltkriegs bis in die Gegenwart. 2010. Thomas Berger-v. d. Heide, Stephan Burrichter, Bettina Mende, Ulrich Mittelstädt, Karl-Heinz Müller, Dieter Potente and Cornelius Schley. Berlin: Cornelsen.

Further References

Ahlrichs, Johanna, Katharina Baier, Barbara Christophe, Felicitas Macgilchrist, Patrick Mielke and Roman Richtera. 2015. 'Memory Practices in the Classroom: On Reproducing, Destabilizing and Interrupting Majority Memories'. Journal of Educational Media, Memory, and Society 7, no. 2: 89–109.

Baier, Katharina, Barbara Christophe and Kathrin Zehr. 2014. 'Schulbücher als Seismographen für Diskursive Brüche: Ein Neuer Ansatz in der Kulturwissenschaftlichen Schulbuchforschung Dargestellt am Beispiel der Analyse von Schulbucherzählungen über den Kalten Krieg', *Eckert. Working Papers* 4. http://www.edumeres.net/urn/urn:nbn:de:0220-2014-00184, last accessed 23 October 2018.

Binnenkade, Alexandra. 2015 'Doing Memory: Teaching as a Discursive Node', Journal of Educational Media, Memory, and Society 7, no. 2: 29–43.

Christophe, Barbara. 2017. '"Eigentlich hingen ja alle mit drin." Entnazifizierung und Kalter Krieg in deutschen Schulbüchern und in den Erzählungen von Lehrenden'. In *Das Geteilte Deutschland im Schulbuch: Die Darstellung des Kalten Krieges am Beispiel Deutschlands in den (Geschichts-) Schulbüchern von*

1945 bis in die Gegenwart, edited by Franziska Flucke and Ulrich Pfeil, 147–164. St. Ingbert: Röhrig Universitätsverlag.

Erll, Astrid. 2011. *Kollektives Gedächtnis und Erinnerungskulturen: Eine Einführung*. 2nd rev. ed. Stuttgart/Weimar: Metzler.

Feindt, Gregor et al. 2014. 'Entangled Memory: Toward A Third Wave in Memory Studies'. *History and Theory* 53: 24–44.

Förster, Peter. 2008. 'Noch Immer Keine Zukunft im Osten! Bericht über Wesentliche Ergebnisse der 22. Welle', http://www.wiedervereinigung.de/sls/PDF/foersterstudie2009.pdf, accessed 22 February 2017).

Förster, Peter. 2011. 'Zwischenbilanz: Zwei Jahrzehnte nach Wende und Deutscher Einheit ist die Generation der Mittdreißiger tief gespalten in Gewinner und Verlierer!' Ergebnisbericht zur 23. Welle der Sächsischen Längsschnittstudie. Leipzig,. http://www.wiedervereinigung.de/sls/PDF/foersterstudie2010.pdf, accessed 22 February 2017.

Foucault, Michel. 1969. *L'Archéologie du Savoir*. Paris: Gallimard.

Iriye, Akira. 2014. *Global Interdependence: The World after 1945*. Cambridge, Massachusetts [u.a.]: The Belknap Press of Harvard Univ. Press.

Jarausch, Konrad H., Christian F. Ostermann and Andreas Etges, eds. 2017. *The Cold War: Historiography, Memory, Representation*. Berlin: De Gruyter.

Kleßmann, Christoph. 2010. '1945: Welthistorische Zäsur und "Stunde Null", Version 1:0'. *Docupedia-Zeitgeschichte* 15 October 2010. http://docupedia.de/zg/1945, accessed 23 October 2018.

Lindner, Bernd. 'Kriterien für ein Modell der Jugendgenerationen in der DDR'. In *Generationalität und Lebensgeschichte im 20. Jahrhundert*, edited by Jürgen Reulecke, 187–215. München: R. Oldenburg Verlag, 2003.

Linde, Charlotte. 1993. *Life Stories: The Creation of Coherence*. New York/Oxford: Oxford University Press.

Lundestad, Geir. 2014. *East, West, North, South: International Relations since 1945*. 7th ed. Los Angeles: Sage.

MacIntyre, Alasdair C. 1984. *After Virtue: A Study in Moral Theory*. Notre Dame, Indiana: University of Notre Dame Press.

Möller, Horst. 1995. 'Die Relativität Historischer Epochen: Das Jahr 1945 in der Perspektive des Jahres 1989'. *Aus Politik und Zeitgeschichte* 18: 3–9.

Müller, Birgit. 2008. 'Erinnerungskultur in der DDR'. *Geschichte und Erinnerung*. Berlin: Bundeszentrale für Politische Bildung. http://www.bpb.de/geschichte/zeitgeschichte/geschichte-und-erinnerung/, accessed 24 October 2016.

Propp, Vladimir. 1968. *Morphology of the Folktale*. Translated by Laurence Scott. Austin: University of Texas.
Reh, Sabine. 2003. *Berufsbiographische Texte ostdeutscher Lehrer und Lehrerinnen als 'Bekenntnisse': Interpretationen und methodologische Überlegungen zur erziehungswissenschaftlichen Biographieforschung*. Bad Heilbrunn: Klinkhardt.
Scott, James C. 1985. *Weapons of the Weak: Everyday Forms of Peasant Resistance*. New Haven, CT: Yale University Press.
Welke, Tina. 2012. *Tatort Deutsche Einheit: Ostdeutsche Identitätsinszenierung im 'Tatort' des MDR*. Bielefeld: transcript.
Wertsch, James V. 2002. *Voices of Collective Remembering*. Cambridge: Cambridge Univ. Press.
Schütze, Fritz. 1982. 'Narrative Repräsentation Kollektiver Schicksalsbetroffenheit'. In *Erzählforschung: Ein Symposium*, edited by Eberhard Lämmert, 568–590. Stuttgart: Metzler.

Open Access This chapter is licensed under the terms of the Creative Commons Attribution 4.0 International License (http://creativecommons.org/licenses/by/4.0/), which permits use, sharing, adaptation, distribution and reproduction in any medium or format, as long as you give appropriate credit to the original author(s) and the source, provide a link to the Creative Commons licence and indicate if changes were made.

The images or other third party material in this chapter are included in the chapter's Creative Commons licence, unless indicated otherwise in a credit line to the material. If material is not included in the chapter's Creative Commons licence and your intended use is not permitted by statutory regulation or exceeds the permitted use, you will need to obtain permission directly from the copyright holder.

Part III

Memory Practices in the Classroom

Part-II

16

Introduction to Part Three: Memory Practices in the Classroom

Peter Gautschi, Barbara Christophe, and Robert Thorp

Teaching is a difficult task. As Lee S. Shulman determined in 1986: 'From the perspective of complexity management, teaching is a far more demanding occupation than is medicine' (Shulman 1986). Doyle (1986, 394-395) has identified six reasons for this complexity: multidimensionality, simultaneity, immediacy, unpredictability, publicity and historicity.

P. Gautschi (✉)
Institute for History Education and Memory Cultures, University of Teacher Education Lucerne, Lucerne, Switzerland
e-mail: peter.gautschi@phlu.ch

B. Christophe
Georg Eckert Institute for International Textbook Research, Member of the Leibniz Association, Brunswick, Germany
e-mail: christophe@gei.de

R. Thorp
University of Stockholm, Stockholm, Sweden

The University of Newcastle, Newcastle, NSW, Australia
e-mail: robert.thorp@edu.su.se; robert.thorp@newcastle.edu.au

© The Author(s) 2019
B. Christophe et al. (eds.), *The Cold War in the Classroom*, Palgrave Studies in Educational Media, https://doi.org/10.1007/978-3-030-11999-7_16

When it comes to the teaching of history, we can add six further reasons for the particular difficulty in this subject area (Gautschi 2007): First, the learning objects usually *elude the primary view*. History lessons address something now in the past and which must, however, be set within a present context and mindset. Second, this universe of history grows with each passing day – there is *increasingly more past* – while the time available for history teaching is becoming increasingly limited and demands are growing with regard to the choice of topic. Third, history teaching is to a large extent confronted with digital change. This is relevant both to the representation and to the visualisation of the past and, of course, as in all other domains, also to the teaching and learning processes themselves. Fourth, history teaching aims not only at teaching knowledge but also at initiating historical thinking, an 'unnatural act', as Sam Wineburg (2001) has put it, which is not simply intuitive and whose facilitation is highly demanding. Fifth, the mediation of history is also always about *individual and social identity*. Jörn Rüsen even wrote in his work *Historik* that 'Identity formation is therefore one of the most important functions, if not the most important function, of historical thinking in the life practice of its time' (Rüsen 2013, 267, trans. PG). Sixth, bringing the past to the present mind always involves the working out of *culturally shaped common memories* which have a say in defining what counts as a relevant history (Ahlrichs et al. 2015). All in all, *history teaching requires navigating* back and forth between different poles: between transmitting knowledge, enabling historical thinking or building up identity, between history and the past as well as between history and memory.

Research into history teaching is no less complex than its research object (Gautschi 2013, 2014). How do we define and describe such a *volatile and multidimensional object of research*? How do we find and formulate relevant questions or hypotheses in view of the complexity and unpredictability of history teaching? How can we access a field that in theory is a public sphere but to which entry is restricted or even denied by a large number of gatekeepers in order to protect teaching processes and personal rights (Gautschi 2012)? How should we address the huge challenges of data collection and ascertain which methods of data evaluation prove appropriate, productive and target-orientated (Diekmann 2017, 194)? In recent years, videography has proved to be a particularly productive way of collecting data for research into history teaching,

16 Introduction to Part Three: Memory Practices in the Classroom

because it allows the scholar to implement the basic idea of field research: 'to examine its subject in as natural a context as possible in order to avoid distortions caused by the intervention of research methods or by the unrealistic external perspective' (Mayring 2002, 54).

Video-based classroom analysis has a number of advantages over traditional methods (questionnaires, interviews and direct observation in the classroom), in particular the fact that videos can be used to view the classroom activities of different people as often as desired and independently of the time of recording (Gautschi 2016). Further, video analysis provides deeper insight into the complexity of teaching processes, allows the researcher to analyse teaching sequences from several perspectives and guided by different questions, and it facilitates the integration of quantitative and qualitative analyses. Secondary analyses of the data material are possible at a later point in time, the communication of results becomes possible on the basis of examples, and the findings can also be reflected back into practice. In short, the result is an enriching combination of research, theory and practice (cf. Seago 2004; Krammer et al. 2008; Rauin, Herrle and Engartner 2016). In particular, instructional videos are an excellent basis for a case-by-case analysis of history teaching, as the following three chapters will unveil.

Research into history teaching can be carried out in six different directions (cf. Gautschi 2014):

a) *Phenomenon research* aims at a sophisticated description and analysis of the realities of teaching; that is, the manifestations and production patterns of historical teaching and learning, of methodological and medial aspects of history teaching, but also the description of conditions such as timeframes, curricula and textbooks.

b) *Outcomes research* aims at collecting and measuring the learning outcomes (performance, interest in the subject, topic-specific attitudes and skills) of students after a history lesson, unit or period, insofar as this teaching effect can be interpreted. The collection of learning outcomes receives an evaluative character by comparing different groups or through clearly defined standards and objectives.

c) *Effectiveness research* deals with the causal analysis of condition-effect relationships in history teaching. Factors which ensure educational success are to be identified. In this context, teaching and learning quality are seen as characteristics of effectiveness in the sense of a multi-dimensional understanding of education: attitudes, learning motivation, topic-specific interest and performance interact and need to be investigated simultaneously (Reusser 2001). Effectiveness research connects phenomena and outcomes research and searches for relations between teaching processes and outcomes. In contrast to descriptive outcomes research, it aims at identifying and determining the conditions needed for successful teaching (Van Drie and Van Boxtel 2008).

d) *Intervention research* generally involves developing, implementing and evaluating concrete teaching sequences, units or products on the basis of didactical and theoretical considerations. Its aim is not to describe the empirical reality of teaching, but rather to create and examine the quality of a *new* reality of teaching. Accordingly, it seeks to improve the process-oriented practice. In the methodological ideal case, intervention research coincides with experimental effectiveness research.

e) Research on *historical consciousness* is concerned with the analysis of the thought paths of individuals in relation to history. Typical questions ask (i) what exactly teachers and students do when they engage in historical thinking (Wineburg 2001), (ii) what kind of historical consciousness they display (Seixas 2006) and (iii) how students perceive key concepts such as time, change, perspective, significance or evidence (Voss et al. 1998).

f) Finally, the sixth direction is research on history teaching as an institutionalised and at the same time socially embedded setting in which we may investigate how people who happen to be teachers and students negotiate the meaning of the past (Ahlrichs et al. 2015; Christophe 2017; Binnenkade 2015; Macgilchrist et al. 2017). In this research, the focus is on the patterns of meaning that emerge during classroom talk and on the many strands that connect these meaning-making processes with wider social and cultural discourses. It deals with memory practices in the classroom. To quote an intriguing phrase coined by Alexandra Binnenkade, teaching is construed as a discursive node of all the discourses to which teachers and students are exposed and in which they take part when watching films, reading newspapers, talking to family and friends, browsing the internet or perhaps also the textbook.

16 Introduction to Part Three: Memory Practices in the Classroom

These six directions are characterised by a clearly recognisable shared objective. They are not clearly defined categories but rather serve *to convey a big picture*. For example, for a long time the fifth research direction was strongly perceptible. In view of the narratives more-or-less handed down in the established nation states of Western democracies, researchers turned to individuals and their *historical consciousness*. However, this has changed notably over the last few years with the increasing awareness of living in plural and fragmented postmodern societies that are divided with regard to interpretations of the past but also the advance of populism.

While most studies follow more than one single research direction, the following three chapters show clear trends. Whereas Barbara Christophe analyses meaning-making in the classroom as politically loaded memory practices, Robert Thorp looks at narratives offered by teachers and students as indicators for a specific type of historical consciousness. Peter Gautschi and Hans Utz, meanwhile, apply a broad range of concepts from history didactics in order to make informed judgements about the quality of history lessons. However, all three chapters share one crucial feature: while other studies in history education primarily analyse what the history classroom as a setting with certain rules and procedures would do with a certain historical topic (Henke-Bockschatz and Mehr 2012; Hollstein et al. 2002), these three studies investigate what the Cold War as a socially contested historical topic does with the history classroom. Moreover, all three of the following contributions implement phenomenon research and are *based on the same data*, namely on the same four videographed history lessons from the different countries, all of which deal with the origins of the Cold War.

The researchers working on these studies and the authors of the following three contributions contacted secondary-school history teachers in Germany, Switzerland and Sweden, with the request that we observe and film their teaching on the Cold War. We also asked the students' permission to observe and film the lessons; only those who consented were filmed. The observed lessons varied in length. The material was transcribed shortly afterwards, and it is these transcriptions and videos that are used in the following analyses. The transcriptions were then translated from German and Swedish into English. The four teachers included in the study were born before 1970 and thus all had personal experience of the Cold War period. The rationale here was that these teachers would have a richer and more complex understanding of the Cold War period and that this socio-political circumstance in itself would have informed their own lives and experiences (Gautschi et al. 2014). The lessons analysed here are *introductory lessons to the Cold War period*, offering an excellent basis for comparison between the four teachers and for insights as to how the Cold War is introduced and framed in the classroom.

The lesson from Sweden was the shortest. It lasted 27 minutes and consisted of four parts: At the beginning of the lesson, the teacher introduced the subject with her own experiences and those of her generation. She then showed the class a film about the rise of the Soviet Union and the USA and their struggle against Hitler's Germany during the Second World War. Subsequently she introduced the three politicians Stalin, Roosevelt and Churchill, presented the Yalta Conference, and showed another film excerpt about the origin of the Cold War and Truman's containment policy. At the end of the lesson, the teacher explained the significance of the Cold War and Sweden's position with formal neutrality and yet an informal belonging to the West.

The lesson from Switzerland, which lasted 60 minutes, also used a film excerpt of the atomic bombing of Hiroshima; however, this was preceded by an introduction to the topic using a caricature entitled 'Tandem or Unicycle?' from a Swiss textbook. The pupils worked in groups to contextualise both caricature and film. Then the teacher and the class discussed the characteristics and interests of the Cold War blocs, recording the results in tabular form on the blackboard. The pupils then received two text sources representative of the two Cold War parties, to be interpreted working in pairs. At the end of the lesson the teacher gave an overview of the prehistory of the Cold War (1941-1945), in particular of the treatment of Germany by the victorious powers in the aftermath of World War II according to the principles of democratisation, denazification, demilitarisation and decentralisation.

We observed two double lessons from Germany on the origins of the Cold War, one from the former West and one from the former East Germany. Each double lesson lasted around 85 minutes. The teacher of the lesson in Lower Saxony began by brainstorming the students' previous knowledge of the Cold War, noting keywords. Interestingly, this teacher also introduced the topic using a caricature, this time with the caption 'Draft of a Memorial to the Victors' (*Entwurf für ein*

16 Introduction to Part Three: Memory Practices in the Classroom

Siegerdenkmal), and a quotation from Stalin. More detailed analyses of these lessons and how they approached the material are given in the following three chapters.

The courses taken by the fronts in Europe at the end of the Second World War were traced in a group effort. The teacher then presented a brief historical outline of the development of Russia and the Soviet Union since the 19th century, subsequently asking the pupils to do the same for the USA on the basis of their previously acquired knowledge. At the end of the double lesson, the pupils elicited the self-images of the two camps on the basis of representative text sources, juxtaposing these with the image of the other side.

Similarly, in the lesson we observed in Saxony-Anhalt the pupils were confronted with the same caricature used by the lesson in Lower Saxony ('Draft of a Memorial to the Victors') at the beginning of the double lesson, to be analysed with the help of worksheets. The evaluation of this working phase took place in class. Then the pupils were presented with text sources on the Truman doctrine and the Shdanov theory and asked 'who?', 'what?', and 'with what cause'? Here, too, the results were discussed in class. Afterwards, the class discussed the term 'Cold War' on the basis of an image of Checkpoint Charlie in Berlin. The learning results were compared with the text from the school history book and led to the definition of the term 'Cold War'. At the end of the double lesson, the topics covered were summarised and reinforced with the help of another worksheet.

Although the following three contributions all implement phenomenon research and are based on the same data, they differ considerably in interpretation as well as methodology. This section of the book thus follows on from a strand of research in history didactics which, with this comparative approach, strives both to sharpen the theories and methods and to provide new insights into the object of research (Meyer-Hamme et al. 2012). These 'crossed glances' result in a more colourful and detailed picture, which is certainly stimulating if not free of contradiction.

Barbara Christophe's contribution on 'Selecting, Stretching and Missing the Frame: Teachers and Students from Germany and Switzerland Making Sense of the Cold War', compares two introductory lessons on the Cold War held in two year-10 classes in western Germany and Switzerland. From a theoretical perspective her analysis is inspired by memory studies; methodologically she draws on a discourse-based frame analysis. Focusing on rich points, on moments when something unexpected is of particular relevance to processes of framing and interaction, the paper raises three questions. It explores (i) to what extent frames offered by the teachers are shared or contested, (ii) how coherent these frames are and (iii) how frames established by teachers and students interact. Christophe arrives at three conclusions: She shows that both teachers mobilise two clearly recognisable, if opposing, frames, both of which have political implications. She also demonstrates that they 'stretch' and 'bend' their preferred frames in order to integrate all the details they wish to mention. And she argues that students regularly miss the frames offered by their teachers by either failing to recognise their narrative and political logic or by tacitly resisting them. Discussing these empirical insights against the backdrop of debates in memory studies and history didactics, Christophe argues that the misunderstandings we observe when teachers and students negotiate the meaning of the past as representatives of different generations appear to be an important third pattern in communication about memory beyond the alternatives of consensus and conflict often discussed in theoretical debates. Moreover, she contends that by missing the chance to explicitly recognise the political character of Cold War memory, teachers contribute to the likelihood of persistent misunderstandings.

In their chapter, 'Learning from Others: Considerations within History Didactics on Introducing the Cold War in Lessons in Germany, Sweden and Switzerland', *Peter Gautschi* and *Hans Utz* compare the four different lessons in which teachers are confronted with the same challenge, namely how to begin teaching a subject such as the Cold War when the teacher is not only an educator but also a witness of the conflict itself, for which there is no universally accepted master narrative. The chapter is structured around basic didactic questions such as: What is taught in the introductory lessons on the Cold War? How do teachers structure the lessons? What is the learning objective? At the end of the chapter the authors recommend that, when teaching contemporary topics, teachers should teach history while consciously broaching the issue of memory. If successful then history education will be instrumental not only in building knowledge but also in constructing identity and developing critical thinking.

In his chapter 'Pedagogical Entanglements and the Cold War: A Comparative Study on Opening History Lessons on the Cold War in Sweden and Switzerland' *Robert Thorp* analyses the two lower-secondary school opening lessons on the Cold War from Sweden and Switzerland. The opening lessons are analysed according to the content covered, the educational media used, and how the teachers interact with their students. The study finds that the opening lessons vary to a great extent. Whereas the Swiss lesson predominantly focuses on establishing a critical narrative of the origins of the Cold War conflict, the Swedish lesson disseminates what could be considered a traditional narrative of the Cold War. The lessons also differ in terms of the different forms of educational media employed by each educator. While the Swiss teacher makes use of caricatures to instigate pupil-oriented discussions about what caused the Cold War, the Swedish teacher uses personal analogies and a video during class. The study, however, finds that neither teacher engages with the contingencies of history culture that affect historical content and how we approach it; instead, both disseminate a closed rendering of the history of the Cold War.

Although the three contributions examine the same introductory lessons on the subject of the Cold War in very different ways, there are some important *common insights*: First, life experiences, memories and teachers' beliefs shape their teaching activities decisively. Second, the situations in which individuals engage with the past, i.e. the persons they talk to, the media they use but also the political issues that dominate in the present moment, all these situational factors have an influence on practices of teaching the past. When we place emphasis on these factors, we construe teaching and learning history as memory practices.

Third, rendering these processes explicit reduces the risk of misunderstandings in history lessons. Being reflective about the contingency of one's own approach to the past is thus not only a requirement of fairness in the plural societies of today; it also enhances cognitive understanding. At the same time, reflection on the contingency of one's own approach to the past appears to be a rarity in societies considered established nation states. When common-sense assumptions are strong and socially effective, the work they perform tends to be invisible. As many studies show (Psaltis et al. 2017; Bentrovato et al. 2016), this contrasts sharply with the conditions of teaching history in post-conflict societies where everybody is painfully aware of the political involved in debates about the past. This leaves us with the insight that history can indeed 'bite' or 'bore', depending on the specific context. It can suffer from both the disappearance and from the overwhelming presence of the political.

The fourth common insight is that the theories, methodologies and convictions of scholars used for teaching research shape their results largely, and finally, all three studies recognise that adherence to these insights reduces the risk of absolute conclusions.

References

Ahlrichs, Johanna, Katharina Baier, Barbara Christophe, Felicitas Macgilchrist, Patrick Mielke and Roman Richtera. 2015. 'Memory Practices in the Classroom: On Reproducing, Destabilising and Interrupting Majority Memories', *Journal of Educational Media, Memory and Society* 7, no. 2: 89–109.

Bentrovato, Denise, Karina Korestelina and Martina Schulze. 2016. *History Can Bite: History Education in Divided and Post-War Societies.* Göttingen: V&R unipress.

Binnenkade, Alexandra. 2015. 'Doing Memory: Teaching as a Discursive Node', *Journal of Educational Media, Memory, and Society* 7, no. 2: 29–43.

Christophe, Barbara. 2017. 'Eigentlich hingen ja alle mit drin. Entnazifizierung und Kalter Krieg in deutschen Schulbüchern und in den Erzählungen von Lehrenden'. In *Das geteilte Deutschland im Schulbuch. Die Darstellung des Kalten Kriegs am Beispiel Deutschlands in den (Geschichts-) Schulbüchern von 1945 bis in die Gegenwart,* edited by Franziska Flucke, Bärbel Kuhn and Ulrich Pfeil, 147–165. St. Ingbert: Röhrig Universitätsverlag.

Diekmann, Andreas. 2017. *Empirische Sozialforschung. Grundlagen, Methoden, Anwendungen.* 17th edn. Reinbek bei Hamburg: Rowohlt-Taschenbuch-Verl.

Doyle, W. 1986. 'Classroom Organization and Management'. In *Handbook on Research on Teaching,* edited by M. C. Wittrock. 3rd edn, 392–431. New York: Macmillan.

Gautschi, Peter. 2007 'Geschichtsunterricht erforschen - eine aktuelle Notwendigkeit'. In *Geschichtsunterricht heute. Eine empirische Analyse ausgewählter Aspekte,* edited by Peter Gautschi, Daniel V. Moser, Kurt Reusser and Pit Wiher, 21–59. Bern: h.e.p. verlag ag.

Gautschi, Peter. 2012. *Guter Geschichtsunterricht, Grundlagen, Erkenntnisse, Hinweise.* 3rd edn. Schwalbach/Ts.: Wochenschau Verlag [2009].

Gautschi, Peter. 2013. 'Erkenntnisse und Perspektiven geschichtsdidaktischer Unterrichtsforschung'. In *Forschungsmethoden und Forschungsstand in den*

Didaktiken der kulturwissenschaftlichen Fächer, edited by Marko Demantowsky and Bettina Zurstrassen, 203–244. Bochum/Freiburg: projekt verlag.

Gautschi, Peter. 2014. 'History Education Research in Switzerland'. In *Researching History Education. International Perspectives and Disciplinary Traditions*, edited by Manuel Köster, Holger Thünemann and Meik Zülsdorf-Kersting, 104–132. Schwalbach/Ts.: Wochenschau Verlag.

Gautschi, Peter, Markus Furrer and Barbara Sommer Häller. 2014. 'Umgang mit Geschichte und Erinnerung in Schule und Hochschule'. In *Der Beitrag von Schulen und Hochschulen zu Erinnerungskulturen*, edited by Peter Gautschi and Barbara Sommer Häller, 7–24. Schwalbach/Ts.: Wochenschau Verlag..

Gautschi, Peter. 2016. 'Fachdidaktik als Design-Science. Videobasierte Unterrichts- und Lehrmittelforschung zum Lehren und Lernen von Geschichte'. In *Visible Didactics – Fachdidaktische Forschung trifft Praxis*, edited by Christa Juen-Kretschmer, Kerstin Mayr-Keiler, Gregor Örley and Irmgard Plattner, 53–66. *Transfer Forschung-Schule*, vol. 2, Bad Heilbrunn: Klinkhardt.

Henke-Bockschatz, Gerhard and Christian Mehr. 2012. 'Von den Möglichkeiten historischen Verstehens im Unterricht als sozialer Praxis'. In *Was heißt guter Geschichtsunterricht? Perspektiven im Vergleich*, edited by Johannes Meyer-Hamme, Holger Thünemann and Meik Zülsdorf-Kersting, 107–122. Schwalbach/Ts.: Wochenschau Verlag.

Hollstein, Oliver, Wolfgang Meseth, Christine Müller-Mahnkopp, Matthias Proske and Frank Olaf Radtke. 2002. Nationalsozialismus im Geschichtsunterricht. Beobachtungen unterrichtlicher Kommunikation. Frankfurt: Universität Frankfurt.

Krammer, Kathrin, Claudia Lena Schnetzler, Nadja Ratzka, Christine Pauli, Kurt Reusser, Frank Lipowsky and Eckhard Klieme. 2008. 'Videobasierte Unterrichtsanalyse in der Weiterbildung von Lehrpersonen: Konzeption und Ergebnisse eines netzgestützten Weiterbildungsprojekts mit Mathematiklehrpersonen aus Deutschland und der Schweiz'.*Beiträge zur Lehrerbildung* 26: 178–197.

Macgilchrist, Felicitas, Johanna Ahlrichs, Patrick Mielke and Roman Richtera. 2017. 'Memory Practices and Colonial Discourse: On Text Trajectories and Lines of Flight', *Critical Discourse Studies* 14, no. 4: 341–361.

Mayring, Philipp. 2002. *Einführung in die qualitative Sozialforschung. Eine Anleitung zu qualitativem Denken*. 5th edn. Weinheim and Basel: Beltz.

Meyer-Hamme, Johannes, Holger Thünemann and Meik Zülsdorf-Kersting. eds. 2012. *Was heisst guter Geschichtsunterricht? Perspektiven im Vergleich*. Schwalbach/Ts: Wochenschau Verlag.

Psaltis, Charis, Mario Carretero and Sabina Cehajic-Clancy. 2017. *History Education and Conflict Transformation. Social Psychological Theories, History Education and Reconciliation.* London: Palgrave.

Rauin, Udo, Matthias Herrle and Tim Engarnter. 2016. *Videoanalysen in der Unterrichtsforschung. Methodische Vorgehensweisen und Anwendungsbeispiele.* Weinheim and Basel: Beltz Juventa.

Reusser, Kurt. 2001. *Bridging Instruction to Learning. A Research Strategy and its Implementation in a National and Cross-cultural Video Study in Switzerland.* Keynote address from the 9th European Conference for Research on Learning and Instruction (EARLY), Fribourg, Switzerland, 31 August 2011.

Rüsen, Jörn. 2013. *Historik. Theorie der Geschichtswissenschaft.* Köln, Weimar, Wien: Böhlau Verlag.

Seago, N. 2004. 'Using Videos as an Object of Inquiry for Mathematics Teaching and Learning'. In *Using Video in Teacher Education*, edited by J. Brophy, 259–286. Oxford: Elsevier.

Seixas, Peter. 2006 'Historical Consciousness: The Progress of Knowledge in a Post-progressive Age'. In *Narration, Identity and Historical Consciousness*, edited by Jürgen Straub, 141–162. New York: Berghahn Publishers.

Shulman, L. S. 1986. 'Those Who Understand: Knowledge Growth in Teaching'. *Educational Researcher* 15, no. 2: 4–21.

Van Drie, Janet and Carla Van Boxtel. 2008. 'Historical Reasoning: Towards a Framework for Analyzing Students' Reasoning about the Past'. Educational Psychological Review 20, no. 2: 87–110.

Voss, James, Jennifer Wiley and Joel Kennet. 1998. 'Students' Perception of History and Historical Concepts'. *International Review of History Education* 2: 307–330.

Sam Wineburg. 2001. *Historical Thinking and Other Unnatural Acts: Charting the Future of Teaching the Past.* Philadelphia: Temple University Press.

Open Access This chapter is licensed under the terms of the Creative Commons Attribution 4.0 International License (http://creativecommons.org/licenses/by/4.0/), which permits use, sharing, adaptation, distribution and reproduction in any medium or format, as long as you give appropriate credit to the original author(s) and the source, provide a link to the Creative Commons licence and indicate if changes were made.

The images or other third party material in this chapter are included in the chapter's Creative Commons licence, unless indicated otherwise in a credit line to the material. If material is not included in the chapter's Creative Commons licence and your intended use is not permitted by statutory regulation or exceeds the permitted use, you will need to obtain permission directly from the copyright holder.

17

Selecting, Stretching and Missing the Frame: Making Sense of the Cold War in German and Swiss History Classrooms

Barbara Christophe

Memory studies present us with two narratives, both of which tend to offer somewhat opposing images of how we should think about collective memory. According to one school of thought, collective memory appears to be strong and powerful, moulding pasts, rather effectively, according to the needs of shifting presents (Hobsbawm and Ranger 1992; Zelizer 1998). According to the second, collective memory is the precarious result of an attempt to square the circle (Assmann 2006). While it has to *decouple* from the polyphonic memories of individual persons in order to achieve coherence, it also has to *tie in* with individual memories in order to be accepted as an appropriate and meaningful frame. It is in line with this second narrative that authors place emphasis on conflict and struggle. When talking about collective memory, one must not expect it to be consensual, coherent or stable (Schwartz 2016, 10), they argue. Memory does not primarily result in social cohesion but instead can serve as an object of contestation (Bodnar 1992; Sturken 1997; Sierps 2014) and

---

B. Christophe (✉)
Georg Eckert Institute for International Textbook Research, Member of the Leibniz Association, Brunswick, Germany
e-mail: christophe@gei.de

fragmentation (Leggewie 2009; Hoskins 2011); it not only clearly orients an individual but also creates ambivalence and inconclusiveness (Ryan 2011; Sturken 1999; Beattie 2008). It does not travel untouched across time and space, but is instead subject to continuous mutation every time it is invoked.

Against the backdrop of these debates, this chapter analyses how teachers and students in a German and a Swiss history classroom 'do' memory (Macgilchrist et al. 2015), when discussing the origins of the Cold War. Conceived of as a meeting place between members of different generations (Menk 2006), the history classroom is studied from the perspective of memory *practices*. Looked upon from that angle, teachers and students whose formative experiences took place in different historical periods and who have been exposed to different discourses could be expected to recall the past rather differently (Schuman and Scott 1989).

Focusing on the discursive frames applied by both groups, this chapter explores (i) to what extent the emerging patterns of interpretation are shared, contested or simply diverse, (ii) how coherently they connect to culturally shaped frameworks and (iii) how they interact with one another. I will proceed in three steps: I begin by looking into the discourses enacted by the two teachers, then continue to examine how coherently both of them use framing strategies. Finally, I focus on patterns of interaction that evolve between teachers and students in both classrooms. Comparing both teachers, I show that they differ in selecting frames with opposing political implications but converge in stretching and bending these frames in order to integrate all the details they wish to mention. Analysing classroom talk as an exchange between members of different generations, I point out that students often appear to miss the frames their teachers use, at times because they fail to recognise the political and narrative logic behind them and at other times because they tacitly resist them. Translating these empirical findings into a theoretically relevant contribution to memory studies, I argue that misunderstanding and misperception constitute a likely third option when members of different generations remember the past, alongside conflict and consensus. I moreover contend that generational differences in judging the past can be linked to the fading of common-sense assumptions as well as to differences in moral demands. With regard to history teaching, I point out that both teachers simultaneously invoke and suppress the political due to how each remembers the Cold War, thus making it considerably more difficult for their students to understand them.

Method

My analysis draws mainly on two video-recorded lessons on the origin of the Cold War.[1] In addition, the interpretation of some particularly dense moments of classroom discourse is corroborated by referring back to different types of interviews[2] conducted with the two teachers, as well as to observational data gathered during ethnographic field work in their respective classrooms.[3] While I do not aspire to present findings representative of German or Swiss history lessons as a whole, I do depict in detail situated classroom talk that should allow us to better understand what happens when members of different generations interpret a contested past like the Cold War.

Conceptually, this chapter is geared towards frame analysis, which aims at identifying the major cognitive schemata people use to organise experience and give meaning to reality (Goffman 1974). Beyond this rather general definition, my understanding of the concept of the frame is based on three crucial claims. First, I take frames to be a 'configuration of positions' (Lombardo et al. 2009, 11), which are not restricted to cognitive schemata alone but also include normatively loaded bias and assumptions of which people are not aware. Accordingly, I pay close attention to hidden assumptions implied but not explicitly stated when approaching the framing of discourses in the classroom. Second, in line with discourse-based approaches I assume that the frames used by individuals are embedded in socially shared networks of frames, which we shall call frameworks for the sake of clarity (Marx Ferree 2009). This leaves me with the task of identifying culturally influenced interpretations of issues and events within the frames used in the two classrooms. Finally, I believe that frames play a vital role in helping us to make sense of the world by reducing complexity and by pointing our attention to certain factors while bracketing out others. Frames order and link events together into packages.

Selecting Different Frames

A first comparison of both lessons quickly reveals that both teachers adhere to surprisingly similar strategies on some levels, while making completely different choices on others. To begin with similarities, both start their lessons with caricatures focusing on the break-up of the Anti-Hitler Coalition. While the German teacher refers to the famous Swiss drawing, 'Draft of a Memorial to the Victors', which features Roosevelt and Stalin sitting on a horse with two heads pointing in opposite directions, the Swiss teacher employs a caricature of Truman and Stalin on a tandem which then breaks apart into two unicycles heading different ways. Moreover, during the latter part of each lesson, both teachers ask their students to use fragments of the famous speeches given by Truman and Stalin in 1947 to illustrate their initial thoughts on the opposing ideas Americans and Soviets stood for. However, as we shall see, each

Fig. 17.1 Cartoon entitled 'Tour du Monde: Tandem oder Einrad?' by Jean Leffel. From German textbook: *Menschen in Zeit und Raum 9,* Edition for Lower Saxony, 113 (Zurich: Schulbuch Verlag plus AG, 2012)

17 Selecting, Stretching and Missing the Frame: Making Sense...

Fig. 17.2 Cartoon entitled 'Entwurf fur ein Siegerdenkmal' or 'Draft of A Memorial to the Victors', published in Schweizer Illustrierte (11 April 1945). Reproduced here from the German textbook: *Entdecken und Verstehen 3,* Edition for Lower Saxony, 99 (Berlin: Cornelsen, 2010)

teacher contextualises these materials in very different ways, integrating them into opposing frames that support conflicting stories on the origin of the Cold War.

The History Teacher from Germany

The most prominent feature in the lesson given by the German teacher, here referred to as Ms. Burmeister, is her outspoken anti-Soviet bias. Although she starts the classroom discussion with the cartoon described above, which seems to equally distribute blame for having caused the Cold War between both superpowers, in the remainder of the lesson she places an almost exclusive focus on the Soviets as the main culprits. In order to contextualise the cartoon she draws her students' attention to the famous speech Stalin gave in April 1945. Asking them to read aloud his unambiguous statement that the victorious powers would impose their social systems on all occupied countries as far as their armies advance, she evokes the image of an aggressive Soviet Union. Something similar happens in the next phase of the lesson.

00:28:37-	Tfem	Would you please look in your atlases for a map that shows where the borders were between the armies after the Second World War?
00:29:00	S8	Um, what it looked like, or the occupying forces?
00:29:03	Tfem	Hm?
00:29:11	S8	Well, what it/ it looked like, or, […] or a map with the whole occupying forces and stuff? #00:29:12-1#
00:29:17-	Tfem	With the occupying forces. We have here 'how/ as far as his armies can reach'. #00:29:17-4#
00:30:08	Tfem	So, now everyone has, no perhaps not. […] Some are still flicking through. #00:30:00-8#
00:30:17	S4	When was the cartoon from again?
00:31:18	Tfem	April '45. But not much changed after that. […] So. How far did the Soviet […] zone of occupation reach? […] Either look at the map on page 62 or on page 92, there look at map 4.

In this scene, we see how the teacher subsequently reframes the task she is giving to her students without reflecting explicitly on the implications brought about by her change of wording. While she initially asks her students to browse the atlas and search for a map that illustrates the borders between the allied powers in 1945, she then suddenly instructs them to look only for the Soviet zone of occupation. In line with this pattern of placing blame on the USSR while remaining silent on the subject of the USA, a large portion of the lesson—34 out of 90 minutes—is dedicated to a presentation which she gives on the role of the Soviets and the Russians, both of which are repeatedly described as being aggressive and backward (Neumann 1999; Macgilchrist 2011; Lawless 2014). She cites the inclusion of Siberia and Central Asia in the Tsarist Empire as an example of Russia's expansionist drive in the nineteenth century. After the Second World War, the USSR is said to have started its 'march towards the west'.[4] At the same time, according to Ms. Burmeister, Russia never really had any chance to compete with a West which proved superior on all levels. Economically and socially, Russia, she argues, is 'fairly undeveloped',[5] even 'very primitive in terms of social equality'.[6] A look at the map illustrates 'that there is not very much [there]', particularly in contrast to 'a map of Germany or maybe Great Britain or France'.[7] The arbitrariness of the Russian Tsar, who was not restrained by any law, contrasts sharply with European monarchies which had adopted constitutions by the nineteenth century at the latest. In terms of abolishing serfdom, Russia lagged behind by more than 70 years according to Ms. Burmeister. In the end, she describes Russia as defeated, as a country where 'reforms did not come to anything',[8] where political disputes triggered either assassinations or civil war with 'all members of the population [...] fighting in groups against one another'.[9]

The History Teacher from Switzerland

Most of the time, the history teacher from Switzerland, here referred to as Ms. Reger, establishes frames that are completely different to those used by Ms. Burmeister. At the beginning of the lesson, she contrasts the cartoon, which depicts the Cold War as the result of a disrupted relationship, with a film that focuses on the atomic bomb dropped on Japan by the Americans in 1945. Ms. Reger thus draws on a source that portrays Americans not only as having killed thousands of Japanese civilians, but also as enjoying unrivalled military superiority. To ensure that they get the message, Ms. Reger asks her students whether the film they have seen 'connect[s] at all with the cartoon'.[10] Subtly preparing the ground for the 'right' answer, she raises the question of 'who's got the better seat on the tandem'.[11] Bringing home her own conclusion, she then emphasises that Truman, who is riding in the front seat, clearly had the better position given that 'the one in front can steer'.[12] Undermining the position articulated by the cartoon, she finally encourages the students to reflect on whether the unicycles are the proper size: 'And [...] are the proportions right at the bottom, the two unicycles? Would they be right at that time, straight after the Second World War?'[13] For her, it is crystal clear that America 'ha(s) got the upper hand'[14] due to its nuclear weapons, a detail which, she points out, is not mentioned at all in the cartoon. Later in the lesson, when she talks about the general situation different countries faced after 1945, she speaks of the USA as 'the number one as a world power [...] economically and [...] of course militarily',[15] as 'a power that can pack a punch'.[16]

While she highlights the power disparities between these two rivals and clearly assigns the position of superiority to America, Ms. Reger downplays political or moral differences, resolutely excluding all traditionalist ideas about a morally superior USA or West. This becomes particularly apparent during a classroom discussion on the Truman and Zhdanov speeches when she asks students to stage a clash of arguments between the two. Summing up the discussion, she concludes 'both have the same roles probably using the same means'.[17]

At the end of the lesson and during a short lecture on Allied policies in occupied Germany, Ms. Reger openly accuses Americans of having cooperated with the same Nazis they fought against in the Second World War.

01:00:52[18]	Tfem	And what then, what happened after that, the rats, or these Nazis, they were recycled, well, that's how it's put according to, in this, um, book. It was like this, they then, or in the Cold War, there were plenty of uses for them. In Latin America, when people wanted communist rabble-rousers tracked down. And an example is, um, Klaus Barbie, he was the Butcher of Lyon. He was one of those who fled and was recruited by the CIA in Bolivia and was one of those responsible for tracking down Che Guevara. [Barbie's] past was irrelevant [to the CIA in recruiting him], but the point is, he was tracked down. (2 sec). So this is referred to as recycling.

She bases her talk on a book that investigates how the Nazis fled legal persecution like rats vanishing through thousands of loopholes.[19] On a purely linguistic level, she persistently neglects to ascribe responsibility. She speaks of the 'plenty of uses' that were made of the Nazis, who were 'recycled', in Latin America where the 'people', i.e. a rather poorly identified historical protagonist, wanted to track down 'communist rabble rousers', apparently with the help of Nazis. However, with the strategically placed example of Klaus Barbie, who despite his criminal past as the 'Butcher of Lyon' was 'recruited' by the American intelligence agency, the CIA, Ms. Reger clearly invites her students to view the USA as the driving force behind these machinations.

Comparison

By framing the stories they offer to their students quite differently, both teachers show us that competing approaches in Cold War historiography, declared prematurely dead by some, still play a vital role in school history.

Probably unwillingly, they moreover remind us of the inescapably political nature that characterises representations in general (Hutcheon 2007) and historical accounts in particular (Sturken 1997).

Stretching the Frame

While the two teachers clearly differ by invoking culturally opposed frames, both of them encounter similar difficulties in integrating all the details they feel should be mentioned. In the end, both stretch and bend their respective frames successfully in order to make them fit the contours of the stories they wish to tell.

The History Teacher from Germany

In the case of the history teacher from Germany, traditionalist discourse is interrupted in two significant instances. The first occurs when Ms. Burmeister is talking about the historical dynamics that led to the October Revolution in 1917.

00:54:15[20]-	Tfem	In 1917 the military situation and the economic situation in Russia were so catastrophic that Tsar Nicolas II decided, and was forced of course really, to abdicate. So he did. Then there was a [...] government, provisional government they were called, that came to power and attempted to er, the [...] to contain the military situation, which ultimately they were not able to do. They were expected, really, to make peace. And they should have addressed social injustice more, and especially they should have helped the farmers. For example they should have divided up the land. And that didn't happen. [...] And then there was a, er, group, has been for a long time, since the end of the 19th century, we had them in Germany too, Social Democrats. A party that spoke for the workers. And on the (clicks on the next slide) erm. On the Russian side there were those known as the Bolsheviks. It means 'majority group'. They were particularly radical. And they wanted social equality, land redistribution. They were responsible for what was really a putsch in October 1917.

In this moment Ms. Burmeister speaks in a rather ambivalent manner about the Bolsheviks. On the one hand, she emphasises the shortcomings of their predecessors, i.e. the provisional government which, according to her, failed to address issues of 'social injustice', thus giving ample cause for upheaval. She even portrays the Bolsheviks as the only historical figures who cared for the viable interests of ordinary men and women and promised 'social equality' and 'land distribution', two things which by today's moral standards appear to be just and fair. On the other hand, Ms. Burmeister describes the same Bolsheviks as 'radical' and as having organised 'what was really a putsch', thus connecting them with two words that definitely have negative connotations in German discourses.

Something similar happens when she introduces Karl Marx as the founding father of Soviet communism.

| 01:04:35[21] | Tfem | They advanced that far. [...] All in the name of a system. The system that was behind it, was called, and is called 'Communism'. [...] Can we now? I'll just turn this off. (Turns the computer screen off.) Er, the idea behind it is [...] from Karl Marx in the 19th century: Society is very unequal. Wealth is very unfairly distributed. Decisions about where money should be spent in a nation are too unfairly distributed. That, how the workers have to live and work, how low their wages are, that is simply not fair. It must be changed. [...] Basically those that own things, should no longer own them. That there should be no more industrialists who decide by themselves 'I'm going to close my firm, or I'm going to produce this and that' but rather it should be under the control of the workers. That is the central idea. [...] |

Marxism is not only presented here as an adequate and legitimate response to a number of unpleasant realities in the nineteenth century – when wealth was distributed unfairly, workers received appallingly low wages and common sense would lead one to the conclusion that 'it must be changed' – but the measures Marxists would have implemented in the event of their success are actually openly praised. There is no doubt that, to Ms. Burmeister, depriving 'industrialists' of the ability to shut down factories sounds like a good idea.

Displaying a surprising degree of attraction to the ideas of Marxism, this teacher is actually close to cracking the traditionalist frame to which she usually refers when telling the story of the Cold War. In such moments, Ms. Burmeister engages a strategy aimed at repairing the damage she may have done to the coherence of her account.

01.02.20[22]	Tfem	And the Soviet Union claimed 'We have realised this. We have done it like this'. [...] It was opposed to for example (Turns computer screen back on and goes to 'Stalinism' slide) um, in agriculture the farmers could no longer decide themselves what, er, they produced, and at what price and so on. That was all decided for them. In businesses the workers could not decide what they produced, and at what prices and so on. It was all set by the state. [...] But the claim was 'We have abolished individual decisions, the individual power of businessmen. We are working for the people'.

Ms. Burmeister's strategy mainly rests on denying the Bolsheviks the right to present themselves as legitimate heirs to Marx and Marxism. She points out that after 1917 they did quite the opposite of what Marx had once demanded. Instead of letting workers and farmers determine what they were going to produce and how much money they would charge for their products, she argues, the Bolsheviks simply replaced the former industrialists with the state, thus altering close to nothing for working people, who were still subject to decisions taken by others. In Ms. Burmeister's account there thus appears to be a huge gap between the values the Bolsheviks claim to represent and the cruel reality they created.

The History Teacher from Switzerland

There is only one moment when Ms. Reger is in danger of transgressing the limits of the revisionist discourse she generally employs: when she talks about the position in which the Western states found themselves after 1945. Broadening the perspective and switching from a hitherto exclusive focus on the USA to allow for a quick glance at the circumstances the United Kingdom was facing at that time, she first of all draws her students' attention to the upcoming end of the British Empire. Putting an emphasis on decolonisation as an important historical process, she touches upon an issue which is regularly raised by authors who argue that the Cold War paradigm is a much too narrow one with which to make sense of all the relevant historical trends that took place across the globe after the Second World War (Conelly 2000; Iriye 2013). However, she herself is far from arriving at this conclusion. Quite the reverse, as becomes evident when she appears anxious to bring the Cold War back in to the discussion. She actually tries hard to explain how an admirable goal like decolonisation was achieved morally under the hegemony of the USA, the world power of which she is otherwise critical.

0:26:31[23]	Tfem	Because, um, in the Atlantic Charter Roosevelt and Churchill spoke of it, of the right of peoples to self-determination. And the inhabitants of the colonies, they were listening carefully, right, and they thought: Yes, absolutely! Only, they of course hadn't meant it like that, or that they [would] give up their colonies, but instead they were thinking of, yes, that the regions occupied by Germany should be given up. And so now, after the Second World War, decolonisation began too.

Ms. Reger mobilises a rather abstract narrative here, according to which events do not necessarily reflect the initial intentions of those who may have caused them but may well be the unintended side-effects of another conscious action. More concretely, she argues that, in setting up The Atlantic Charter and in subscribing to the principle of self-determination, Roosevelt and Churchill would primarily have had in mind the European countries formerly occupied by Nazi Germany as beneficiaries of their actions. To Ms. Reger, it is clear that these two leading Western politicians simply failed to anticipate that the same principle could be applied to colonised parts of the world as well. 'Of course they hadn't meant it like that', Ms. Reger says, 'drawing authority from an unspoken premise' (Geertz 1992, 6) by presenting her judgment as a fact that anybody with a clear mind would spontaneously grasp and embrace.

Comparison

Both teachers successfully walk the line between stretching and bending the frame while preventing it from breaking. Both appear to have similar reasons to deviate from culturally shared narratives. From the life-story interviews we conducted with them, we know that in both cases the historical details they could not help but mention, although they have the potential to undermine the coherence of the overall account, are biographically relevant to them. While Ms. Burmeister spent a lot of time reading Marx in circles of politically active students as a young adult,[24] Ms. Reger had made many trips to postcolonial countries such as Vietnam or Cuba.[25]

Differences between these two educators in dealing with ambivalences mainly pertain to the repair strategies they apply in the process of modifying the frames they have selected. Portraying the USA as a power which by sheer miscalculation happened to be supportive of the noble goal of decolonisation, Ms. Reger largely preserves the picture she has previously drawn within a revisionist frame. At the same time, Ms. Burmeister allows more ambivalences to enter her discourse. While she mostly draws a rather bleak picture of the Soviet Union, she also admits that the Soviet system was based on noble ideas dating back to Marx. Although she reconciles both perspectives by pointing to an implementation gap, she nevertheless also credits the Soviets with good intentions.

Missing the Frame

As I argue above, frames are culturally shaped cognitive schemata which help us to recognise a 'messy' reality by imposing a structure upon it. Yet, in order to be readable to people, they are also dependent on culturally shaped common-sense assumptions. As soon as these common-sense assumptions are no longer shared socially, frames may be overlooked. This is what we can observe in both classrooms. In some situations, teachers and students talk at cross purposes. They fail to recognise each other's frames because they are unable to infer the other's preferred frame from what has been said.

The History Classroom in Germany

In the German history class we observed, the students were most actively involved during the last phase of the lesson when they were asked to stage a discussion between Americans and Russians, based on their reading of the famous Truman and Zhdanov speeches from 1947. They were split into four groups with each being instructed to identify either with the Soviets or with the Americans. More specifically, they were tasked with deriving images of the 'self' and the Cold War 'other' from the two speeches. However, all groups had considerable difficulty grasping what the teacher viewed as the bottom line of the claims made by both historical parties.

Looking at the two American groups, we came across two striking moments. Generally speaking, much of the pathos in Truman's speech in 1947 was completely lost in the representation offered by the students. While the American president spoke dramatically about two lifestyles opposing each other, contrasting freedom with oppression and promising help to all free nations ready to resist submission, the students spoke rather dryly of the economic and financial support offered by the USA to the free nations. Moreover, in one particularly striking moment, one female student, here referred to as Marie, who was given the task of summing up Truman's accusations against the USSR, misreads the core words. While the American president spoke about his firm commitment 'to support free peoples who are resisting attempted subjugation *by* armed minorities or by outside pressures',[26] Marie speaks of 'the subjugation *of* the armed minorities as a result of external pressure'.[27] According to her, the Soviets are thus not guilty of having allowed armed minorities to oppress others; rather, they are charged with having subjugated armed minorities. The teacher quickly corrects Marie by drawing attention to how she has replaced 'by' with 'of'. She also offers her own summary according to which the Soviets did not 'really want to create a democracy' but were 'in fact [...] doing the opposite and oppressing'.[28] Surprisingly,

17 Selecting, Stretching and Missing the Frame: Making Sense... 375

and despite the political disparities between the two versions that are brought to the table by the teacher and Marie, the intervention of the former meets with neither resistance nor further enquiries. Obviously, Marie has failed to make sense of the Truman speech, because she had neither enough historical knowledge nor sufficient stereotypical ideas about the Soviets to compensate for her lack of knowledge. The fact that she does not see any reason to defend her version of the story seems to point to either a lack in awareness about the clash of positions she has just contributed to or to an indifference towards history teaching in general and history teaching about the Cold War in particular. In any case, it seems that the history of the Cold War does not hold enough relevance for Marie for her to make significant effort towards an appropriate interpretation (Schwartz 2016).

If we turn to the groups that were set the task of identifying with Zhdanov, things seem initially to go more smoothly. The ease with which the students seem to grasp the logic behind the Soviet position is perhaps somewhat surprising given Ms. Burmeister's extensive othering of Russia and the USSR earlier in the lesson. The students cast in the role of the Soviets counter the altruistic American self-image the other group had difficulty articulating, claiming that all this was in fact only about imperialism and that the Americans 'just want that so that they can be a world power'.[29] In addition, they correctly reconstruct the Soviet self-image by pointing out that they, the Soviets, wanted 'to reintroduce democracy and to act against, er, against American imperialism'[30] and 'to beat fascism and, er, act in the name of our people'.[31]

However, at one point, the smoothness of the students' identification with the Soviets is interrupted, although it seems unclear what is actually happening in the following situation:

00:34:38[32]-4	Tfem	So let's have the opposite-um-version. How does the Soviet Union present itself? And the Americans have to respond [...] Go, S13, S7, S18, now it's your turn. How do you see yourselves?
00:34:43	S13masc	We want to destroy democracy
00:34:46	Tfem	You want to destroy democracy?
00:34:48	S13masc	Yes. We want to destroy democracy.

00:34:54		Tfem	I think there's a bit of a misunderstanding there, S13. The Soviets wouldn't say that about themselves. (General restlessness and some laughter.)
00:35:09		S13masc	Yes, first we want er, the position, the same economic position as America, that's what we want to achieve.

At first glance, the student who is talking here, whom we henceforth refer to as Markus, seems to start off on the wrong track. Trying to contribute to the construction of the Soviet self-image, he says, 'we want to destroy democracy'. His classmates respond with laughter. They immediately seem to understand that Markus is violating the general rule of the game by vilifying, instead of glorifying, the Soviet self he was told to identify with.

But what has actually happened? Has Markus made a mistake? The ease with which he presents a better, a more accurate alternative soon after the corrective intervention by the teacher sows doubt. This doubt increases if we look at how Markus behaved in the other lessons we observed. To give one telling example: Asked to describe the feelings of school children who were receiving CARE parcels in the aftermath of the Second World War, he responded with open irony to what appears to him to be a ridiculously simple and obvious task. In contrast to the positive responses of his classmates, who even elaborated on the difference between the truly grateful children of that time and themselves as the spoiled youngsters of today, he made a witty comment suggesting that CARE actually stood for '*Calorien-armes-Reste-Essen*' (low-calorie leftovers).[33]

Is something similar happening in the role-play? Maybe Markus is simultaneously exploiting and undermining the role ascribed to him with his strangely inappropriate self-description of the Soviets as democracy-destroying monsters? Perhaps he wishes to unveil the hidden transcript of the lesson according to which these Soviets are always the bad guys? Or possibly he is not the slow but the smart pupil who subtly points to the paradox of staging a seemingly open-ended debate between Soviets and Americans after having been told how backward, evil and violent the Soviets were?

According to this line of thought, Markus acts as a discourse analyst (Macgilchrist et al. 2017) who uncovers the rules of a discourse according to which it is beyond question that the Soviet are the culprits. We cannot prove this interpretation, but looking at all the mishaps and glitches discussed so far, it is clear that the role-play turned out to be full of lapses and misunderstandings.

The History Classroom in Switzerland

In the Swiss case, the most obvious instance of missing the frame occurred during a classroom discussion on the peculiarities of the situation the Soviet Union faced on the eve of the Cold War. We observed the following exchange between Ms. Reger and two of her most actively engaged students.

0:26:31[34]	Tf	OK then, so now there's, um, the Soviet Union here (2 sec). Where does the Soviet Union stand, or what is there to say here about [...] this state at the end of the war? (16 sec) SmA?
0:27:08	SmA (Peter)	It pulled out, I mean, from this [...] I mean, after the world [...] you know, after the two world wars it was [...] it's shown, there's like a conflict, or sort of a silent conflict between the two ideologies.
0:27:20	Tf	Hmhm, hmhm.
0:27:22	SmA (Peter)	And I have the feeling, I mean, America's scared of this communism thing.
0:27:26	Tf	Hmhm.
0:27:27	SmA (Peter)	And the Soviet Union is making propaganda against capitalism [...] like sort of on two fronts.
0:27:34	Tf	Yes, exactly, that's what happens now. But actually, to complete this here, basically: that was the [...] here: the coalition against Hitler, right? (4 sec). At the end of the war. So we can see that here. That's it, the, the tandem you can see [...] see in the cartoon [...] And now... yes? SmA?
0:28:12	SmA (Peter)	Perhaps there's also [...] gaining land [...] Germany gets divided up.
0:28:18	Tf	That's it. Yes, precisely.
0:28:20	SmA (Peter)	And [...] afterwards, after Europe, this, this, um, Iron Curtain becomes very strongly felt between East and West.

0:28:28	Tf		Hmhm, hmhm. Exactly. Let's look at the war now... Perhaps you remember the US entering the war or, put a better way, um, the Soviet... the Soviet Union was attacked and the consequence was – was – huge losses [...] millions of victims (4 sec). And in spite of this: where in the ranking – to come back to the ranking – where are, where's the Soviet Union? (4 sec) Yes, um, SmB?
0:29:08	SmB		Actually in second place, because it['s] actually still a really, really big military power.
0:29:13	Tf		That's right. (8 sec) Number two. (10 sec)
0:29:35	Tf		That's certainly, um, a point. And SmA said it already: Expansion to the west, that's a given, right? (11 sec)
0:29:55	Tf		And someone said that already, it's like this: (If I [could] just a bit [...]) They, I mean, they're winners too, aren't they? And they're winners, they're both winners, but it became clear that communism's an alternative to this liberal, this liberal democracy. Clear as day, that's the alternative. And why shouldn't communism be the best model? With a [...] with communism you can [...], I mean, you can win wars. So here: communism as an alternative form of society.

The first striking thing to be observed in this intense scene is the careful manoeuvring of the student, 'Peter', who is responding to the teacher's introductory question. He starts to talk only after a rather long period of silence where none of his fellow classmates appear to have sufficient prior knowledge on the Soviets to answer the question. Upon closer examination we can clearly see that even Peter is not really sure about the point he wants to make. We see him cautiously probing, withdrawing and offering contradictory stories of how the Soviets have acted while paying close attention to his teacher's reactions.

Initially, he talks about the Soviets pulling out and thus seems to be invoking a revisionist frame according to which the Soviets would be an exhausted and therefore cautious power. Describing the Soviets as being in retreat in the literal sense of moving back from occupied territories, he is, however, referring to incorrect historical facts. Accordingly, Ms. Reger's reactions are hesitant at best. Mumbling a somewhat indeterminate 'hm', we see in the video that her face clearly shows disapproval.

17 Selecting, Stretching and Missing the Frame: Making Sense... 379

Given her general inclination towards revisionism, she is, in all likelihood, not disapproving of the overall line of thought that the student is offering but rather of his failure to provide convincing proof.

Reading her face correctly, while probably failing to understand the reasons for her lack of enthusiasm, the student intuitively performs a radical turnaround. Without reflecting on the change in his attitude, he starts to speak about the propaganda war the Soviets have been waging against the Americans who, according to him, were fearful of the Soviets he now suddenly describes as representing a threat. Encouraged by a fellow student who is nodding approvingly at him, Peter continues to elaborate more resolutely the traditionalist frame he has easily switched to by talking about the Iron Curtain the Soviets had erected and the territorial gains they had made.

Ironically, the evolving conversation aptly demonstrates that he could not have missed his teacher's preferred frame more clearly. Again, he is misled by Ms. Reger's ambivalent feedback. While Peter seems to take encouragement from the repeated phrases 'yes, exactly', 'yes, precisely', he simultaneously seems to ignore the critique she is raising.

As soon as he has finished his description of the aggressive and expansive Soviets, Ms. Reger begins to give a kind of counter-speech. However, it is only the concessive phrase 'but actually' that reveals her intention to break with what Peter just has said. She then makes two claims, both of which are clearly meant to reintroduce the revisionist frame that Peter referred to at the beginning of this scene and was unable to substantiate with appropriate evidence. Ms. Reger recalls the enormous losses the USSR experienced in the Second World War after they were attacked, and she emphasises how attractive the Soviet Union and the social order it stood for must have been in the eyes of contemporaries who had just seen them winning the war against the Nazis.

There are four interesting insights to be gained so far: Firstly, in order to satisfy his teacher, Peter is ready to alter his account. Secondly, Peter repeatedly misjudges his teacher's preferences. Thirdly, Ms. Reger picks up only on those comments from the classroom talk which fit her preferred frame, without even mentioning any tension between her own claims and the claims put forward by students. Finally, her story quickly acquires authoritative status without any resistance. As a result, the meaning of the Cold War is quickly fixed, despite the fact that it had been mutable just a moment before. All participants in the discussion simultaneously collude in rendering invisible the disagreements and misunderstandings that preceded the fixing of meaning.

Another scene from the Swiss classroom shows that, at times, something more fundamental is involved than simply an array of different assumptions about the Cold War and its main participants. The following exchange takes place during the discussion about the cartoon depicting Truman and Stalin riding a tandem.

0:12:03[35]	Tf (Reger)	And, um, [...], what do you think? [...] The top part of the picture [...] this tandem, who's got the better seat on the tandem? (2 sec) Yes? SfC?
0:12:18	SfC (Anne)	(Smiling) Yes, it's Stalin. Because he actually has to do, you know, less work. I mean, he has to do less pedalling, but he doesn't get to decide [where to go].
0:12:23	Tf (Reger)	Yes, precisely. So you think that the back seat's the better one? (brief laugh)
0:12:28	SfC (Anne)	(Smiling) Yes, then nobody sees if he doesn't do anything. I mean, he's working, the one in front, and the one at the back can put his feet up.
0:12:34	Tf (Reger)	Hmhm. Quite. But on the other hand, as you said, the one in front can steer.
0:12:40		Now, um, what about, um, this film, I mean, what's it saying? How can we link it in to this [...] cartoon? SfB?

Ms. Reger's question concerning which of the two leaders had the better seat on the tandem produces a discord which is not openly addressed. Whereas Anne clearly points to Stalin as the privileged one who could relax in the back seat while letting Truman do all the work, Ms. Reger sees the advantages on the side of the American president who was able to direct the tandem.

At this point, significant differences in value orientation emerge. For the teacher it seems beyond question that what really counts, especially in politics, is having power over others and thus the ability to shape the world according to your ideas. Anne clearly has other priorities. To start with, she bases her judgement on her own everyday experience, which seems to tell her that in an age where one is constantly seeking self-enhancement (Ehrenburg 1998), you are well advised to escape additional responsibilities and get as much rest as you can. Such assumptions and the values behind them are clearly at odds with the quintessential logic in many narratives of the Cold War, which is portrayed as a fierce competition between two rival powers, both striving to impose their own social system upon the rest of the world.[36]

Comparison

At first glance, teachers and students in the two classes seem to adopt opposing stances. However, if we look at structural issues and focus on the interaction between the two sets of protagonists, we discover surprising similarities. While the German teacher clearly articulates traditional, anti-Soviet perspectives, her students show much more scepticism and restraint with regard to the USA. And whereas the Swiss teacher plays the revisionist card, being much more critical towards the USA, students tend to blame the USSR more strongly. Hence, in both cases we see a degree of mismatch between the positions taken by teachers and their students.

Obviously, students do not relate with the same naturalness to the competing ways of framing the Cold War as do the two teachers, who were for many years exposed to discourses surrounding the conflict. As we can see from the example of Ms. Reger in Switzerland, teachers may oppose the discourses they have grown up with and question the common-sense assumptions upon which these are built. However, at the same time, they have apparently deeply internalised the binary oppositions that come with them. None of this seems to be true for the students as members of a younger generation born long after the end of the Cold War.

Some, like Peter from Switzerland, switch frames with astonishing ease when trying to come up with an 'appropriate' story on the USSR. Others, like Marie in Germany, confuse words when trying to summarise the American point of view. Phrasing the same observations in the language of frame analysis, we can state that the two teachers are using Cold War frames as a configuration of positions to package beliefs about social stakeholders in more or less coherent parcels. Yet students pick up individual elements while mostly ignoring relationships and connections as the key units of frames (Marx Ferree 2009). While teachers use, recognise and remember those frames as being embedded in social discourses that structured the political universes in which they grew up, the same frames do not seem to have any practically relevant meaning for the students.

Discussion

Translating the empirical insights I have presented so far into a more general contribution to the fields of memory studies and history didactics, I would like to make the following points.

Neither Resisting Nor Complying: The Mnemonic Weapons of the Weak

In the introduction to this chapter I briefly touch upon the opposition between two perspectives on social processes of remembering, with one emphasising consensus and the other stressing conflict. Against the backdrop of this controversy, the most intriguing observation we have made in the two history classrooms pertains to patterns of interaction between teachers and students. We do not see them achieving a consensus on how to make sense of the Cold War. But nor do we see them clashing over competing interpretations. Rather, we observe frequent instances of troubled communication when both students and teachers come up with statements that are either irritating or incomprehensible to the other party.

Reflecting on the likely causes for this phenomenon, a typical feature of the history classroom comes to mind. Teaching has often been described as a rather asymmetrical setting (Gies 2004, 172; Pandel 2017, 44). As we know from anthropological research, these kinds of settings encourage neither resistance nor full compliance (Scott 1985). Those who are in a subordinate position are more likely to simulate the acceptance of the status quo while simultaneously striving to undermine it. Some scenes in the German classroom can be seen as fitting into this picture. One student in particular seems to play the role of the joker, on the surface unable to deal properly with the tasks assigned to him while actually mocking the whole idea behind the task. His predominantly ironic attitude thus prevents him from either accepting or rejecting the mnemonic frames offered by his teacher. Berthold Molden (2016) has described something intriguingly similar when discussing how many older people in post-socialist Central Eastern Europe simply ignore the hegemonic narratives about a totalitarian regime that had allegedly taken an entire population hostage and subjected it to relentless oppression. As they would not risk waging a fight they could not hope to win, they did not resist official memory frames but simply undermined them by recalling how normally and even happily they had lived under communism. Above all, these frames appear to be fairly powerful, as they resonate with corresponding stories told in the West about the triumph of freedom and democracy.

Fading Common Sense: The Missing Link in the Transgenerational Transmission of Mnemonic Frames

We can only compare the situation the students in the two history classrooms – and the older Eastern Europeans – face, however, in terms of power asymmetries. They differ dramatically in one crucial respect: While the Eastern Europeans discussed by Molden were contemporaries of the Cold War, our students cannot rely on personal experiences to define their relationships with the frames imposed upon them. As a result, they are indifferent rather than sceptical. Usually, excepting the example above, they do not respond with irony but with dispassionate inattention to the narrative given by their teachers. This attitude contrasts starkly with that of the teachers, who strive to use the frames coherently even in those rare moments when they stretch and bend them. The fact that they are then eager to engage in 'repair strategies' suggests that they must be aware of the strain they are putting on these frames.

Simultaneously, students generally appear to be relatively poor at recognising frames. This is particularly evident when individual students try to please their teachers and ultimately fail. It is as if the teachers have provided the students with a rough sketch, clearly expecting them to be able to complete the picture they themselves have in mind, while the students see only isolated items randomly pinned together with little indication as to how to proceed. At the core of this issue is that the common-sense assumptions the teachers grew up with appear to have faded away or simply lost their relevance to the lives of the young people they are teaching. As we know from discourse analysis (Fairclough 1989), common-sense assumptions play a vital role in helping people to fill the voids inevitably left by each discourse. It is thus those implicated but not explicated common-sense assumptions that assure the comprehensibility of social discourse and ways of framing these discourses.

Speaking Different Moral Languages: The Deep-seated Roots of the Mnemonic Divide

The interactions in the Swiss classroom especially reveal that students, as members of a post-Cold War generation, not only lack something in comparison to their teachers who constitute the 'Cold War generation', but also possess something peculiar. This was illustrated during the classroom discussion of the cartoon showing Stalin and Truman riding a tandem. As I have argued, perceiving the figure able to take a rest in the back seat as the more privileged in comparison to the figure in the front seat who has to do all the work, students display hierarchies of values that clearly differ from the attitude expressed by their teacher, who takes it for granted that everyone would be eager to steer from the front seat.

To a certain extent, this finding challenges an observation made by the memory researcher James Wertsch (2008), who suggests some useful analytical categories that should help us to make sense of empirical data on the trans-generational transmission of memory. Comparing accounts of the Second World War given by members of different generations in Russia, he introduces a distinction between what he calls specific narratives on the one hand and schematic narrative templates on the other. While the former transform concrete, temporally situated events into a story, the latter offer 'a generalised narrative form,' 'an underlying pattern', that may be instantiated in many different situations talking about many different events (Wertsch 2008, 56). Based on this distinction, and referring to his empirical research, Wertsch argues that schematic narrative templates have a better chance of surviving generational change than specific narratives, as repeated use has deeply inscribed them into the cultural repertoire of each society.

In the Swiss classroom we observe something slightly different. Apparently, what sets the teacher's accounts of the origin of the Cold War from those of the students are rather general and abstract patterns of sense-making, patterns which delineate what humans can be expected to strive for. We see the two groups speaking different moral languages and thus, perhaps inevitably, failing to understand each other.

We can assume that these different languages are shaped by two primary factors. On the one hand, we might expect generational differences to be at play in such a situation; the teacher belongs to a generation that believes in the possibility of social change through political organisation, whereas the students live in 'cynical, post-hegemonic times' when 'everybody knows […] that politics is deceit' (Beasley-Murray 2010, ix). Yet, on the other hand, the peculiarities of the school setting, with its rigid and institutionalised roles, are also a significant factor. Charged with steering the learning process, teachers must be constantly aware of their objective to give direction to others and take control of situations. At the same time, performing their 'job' as students (Breidenstein 2006), young people have a tendency to minimise their efforts. Maintaining a certain image among peers may oblige them to disparage any over-achievers and thus avoid being identified with them.

From this perspective and in accordance with a new trend in memory research (Feindt et al. 2014), the differences between the schematic narrative templates articulated by the teacher and those of her students would be perceived as not only expressions of a generational divide but also as the fluid results of the specific situation.

Being Political Without Admitting It: The Illusion of Mnemonic Hegemony

Looked upon from the angle of history didactics, the empirical material I have presented seems to speak of the salience of one oft-forgotten aspect: Both teachers I observed reveal themselves to be persons with easily recognisable political beliefs. But although these beliefs clearly determine the selection choices they make as teachers, as well as the judgements they pass, they are not made explicit. The political is thus simultaneously invoked and backgrounded. The teachers are political without admitting to it.

What we are dealing with, then, are arguably not so much the individual attitudes of two teachers but instead deeply ingrained social habits. The settled societies of the Global North seem to have moved beyond mnemonic conflict, at least in the imagination of part of the cultural elite. Open contestation is often perceived to be an exclusive feature of post-conflict settings or of newly (re)emerging nation-states (Sindbæk-Anderson and Törnquist-Plewa 2016). The ease with which the master-narratives of successful democratisation and westernisation have come to dominate public discourse in Germany (Hertfelder 2017) appears to be a case in point, as does the familiar statement that we have moved beyond old controversies when it comes to the Cold War. Certain tendencies in history didactics also seem directed towards putting constraints on what can be contested legitimately. While some authors would agree that students should be introduced to competing frames of interpreting the past, they would simultaneously insist on teaching them the undisputable facts of the past first (Garske 2017). This whole concept seems to be based on the idea that frames and facts exist independently of each other. However, the two lessons I have discussed here suggest that facts and frames are closely interrelated. The frames the two teachers draw on emerge only as a result of their attempts to establish connections between the facts they mention. The facts the teachers rely on are constituted as relevant and part of important historical evidence only by the frames they are meant to support.

Neglecting these insights means neglecting the persistent presence and even the usefulness of conflict between competing historical frames, potentially with serious repercussions for both remembering and teaching the past. While Michael Kammen (1993, 13) argues that 'memory is more likely to be activated by contestation and amnesia is more likely to be induced by the desire for reconciliation', my analysis shows that the absence of conflict also deprives students of the opportunity to comprehend memory narratives against the background of counter-narratives.

Notes

1. The German lesson took place on 12 October 2014 in Year 10 of a comprehensive school; the Swiss lesson took place on 13 October 2014 in Year 10 of a grammar school (*Gymnasium*). The lessons were recorded, transcribed and rendered anonymous by giving code names to persons and places mentioned. I quote them by indicating the file name and the location of the quote in minutes of recording as indicated in the transcription. The quotes I use in the text were translated from German by the author. The original files can be consulted at the Georg Eckert Institute in Braunschweig on the understanding that the privacy rights of the people involved are respected and guaranteed.
2. In 2014 my Swiss colleague Nora Zimmermann and I conducted biographical-narrative interviews and guideline-based interviews on textbook representations with 10 history teachers in Germany and a further 10 in Switzerland. All teachers were born before 1970 and were thus eyewitnesses of the Cold War period themselves. The interviews which were recorded and transcribed are cited by their number, date and the interviewee's country of origin (WG for western Germany, CH for Switzerland).
3. The field notes are quoted by indicating the date when the lesson took place, the number we assigned to the teacher who gave it and the location.
4. 2014_10_12_Video_T2_WG_B, 00:14:33-2.
5. Ibid. 00:01:16-5.
6. Ibid. 00:01:25-5.
7. Ibid. 00:00:19-9.
8. Ibid. 00:04:02-8.
9. Ibid. 00:09:20-8.
10. 2014_10_13_Video_T1_CH, 0:09:20.

11. Ibid. 0:12:03.
12. Ibid. 0:12:34.
13. Ibid. 0:13:10
14. Ibid. 0:13:59
15. Ibid. 0:23:24
16. Ibid. 0:24:08
17. Ibid. 0:44:27
18. Ibid.
19. Rena und Thomas Giefer: *Die Rattenlinie. Fluchtwege der Nazis.* Beltz, Weinheim 1992.
20. 2014_10_12_Video_T2_WG_B
21. Ibid.
22. Ibid.
23. 2014_10_13_Video_T1_CH
24. WG Teacher 2 biographical-narrative interview 2 (3.06.2014)
25. CH Teacher 1 biographical-narrative interview 11 (12. 05. 2014)
26. http://avalon.law.yale.edu/20th_century/trudoc.asp (accessed 14 May 2019).
27. 2014_10_12Video_T2_WG_B, 00:37:00-0.
28. 2014_10_12Video_T2_WG_B, 00:37:17-9.
29. 2014_10_12Video_T2_WG_B, 00:34:09-0
30. 2014_10_12Video_T2_WG_B, 00:35:56-9
31. 2014_10_12Video_T2_WG_B; 00:37:22-9
32. 2014_10_12Video_T2_WG_B.
33. 2015_01_07_FN_WG_teacher2.
34. 2014_10_13_Video_T1_CH.
35. Ibid.
36. Observations I made in another history classroom support the assumption that differences between the values taken for granted by teachers and students have learnt to take for granted can contribute to misunderstandings. In 2015 students in a tenth grade class in western Germany were working in pairs for several weeks preparing presentations on Cold War topics. Two girls had just started to look for material they could use to compare popular culture in East and West Germany during the Cold War. Their teacher, who was born in 1950, recommended that they browse the internet to gather information on the case of Udo Lindenberg. Quickly they ascertained that Lindenberg was a West German singer-songwriter who tried for a long time to organise a concert in the GDR

before finally receiving an invitation. Initially, the ruling party, the SED, would not give him a permit because they suspected him of being too critical of authority in general. The two girls had great difficulty understanding why Lindenberg had been so keen to travel to East Germany in the first place. Based on their common-sense knowledge, East Germany was a grey and dull place nobody would have wanted to visit but everybody tried to escape. The teacher, for whom it was natural that citizens of the FRG would want to keep in touch with their co-nationals in the GDR, had a hard time comprehending the confusion the girls felt. Cf. 2015-01-23-FN-WG-teacher3.

Bibliography

Textbooks Cited

Menschen in Zeit und Raum 9. 2012. Edition for Lower Saxony. Zürich: Schulbuch Verlag plus AG.
Entdecken und Verstehen 3. 2010. Edition for Lower Saxony. Berlin: Cornelsen.

Further References

Assmann, Aleida. 2006. *Der lange Schatten der Vergangenheit. Erinnerungskultur und Geschichtspolitik.* München: C.H. Beck.
Beasley-Murray, Jon. 2010. *Posthegemony. Political Theory and Latin America.* Minneapolis/London: University of Minnesota Press.
Breidenstein, Georg. 2006. *Teilnahme am Unterricht. Ethnographische Studien zum Schülerjob.* Wiesbaden: Verlag für Sozialwissenschaften.
Beattie, Andrew H. 2008. *Playing Politics with History. The Bundestag Inquiries into East Germany.* New York: Berghahn, 2008.
Bodnar, John. 1992. *Remaking America: Public Memory, Commemoration and Patriotism in the Twentieth Century.* Princeton: Princetown University Press.
Conelly, Matthew. 2000. 'Taking off the Cold War Lens: Visions of North–South Conflict during the Algerian War of Independence'. *American Historical Review* 105, no. 3: 739–69.
Ehrenburg, Alain. 1998. *Fatique d'etre soi.* Paris: Odile Jacob.

Fairclough, Norman. 1989. *Language and Power*. Essex: Pearson Education Limited.

Feindt, Gregor et al. 2014. 'Entangled Memory: Toward a Third Way in Memory Studies'. *History and Theory* 53, no. 1: 24–44.

Garske, Lucas. 2017. 'Zwischen Historischem Denken und Basiswissen. Der Streit um das Berlin-Brandenburgische Kerncurriculum als Debatte um das Grundverständnis des Geschichtsunterrichts'. *Zeitschrift für die Didaktik der Gesellschaftswissenschaften* 8, no. 1: 119–131.

Geertz, Clifford. 1992. 'Common Sense as a Cultural System'. *The Antioch Review* 50, nos. 1–2: 5–26.

Gies, Horst. 2004. *Geschichtsunterricht. Ein Handbuch zur Unterrichtsplanung*. Köln/Weimar/Wien: Böhlau.

Goffman, Erving. 1974. *Frame Analysis. An Essay on the Organization of Experience*. Cambridge: Harvard University Press.

Hertfelder, Thomas. 2017. 'Opfer, Täter, Demokraten. Über das Unbehagen an der Erinnerung und die neue Meistererzählung der Demokratie in Deutschland'. *Vierteljahreshefte für Zeitgeschichte* 65, no. 3: 365–394.

Hobsbawm, Eric and Ranger, Terence. 1992. *The Invention of Tradition*. Cambridge/New York: Cambridge University Press.

Hoskins, Andrew. 2011. 'Media, Memory, Metaphor: Remembering and the Connective Turn'. *Parallax* 17, no. 4: 19–31.

Hutcheon, Linda. 2007. 'The Postmodern in Retrospect and Gone Forever, But Here to Stay: The Legacy of the Postmodern'. In *Postmodernism: What Moment?* edited by Pelagia Goulimari, 16–18. Manchester: Manchester University Press.

Iriye, Akira. 2013. 'Historicizing the Cold War'. In *The Oxford Handbook of the Cold War*, edited by Richard H. Immerman and Petra Goedde, 15–31. Oxford: Oxford University Press.

Kammen, Michael. 1993. *Mystic Chords of Memory. The Transformation of Tradition in American Culture*. New York: Vintage Books.

Lawless, Katerina. 2014. 'Constructing the Other: Construction of Russian Identity in the Discourse of James Bond Films'. *Journal of Multicultural Discourses* 9, no. 2: 79–97.

Leggewie, Claus. 2009. 'Zur Einleitung: Von der Visualisierung zur Virtualisierung des Erinnerns'. In *Erinnerungskultur 2.0: Kommemorative Kommunikation in digitalen Medien*, edited by Erik Meyer, 9–28. Frankfurt am Main: Campus.

Lombardo, Emanuela, Petra Meier and Mieke Verloo. 2009. 'Stretching and Bending Gender Equality. A Discursive Politics Approach'. In *The Discursive Politics of Gender Equality: Stretching, Bending and Policymaking*, edited by Emanuela Lombardo, Petra Meier and Mieke Verloo. Abingdon/New York: Routledge.

Macgilchrist, Felicitas. 2011. *Journalism and the Political: Discursive Tensions in International News Coverage of Russia*. Amsterdam: John Benjamins.

Macgilchrist, Felicitas, Johanna Ahlrichs, Patrick Mielke and Roman Richtera. 2017. 'Memory Practices and Colonial Discourse: On Text Trajectories and Lines of Flight'. *Critical Discourse Studies* 14, no. 4: 341–361.

Macgilchrist, Felicitas, Barbara Christophe and Alexandra Binnenkade. 2015. 'Memory Practices and History Education.' *Journal of Educational Media, Memory, and Society* 7, no. 2: 1–9.

Marx Ferree, Myra. 2009. 'Inequality, Intersectionality and the Politics of Discourse: Framing Feminist Alliances'. In *The Discursive Politics of Gender Equality: Stretching, Bending and Policymaking*, edited by Emanuela Lombardo, Petra Meier and Mieke Verloo. Abingdon/New York: Routledge.

Menk, Peter. 2006. *Unterricht – Was ist das? Eine Einführung in die Didaktik*. Norderstedt: Books on Demand.

Molden, Berthold. 2016. 'Resistant Pasts versus Mnemonic Hegemony: On the Power Relations of Collective Memory'. *Memory Studies* 9, no. 2: 25–142.

Neumann, Iver B. 1999. *Uses of the Other. 'The East' in European Identity Formation*. Minneapolis: University of Minnesota Press.

Pandel, Hans-Jürgen. 2017. *Geschichtsdidaktik. Eine Theorie für die Praxis*. Schwalbach: Wochenschau Verlag.

Ryan, Lorraine. 2011. 'Memory, Power and Resistance: The Anatomy of a Tripartite Relationship'. *Memory Studies* 4, no. 2: 154–189.

Schuman, Howard and Jacqueline Scott. 1989. 'Generations and Collective Memories'. *American Sociological Review* 54, no. 3: 359–381.

Schwartz, Barry. 2016. 'Rethinking the Concept of Collective Memory'. In *Routledge International Handbook of Memory Studies*, edited by Anna Lisa Tota and Trever Hagen, 9–20. London/New York: Routledge.

Scott, James C. 1985. *Weapons of the Weak. Everyday Forms of Peasant Resistance*. New Haven/London: Yale University Press.

Sierps, Aline. 2014. *History, Memory and Trans-European Identity. Unifying Divisions*. London: Routledge.

Sindbaek-Andersen, Tea and Barbara Törnquist-Plewa, eds. 2016. *Disputed Memories: Emotions and Memory Politics in Central, Eastern and South-Eastern Europe*. Berlin/Boston: Walter de Gruyter.

Sturken, Marita. 1997. *Tangled Memories: The Vietnam War, the AIDS Epidemic, and the Politics of Remembering*. Berkeley: University of California Press.

Sturken, Marita. 1999. 'The Wall, the Screen and the Image: The Vietnam Veterans Memorial'. In *The Visual Culture Reader*, edited by N. Mirzoeff, 357–70. New York: Routledge.

Wertsch, James V. 2008. 'The Narrative Organization of Collective Memory'. *Ethos* 36, no. 1: 120–35.

Zanazanian, Paul and Sabrina Moisan. 2012. 'Harmonizing Two of History Teachings Main Functions: Franco-Quebecois History Teachers and their Predisposition to Catering to Narrative Diversity. *Education Sciences* 2, no. 4: 255–275.

Zelizer, Barbie. 1998. *Remembering to Forget. Holocaust Memory through the Camera's Eye*. Chicago: University of Chicago Press.

Open Access This chapter is licensed under the terms of the Creative Commons Attribution 4.0 International License (http://creativecommons.org/licenses/by/4.0/), which permits use, sharing, adaptation, distribution and reproduction in any medium or format, as long as you give appropriate credit to the original author(s) and the source, provide a link to the Creative Commons licence and indicate if changes were made.

The images or other third party material in this chapter are included in the chapter's Creative Commons licence, unless indicated otherwise in a credit line to the material. If material is not included in the chapter's Creative Commons licence and your intended use is not permitted by statutory regulation or exceeds the permitted use, you will need to obtain permission directly from the copyright holder.

18

Learning from Others: Considerations within History Didactics on Introducing the Cold War in Lessons in Germany, Sweden and Switzerland

Peter Gautschi and Hans Utz

Every beginning is hard, yet, as the saying goes, well begun is half done. As regards getting things started, we could use a number of other aphorisms, and almost all of them emphasise the significance of the beginning. That holds true in the context of teaching as well, since here the start of a lesson or topic, in fact, constitutes a key phase and is plannable like no other teaching situation (Gautschi 2012, 114–117). It is particularly difficult to begin teaching the topic of the Cold War, because there does yet not exist any unanimously accepted master narrative about it (Furrer and Gautschi 2017, 16–21).

How, then, does history teaching on the Cold War begin? We compare the introductory lessons on the topic of the Cold War in four school classes, one in the former East Germany, one in the former West Germany,

---

P. Gautschi (✉)
Institute for History Education and Memory Cultures, University of Teacher Education Lucerne, Lucerne, Switzerland
e-mail: peter.gautschi@phlu.ch

H. Utz
University of Teacher Education Lucerne, Lucerne, Switzerland
e-mail: hans.utz@phlu.ch

© The Author(s) 2019
B. Christophe et al. (eds.), *The Cold War in the Classroom*, Palgrave Studies in Educational Media, https://doi.org/10.1007/978-3-030-11999-7_18

one in Switzerland and one in Sweden. This comparison allows us, firstly, to identify the similarities and differences between the observed lessons. Secondly, the teaching settings which are actually realised in these classrooms can be compared with possible alternatives, on the basis of considerations guided by theory. Thirdly, criteria can be proposed and applied[1] which allow us to judge how successfully each chosen introduction to each of the four lessons ensures historical learning.

This chapter intends to draw teachers' attention to different ways of introducing topics in history lessons and to generally encourage teachers to reflect on their own role in teaching history lessons. At the same time, it is aimed at scientists who observe, analyse and interpret history teaching. It will provide them with theories and possible approaches for discussion, and is structured around three sets of basic questions concerning history didactics: What issues and debates do teachers tackle in introductory lessons on the Cold War? What subjects, terminology, concepts and narratives are discussed? What perspectives do teachers approach past events from? The second set of questions allows us to ask: How are these perspectives related? How do teachers design their lessons? What processes and structures do they use and what forms of teaching, learning opportunities and presentation concepts are offered? Finally, we introduce the following questions: What purpose does this method of teaching serve? What new knowledge and skills will students acquire and what are the opinions and attitudes that they will build up and be able to differentiate between?

Learning Subjects: The 'What?' of History Teaching

While the topic 'the Cold War' can be covered in many different school subjects, three particular aspects render this topic a learning subject for history teaching: (a) If development contexts, meaning the causes and effects of the event and continuity and change over the course of time, are discussed. The teacher might ask what happened before and after the event, and what the reasons for and consequences of the phenomenon were. (b) The Cold War also becomes a topic for history education if individuals' actions and issues of identity are explored, especially in regard to social practice concerning rule, economy and culture. Who acted? Who had to bear the consequences? How do past events concern different groups of people? Finally (c), the topic becomes relevant for the history classroom if concrete examples, methods and principles of historical knowledge are included in the lesson. What are the findings from the sources? Are there any contradictory sources and representations? How does historiography differentiate between the memories of people involved in the event and the current objectivities of historical and memory cultures? (Gautschi and Fink 2016, 138–140). One and the same subject can be taught in radically different ways. In other words: With respect to the 'what?' of history teaching, the narratives presented and tackled in these lessons are thus of particular interest (Mayer 2005, 223–228).

Development Contexts

Whoever wants to document, characterise and analyse the 'what?' of history teaching, first of all, must record the chronological markers which can be found in teaching. It is particularly important to note whether the date, duration and sequence of events and processes are precisely laid out and how changes are depicted. For example, the teacher in the lesson taking place in Lower Saxony refers back to the Russian Revolution when explaining the prehistory of the Cold War:

> 02:04 Tf In that time there was, however, a war against Japan in 1905 in which the Russians were without much ado defeated. This was the trigger for more and more violent protests in the cities. So that certain reforms were initiated, but [...] in 1914 war broke out from the part of Russia and from the part of Germany. And the reforms for the time being got stuck again.

The causes and consequences of the event being taught also need to be identified in historical development contexts. Indicators for these are word particles like 'afterwards', 'therefore', 'eventually', 'thus' or 'because' which are, for example, used by a student in Saxony-Anhalt:

| 21.09 | PmA | Yes, there were no active actions happening between both the powers because they knew that they both were very strong, they were in possession of nuclear arms. Thus, the deterrence was, in fact, also mutual since they knew that if they now started a war, perhaps also the world or a Third World War, that they were not going to survive it. And, therefore, these acts of war did, in fact, partly not happen either. And then, the situation was actually so tense because they had partly also provoked each other. But, in fact, they knew that the deterrence actually existed. |

If one compares to what extent development contexts occur in the four lessons the following picture emerges:

Fig. 18.1 shows that the date, duration and sequence of events and processes can generally be designated precisely. In almost all cases, we can see that the emergence of the two 'fronts' of the Cold War, after their alliance in the Second World War, is clearly explained and the histories of the USA and the Soviet Union contrasted. Only in the Swedish lesson is the focus more strongly put on people's everyday experience in Sweden during this period. The lesson in Lower Saxony stands out because of the

		−	0	+	++
1. Scheme of changes over time and of development contexts	a. The description of the date, duration, sequence of events and processes is precise.		●	◆OX	
	b. Changes are depicted.		O	X●	◆
	c. The differences of phenomena in different time periods are delineated.		◆ O●X		
	d. Possible alternative courses of events are depicted.	◆O●	X		
	e. Causes, preconditions of events and actions are explored.		O	●X	◆
	f. Consequences, effects of events and actions are described.		OX	◆●	

Key: −: not true, 0: just true, +: very true, ++: pronouncedly true

Fig. 18.1 Table of the Scheme of Changes over Time and of Development Contexts (Gautschi 2012, 97); Lower Saxony (◆), Saxony-Anhalt (O), Sweden (●), Switzerland (X)

fact that causes as well as preconditions of events and actions are clearly delineated. It is surprising that, in these introductory lessons, teachers don't touch upon the possible results of the Cold War, or what might have happened had the superpowers not come to an agreement with the intervention of the United Nations. Here the students can imagine how different the results of the Cold War could have been.

Human Action in Social Practice

The central subject of history is the individual human agent, inescapably bound in the structural contexts of the time period within which they live. Whoever wants to investigate the 'what?' of history teaching thus, for example, must therefore ask how people and institutions are represented. Who is described as the actor, who as the sufferer? The teacher from Sweden, for example, presents herself and her parents as contemporary witnesses to the period right at the beginning of the lesson:

02:50   Tf   [I say] that I was born in 1959. Thirty years I was thus living in a historical epoch which is called 'the Cold War'. Your parents as well and especially my mother and parents are really marked by this time period.

Furthermore, it is interesting to note the areas of meaning formation which become subjects of discussion in the process of teaching the Cold War. According to Hans-Ulrich Wehler by areas of meaning formation the three equal, continuously ongoing dimensions of society are meant: rule, economy and culture (2006, 7). Of course, the Cold War can be dealt with from political perspectives and approached from different viewpoints in class. But economic and cultural issues also play an important role especially when it comes to this particular topic.

An analysis of these lessons makes clear that in the introductory lessons in Switzerland, in Sweden and in Lower Saxony humans become particularly visible as actors (Stalin, Roosevelt, Churchill and others, for example), as well as emphasising the idea that the Cold War is best dealt with from political viewpoints, seen as a conflict which emerged because

		−	0	+	++
2. Thematisation of human action in social practice.	a. Humans are visible as actors.		●	◆XO	
	b. Rule and participation are thematised.		◆●X	O	
	c. Poverty and wealth as well as work are thematised.	O●X	◆		
	d. Culture is thematised.	O●X	◆		

Key: −: not true, 0: just true, +: very true, ++: pronouncedly true

Fig. 18.2 Table of Evaluation of the Thematisation of Human Action in Social Practice in Four Introductory Lessons on the Cold War; Lower Saxony (◆), Saxony-Anhalt (O), Sweden (●), Switzerland (X)

of a contrast between two worldviews (see Fig. 18.2). Surprisingly enough, within these lessons, economic and cultural factors are practically ignored. However, popular songs from both camps, historical monuments, comics or the recorded memories of ordinary people about their youth in the East and the West, that is to say relevant cultural artefacts, for example, would be useful as starting points when introducing the topic of the Cold War, and perhaps would generate more interest among students.

Principles and Methods of Historical Knowledge

In order to teach the topic of the Cold War in history lessons in particular teachers must both carefully select content and also present methods and principles of approaching historical knowledge. Since the past is past and cannot be directly observed, because history is thus always constructed, the examination of the validity of these constructions is an important task. At the same time, whenever possible controversial sources and multi-perspectival representations need to be consulted (Pandel 2006, 16). As regards the topic of the 'Cold War', this is often very well achieved in the observed lessons, with the exception of the Swedish lesson, as the following excerpt from the Swiss lesson illustrates:

	–	0	+	++
3. Exemplary and target-group-adjusted representations	O	♦	X●	
4. Validity, multi-perspectivity, controversy		●	O	♦X
5. Reference to the present			♦O●X	
6. Reference to the learners' living environments		♦O●X		
7. Methods of historical knowledge	O	♦X●		

Key: –: not true, 0: just true, +: very true, ++: pronouncedly true

Fig. 18.3 Table of Evaluation of Principles and Methods of Acquiring Historical Knowledge in Four Introductory Lessons on the Cold War; Lower Saxony (♦), Saxony-Anhalt (O), Sweden (●), Switzerland (X)

> 33:34 Tf Well, your task is the following: In the book there is a source by Truman, the American president who talks about the Soviet Union, and there is a source by Zhdanov, the secretary of the Central Committee. And it is your task, that means somebody adopts the role of Truman, somebody the role of Zhdanov, and you work out the core messages of this source and you will try and convince the other of what, in fact, is good about Communism or likewise Capitalism.

Teachers can better ensure that their students acquire historical knowledge if references to the present and the living environment are provided and if the dealing with sources, representations and historico-cultural factors follows methodological rules which can be taught and learned. As Fig. 18.3 shows the four lessons are similar in that all of them hardly make any mention of living environments but do make reference to the present. With a view to the other criteria, differences are rather stark.

Core Content of the Introductory Lessons

Whereas the criteria discussed so far allow for interesting comparisons about the learning subject, they do not expound at all upon narrative meaning formation. If we refer back to the concept of 'narrative templates', a term coined by James V. Wertsch (2008, 133–156), we can see just how important this understanding is. According to Wertsch, narrative templates differ from 'formal history' as they make use of 'templates' at two levels: 'Specific narrative templates' contain concrete data-supported (not necessarily objective, scientific-based) messages which give their validity to a narrative through concrete events. 'Schematic narrative templates' are based on universal convictions shared by the narrator as well as the addressee. These convictions establish a connection between individual events in a narrative, which reveals itself to the addressees even when the explanation lacks detail.

If we compare the four lessons by referring back to the narrative templates used each time, we discover startling similarities with regard to the 'schematic narrative templates', which can be summarised in four points made by the teachers: Firstly, a common enemy brings two entities together in an attempt to overwhelm that enemy with joint forces. Secondly, in each lesson the teacher poses the question of whether indeed such a union can be achieved, pointing to how, afterwards, the differences between the two forces prevail once again, causing conflict. Thirdly, the teachers argue that, because the two forces do not want to have another conflict after the first, they distance themselves from each other. The fourth point the teachers make, which accords with this 'schematic narrative template', is that, instead of a violent fight with severe losses, an indirect, dogged, 'cold' conflict breaks out, namely the Cold War. This 'schematic narrative template' dates back to a post-revisionist interpretation of the Cold War, according to which neither the Soviet Union nor the USA can unequivocally be made responsible for its beginning. It not only serves as an explanation for the Cold War, but can also applied to both inter-human or socio-political constellations. For example, the female student PfB illustrates this at the start of the lesson: The students first discuss their partner work, which is to analyse a caricature. Amongst other things, they find out that Truman and Stalin are depicted in it, and that the two of them are first portrayed together and then separately. Afterwards they start reflecting on the reason for their separation.

02:34 PfB The reason for which they separated? Yes, what does Stalin want? What does, what does the USA want? What does the Soviet Union want?
02:42 PfC Yes, already clearly together, but you know how they before together [...] together fought. (Afterwards) simply because [...]

02:47 PfB	Yes, because there is no reason anymore which they fight for.
02:48 PfC	Yes, that is also true again.
02:50 PfB	That is, in fact, sometimes also the case with political parties, they fight for something, and after that election it is over because [...] they actually want totally different things. But sure, for this they are [...]
02:57 PfC	Yes, yes. This is actually clear.
02:58 PfB	Because, it had the advantage for both that – that Hitler was, for example, overthrown.

At the level of the 'specific narrative templates', different narratives are developed in the four classrooms.

The Process: The 'How?' in History Teaching

Apart from the 'what?', the question as to the 'how?' always arises when teaching history. Here, three factors play a central role, namely the chosen form of teaching, the ensuring of an efficient and, at the same time,

Fig. 18.4 Table of a Common 'Schematic Narrative Template' and Different 'Specific Narrative Templates' in Four Introductory Lessons on the Cold War

clear classroom management and the form of presentation preferred by the teacher.

The Form of Teaching, Functional Rhythm and Media

History can be approached and staged in class through four different forms of teaching, which we refer to as 'presenting', 'dialogue-oriented', 'task-based' and 'discovery' history teaching.

Presenting history teaching can be identified when the teachers explain or narrate something. Therefore, the teachers might read out or present texts freely. Of course, here the teacher can enrich the learning experience with further materials, such as pictures or film extracts. Sequences in which the form of teaching remains the same during five minutes are referred to as presentations. In this regard, the observed introductory lessons on the Cold War can be divided into two groups and two lessons fall into each one: Firstly, in the lessons from Sweden and Lower Saxony the presentations take up a lot of time: In Sweden the female teacher narrates the prehistory of the Second World War and the development of the Soviet Union, respectively, and shows a narrative film, which together occupy almost half of the short lesson (min. 15–27). In Lower Saxony, a teacher gives a speech about the Russian/Soviet history of the second half of the nineteenth century up to the Stalin era, which, including interruptions, lasted eleven minutes. Secondly, in both the other lessons there are only short (content-based) presentations which aren't central to the lesson. The presentation explicitly labelled as a 'teacher speech' by the female teacher in the Swiss lesson (min. 55–60) refers to an excursus, a book about the flight of former Nazi functionaries before punishment. The presentation of the teacher in the lesson of Saxony-Anhalt (min. 72–75) does not even last five minutes and takes the form of a mere recapitulation.

Dialogue-oriented history teaching must be distinguished from presenting history teaching. This form can be recognised by the fact that teachers and learners engage in a conversation or mutual exchange in order to deal with a topic. Often teachers ask questions which learners should answer. Teachers and students become aware of things together, explore, interpret and develop common value judgements. Dialogue-oriented history teaching is demanding for the learners as well as for the teachers. The four lessons we observed and analysed once again strongly differ from each other: In Lower-Saxony and in Switzerland dialogue-oriented history teaching, in the form of a class discussion, takes up a lot of space. In the lesson from Lower-Saxony the dialogue-oriented teaching lasts 29 minutes (min. 18–47): This approximate half-hour teaching sequence – by far the longest one out of the four lessons – is devoted to the interpretation of a caricature which showed Stalin, Roosevelt and Churchill back to back mounted on horse with two heads (the two halves of which are supposed to trot in the opposite direction). The female teacher gathers the observations of the class and links them with information about the emergence of the conflict between the super powers. Thus, in the course of the lesson the students work out the prehistory of the Cold War through engaging in a dialogue guided and enriched by the teacher. In the lesson from Switzerland the dialogue-oriented teaching lasts twelve minutes (min. 17–29): This teaching sequence also takes place at the beginning of the lesson. From the prior knowledge and the assumptions of individual students, the female teacher delineates the situations in which the victors, the defeated and the different countries in the 'third world' find themselves after the end of war. However, in the lessons in Saxony-Anhalt (min. 32–37) and Sweden (min. 6–14) the sequences of dialogue-oriented teaching are considerably shorter. They are, as it were, pushed to the fringes by the task-based (Saxony-Anhalt) and the presenting teaching (Sweden) methods.

In sequences where the teachers use task-based and discovery history teaching methods, they do not directly control the 'what?' and the 'how?' of the teaching any more. Instead of mediating knowledge, they instead find themselves in the role of the coaches and the learning guides. In task-based history teaching, the learners are given mostly sources or representations as well as written questions, prompts and assignments. They receive a task and work independently and, guided by their individual assignments, deal with historical documents directly. In discovery history teaching, neither the 'what?' (sources and representations) nor the 'how?' is given straightforwardly to the students. In a self-directed fashion, the students discover things for themselves, explore, interpret, judge and present. Such teaching is usually referred to as 'project teaching'. The task-based history teaching takes place most intensively in the lesson in Saxony-Anhalt: In the space of 90 minutes the students are given seven assignments, pausing often to regroup and analyse the processes with which they are working. They, in fact, work independently, but are nevertheless kept on a short leash, with tasks aimed at generating short, closed answers. The lessons in Lower Saxony and in Switzerland include task-based teaching at the beginning, obviously in order to engage the students, and then once again after half (Switzerland) or two thirds (Lower Saxony) of the elapsed time, probably to counter the students' tiredness by introducing something new. The tasks thereby require from students not only the competence *to draw information from historical sources and accounts* but also the competence *to interpret historical events* as well as, partly, the ability to *position themselves in relation to past experiences*. The students must analyse materials, draw connections between them and form their own opinions based on the arguments they (and other students) have made. In the lesson from Sweden task-based teaching is not prominent. All these forms of teaching can be used in different classroom formats, including individual work, partner work, small-group and large-group work, as well as summarising sessions.

Fig 18.5 shows what the profile of the Swiss lesson looks like if for each minute respective codes are assigned. This lesson is characterised by a frequent change of teaching forms. In the first quarter of an hour task-based and presenting history teaching is most prominent. The students are engaged in partner work and watch a film extract. In the second quarter of an hour dialogue-oriented teaching follows. In the third quarter of an hour, task-based teaching predominates, and in the last quarter of an hour presentations occur again, taking the form of explanations by the teacher.

In order to compare several lessons, profiles which only present the three teaching forms and in which we can assign a code every five minutes are most useful. Table 18.1, for example, allows us to compare the four introductory lessons. At first glance, the structural similarity of the lessons from Switzerland and Lower Saxony becomes evident. These are double lessons with a central focus based in a long class discussion. Presenting and task-based teaching lead up to it and away from this focus, respectively. Concerning the Swiss lesson, these forms of teaching are divided into shorter steps than in the Lower-Saxony lesson.

The lesson in Saxony-Anhalt is almost entirely built up on task-based teaching. The tasks are evaluated in a group session before the next task is

18 Learning from Others: Considerations within History... 405

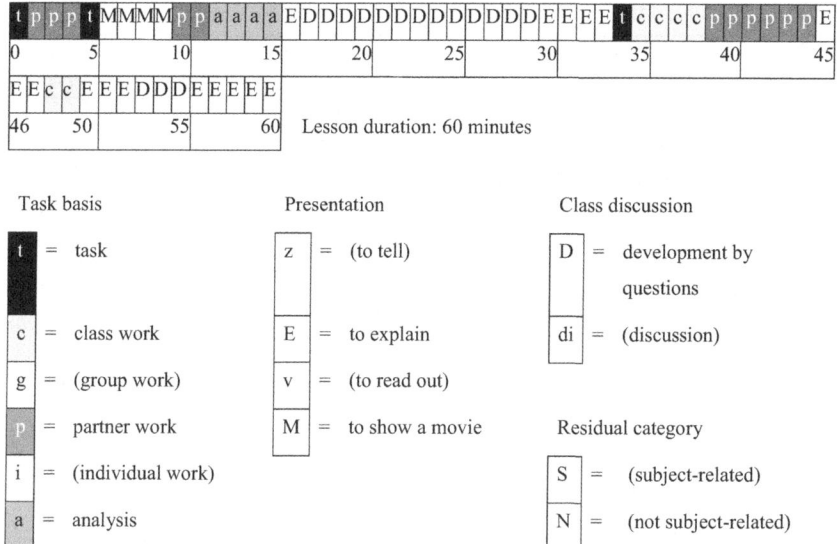

Fig. 18.5 Table of Presentation of the Form of Teaching: Profile of the Swiss Lesson in Coding per Minutes (in brackets: teaching forms not occurring here)

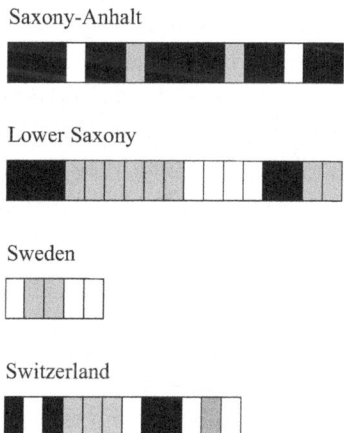

Fig. 18.6 Table of Presentation of the Form of Teaching in Five Minute Coding: 'Task-based' (black), 'Presenting' (white) and 'Dialogue-oriented' (grey) Forms

Table 18.1 Table of the Teaching Forms of the Four Analysed Lessons in Comparison

		Saxony-Anhalt	Lower Saxony	Sweden	Switzerland
1a	Share of task-based teaching	78%	37%	0%	40%
1b	Share of presenting teaching	6%	17%	65%	33%
1c	Share of dialogue-oriented teaching	16%	46%	35%	27%
	In total	100%	100%	100%	100%
2a	Average duration of a task-based, presenting and a class-discussion sequence	7 min.	12 min.	4 min.	5 min.
2b	Standard deviation from 2a	5.5	9.4	2.4	3.6
2c	Median value analog to 2a	6 min.	12 min.	4 min.	4 min.

introduced in class teaching. This rhythm is strictly adhered to over the length of a double lesson.

In the short lesson in Sweden task-based teaching is, however, missing. The female teacher provides an introduction into the topic of the Cold War through an explanation. The class discussion is thus given a frame, and it obviously serves to involve the students in the discussion. This finding is supported by the more detailed quantitative evaluation.

The four lessons differ as regards teaching forms, but also concerning the staged learning processes. At all times the teachers obviously had found their own functional rhythms to best teach their students. It is important to consider how a complete learning process is correctly built up. In the Swiss lesson, for example, the female teacher tries to spark the students' curiosity and to engage them at the beginning of the lesson. Afterwards the students repeat the things they have learned, linking these with what they have learnt previously. After that the students work on learning tasks which serve to deepen their new knowledge, and at the end the teacher first provides a thematic overview once again, so that the students' new knowledge is reinforced, and then gives a summary on other interesting topics which will be dealt with in future lessons.

Such a learning process ensures a wide variety of stimulating, engaging and appropriate learning opportunities. If one compares the four lessons

		–	0	+	++
8. Ensuring stimulating, engaging and appropriate learning opportunities	a. The teacher adjusts the learning tasks according to the students' knowledge. He/she makes sure that the majority of the students can master them.		O●	◆X	
	b. The teacher adjusts the complexity of the topic according to their students' stage of development.		O	◆	●X
	c. The teacher chooses student activities which are well-suited for achieving the objectives and ensure efficient learning.	●	◆O		X
	d. The teacher makes sure that all the learners are cognitively engaged.		●	◆OX	
	e. The teacher makes sure that the students' new knowledge will be long term. He/she links new content with already existing knowledge.	●	◆	X	O

Key. –: not true, 0: just true, +: very true, ++: pronouncedly true

Fig. 18.7 Table Ensuring Stimulating, Engaging and Appropriate Learning Opportunities: Lower Saxony (◆), Saxony-Anhalt (O), Sweden (●), Switzerland (X)

from the perspective of these criteria, the lesson from Switzerland obtains the best rating.

Apart from the form of teaching and the functional rhythm, the media used in each lesson allows us to see the inclusion of the 'how?' of history teaching to a considerable extent. Besides the traditional media such as text sources, pictures or maps, various other types of other media, for example caricatures, comics, films or hypermedia, are also used in these lessons. In the Swiss lesson the variety of media used is stark compared to the other three lessons. The lesson starts with the interpretation of a projected caricature, which was also handed out on paper (min. 1) and its message is compared with a film on YouTube (min. 5–9). The second sequence relies on a partly prepared, partly dialogue-oriented blackboard text in tabular form (min. 15). The third sequence is based on two text sources in the textbook, which in partner work are opposed and compared to each other (min. 35). Afterwards (min. 45), the female teacher presents a chronological overview of the period in the form of a PowerPoint presentation, draws the division of Germany onto a map projected onto a screen (min. 47) and shows her students a book, the content of which she briefly summarises (min. 56).

Classroom Management, Classroom Climate and Clarity

Classroom management and the use of time in the class, the classroom climate as well as clarity and structure of the teacher's explanation also play an important role when designing teaching lessons (Gautschi 2012, 81–88). In order to manage a class efficiently and to use the teaching time well, it is important for teachers to set clear rules and make sure they are followed. Here rituals which support learning are useful. Special attention should be paid to the start and the end of the teaching: Are the teaching forms used here appropriate to the situation? Do they support the management of the class? Teachers can ensure that they use as much available teaching time as possible if they keep transitions streamlined. Good time management also leads to successful learning. Figure 18.8 shows the evaluation of the four lessons in this area. Here again, the Swiss lesson comes out best.

Gerhard Schneider outlines four different ways teachers might start a lesson: They can arouse interest in the topic (A), activate the prior knowledge and the prior experiences of their students (B), problematise the topic (C) or calm down the class (D) (2008, 26). In the lessons we analysed, types A, B and C occur. Type A stops the teacher from giving merely

	–	0	+	++
9. Ensuring efficient classroom management and use of time		◆●	X	O
10. Fostering a supportive classroom climate		O	◆●X	
11. Ensuring appropriate clarity and structure		O●	◆X	

Key: –: not true, 0: just true, +: very true, ++: pronouncedly true

Fig. 18.8 Table Ensuring a Classroom Environment Conductive to Learning: Lower Saxony (◆), Saxony-Anhalt (O), Sweden (●), Switzerland (X)

an explanatory introduction and instead suggests that the teacher confront the class with a source, despite their lack of knowledge. The gaps in the students' knowledge mean they are more engaged, as they want to fill these gaps. In contrast, type B possibly activates existing prior knowledge but it also draws on the students' assumptions, thus falling back on ideas from the sphere of historical culture. Type B represents a 'sound of the bell' type of teaching, enriched with content: The lesson starts, the class engage with and focus on the topic.

Table 18.2 Table of Beginning a Lesson, according to Gerhard Schneider (2008)

	Saxony-Anhalt	Lower Saxony	Sweden	Switzerland
Type	A	B	D	A
Characteristic	Interpreting a caricature on the emergence of the bipolarity of the Cold War in individual work	Brainstorming on assumptions and associations about the Cold War in group work	Organisation of the lesson setting, catching the attention of the students, narrative recapitulation	Interpreting a caricature on the emergence of the bipolarity of the Cold War in individual work
Duration	16 min., with two assignments and evaluation	17 min., thereof 9 min. of evaluation	2 min., without student activity	4 min., without immediate evaluation
Student activity	Individual work, written form, various, mostly wait-and-see	Group work, written form, different as regards results	–	Individual work, opportunity for written form, assumingly concentrated
Link to the lesson	Coherent	Coherent	Coherent	Coherent
Referred to again in the lesson	In the summary	Not any more	Motif of the memory of the parent/teacher generation is taken up one single time	At the beginning of the dialogue-oriented part

The teachers in Sweden and Lower Saxony introduce the topic and the term 'Cold War' when they start the lesson, whereas the teachers in the two other lessons, with the type A method of starting a lesson, do not (Switzerland, min. 0: 'I still do not exactly tell you what the [topic] is'). Thus, the teachers seem to want to avoid pre-empting any interpretation of the caricature presented and used as an introduction.

Presentation Concepts

According to Michele Barricelli, we can distinguish six presentation concepts which, on the one hand, constitute a basic pattern of historiography, but, on the other, are also applicable to teaching (2012, 202–223; see also Table 18.3).

Table 18.3 Table of Presentation Concepts according to Barricelli

Presentation concept	Principle	Characteristic(s)
Genetic-chronological narrative	Presenting and explaining history over the course of time, arbitrary beginnings and ends	Linking additive, temporal, adversative, conditional
Longitudinal cut	Concentration of the genetic narratives on one single topic relevant to the present	No historical but thematic linking, marked gaps in continuity
Cross section	Concentration on a time period in one area including many historical areas (society, politics, culture, economy)	Linking of contexts
Case analysis	Reduction of complexity of information; on the other hand, focus on opinion and decision making on the part of the students	Reference to a problem relevant also today; discovery-exploratory learning
Constellation analysis	Presenting and working out models on connections within a historical constellation	Visualisation, forming models
Individualising and biographical procedure, respectively	Focus on the human being in history, in the sense of personification, often in the form of collective biographies	Vividness, concreteness

An analysis of the lessons as regards the presentation concepts again reveals a striking similarity between them: All four teachers put into practice a constellation analysis (Fig. 18.9). The political, economic and (partly) ideological constellation of the Cold War is brought into focus. In all cases, both the camps are opposed to each other in verbal as well as visual terms and compared with one another with respect to economic order, the function of the state or the weighting of the individual. A chronological-genetic derivation of this constellation is touched upon in three of the four lessons but does not in any of the cases contribute to the explanation of the emergence of the Cold War. Events mentioned, such as the nuclear bomb, the

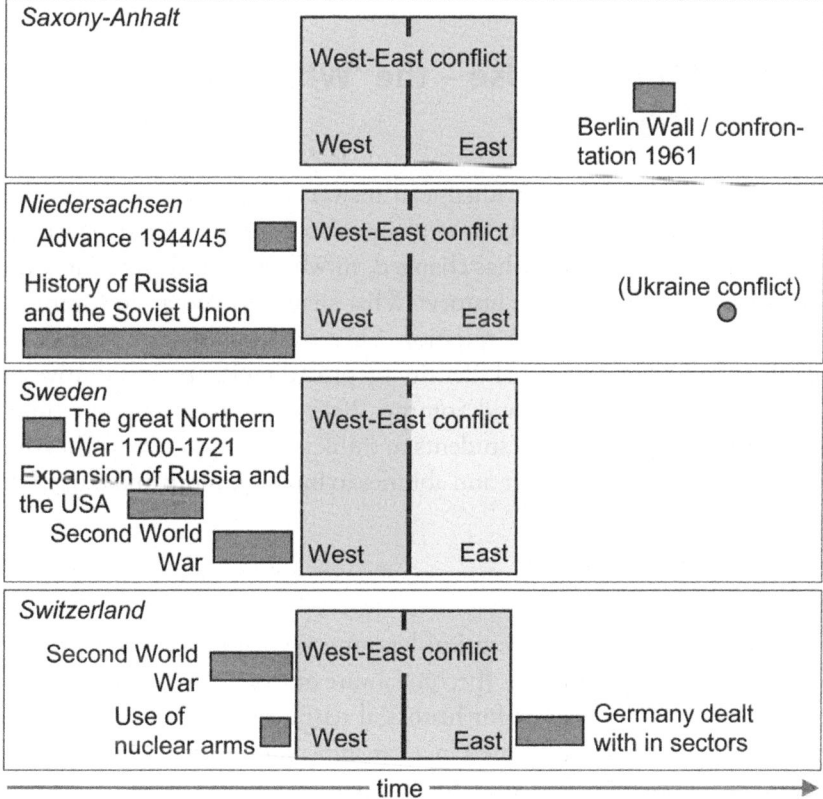

Fig. 18.9 Table of Visualisation of the Presentation Concepts according to Barricelli on a Timeline in the Four Lessons

Second World War, the Great Northern War or the Berlin Wall, are there mainly to reinforce the students' knowledge and thus serve the purpose of illustration. The illustration makes up for the weakness of a constellation analysis which as an abstracting model hardly allows a teacher to draw on the students' own daily lives. On the other hand, it allows for an overview and proffers easy-to-learn knowledge by reducing complexity.

At the same time, the constellation analysis, which allows the students to see an overview of the issues and acquire knowledge easily, requires a great deal of intellectual preparatory work from the part of the teacher. The teacher must first understand these constellations, so must fall back on both specialised literature and their own knowledge of the topic.

For the Students' Use – the 'What for?' of Teaching History

By dealing with history, individuals can answer crucial questions regarding their existence: How have I become the person I am today? How have we become what we are? What has changed, in what way and why? How do I arrive at my judgement on history? What shall I do? What do I want to do? In helping tackle these questions, history teaching contributes to building individual and social identity by providing the basic narrative of a society (Gautschi, Furrer and Sommer 2014, 9–12). At the same time, history teaching also enables students to think in historical terms. They are able to acquire the knowledge and abilities to build opinions and attitudes.

Historical Learning

For teachers and learners historical learning involves four different, but interwoven, mental processes (become aware of things, explore, interpret, orient oneself) which allow for historical narration. In Fig. 18.10, these mental operations are illustrated in a *structure and process model*: The processes are represented as arrows, the products as squares.

Historical learning takes place when an individual, imbedded in society and thus in change over time, approaches a certain period of history.

18 Learning from Others: Considerations within History...

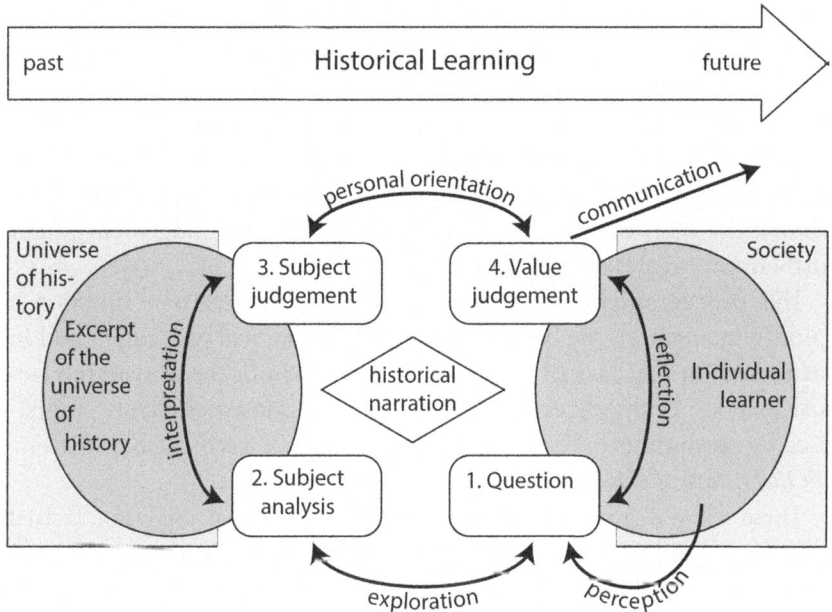

Fig. 18.10 Structure and Process Model of Historical Learning

Historical learning starts when learners specifically focus their attention on a section of the past and *become aware of* facts from this period (sources, representations) or when they encounter people who represent or narrate history. The learners *draw information* from their findings, reconstructing narratives of the period from historical testimonies. They work out a *'factual analysis'* (Jeismann 2000, 63) in which 'factual findings' (Weymar 1970, 202) are presented by them. In a next step they *interpret* these factual findings, establish relations to other historical testimonies and, in doing so, place their findings in a larger context of causes and effects. Thus, they arrive at a *'historical factual judgement'* (Jeismann 2000, 64). Then the learners can establish a relation between this historical factual judgement and their own personal opinion. They arrive at a *'historical value judgement'* (Ibid., 64) with respect to present or future, individual or social situations and problem areas. The value judgement will eventually be compatible with the currently valid and accepted moral values of the present society in which the individual lives, and, therefore, it needs to be examined on the basis of this. This happens within the *'objectivity-forming discourse'* in which the *'normative validity'* is established by means of *'reflection and justification'* of one's own viewpoint (Rüsen 1997). Therefore, the value judgement becomes the starting point for dialogue with others, which in itself is again the cause of further questions about history, the past, the present or the future. The value judgement might furthermore trigger an individual to act.

This process might also happen in reverse: The learners question a value judgement on the basis of the underlying factual judgement and in turn question that factual judgement on the basis of the underlying factual analyses. Both processes, both of de- and reconstruction, are emphasised by the authors of the working group 'FUER Geschichtsbewusstsein' *(FOR Historical Awareness)* (Schreiber et al. 2007, 21).

These mental processes between questions, factual analyses, factual judgements and value judgements come up in *'historical narration'* (Rüsen 2008, 75). Therefore, 'historical narration' is represented as a basic competence in Fig. 18.10 (centre).

The Role of the Learner in History Teaching

In what way is such historical learning then fostered in the four lessons? Overall, it must be said that in the observed lessons little historical learning can, in fact, be observed. The lessons are knowledge-oriented, especially the ones from Switzerland and from Saxony-Anhalt.

It comes as no surprise that students hardly have the opportunity to become aware of things by themselves, as Criterion 11 in Fig. 18.11 shows. If teachers include selected topics with a constellation analysis, there is hardly any space for the learners' own awareness to develop.

What is more successful in the observed lessons is the ability of the students to interpret (Criterion 13). Because interpreting (Criterion 15) is closely linked to acquiring knowledge, this assessment is not surprising.

In the observed lessons the students hardly have a chance to orient themselves. Only very few value judgements are openly made. This might also be a characteristic of introductory lessons. Possibly the students

11. Awareness of historical testimonies and of changes over time	OX	◆●		
12. Exploring, examining and presenting of historical factual analyses (competence to draw information from historical sources and accounts)		◆O● X		
13. Interpretation (analysis and interpretation of history (competence to interpret historical events)		O●	◆X	
14. Orientation: Meaning formation via past experiences and value judgement examination on the basis of past experiences (competence to position oneself in relation to past experiences)	O	◆●X		
15. Acquiring and reproducing knowledge about past events and the understanding of history		◆●	OX	

Key: –: not true, 0: just true, +: very true, ++: pronouncedly true

Fig. 18.11 Table of Evaluation of the Use of History Teaching; Lower Saxony (◆), Saxony-Anhalt (O), Sweden (●), Switzerland (X)

might have developed only very few factual analyses and factual judgements as yet and are therefore not confident enough to make any value judgements, which, in fact, can be considered rather positive.

Conclusion

Overall Evaluation of the Lessons

Fig. 18.12 summarises the results of applying the above findings to the four introductory lessons. Two aspects are particularly striking: First of all, differences mainly emerge in the process of history teaching, in criteria which are independent of both the topic being taught and general didactic expectations. Secondly, we can see that, overall, only few similarities exist between the lessons observed, despite the fact that in all four lessons the same 'schematic narrative template' and the same presentation rationale was used.

Generally, we can ascertain that (a) in all 4 lessons a reference to the present was made, without, however, drawing upon the students' own

		−	0	+	++
Learning subject: Contents, topics and media	1. Significant topic			◆●XO	
	2. Thematisation of changes over time and development contexts		O●	◆X	
	3. Thematisation of human action in social practice		◆OX●		
	4. Exemplary and target-group-adjusted representations of history	O	◆	●X	
	5. Validity, multi-perspectivity and controversy		●	O	◆X
	6. Reference to the present			◆●XO	
	7. Reference to the students' living environment		◆O●X		
	8. Methods of historical knowledge	O	◆X●		
Process structure: Lesson design teacher	9. Ensuring of an efficient classroom management and use of time		●◆	X	O
	10. Fostering a supportive classroom climate		O	◆●X	
	11. Ensuring of stimulating, engaging and appropriate learning opportunities		●O	◆X	
	12. Ensuring appropriate clarity and structure		O●	◆X	
Use: Subject-specific	13. Awareness of historical testimonies and of changes over time	OX	●◆		
	14. Exploring, examining and presenting of historical factual analyses		●X◆O		
	15. Interpretation (analysis and interpretation) of history		O●	◆X	
	16. Orientation: Meaning formation via past experiences and value judgement examination on the basis of past experiences	O	◆●X		
	17. Acquiring and reproducing of knowledge about past events and understanding of history		◆●	OX	

Key: −: not true, 0: just true, +: very true, ++: pronouncedly true

Fig. 18.12 Table of Overall Evaluation of the Lessons after Points; Lower Saxony (◆), Saxony-Anhalt (O), Sweden (●), Switzerland (X)

experiences, (b) in 3 of 4 lessons, significant topics were taught; (c) 3 of 4 lessons were factually correct, multi-perspectival and controversial; (d) 3 out of 4 lessons featured engaging and appropriate learning opportunities; d) hardly any attention was given to human action in societal practice, and finally (e) the students had only few opportunities for their own perceptions, to draw information from historical sources, or for their own orientation. We therefore conclude that little historical learning occurred in the lessons observed.

Students at the Focus!

What was the reason for the pronounced lack of historical learning in these lessons? One explanation might be that, in introductory lessons in particular, teachers often think from the angle of the topic per se. This may be reinforced by particularly demanding analysis that was selected in order to present that subject matter.

When it comes to selecting a presentation concept, there are other opportunities which would allow teachers to reference both the present and the daily lives of their students. We shall briefly outline 4 alternatives here. Firstly, there is the longitudinal cut, in which students would be taught the history of the Ukraine, for instance, from the brief period of independence (1917–1920), through the Second World War, the integration into the Eastern bloc, the independence in 1991 until the annexation of Crimea and the separatism of Eastern Ukraine. Secondly, teachers may opt for a cross-section, which would examine the situation in 1945 and the lives of those in war ravaged countries as well as those spared from war, further allowing students to look at society, economy and culture. Thirdy, a case study would present a specific scenario, such as the abduction of the lawyer Dr. Walter Linse from West Berlin into the East sector on 8th July 1952, as well as the mechanics of the Cold War at the level of the population, the governments in East and West Berlin and even in the USA and the Soviet Union. All of this can be demonstrated vividly, rendering clear to students the impact of the Cold War on individuals. Fourth, teachers might select an individualising procedure, covering, for instance, the history of displaced people from East Prussia in 1945 and their later integration in the FRG.

In order to ensure that historical learning does take place, even in introductory lessons, teachers must stress the relevance of the topic to the students' own living environments. The learners' question when confronted with the Cold War, 'and what has this got to do with me?' (cf. Thurn 1993[2]), can be answered in different ways; however, it is crucial that students recognise and understand 'what reflecting on past events has got to do with their present and future' (Bergmann 2004, 91–92). When learners apply historical learning as their method, they have to first know what *historical learning* is. This idea has as yet not been given enough attention. However, the standard history textbooks all feature explanations in their preliminary pages as to what history is, also providing definitions of terms such as 'sources', 'representations', 'chronology' or 'archaeology'. Yet what exactly historical teaching is and wherein historical thinking differs, for example, from mathematical thinking is not explained (cf. Fuchs et al. 2016, 4–5)[3].

It is evident that students learn best if they know the reasons why they are studying certain topics and why they are being taught via certain methods (Cf. Beck et al. 1995; Messner 1998). Successful students begin to learn with the prior knowledge of how they will be taught. They observe and reflect upon how they themselves learn and control their own learning efficiently. In contrast to the less successful students, the successful ones learn with awareness (Messner 1998). It is certainly not a new discovery that students themselves must reflect upon their own ways of learning or that history teaching should relate to the students' own living environments and offer them the opportunity to be a part of guiding their own learning. The popularity of student-oriented history teaching has increased in the last few years, particularly in regards to competence orientation. Obviously, however, such an approach to teaching history does not occur on a day-to-day basis. Our analysis of the four introductory lessons suggests that subject- and science-driven approaches still predominate when it comes to teaching history (Rohlfes 1986, 177). Those involved in teaching history must ensure that in the future students come even further into the focus!

Notes

1. The evaluation of the lessons was carried out by Peter Gautschi and Hans Utz together with research assistant Antje Suter and student assistant Jasmine Steger, using the criteria on a four-point scale. The four evaluations were averaged and rounded. No examination of the inter-rater reliability was conducted due to the explorative character of the procedure.
2. Cf. Susanne Thurn: '[...] und was hat das mit mir zu tun?': Geschichtsdidaktische Positionen (Pfaffenweiler: Centaurus). She presents the objectives of her own teaching in regards to history education and writes: 'I would like that my students [...] when having pressing – pressing them and pressing our society – problems ask inquiring historical questions because they have learnt that the historical dealing with intentions, conditions restricting action and hindrances of all sorts might be useful for them' (Thurn 1993, 255).
3. An exception is the school history textbook Zeitreise, which at the beginning of each volume, on the basis of a monument, defines historical learning (Fuchs et al. 2016).

Bibliography

Textbooks Cited:

Fuchs, Karin, Peter Gautschi and Hans Utz. 2016. Zeitreise 1. Das Lehrwerk für historisches Lernen im Fachbereich 'Räume, Zeiten, Gesellschaften'. Edition for Switzerland. Baar: Klett und Balmer.

Further References:

Barricelli, Michele. 2012. 'Darstellungskonzepte von Geschichte im Unterricht'. In Handbuch Praxis des Geschichtsunterrichts. Volume 2, ed. by Michele Barricelli and Martin Lücke, 202–223. Schwalbach/Ts.: Wochenschau Verlag.

Beck, Erwin, Guldimann, Titus, Zutavern, Michael. 1995. 'Eigenständig lernende Schülerinnen und Schüler'. In Eigenständig lernen, ed. by Erwin Beck, Titus Guldimann and Michael Zutavern, 15–58. St. Gallen: UVK, Fachverlag für Wissenschaft und Studium.

Bergmann, Klaus. 2004. 'Gegenwarts- und Zukunftsbezug'. In *Handbuch Methoden im Geschichtsunterricht*, ed. by Ulrich Mayer, Hans-Jürgen Pandel and Gerhard Schneider, 91–112. Schwalbach/Ts.: Wochenschau Verlag.

Furrer, Markus, Gautschi, Peter. 2017. 'Memory Cultures and History Education. Introduction'. In *Remembering and Recounting the Cold War*, ed. by Markus Furrer and Peter Gautschi, 11–26. Schwalbach/Ts.: Wochenschau Verlag.

Gautschi, Peter. 2012. *Guter Geschichtsunterricht, Grundlagen, Erkenntnisse, Hinweise.* 2nd Edition. Schwalbach/Ts.: Wochenschau Verlag.

Gautschi, Peter, Furrer, Markus, Sommer Häller, Barbara. 2014. 'Umgang mit Geschichte und Erinnerung in Schule und Hochschule'. In *Der Beitrag von Schulen und Hochschulen zu Erinnerungskulturen*, ed. by Peter Gautschi and Barbara Sommer Häller, 7–24. Schwalbach/Ts.: Wochenschau Verlag.

Gautschi, Peter, Fink, Nadine. 2016. 'Lehrplanlyrik und Unterrichtsalltag in der Schweiz: Einblicke in fächerverbindendes historisches Lernen in der deutsch- und französischsprachigen Schweiz'. In *Geschichte im interdisziplinären Diskurs. Grenzziehungen – Grenzüberschreitungen – Grenzverschiebungen*, ed. by Michael Sauer, Charlotte Bühl-Cramer, Anke John, Astrid Schwabe, Alfons Kenkmann and Christian Kuchler. 131–150. Göttingen: V&R Uni Press.

Jeismann, Karl-Ernst. 2000. *Geschichte und Bildung: Beiträge zur Geschichtsdidaktik und zur Historischen Bildungsforschung.* Paderborn: Ferdinand Schöningh Verlag.

Mayer, Ulrich. 2005. 'Qualitätsmerkmale historischer Bildung. Geschichtsdidaktische Kategorien als Kriterien zur Bestimmung und Sicherung der fachdidaktischen Qualität des historischen Lernens'. In *Zeitgeschichte und historische Bildung. Festschrift für Dietfrid Krause-Vilmar*, ed. by: Wilfried Hansmann and Timo Hoyer. 223–243. Kassel: Jenior.

Helmut Messner. 1998. 'Die kompetente Lernerin, der kompetente Lerner'. *Forum Schule Heute* 12 (4). 3–6.

Pandel, Hans-Jürgen. 2006. *Quelleninterpretation. Die schriftliche Quelle im Geschichtsunterricht* 3rd Edition. Schwalbach/Ts: Wochenschau Verlag.

Rohlfes, Joachim. 1986. *Geschichte und ihre Didaktik*. Göttingen: Vandenhoeck & Ruprecht.

Rüsen, Jörn. 1997. 'Objektivität'. In *Handbuch der Geschichtsdidaktik* 5th Edition, Revised Edition, ed. by Klaus Bergmann, Klaus Fröhlich and Annette Kuhn, 160–163. Seelze-Velber, Kallmeyer.

Rüsen, Jörn. 2008. *Historisches Lernen. Grundlagen und Paradigmen* Volume 2, Revised and Extended Edition. Schwalbach/Ts.: Wochenschau Verlag.

Schneider, Gerhard. 2008. *Gelungene Einstiege. Voraussetzung für erfolgreiche Geschichtsstunden* 5th Edition. Schwalbach/Ts.: Wochenschau Verlag.

Schreiber, Waltraud, Körber, Andreas, von Borries, Bodo. 2007. 'Historisches Denken. Ein Kompetenz-Strukturmodell'. In *Kompetenzen historischen Denkens. Ein Strukturmodell als Beitrag zur Kompetenzorientierung in der Geschichtsdidaktik*, ed. by Andreas Körber / Waltraud Schreiber and Alexander Schöner. 17–53. Neuried: Ars Una [Kompetenzen: Grundlagen – Entwicklung – Förderung].

Thurn, Susanne. 1993. *'[...] und was hat das mit mir zu tun?': Geschichtsdidaktische Positionen*. Pfaffenweiler: Centaurus.

Wehler, Hans-Ulrich. 2006. *Deutsche Gesellschaftsgeschichte*. Volume 1, 4th Edition. München: C.H. Beck.

Weymar, Ernst. 1970. 'Werturteile im Geschichtsunterricht'. *Geschichte in Wissenschaft und Unterricht* 21 (3): 198–215.

Wertsch, James V. 2008. 'Collective Memory and Narrative Templates'. *Social Research* 75 (1): 133–156.

Open Access This chapter is licensed under the terms of the Creative Commons Attribution 4.0 International License (http://creativecommons.org/licenses/by/4.0/), which permits use, sharing, adaptation, distribution and reproduction in any medium or format, as long as you give appropriate credit to the original author(s) and the source, provide a link to the Creative Commons licence and indicate if changes were made.

The images or other third party material in this chapter are included in the chapter's Creative Commons licence, unless indicated otherwise in a credit line to the material. If material is not included in the chapter's Creative Commons licence and your intended use is not permitted by statutory regulation or exceeds the permitted use, you will need to obtain permission directly from the copyright holder.

19

Pedagogical Entanglements and the Cold War: A Comparative Study on Opening History Lessons on the Cold War in Sweden and Switzerland

Robert Thorp

The Cold War was a complex series of events that came to have a great impact on most countries in Europe. This article analyses two lower secondary schools' opening lessons on the Cold War, one taught in Sweden and the other in Switzerland. The study finds that the opening lessons vary to a great extent, regarding both *what* content is covered but also *how* that content is covered. Whereas the Swiss lesson predominantly focuses on establishing a critical narrative of the origins of the Cold War conflict, the Swedish lesson disseminates what could be considered a traditional narrative of the Cold War. The lessons also differ due to the different forms of educational media employed by each teacher. While the Swiss teacher makes use of caricatures to instigate pupil-oriented discussions about what caused the Cold War, the Swedish teacher uses personal analogies and a video during class. The study, however, finds that neither teacher engages with the contingencies of history culture that affect historical content and how we approach it; instead both disseminate a closed rendering of the history of the Cold War.

R. Thorp (✉)
University of Stockholm, Stockholm, Sweden

The University of Newcastle, Newcastle, NSW, Australia
e-mail: robert.thorp@edu.su.se; robert.thorp@newcastle.edu.au

Introduction

Teaching history is a complex enterprise. There are always a number of factors that come into play when a teacher sets out to disseminate a certain historical content. Not only should the teacher reflect on what content to cover in a teaching situation, but he or she also needs to reflect on how that content should be presented to the pupils. Here, the preconceptions and prior knowledge of the pupils needs to be taken into account (Duraisingh 2017; Stymne 2017), as well as that of the teacher (Thorp 2016). Furthermore, history education can also be understood as a kind of cultural endeavor in which collective memories, personal experiences, beliefs and opinions as well as official curricula are at work (Furrer and Gautschi 2017). History teachers have to navigate these challenges whenever they set out to teach their subject. Approaching history teaching from this perspective means that we come to regard such a process as a kind of entangled activity where both subject-related constraints and social and cultural constraints come into play (Parkes 2013; Thorp 2016).

Indeed, the subject of history itself might also be regarded as subject to a similar kind of entanglement. One important aspect of history is the study of the past with the aim to understand how it has influenced societies today. However, and this is another important aspect, history must always be reconstructed and is, thus, contingent on this reconstruction. With this view, it follows that knowing history basically means grasping two different but inter-related concepts: the existence of facts about the past and its events and the concept that history is also always a reconstruction of this past (Wineburg 2001; Parkes 2011). Moreover, whenever we make use of history we continuously reconstruct the reconstruction of the past in what perhaps might be called a never-ending cycle of reconstruction. German philosopher Hans-Georg Gadamer posited the idea that an awareness of how history is always constructed within a certain context for certain purposes, how it is always the subject of historicity, was one of the greatest achievements of modern thought (Gadamer 1975). This awareness of historicity, or historical consciousness, it could be argued, is an essential component in an understanding of history that seeks to disentangle an entangled historical subject. This in itself poses another difficult challenge to history teachers. Following this line of argumentation, the Cold War can serve a particularly interesting historical topic to study due to its historical proximity and looming consequences for many (if not all) European countries. Furthermore, the Cold War as a historical topic allows historical and didactical entanglements to come to the fore. It is a historical event that goes beyond simply having a historical relevance since it also affects ideological, social and cultural conceptions of ourselves, our national and international affairs (Furrer 2017). From a disciplinary perspective, the Cold War is also the perfect case study because it is still close to us; we have, therefore, an excellent opportunity to explore how it has been constructed as a historical event. The binary opposition between the USA and the USSR at the core of the event also makes it ideal for these purposes, since we have two agents who deliver different narratives in regards to the same historical event. However, since the Cold War is an historical event that goes beyond just being an historical event, it can also pose great challenges to history teachers, since it feeds into our basic common sense assumptions of how we should understand people, politics and the world, playing such a prominent part in European post-war societies. In other words, we might argue that the Cold War itself is a highly entangled historical subject.

In order to tease out what implications the interplay and ensuing entanglement between history, collective memory, personal experiences and classroom teaching practices have for the teaching of history, I wanted to study how teachers from two different national contexts taught the same historical subject. For these reasons, secondary school history teachers in Sweden and Switzerland were observed when they introduced a teaching unit on the Cold War to their students. The rationale here was not that I would be able to get at the historical cultures of these countries, or to be able to say something about how teachers in these two countries teach the Cold War in general. Rather, it was seen as an excellent opportunity to study how two teachers from two different contexts, who taught the same historical topic, went about delivering that same topic to their pupils. Thus, the focus of this study was to more deeply understand how these teachers dealt with the complexities and entanglements I have outlined above. Recent research on teaching history, assuming not only disciplinary difficulties in teaching history but also social and cultural ones has shown that matters of curricular demands, collective memory, cultural entanglement and awareness of historicity all play prominent roles in how history teachers perceive their subject, their own roles as educators and how to best teach the subject (Persson and Thorp 2017; Persson 2017; Thorp 2017; Zanazanian 2009). This study should be seen as a further exploration of this field of research into educating students in the subject of history.

Consequently, the aim of this article is to analyse how two history teachers from two different contexts approach the Cold War in a teaching situation and how they engage with the historicity of the historical content they disseminate. Attention will be given to the strategies and educational media the observed teachers used, as well as to how particular content was covered. The presentation below will start with an outline of the theoretical and methodological concerns regarding the teaching of history. Following on from this explanation, I will present the main results of the study, and then discuss how these results might be used to encourage further understanding of the cultural entanglements that characterise the teaching of history.

Approach

Theoretical assumptions

A basic theoretical assumption that has been made here is that history inevitably is a reconstruction of past events. This reconstruction in turn is subject to historicity in the sense that it is always contextually contingent (Thorp 2016). Historians (and others who produce accounts of history) always meticulously select and interpret past sources in order to construct history. In this sense history is always alienated from the past it wishes to reconstruct (cf. Roth 2012), and it is this alienation that gives rise to history as a serious methodological and critical study of past events (cf. Wilschut 2012, 47–52). Because of this inherent contingency in history, any historical narrative is open to scrutiny and is, in a way, provisional: other perspectives, methodologies and interests may generate other historical accounts using the same source material. Thus, it might be argued that the merits of any historical account lie not so much in the actual history it conveys, but instead in the methodological aspects of how that particular historical narrative was produced. This means that epistemological concerns take the front seat, particularly when it comes to the academic subject of history (Thorp 2016).

Yet there is also another aspect of history that needs to be taken into account, especially when it comes to teaching history. History is not only the careful reproduction of past events through a critical methodological inquiry, it is also a central component of how we construct meaning, in regards to both ourselves, our fellow human beings and the world. Thus, history shapes existential, ideological, moral and pedagogical aspects of our lives. If we want to argue or establish something about ourselves or our societies, we often use history to do so (cf. Karlsson 2014). Following this line of argumentation, we can say that there is a kind of inherent tension in history: It is something which we both use to make sense of things and which we, more or less, may come to take for granted (or even should take for granted). Yet it is also something that is constructed, provisional, contingent and, thus, dynamic. A challenge for any history teacher is to try to relate to this tension whenever he or she teaches history. Furthermore, history teachers are also individuals with personal experiences, interests and beliefs that affect how they view themselves, their fellow beings, the world and, therefore, history. From a perspective on pedagogical approaches to history, then, it becomes a matter of whether these approaches engage with this tension, or if they are particularly orientated towards representing and reproducing specific historical narratives. There is a strong consensus in history education research that pedagogical approaches ignoring the constructed nature of history are problematic, since they may foster a limited understanding of history and result in chauvinism and intolerance. The proposed solution is to teach history as critical inquiry and to foster historiographical insights, instead of merely presenting a particular historical narrative (Foster and Padgett 1999; Lévesque 2008; Seixas 2000; Wineburg 2001). Through a rational, autonomous stance towards the subject of history, a position commonly referred to as historical thinking, pupils (and others) will be able to approach historical narratives and history carefully and will not be swayed by the normative pull of history. I argue, however, that this is a formidable challenge due to the role history plays in our commonsense assumptions about ourselves and the world. Additionally, the education students receive in the subject is always a cultural and ideological enterprise; the subject matter which we apply our historical thinking to therefore goes beyond matters of critical inquiry (Thorp 2017). Even historians are affected by the cultural contexts in which they live and work.

I argue that an important means of acknowledging and involving this tension in our study of history and our pedagogical methods of teaching the same subject is to focus on matters pertaining to historicity and historical consciousness, i.e. an awareness of how all historical narratives and all our encounters with these narratives exist in time. This means that everything historical is contingent on historical factors and is thus open for reinterpretation. Historical consciousness should here be understood as the ever-present awareness that all human beings and all forms of social integration they have created exist in time, i.e. they are subject to historicity. Historical consciousness is manifested in human representations and conceptions, and results in an understanding or appreciation of how contextual contingency is inherent in these representations and conceptions, thus safeguarding common human rationality (Jeismann 1979). In this sense historical consciousness should be regarded as a kind of epistemic stance towards history that enables the individual to appreciate how history is reconstructed but at the same time omnipresent in all our encounters and uses of it. Approaching historical consciousness like this puts focus on the inherent tension in history outlined above: history is there for us to critically scrutinise and construct, but it is also the fabric of the historical meaning we make. This means that the critical gaze should not only be turned outwards towards historical accounts that we encounter, but also inwards towards our own meaning making and conceptions of history (Parkes 2011).

In order to empirically analyse how we epistemologically approach history and historical narratives, I devised a model of *narratological uses of history* in order to exemplify and categorise how we make use of history from the perspective of historical consciousness. Borrowing from and modifying Jörn Rüsen's typology of historical narratives (2012), I formulated three cognitively and narratologically different ways of using history: (i) A *traditional* narratological use of history presents history as static and acontextual, (ii) A *critical* narratological use of history attempts to destabilise other historical narratives or presents alternative historical narratives; and (iii) A *genetic* narratological use of history portrays history as dynamic, contingent and characterised by continuity and change (Thorp 2017, 132).

If we understand historical consciousness as an awareness of historicity, we can claim that historical consciousness should be understood as an epistemic approach towards history. If we are aware that history is a result of interpretation and reconstruction that historians (and others) make, we have a different kind of understanding of history than if we did not possess such an awareness. These different kinds of understanding of history correspond to the narratological uses of history above. A traditional use of history disregards how history is always the result of interpretation and reconstruction and instead presents history in a factual way; it purports that when we study history we can understand what *really* happened. A critical use of history uses history in a way that straddles the distance between the traditional and the genetic uses of history, since history is perceived as something that is contingent on perspective and interpretation, although there remain correct ways of understanding history. This can either result in a kind of relativistic stance towards history (meaning that all historical accounts are equally true or false) or in an understanding that claims that some historical accounts are 'true' and others are not (in the traditional sense of the term). A genetic use of history instead focuses on how all historical accounts and all approaches to history are characterised by interpretation, perspective and meaning making and is inevitably contingent on these factors. Here we can see a close theoretical connection to historical consciousness, as an awareness of historicity.

If we relate this framework to the study at hand, it becomes important to look not only at the content covered in class and the framing of that content, but also at the *presentation* of the content. Do the teachers engage with the entanglements of the Cold War, or do they present the pupils with a traditional narrative of how the events unfolded? It becomes more relevant to analyse the tasks and assignments the students are presented with: do they invite discussions of the complexity of the historical event at hand and the multitude of possible relationships to it, or are the pedagogical approaches used aimed at inculcating students with a particular historical account of the Cold War which they then unconsciously internalise?

In my initial analysis of the material, I analysed the teaching methods and materials the teachers employed when introducing the Cold War. I further analysed what pedagogic approach each teacher used in their respective classroom. For instance: Was the lesson focused on pupil activity or was it more of a session to orient the pupils? The next step in the analysis was to look at the content covered in these opening lessons. Who were the most prominent figures, what was the Cold War about? What aspects of the Cold War were highlighted and how was this content framed? The final stage of the analysis was directed at analysing how the teachers approached the lesson content from the perspective of engaging historical consciousness and narratological uses of history. This means that particular attention was paid to how the two teachers engaged with the entanglements and tensions of history and the teaching of history which were highlighted above.

Results

Teaching strategies and educational media

The two observed lessons show two distinctly different teaching strategies, but also some important similarities. The Swiss lesson could be characterized as pupil centered, although the teacher was in full control of the assignments and the content covered. The class began with the teacher showing the pupils the cartoon 'Tour du Monde: Tandem oder Einrad' by Jean Leffel, printed in the German textbook *Menschen in Zeit und Raum 9* (2012, 113; see the introduction to this section). This cartoon depicts Harry S. Truman and Joseph Stalin riding bicycles. In the above picture we see them riding a tandem bicycle. Truman is in front and seems to be in charge of the direction they're going, with Stalin helping him. We could interpret this as relating to the relationship between the two during the Second World War and the fight against Hitler. The expressions on their faces are those of contention. The picture underneath shows Stalin and Truman riding unicycles in opposite directions. Their bodily poses and facial expressions are equally defiant. What I find particularly interesting with this cartoon is the historical message it seems to convey: Stalin and Truman (i.e. the USA and the USSR) both acted defiantly after the end of the Second World War, and thus both could be blamed for the escalation of the Cold War conflict. This is at odds with the typical Western view of the Cold War, which posits Stalin and the USSR as solely responsible for the Cold War (Holmén 2006; Ritzer 2012; Thorp 2015).

The pupils in the Swiss classroom were instructed to reflect on how the cartoon relates to a film about the American bombings of Hiroshima and Nagasaki and the extent of the destruction it caused. The teacher then returned to the cartoon and asked the pupils to discuss how they thought the cartoon related to the film they had just been shown. The most part of the lesson was devoted to this activity. While the pupils' answers drove the ensuing discussion in class and they were quite active, the teacher was still in control of the direction of the discussion, using various prompts and leading questions. The pupils were then asked to perform a role play activity, in which they read quotations by Harry S. Truman and Andrei Zhdanov, each arguing that the political orientations of their respective countries after the Second World War were the correct ones. The pupils were then asked to perform mock debates where they pretended to be either Truman or Zhdanov. At the end of the lesson the discussion in class was directed towards Germany and Japan and the culpability these nations should share for their actions during the Second World War. German nationalism, for instance, was problematized in relation to how the Germans celebrated the World Cup victory in football with flags. Pupils commented on how this outburst of national pride in particular made some Germans feel uneasy due to their past experiences with nationalism. Finally, the teacher directed the discussion towards the agenda the Allied forces decided on in relation to Germany.

The Swedish teacher used a different strategy. The lesson started with the teacher briefly, but still comprehensively, introducing the Cold War. The teacher's narrative was oriented towards giving the pupils an understanding of what the Cold War was and when it took place, and the narrative focussed on the conflicts of the Cold War; the teacher stressed that it was a war between the USA and the USSR fought by proxy. She also, when discussing Sweden's role during the Cold War, emphasised how Sweden was neutral in the conflict but that there was also a long tradition of conflict with Russia in Sweden, which prompted the Swedish government to orientate themselves towards the West and the USA. The next activity involved showing the pupils a French documentary film about the origins and escalation of the Cold War conflict. As an introduction to this activity the teacher introduced historiographical aspects, focussing on how history is always presented for a purpose and that it is contingent on this purpose. She then asked the pupils to reflect on whether the film might present a Western or Eastern perspective on the conflict, given that it is of French origin. The pupils replied that the film would probably be told from a Western perspective.

In brief, the film's narrative of the conflict focussed on the USA and USSR as two countries with similar pasts that cooperated during the war against Germany, but then came to oppose each other. In my view, the reason for the conflict between the USA and USSR is related to Stalin's breach of the Yalta conference agreement and the imposition of communist dictatorships in the countries that were occupied by the Red Army. These actions then made the USA realise that there was a communist threat and that they had to act upon this threat. This is what could be called the traditional Cold War narrative (Lundestad 2004). Throughout the showing of the film the teacher commented on what she perceived to be key aspects of the film's narrative. The teacher then ended the lesson by summing up and stressing the key features of the lesson: (i) the Cold War is a period that has shaped our present society, (ii) it was a troublesome period and (iii) Sweden was frightened of the USSR and chose to orient itself towards the West.

Historical content

The Swiss lesson centred around two aspects of the Cold War period, i.e. the origins of the conflict and the reverberations of the Second World War on Germany and Japan. Regarding the origins of the conflict, the Swiss teacher placed great emphasis on explaining the conflict as a power struggle between the USA and the USSR and tried to ascribe agency to both actors. The cartoon used in the beginning of the lesson illustrated this well: in it, both Truman and Stalin are both unwilling to cooperate and thus both responsible for the escalation of the conflict. Furthermore, Truman and the USA are depicted as in charge of the course of events before the end of the Second World War and might in this sense be regarded as having the upper hand in the relationship between the two. This impression was further accentuated by the film portraying the American atomic bombings in Hiroshima and Nagasaki the teacher chose to show her pupils, and the assignment she gave them to relate the cartoon to the film's content. The aim here seemed to be to show that the USA and their military capacities did pose a threat towards Joseph Stalin and the USSR. This conclusion was further strengthened by the discussion between the teacher and the pupils that followed after the film.

To begin with, the teacher asks her pupils 'OK, right then, this film, what it showed, does that connect at all with the cartoon? And if so, how?' A pupil replies after some reflection:

> Yes, it is easy to explain, first they worked together. And then [...] Hiroshima happened. And then they [the USA and the USSR] split up and that made the world split up, actually.

In this interpretation, that went unchallenged by the teacher, you could argue that the USA caused the conflict through its atomic bombings in Japan. The teacher then instructed her pupils to look at the top picture of the cartoon (showing Truman and Stalin riding a tandem bicycle) and asked them 'Who's got the better seat on the tandem?' A pupil then replied, 'Yes, it's Stalin. Because he actually has to do, you know, less work. I mean, he had to do less pedalling, but he couldn't decide [where to go]'. The teacher is not entirely content with this interpretation and replies: 'Quite. But on the other hand, you already mentioned, the one in front can steer', suggesting that Truman had the better seat, after all.

Focus then shifted towards the bottom picture of the cartoon (showing Stalin and Truman riding unicycles in opposite directions). The teacher asked the students 'Are the proportions right in the bottom [picture], the two unicycles? Would they be right at that [particular] time [in history]?' The teacher here wanted her pupils to reflect upon whether the USA and the USSR entered the conflict on equal terms, as is suggested by the picture. Two pupils replied that they thought the proportions were right due to the spread of communism in the world after the Second World War. The teacher then replied:

> Yes, that's right. From the point of view of population numbers, it's a good idea. Which aspect of [the relationship between the USA and the USSR] is not featured here? What else should there be here, again relating to the USA? Perhaps, [...] they've got the upper hand? For what reason, at this particular moment in time? (Swiss teacher)

To which a pupil replied, 'Because they're the only country in the world that had the atom bomb'. This reply seemed to satisfy the teacher as she replied: 'Yes, precisely. OK, then, I think you have interpreted this cartoon here well'. The teacher here seemed to be intent on stressing the role of the USA in the conflict, even though her pupils seem more inclined towards thinking that Stalin and the USSR did indeed pose a threat and had the upper hand in the conflict. The teacher then asked the pupils to rank the USA's world standing after the Second World War, and a pupil replied that they were number one both economically and militarily. The teacher confirmed this and then asked the pupil to explain why the USA should be ranked as number one militarily; the pupil then replied that it was because of the atom bomb.

When asked how they might rank the USSR, a male pupil replied that 'America's scared of this communism thing. And the Soviet Union is making propaganda against capitalism [...]'. He further added that that USSR was also gaining land, which he connected to the fall of the Iron Curtain and the division of Europe into East and West. To this the teacher replied: 'Exactly. Let's look at the war now. Perhaps you remember the US entering the war or, put a better way, the Soviet Union was attacked and the consequence was huge losses, millions of victims', again stressing the inferiority of the USSR compared to the USA. A pupil then replied that the USSR should be ranked in second place. The teacher then went on the sum up the discussion:

> They [the USSR], I mean, they're winners too, aren't they. [...] It became clear that communism is an alternative to this liberal democracy. Clear as day, that's the alternative. And why shouldn't communism be the best model? With communism you can win wars. So here: communism as an alternative form of society. (Swiss teacher)

Here, the teacher reiterated what, it could be argued, is a part of her own agenda with the assignment: In 1945 the USA was by all means the world leader and was in possession of the atom bomb. The USSR had suffered great losses in the war and was therefore inferior to the USA. Furthermore, by winning the war against Germany, the USSR had also shown that communism was a legitimate alternative to the liberal capitalist democracy.

The next activity was a role play activity in which pupils were given quotations by Truman and Zhdanov and were asked to perform a mock debate where they should argue that their country's trajectory after the Second World War was a legitimate one. According to the pupils, Truman's main argument was that the USA is there to protect 'free people, [...] people should choose for themselves'. Zhdanov's argument was interpreted by a pupil as a kind of 'conspiracy theory',

> I mean [they actually said that] America just because of their economic interests took part in the war and that [it] has imperialistic features, [...] and that the communist and democratic countries, to which [the USSR] count themselves, are fighting against this [imperialist] injustice. (Male Swiss pupil).

Here the pupil distanced himself from Zhdanov's interpretation of why the USA entered the Second World War. He then continued:

> I have the feeling that both major powers want to put themselves, I mean, in a good light and [...] have a sort of trailblazing role. I mean for instance when America says: "Yes, we want to respect everyone, we want everyone to decide things for themselves". And Russia's doing exactly the same, but

history shows us something else. That afterwards they actually didn't independently or selflessly support other countries, if we look at, for example, the war in Afghanistan.

To which the teacher replied: 'So both [have] the same role, probably using the same means. We'll see this later on'. The teacher then shifted attention from the USA and the USSR towards Germany and Japan at the end of the Second World War. She asked her pupils 'Now at the end of the war [...] what image [...] does humanity have of these two states [Germany and Japan]'. A pupil replied that people thought that Germany and Japan had to suffer the consequences of being 'megalomaniac', suggesting that their fault lay in being too hungry for power and world domination. The teacher, however, seemed to have something else in mind as well. She asked:

> And on top of that? I mean, [what about] what happened in Germany with the racial ideology that was put into practice? And Japan also committed unbelievable atrocities [during] the war. How is that received, how do people approach the Japanese and the Germans [...] after everything that people realized was happening there? (Swiss teacher)

A pupil here replied that people became aware that 'people were capable of a lot [more] than we used to think'. Another pupil then went on: '[...] People had suddenly found the scapegoat for everything'. The Germans and Japanese 'had to pay' for the war. The teacher then stressed another aspect of this and asked her pupils to reflect upon how people still regard Germany and Japan morally, 'to this day'. One female pupil replied that:

> Yes, it's the same to this day. But for them personally as well. [...] I was at a camp there were three Germans there and we were talking about it and they said it was so extreme that the first time they could hang German flags again was four years ago when the World Cup [in football] was on. (Swiss female pupil B)

The pupil here suggested that this sentiment still affects Germany and Germans today. The remainder of the lesson was devoted to outlining the denazification process in Germany after the war and how Nazis managed to escape justice because of a lax effort on the part of the Allied forces and the USA in Western Europe and the active support of the Vatican.

The Swedish lesson was introduced comprehensively by the teacher, as she outlined what the Cold War was about and then tried to relate it to the Swedish national context. When discussing the definition of the Cold War, she warned her pupils not to think of the Cold War as related to winter but instead asks her pupils to imagine a metaphor:

> Imagine that you just entered a room where your mother and father just had a row, or two of your friends had a row, or something similar. You enter the room and feel […] in the atmosphere that something has happened, or that there is a risk that something will happen. You maybe have been in a fight with someone and argued and you have been very close to losing control, and that is a symbol of what the Cold War is. (Swedish teacher)

She then went on the explain that the Cold War was a war fought by proxy between the USSR and the USA, with Sweden being neutral but caught in between the two powers. Concerning Sweden's stance towards the USA and the USSR, the teacher stressed that:

> We are neutral, and that means that Sweden during this period in history and still today lie in-between [the USA] and [the USSR]. But then we also have a tradition. If you ask grown-ups at home, they will tell you that they are a little bit more scared of [the USSR]. And historically we can explain this by Sweden more often […] having fought [the USSR] than [the USA]. (Swedish teacher)

The teacher then asked her pupils to reflect on what the Cold War can be if it is not a traditional war fought between two belligerents. The pupils replied that it was a war about politics, technology and Germany, to which the teacher repeated that this was a war fought by proxy and asked her pupils to imagine a situation where they are unfriendly with someone and asks their friends to attack this person. The teacher then went on to introduce a film about the emergence of the Cold War conflict, but before she shows the pupils the film she asks them to reflect on historiographical aspects of history:

> When you study history it's extremely important that you always think, and this is not only in relation to the Cold War, but also when we write history today, when your grandchildren will read the history books they will assess "Who wrote this?" and "Did this really happen?" […]. It's really important when you study history, when something has been passed on [or told by someone else], [to reflect] on whether it's true or false and if it has been written for a specific purpose. (Swedish teacher)

She then told her pupils that the film they are about to watch is French and whether France was on the American or Soviet side of the conflict. A pupil replied that they were on the side of the USA. This was confirmed by the teacher, who adds 'and then maybe they regard the conflict in a certain way'. She then left the historiographical aspect to one side and played the film to the class.

In the film a voice over narrates a history of the emergence on the conflict centered on how US and British troops advanced into Germany from the west and Soviet troops advanced from the east. It is then explained that the USSR was a 'dictatorship of the proletariat' and that Soviet economy and political activity was state controlled. The USA is described as a country where the government's power is regulated and where private ownership and free competition is regarded as a guarantee for the well being of its citizens. Regarding the escalation of the conflict between the USA and the USSR, Stalin's breach of the Yalta conference agreement and imposition of communism in the countries occupied by the Soviet troops is presented as a key event, which made the USA realise that the USSR posed a threat to world peace and security, prompting Truman to issue his declaration. Here, the Swedish teacher interjected with: 'In Sweden you said: "The Russian is coming, the Russian is coming, be wary of the Russian […]'. The lesson was then ended by the teacher summing up the content of the day's lesson:

> What we have started with today and will study in the coming two weeks is a period that has meant a lot to me because I have lived during this

period. It has also meant a lot to your parents and grandparents because there was a situation in the world [...] where [the USSR] and [the USA] distrusted each other, they were very afraid of each other and sometimes during this period, starting 1945, things got heated [and war was very close]. So, it's a troublesome time and Sweden tries to be neutral but from tradition we have been more afraid of [the USSR], and therefore we approached [the USA]. (Swedish teacher)

Narratological uses of history

As has been shown above, these two lessons provide us with two rather different approaches to introducing the Cold War, but there are also similarities between the two pedagogical approaches in regards to how history is used narratologically. In the Swiss lesson, the teacher seemed to have a personal agenda with an introduction that was oriented towards destabilising the traditional grand narrative of the Cold War as a result of Soviet aggression. The teaching material used, i.e. the cartoon, the film segment and the quotations from Truman and Zhdanov, all seem to support this conclusion. The cartoon shows us how Truman and the USA were in charge of matters and how Stalin *and* Truman defiantly headed in different directions at the end of Second World War. The film segment highlights how US bombings in Japan wreaked havoc and that the USA had a terrible weapon of mass destruction that they were willing to deploy. Furthermore, the quotations from Zhdanov and Truman ascribe agency to both actors and gives voice to the Soviet interpretation of what was happening in Europe and across the world, i.e. that the USA was an imperialist force intent on imposing their model of society on the world. Throughout the lesson the pupils did, however, give voice to what may be the implicit commonsense assumptions concerning the conflict in Swiss historical culture. This was evidenced, for example, when a pupil interpreted Zhdanov's view of the world as a conspiracy theory and an example of hypocrisy. The teacher engaged with these views throughout and attempted to direct the discussion towards an understanding of how the USA was also an aggressive force, one which had the upper hand in relation to the USSR in 1945. Perhaps the teacher was trying here to show an alternative way of interpreting events after 1945, to challenge commonsense assumptions about the Cold War. This could be a risky enterprise since the teacher could come across as politically and ideologically motivated (and therefore less credible) in trying to put forward an alternative view of the Cold War, but there are no indications that the pupils perceived her this way.

From a pedagogical perspective on history, it could be argued that the repeated clashes between the teacher's agenda and the pupils' insistence on a traditional rendering of the Cold War provided many opportunities for a discussion about the role perspective plays in how we understand history, highlighting how history both underlies our understanding of the world, but also remains contingent on how we approach it. This opportunity was, however, not explicitly grasped by the teacher who instead repeatedly challenged her pupils' interpretations and directed them towards accepting her own interpretations of both the media used in the class and the reasons behind the Cold War. In this sense, you could say that the Swiss teacher chose to use history critically, seeking to destabilise one way of understanding the origins of the Cold War by proposing another approach to the topic.

The Swedish lesson differed in that the Cold War was addressed by the class as a whole. The teacher (and then a film) narrated a version of the Cold War. Here we might argue that the pedagogical approach taken facilitated an understanding of the conflict and history as something fixed and stable, the teacher spelling out the origins of the Cold War. The teacher repeatedly reached out to her pupils during her presentation and tried to engage them in the subject with personal and private analogies, i.e. the Cold War as a family row, the war by proxy as attacking someone through your friends. These analogies were, however, directed towards facilitating an understanding of the Cold War. In this sense history is presented transparently: no specific perspective or construction is discernable (cf. Ankersmit 2013).

One interesting facet to this lesson was that the teacher introduced historiographical aspects before the showing of the film. She urged her pupils to think about how history can be constructed for particular purposes by different groups of people, both in the class and in the future. She further remarked on how narratives can become distorted when they are retold or passed on by people. The Swedish teacher here addressed two aspects of history and historical truth: the idea that history is always contingent on perspective (and therefore suspicious), and the difficulty of knowing what is 'true' in history. It could therefore be argued that the Swedish teacher pushed toward her pupils a kind of relativistic notion of history (it is only a matter of perspective) and the idea that historical truth concerns primarily whether the narrative at hand corresponds with or does not correspond with original events. These two views on historical truth might be understood as conflicting, since one is relativistic in relation to truth, and the other is what could be called a classical positivist notion of truth and history. This makes it difficult to understand what message the Swedish teacher intended to convey to her pupils. Here the teacher had what could have been an excellent opportunity to discuss the historiographical aspects of the narrative presented by both herself and the film and to engage with the Western historical cultural context of these interpretations of the Cold War, but instead the teacher chose to resume the lesson with the narrative at hand. Thus, you could argue that the Swedish teacher used history traditionally in the observed lesson, since the pupils were presented with one narrative and one perspective on events after 1945.

Discussion: cultural entanglements and historicity

The results above reveal that the perception of the Cold War as a conflict between the USA and the USSR is a commonly held assumption when it comes to defining the Cold War, regardless of who might be at fault for causing it. Both lessons centred around this frame when addressing the period after 1945 and no teacher mentioned, for instance, that the period after 1945 was also one of unprecedented improvement in living standards for people in Switzerland and Sweden. The period furthermore saw the introduction of the welfare state in these countries and in most cases further democratisation, historical examples which can be used to problematise the commonsense understanding of the Cold War.

The Swiss lesson was characterised by the teacher's method of engagement with the past and her encouragement to her pupils to do the same: the definition of the Cold War is not something that is once and for all settled but it is still contingent on whose version we are getting. In this way the Cold War is a topic used to provoke not only ideological but also moral discussions, as in the example of how the world viewed Germany and Japan after the Second World War. In this sense, the teacher showed that the Cold War is an event that still affects us and shapes how we view the world. There was, however, a kind of distancing in the Swiss lesson that was brought about by the focus on international affairs and international politics. Switzerland and its role in the world after 1945 was not mentioned at all in the observed lesson.

The Swedish lesson was also characterised by engagement, but in contrast to the Swiss lesson, this engagement did not concern how we might understand the Cold War. Instead, the engagement in this lesson was related to how the teacher perpetually related the events after 1945 to national and personal perspectives, portraying Sweden as caught in-between the USA and the USSR, perhaps even helpless. This was accentuated by the teacher's repeated gesturing to a long Swedish tradition of war with Russia, which pushed Sweden towards the USA and the West. Concerning such engagement, we might note how the teacher related the Cold War to her own upbringing and her pupils' parents and grandparents, emphasising that it was an event that affected these groups a lot and, furthermore, how the pupils' older relatives might also vouch for Russia and the USSR traditionally having posed a threat to Sweden. Significant too, in the Swedish lesson, was the stress the teacher put upon the atmosphere of the Cold War period as one which was fearful and troubled. Sweden was afraid of the USSR, and the USA and the USSR were also afraid of each other. Thus, the Swedish lesson reproduced cultural aspects of fear and distrust towards the USSR and Russia and, in a sense, might have even contributed to the reproduction of Russia as Sweden's eternal enemy. This is a trend that is strong in the Swedish historical culture of the Cold War (cf. Holmén 2006; Thorp 2015, 2017; Persson in this volume). Therefore, the Swedish teacher in this lesson presented the Cold War from a national and personal perspective: the conflict, either viewed from a national perspective or as part of wider international politics, she emphasised, is related to personal experiences (i.e. family relations or relations to friends) or personal feelings (e.g. the fear of the USSR and Russia).

Concerning how the observed lessons relate to the aspects of historicity and the ensuing inherent tension within the subject of history, we can say that even though the two teachers in our case studies manifested a variety of pedagogic strategies and approaches to the Cold War, none of these seemed directed towards raising questions regarding how our own positions might affect how we render history and make sense of the past. Instead, we observed that both teachers chose to approach history as a knowable past impervious to perspective and interpretation. While the Swiss teacher seemingly aimed to destabilise one particular perspective on the Cold War, she nevertheless constructed an alternative understanding that is posited as more legitimate. The Swedish teacher presented one narrative of the Cold War in a personal and affectionate manner, seeking to engage her pupils on a personal level, but this narrative did not invite her pupils to relate to either the Soviet or Eastern perspective in a personal sense, even though this would also have been possible. Consequently, both lessons reproduced perspectives of history which disregard how history is always, and must be, contingent on both how and why different parties choose to approach it.

Concluding remarks

As I pointed out in the introduction to this article, the teaching of history is a complex enterprise that poses challenges to history teachers for a variety of reasons. The lessons described here provide good examples of how a historical topic might be approached in the course of teaching history. Lessons in which pupils are active and contribute to shaping the historical topic presented provide rewarding ways of prompting pupils to engage with and relate to the historical topic at hand. When pupils are presented with narratives which invite them to reflect on the historical topic on a personal level, in order to make sense of what is portrayed, we witness another potentially effective method of bringing history to life for these students and showing them how it has personal relevance for all learners.

Still, the examples presented here also stress the challenges of teaching history, which inevitably crop up due to the subject matter, and reveal the importance of historical self-awareness and historical consciousness. Such recognition is important in order to enable us to engage with the provisional, contingent and dynamic character of history at the same time as we reconstruct and make sense of it. This may be an easy task to describe in theory, but it is a lot harder to do in practice. It is my wish that this chapter may be used to inspire new perspectives on how we may approach the teaching of history, both to highlight the pedagogical challenges and complexities of the subject and to emphasise the importance of history as a subject in schools and elsewhere.

Bibliography

Textbook Cited

Menschen in Zeit und Raum 9. Edition for Lower Saxony. Zürich: Schulbuch Verlag plus AG, 2012.

Bibliography

Ankersmit, Frank. 2013. 'Representation as a Cognitive Instrument'. *History & Theory* 52, no. 2:171–93.

Duraisingh, Elizabeth Dawes. 2017. 'Making Narrative Connections? Exploring How Late Teens Relate their Own Lives to the Historically Significant Past'. *London Review of Education* 15, no. 2: 174–93.

Foster, Stuart J. and Charles S. Padgett. 1999. 'Authentic Historical Inquiry in the Social Studies Classroom'. *The Clearing House: A Journal of Educational Strategies, Issues and Ideas* 72, no. 6: 357–63.

Furrer, Markus. 2017. 'A View of the Cold War in the Swiss Historical Narrative'. In *Remembering and Recounting the Cold War: Commonly Shared History?*, ed. by Markus Furrer and Peter Gautschi. 111–28. Schwalbach: Wochenschau Verlag.

Furrer, Markus and Peter Gautschi. 2017. 'Memory Cultures and History Education. Introduction'. In *Remembering and Recounting the Cold War: Commonly Shared History?*, ed. by Markus Furrer and Peter Gautschi. 11–26. Schwalbach: Wochenschau Verlag.

Gadamer, Hans-Georg. 1975. 'The Problem of Historical Consciousness', ed. by Erick Raphael Jimenez, Matthew Lampert, Christopher Roberts, and and Rocío Zambrana. *Graduate Faculty Philosophy Journal* 5, no. 1: 8–52.

Holmén, Janne. 2006. 'Den politiska läroboken: Bilden av USA och Sovjetunionen i norska, svenska och finländska läroböcker under kalla kriget'. *Studia Historica Upsaliensia* 0081-6531; 221. Uppsala: Acta Universitatis Upsaliensis.

Jeismann, Karl-Ernst. 1979. 'Geschichtsbewußtsein'. In *Handbuch der Geschichtsdidaktik*, ed. by Klaus Bergmann, Annette Kuhn, Jörn Rüsen, and Gerhard Schneider, 1st ed. 42–45. Düsseldorf: Pädagogischer Verlag Schwann.

Karlsson, Klas-Göran. 2014. 'Historia, historiedidaktik och historiekultur - teori och perspektiv'. In *Historien är närvarande: Historiedidaktik som teori och tillämpning*, ed. by Klas-Göran Karlsson and Ulf Zander. 13–89. Lund: Studentlitteratur.

Lévesque, Stéphane. 2008. *Thinking Historically: Educating Students for the Twenty-First Century.* Toronto: Buffalo.

Lundestad, Geir. 2004. *Öst, väst, nord, syd: Huvuddrag i internationell politik efter 1945* Lund: Studentlitteratur.

Parkes, Robert J. 2011. 'Interrupting History: Rethinking History Curriculum after "The End of History"'. In *Counterpoints: Studies in the Postmodern Theory of Education*, 404. New York: Peter Lang Publishing.

Parkes, Robert J. 2013. 'Postmodernism, Historical Denial, and History Education: What Frank Ankersmit Can Offer to History Didactics'. *Nordidactica: Journal of Humanities and Social Science Education* 2 (2013): 20–37.

Persson, Anders. 2017. 'Lärartillvaro och historieundervisning: innebörder av ett nytt uppdrag i de mätbara resultatens tid'. *Umeå studies in history and education* 18. Umeå: Umeå universitet.

Persson, Anders and Robert Thorp, 2017. 'Historieundervisningens existentialiserande potential'. *Nordidactica: Journal of Humanities and Social Science Education* 2 (2017): 59–74.

Ritzer, Nadine. 2012. 'The Cold War in Swiss Classrooms: History Education as a "Powerful Weapon against Communism"?' *Journal of Educational Media, Memory, and Society* 4, no. 1: 78–94.

Roth, Paul A. 2012. 'The Pasts'. *History & Theory* 51 (October): 313–39.
Rüsen, Jörn. 2012. 'Tradition: A Principle of Historical Sense-Generation and Its Logic and Effect in Historical Culture'. *History and Theory* 51, no. 4: 45–59.
Seixas, P. 2000. 'Schweigen! Die Kinder! or, Does Postmodern History Have a Place in the Schools?' In *Knowing, Teaching, and Learning History: National and International Perspectives*, edited by P.N. Stearns, P. Seixas and S. Wineburg, 19–37. New York: New York University Press.
Stymne, Anna-Karin. 2017. *Hur begriplig är historien? Elevers möjligheter och svårigheter i historieundervisningen i skolan*. Stockholm: Stockholm University Press.
Thorp, Robert. 2015. 'Representation and Interpretation: Textbooks, Teachers, and Historical Culture'. *IARTEM E-Journal* 7, no. 2: 73–99.
Thorp, Robert. 2016. 'Uses of History in History Education'. *Umeå Studies in History and Education* 13. Umeå: Umeå universitet.
Thorp, Robert. 2017. 'Experiencing, Using, and Teaching History: Aspects of Two History Teachers' Relations to History and Educational Media'. *Journal of Educational Media, Memory, and Society* 9, no. 2: 129–46.
Wilschut, Arie. 2012. *Images of Time: The Role of an Historical Consciousness of Time in Learning History*. Charlotte, NC: Information Age Publishing.
Wineburg, Sam. 2001. *Historical Thinking and Other Unnatural Acts: Charting the Future of Teaching the Past*. Philadelphia: Temple University Press.
Zanazanian, Paul. 2009. *Historical Consciousness and the Construction of Inter-Group Relations: The Case of Francophone and Anglophone History School Teachers in Quebec*. Montréal: Université de Montréal.

Open Access This chapter is licensed under the terms of the Creative Commons Attribution 4.0 International License (http://creativecommons.org/licenses/by/4.0/), which permits use, sharing, adaptation, distribution and reproduction in any medium or format, as long as you give appropriate credit to the original author(s) and the source, provide a link to the Creative Commons licence and indicate if changes were made.

The images or other third party material in this chapter are included in the chapter's Creative Commons licence, unless indicated otherwise in a credit line to the material. If material is not included in the chapter's Creative Commons licence and your intended use is not permitted by statutory regulation or exceeds the permitted use, you will need to obtain permission directly from the copyright holder.

Index[1]

A

Afghanistan, 188, 192, 436
Africa
  Algeria, 67, 68, 193
  Angola, 68, 70, 211, 212, 215–217
  Botswana, 68
  Cameroon, 68
  Congo, the, 68, 169, 211, 213, 215
  Gabon, 68
  Ghana, 68
  Kenya, 68
  Sub-Saharan, 169
African-American history
  Birmingham demonstration, 126
  Black Panthers, 190, 216
  bus boycott of Alabama, 126
  Evers, Medgar, 126
  Montgomery church burnings, 126
  Parks, Rosa, 126
  Till, Emmet, 126
  See also Civil Rights Movement
African National Congress (ANC), 217
Agent Orange, 306
Albania, 37, 120, 195
Alessandri, Jorge, 232
Allende, Salvador, 17, 222, 227, 229, 231–236, 238, 239, 243
Allies, 54, 58, 59, 61, 70, 100, 118, 162, 186, 197, 233, 266, 305, 308, 319, 325, 326, 331
Al-Qaida, 189

[1] Note: Page numbers followed by 'n' refer to notes.

Ambivalence, 4–8, 18, 77, 141, 253, 254, 259–281, 290, 295, 317, 319, 322, 333, 362, 373
America, United States of, *see* USA
Angola, 68, 70, 211, 212, 215–217
Anti-communism, 19, 139, 141, 143, 145–148, 150, 152, 183, 209, 212, 213, 218, 255, 276, 289, 290, 294, 299–301
Anti-Hitler Coalition, the, 364
Apartheid, 17, 193, 207–209, 211, 213, 216–218
Arendt, Hannah, 108, 109, 126, 128
Arms race, 169, 171, 174, 187, 191, 200
Artillery, 142
Asia, vii, 33, 34, 56, 57, 64, 67, 69, 70, 78, 87, 169, 204n7, 303, 366
Atlantic Charter, the, 199, 372
Atomic bomb, 31, 89, 125, 142, 148, 191, 352, 367, 433
Austria, 66, 147

B

Belgium, 8, 40, 162, 163, 167, 172, 175
Benjamin, Walter, 145
  philosophy of history, 138
Berlin
  airlift, 39, 44, 61
  blockade, 40, 61, 63, 119, 168, 214
  crisis of 1948, 61, 64, 65, 187
  monetary reform in West Berlin, 61
  Wall, the, vii, 63, 85, 90, 119, 138, 150, 151, 169, 176, 217

Black Panther Party, 190, 216
Blumenberg, Hans
  metaphorology, 141
Boehm, Gottfried, 141
  Iconic turn, the, 140
Bolshevism, 115, 127, 267, 370, 371
Brandt, Willy, 169
Brezhnev Doctrine, 169, 296, 297
Britain, 40, 59, 69, 70, 118, 121, 124, 183, 185, 198, 265, 332, 366
British Empire, the, 372
Budapest, 190
Bulgaria, 37, 120, 195, 265
Butler, Judith, 261

C

Cambodia
  Khmer Rouge, 192
Canada, 40
Capitalism, 20, 23, 28, 29, 37, 43, 70, 96, 99, 110, 162, 170, 214, 217, 255, 289, 294, 302, 308, 317, 333, 434
Caribbean Crisis, the, 64–66
Caricatures, *see* Media
Carlyle, Thomas, 160
Castro, Fidel, 67, 124, 170, 191, 216, 231, 234, 244
Catholic Church, 302
Ceaușescu, Nicolae, 172
Chile, 8, 17, 169, 222–226, 230, 231, 233, 236, 239, 241, 243, 244
Chilean Intelligence Agency (DINA), 236, 240, 245n8
China, 8, 17, 56, 64, 69, 75–79, 83, 84, 86–90, 92, 93, 98–102,

123, 192, 211, 212, 214, 215, 303, 307
Chrustjev, Nikita, 116
Churchill, Winston, 19, 38, 39, 185, 194, 195, 198, 199, 327, 328, 352, 372, 397, 403
CIA, 170, 184, 221, 224, 368
Civil Rights Movement, 122, 190, 215, 216
Coherence/coherent, 23–46, 77, 161, 163, 178, 210, 262, 318, 320, 322, 327, 354, 361, 371, 373, 382
Colonialism, 208, 300, 306, 308
Comecon, 168, 214
Comics, *see* Media
Common sense/commonsensical, 4, 7, 15, 16, 45, 355, 362, 370, 373, 381, 383–384, 389n36, 425, 428, 439, 440
Communism, 28–31, 33, 34, 36–38, 66, 87, 96, 99, 117, 119, 123, 141, 143, 162, 169, 170, 176, 192, 196, 210, 211, 215, 217, 236, 255, 290, 292–299, 301–308, 370, 383, 434, 435, 438
Communist Worker's Party, 143
Concrete hedgehog, *see* Switzerland, defences
Condor Operation, 221
Congo, 68, 169, 211, 213, 215
Conspiracy theory, 435, 439
Containment, 26, 33, 37, 38, 168, 192, 197, 214, 307, 352
Crimea, 2, 417
Critical Discourse Analysis (CDA), 261–262

ČSSR, 61, 292–300, 308
Cuba, 65, 67, 119, 124, 148, 169, 191, 211, 212, 215, 216, 231, 234, 235, 239, 373
Cuban Missile Crisis, 65, 85, 87, 90, 91, 169, 171, 174, 188, 191, 214
See also Caribbean Crisis, the
Cuito Canavale, 216, 217
Cultural changes, 167
Curriculum, 23, 112, 162–164, 209–213, 223, 224, 321
Russia, 52, 53

D
DDR, *see* German Democratic Republic (GDR)
De Gaulle, Charles, 84, 193
Decolonisation, 52, 56, 62, 67, 91, 99, 167, 169, 189, 192–194, 208, 209, 211, 308, 372, 373
Democracy, 26, 28, 30, 38, 42, 43, 56, 62, 111, 117, 119, 120, 122, 124, 128, 146, 150–151, 164, 169, 183, 185, 195, 199, 204n7, 208, 210, 213–215, 223, 230, 235–237, 241, 243, 264–267, 269, 270, 275–277, 290, 292, 296, 301, 306, 307, 331, 332, 334, 351, 374–376, 383, 435
Denazification, 335–338, 352, 437
Denmark, 110
Depression, 29, 30, 85
Détente, 65, 66, 168, 169, 171
Dialogue, vi, 66, 175, 273, 321, 331, 337, 402, 403, 414

Dialogue-oriented teaching, 403, 404
Dictatorship, 26, 28, 118, 221–244, 264, 276, 334, 432, 438
Didactics, x, 55, 108, 112, 145, 351, 353, 354, 382, 386, 393–418
Discourse, vii, 2, 3, 5–7, 20, 26, 35, 45, 51, 60, 99, 100, 143, 146, 147, 152, 160, 165, 173, 174, 203n2, 222, 223, 226–230, 233–237, 239, 240, 243, 244, 254, 261–263, 265–268, 271, 272, 274, 278, 279, 300–302, 308–310, 317–339, 350, 353, 362, 363, 369–371, 373, 377, 381, 382, 384, 386
Discovery history teaching, 402, 403
Domino theory, 301, 303, 307, 308
Dresden, 326, 329–331
  Frauenkirche, 330

E

East Germany
  education system, 318
  university, 321–322
  welfare (*see* Welfare state)
Eastern Europe, 20, 26, 38, 42–44, 56, 57, 59, 63–66, 71, 90, 118, 119, 160, 169–172, 174, 176, 197, 264, 266, 267, 272, 275, 277, 292, 299, 383
East Prussia, 418
Eco, Umberto, 259, 281
Economic liberalism, 265, 266
Eisenhower, Dwight D., 66, 170
Elbe, 35, 329

Elections, 42, 125, 183, 191, 217, 229, 233, 239, 243
Environmental problems, 167
European Union, 100, 144

F

Fascism, 141, 300, 307, 335, 375
FBI, 195
Federalisation, 167
Federal Republic of Germany (FRG), 18, 61, 63, 148, 175, 317–319, 339n1, 389n36, 418
Federal State Educational Standards (FSES), 52, 53, 72
Ferro, Marc, 52
Finland, 110
First World War, the, 60, 123, 267
Flanders, 162–165, 167
Flemish, 159–178
  Ministry of Education and Training, 163
Foucault, Michel, 318
France, 40, 59, 69, 70, 84, 114, 118, 124, 197, 303, 307, 332, 366, 438
Frei, Eduardo, 232, 289, 293, 294
Frisch, Max, 142, 147
FUER Geschichtsbewusstsein (*FOR Historical Awareness*), 414

G

Gadamer, Hans-Georg, 424
Gaddis, John Lewis, 90, 264, 265
Gagarin, Yuri, 191
Gandhi, Mahatma, 193
Gdansk, 171

Geistige Landesverteidigung/spiritual national defence, 290
German Democratic Republic (GDR), 18, 62, 63, 65, 88, 168, 175, 254, 265, 272–274, 276, 279, 282n4, 317–319, 321–323, 332, 334–339, 339n1, 339n3, 388–389n36
Germany
 division of, 85, 91, 138, 322, 328, 408
 East Germany (*see* German Democratic Republic (GDR))
 German victimhood, 32, 45, 319
 pre-war, 203n1
 refugees, 32, 35
 reunification, 90, 138, 317, 318
 West Germany (*see* Federal Republic of Germany (FRG))
Gomulka, Vladislav, 64
Gorbachev, Mikhail, 89, 90, 102, 116, 169–171
Gramsci, Antonio, 261
Great Northern War, the, 412
Great Patriotic War, *see* Second World War, the
Greece, 214
Greek civil war, 197
Guérilla tactics, 308
Guevara, Che, 301
Gulag, 116, 168, 190

H

Hegemony, 3, 6, 15, 18, 25, 82–88, 94, 99–101, 222, 254, 259–281, 372, 386–387
Helsinki agreements, 169
Hiroshima, 125, 131–132n24, 132n37, 148, 352, 431, 433
Historical learning, 412–414, 417, 418
Historiography, 7, 45, 51, 52, 54, 59, 63, 71, 77, 99, 149, 165, 172, 184, 189, 213, 273, 368, 395, 410
History
 critical narratological use of, 429
 genetic narratological use of, 429
 traditional narratological use of, 429
Hitler, Adolf, 29, 115, 293, 301, 352, 431
Hobsbawm, Eric, 141, 145, 361
Hungary
 Hungarian crises, 62, 142
 Hungarian refugees, 147, 149

I

Imagined communities (Benedict Anderson), 160
Imhof, Kurt, 143, 290, 300, 301
Immigration, 120–121, 127
Imperialism, 78, 91, 94, 204n7, 295, 300, 308, 333, 375
India, 67, 69, 92, 169, 188, 193
Indochina, 56, 68, 69, 87, 188, 193, 290, 300, 303, 304, 308, 309
Integrated generation, *see* Lindner, Bernd
International Monetary Fund (IMF), 81, 86, 217
Intertextuality, 262
Iran, 169, 214

Iron Curtain, the, 8, 20, 27, 38, 39, 83, 137, 151, 171, 183, 186, 194, 197–200, 269, 271, 328, 379, 434
Islam, 2, 69
Israel, 62, 187
Israeli-Palestinian conflict, 167, 169
Italy, 169, 197

J

Japan, 29, 100, 124, 125, 131–132n24, 133n37, 193, 367, 431, 433, 436, 439, 442

K

Kennedy, John F., 65, 169, 170, 174, 214, 239, 241
Khrushchev, Nikita S., 63, 65, 67, 88, 169, 170, 190, 191
King, Martin Luther, 190, 195
Knowledge
    cultural knowledge, 259–261
    hegemonic knowledge, 15
    official knowledge, 5, 45
Korea, 61, 64, 66, 83, 84, 87, 95, 99, 188, 191, 192, 303, 305
    Kim Il-Sung, 192
Korean War, the, 56, 84, 95, 168, 191, 290
Kreis, Georg, 144, 151, 291
Kremlin, the, 54, 137, 190, 194

L

Laos, 192, 302
Latin America, vii, 56, 57, 62, 70, 78, 87, 124, 163, 169, 222, 229, 231–239, 243, 244, 368

Lausanne, 142, 149
Lenin, Vladimir, 29, 115, 119
Letelier, Orlando, 239, 240
Lindner, Bernd, 318, 319
Lippman, Walter, 118, 130n18
Lower Saxony, 274, 352, 353, 395–399, 402–404, 407, 408, 410, 415
Luxembourg, 40

M

MAD doctrine, 169
Malaysia, 338
Manchuria, 57
Mandela, Nelson, 216, 217
Marshall, George C., 33, 41, 167, 195, 196
Marshall Aid, *see* Marshall Plan, the
Marshall Plan, the, 19, 20, 26–28, 32–35, 41–42, 44, 55, 83, 84, 86, 123, 167, 168, 188, 196, 200–202, 204n7, 204n8, 214, 264
Marx, Karl, 370, 371, 373
Marxism, 97, 178, 184, 234, 243, 370, 371
McCarthy, Joseph, 18, 66, 168, 174, 190, 191
McCarthyism, 66, 122
Media
    caricatures, 355, 407, 423
    comics, 407
    cultures, ix, x, 88, 331, 417, 423
    films, 5, 85, 88, 201, 202, 351, 352, 367, 402, 404, 407, 431–433, 437–441
    hypermedia, 407
    memory alternative, 222, 354

official, 5, 60, 97, 139, 184, 210, 222–224, 230, 243, 244
practices, v–vii, 1–8, 15, 17, 20, 162, 185, 395, 397–398, 425
studies, vi, vii
See also Television
Middle East, 66, 70, 169
Minh, Hồ Chí, 305, 307
Modernity, 96, 99, 160, 208
Moitt, Ronni, 239, 240
Moscow, 37, 38, 55, 58, 61, 68, 75, 118, 137, 208, 295, 330
Multiculturalism, 53
My Lai Massacre, 255, 304

N

Nagasaki, 125, 131–132n24, 133n37, 149, 431, 433
Napalm, 126, 304, 306, 307
Narrative templates, *see* Wertsch, James V.
Narratological uses of history, *see* History
Nationalism, 143, 162, 431
National Socialism, ix, 141, 319
Native Americans, 111, 120, 125, 127
Nazism, 336, 337, 368, 379, 437
Neo-colonialism, 194, 212, 215
Netherlands, the, 40, 69
New Deal, 122
New Thinking, 52
Ngo Dinh Diem, 302
Nicholas II, Tsar, 369
Nine eleven, 2
Non-alignment, 112, 212

North Atlantic Treaty Organization (NATO), 26–28, 33, 40–41, 44, 45, 61, 65, 69, 83, 85, 99, 102n1, 110, 112, 142, 148, 168, 169, 187, 195, 198, 214, 303
Double-Track Decision, 148
Norway, 40, 110
Novick, Peter, 261, 280
Nuclear bomb, *see* Atomic bomb
Nuclear war, 3, 20, 90, 142, 191, 204n7, 318

O

Obama, Barack, 159, 216
October Crisis, *see* Caribbean Crisis, the
October Revolution, the, 369
Orthodox, 26, 40, 77, 172, 173, 214, 294

P

Pedagogy, 5
People's Republic of China (PRC), 65, 75, 212, 304
Periodicals, 290–295, 301–302, 310n1
Pinochet, Augusto, 222–224, 229
Poland, 8, 19, 20, 32, 37, 42, 63, 64, 169, 176, 183–190, 192–196, 198, 201, 203, 203n1, 203n4, 204n6, 265
uprising, 63, 64, 169, 190
Polysemy, polysemeous, 266
Postcolonial, 68, 101, 204n6, 264, 373

Post-revisionism, 45
Post-revisionist, 3, 24–28, 30–32, 34–39, 42, 44, 45, 54, 172, 173, 176, 185, 186, 196–198, 200, 202, 214, 264, 269, 275, 278, 317, 325, 400
Post-structuralism, 160
Potsdam Conference, the, 31, 32, 188, 265
Prague Spring, the, 61, 190, 255, 289–300, 307, 309, 310
Presenting history, 402, 404
Proletariat, 438
Propaganda, 145, 183, 189, 196, 199–201, 203, 203n1, 210, 217, 229, 238, 379, 434
Protests
 Bern, 293, 299, 301
 Bratislava, 299
 San Francisco, 301
Proxy war, 141, 171, 210, 212, 255, 290, 307, 308

R

Racial segregation, 210
Racism, 18, 85, 122, 210
Radio Free Europe, 184, 201
Reagan, Ronald, 170, 215, 240, 241
Reconciliation, 254, 322, 323, 325, 329, 331, 337, 387
Red Army, the, 189, 267, 334, 432
Red Cross, 32
Red Scare, 190, 195
Referendum, 183
Revisionism/revisionists/revolution, 2, 17–19, 24–31, 34, 35, 39–45, 54, 59, 67, 69, 71, 78, 79, 94, 96, 97, 101, 117, 119, 165, 172, 173, 185, 186, 197, 214, 227, 231–236, 238, 239, 243, 244, 253, 264–268, 273, 274, 278, 292, 301, 317, 319, 333, 338, 371, 373, 378, 379, 381, 395
Ricoeur, Paul, 226
Romania, 37, 60, 172, 195, 265
Roosevelt, Franklin D., 30, 327, 352, 364, 372, 397, 403
Rosenberg, Ethel and Julius, 172, 190, 191
Russia
 Bolsheviks (*see* Bolshevism)
 Civil War, 114
 Russian serfs, 114
 Secret Police, 127
 Tsarist, 114, 276, 366
Russian Revolution, the, 165, 395

S

SALT, 169
Samizdat literature, 187
San Francisco, 36, 187, 188, 301
Satellite nations, 32–34, 37
Saxony-Anhalt, 274, 353, 396, 398, 399, 402–404, 407, 408, 414, 415
Schweizerische Lehrerzeitung (SLZ), 291–295, 301, 302, 310n1
Second World War, the, 3, 26, 28, 31, 35, 43, 54, 58, 63, 69, 123, 141, 151, 162, 165, 166, 174, 188, 189, 193, 203n1, 214, 264, 267, 272, 275, 352, 353, 366–368, 372, 376, 379,

384, 396, 402, 412, 417, 431, 433–436, 439, 442
Seixas, Peter, 6, 160–162, 263, 350, 427
Sino-Soviet split, 78, 89, 100, 169
SLZ, *see* Schweizerische Lehrerzeitung
Social Democrats, 297, 336, 337
Socialism, 61, 63, 70, 71, 96, 99, 110, 211, 229, 233, 235, 236, 239, 289, 292–294, 297, 298, 300
Social studies, 23
Solidarity trade union, 183
South Africa, 8, 17, 20, 68, 193, 207–213, 215–218
South America, *see* Latin America
Soviet Union
  aggression, 19, 23, 26, 33, 37, 40, 118, 124, 214, 267, 366, 379, 439
  occupation zone, 328, 329, 335, 336
  security concerns, 18, 28, 29, 265, 266, 273, 274
Space race, 189, 191
Spheres of interest, 214
Spühler, Willy, 291
Stalin, Joseph, 31, 37–39, 42, 54, 58, 63, 66, 88, 90, 115, 116, 118, 119, 127, 128, 129n9, 130n18, 163, 170, 173, 174, 185, 187, 190, 192, 195, 196, 265, 267, 282n3, 327, 352, 353, 364, 365, 380, 384, 397, 400, 403, 430–434, 438, 439
Sturken, Marita, 4, 6, 260, 262, 279, 361, 362, 369
Suez crisis, the, 33
Surveillance state, 149
Sweden, x, 7, 20, 110, 112, 351, 352, 354, 355, 393–418, 423–444
Switzerland
  anti-communism, 139, 143, 145, 147, 148, 276
  anti-slavism, 143
  defences, 139, 149
  Expo 1964, 142
  folklore, 143
  Marxism, 143
  neutrality, 139, 143, 144, 255
  social tensions, 143
  sovereignty, 142, 144
Systemic Functional Linguistics, 226

T

Tambo, Oliver, 217
Tanzania, 211, 213, 215
Task-based history teaching, 402–404
Tehran, 187
Televisions, 85, 116, 141, 300, 330
Texan State Board of Education, the, 23
Thatcher, Margaret, 170, 172
Third World, xi, 8, 19, 24, 56, 70, 77, 78, 82, 91, 92, 98, 100, 170, 194, 208, 215, 233, 255, 264, 290, 300, 303, 306, 310, 403
Tito, Josip Broz, 170
Tonkin Incident, 304, 305
Totalitarianism, 142, 192, 199, 264, 319, 383

Traditionalism, vi, 19, 25, 38, 46, 58, 59, 71, 110, 124, 144, 190, 192, 194, 197, 265, 278, 318, 325, 331, 332, 334–338, 349, 355, 381, 407, 423, 429, 432, 437, 439–442
Truman, Harry S., 31, 37, 38, 42, 123, 170, 173, 195, 352, 364, 367, 368, 374, 375, 380, 384, 400, 430, 431, 433–435, 438, 439
Truman Doctrine, 39, 44, 55, 168, 187, 188, 201, 214, 353
Tsarist Empire, *see* Russia
Turkey, 65, 169, 214

U

Ukraine, 417
United Nations (UN), 26, 36, 44, 68, 69, 92, 94, 188, 191–193, 397
USA
  altruism, 31, 32
  America, United States of, 56, 57, 62, 70, 124, 163, 169, 192, 222, 229, 231–239, 243, 244, 309, 367, 435
  atomic monopoly, 264
  Civil Rights (*see* African-American history; Civil Rights Movement)
  culture, 45, 85, 88, 122, 189
  Disney, Walt, 122, 127
  economic agenda, 270
  exceptionalism, 23
  expansionism, 174, 184, 253, 271
  Ford, Henry, 122, 127, 177
  free enterprise, 23, 30
  Hollywood, 122
  industry, 42, 122
  intervention in Vietnam (*see* Vietnam)
  isolationism, 26, 40
  troops, 32, 57, 128, 266, 438
USSR, 3, 19, 20, 51–55, 57–62, 64, 65, 67–71, 75, 76, 78, 80–83, 85, 87–90, 96, 98, 100, 107, 110, 111, 114–121, 123, 127, 128, 150, 185, 189, 193, 196, 198, 199, 210–217, 239, 264–269, 271, 273–276, 278, 290, 298, 300, 307, 366, 374, 375, 379, 381, 425, 431–439, 441–443

V

Vagueness, 4, 8, 18, 261
Vatican, the, 194, 437
Viet Cong, 301, 304–306, 308
Viet Minh, 304, 311n10
Vietnam, 83, 84, 99, 125–126, 188, 190, 192, 193, 211, 214, 255, 262, 279, 289, 290, 295, 300–310, 373
Vietnam Veterans Memorial, 262
Vietnam War, 64, 91, 125, 137, 141, 148, 169, 255, 279, 290, 300–310
Visual thinking, 138, 140, 152, 153

W

Warsaw Pact, the, 65, 88, 168, 187, 198, 214, 291, 292, 295, 297, 298
Watergate, 195

Welfare state, 3, 86, 169, 194, 318, 441
Wertsch, James V., 226, 254, 320, 321, 339n7, 384, 385, 399
Westad, Arne Odd, 3, 173, 208, 212, 218, 290
Western Europe, 33, 34, 38, 41, 91, 100, 117, 123, 167, 194, 301, 328, 437
West Germany, 59, 65, 202, 266, 268–272, 278, 279, 282n4, 318, 328, 388n36, 393
Western European, 167, 172
Williams, William Appleman, 27, 278
Wilschut, Arie, 161, 252, 426
Wineburg, Sam, 1, 6, 252, 253, 348, 350, 424, 427
Wrocław, 184, 186, 187, 197
WTO, 217

Y

Yalta, 187, 214
Yalta Conference, 352, 432, 438
Yefimov, Boris, 202
Yugoslavia, 85, 99, 102n1, 195

Z

Zedong, Mao, 93, 97, 301
Zhdanov, Andrey Alexksandrovich, 368, 374, 375, 431, 435, 439
Zürich, 153n2, 295, 300, 301

The manufacturer's authorised representative in the EU is Springer Nature Customer Service Centre GmbH, Europaplatz 3, 69115 Heidelberg, Germany. If you have any concerns regarding our products, please contact ProductSafety@springernature.com

Printed and bound by CPI Group (UK) Ltd, Croydon, CR0 4YY

23/03/2026

02076684-0003